The Shamrock and the Cross

THE
SHAMROCK

AND THE
CROSS

Irish American
Novelists Shape
American Catholicism

EILEEN P. SULLIVAN

University of Notre Dame Press
Notre Dame, Indiana

University of Notre Dame Press
Notre Dame, Indiana 46556
www.undpress.nd.edu

Manufactured in the United States of America

Library of Congress Cataloging-in-Publication Data

Names: Sullivan, Eileen P., 1941– author.
Title: The shamrock and the cross : Irish American novelists shape
American Catholicism / Eileen P. Sullivan.
Other titles: Irish American novelists shape American Catholicism
Description: Notre Dame, Ind. : University of Notre Dame Press, 2016. |
Includes bibliographical references and index.
Identifiers: LCCN 2015047725 | ISBN 9780268041526 (pbk. : alk. paper) |
ISBN 0268041520 (pbk. : alk. paper)
Subjects: LCSH: American fiction—Irish-American authors—History and
criticism. | American fiction—Catholic authors—History and criticism. |
American fiction—19th century—History and criticism. | Catholics—
United States—Intellectual life. | Catholic fiction—History and criticism. |
Catholic Church—In literature. | Catholics in literature.
Classification: LCC PS153.I78 S85   2016 | DDC 813/.3099415—dc23
LC record available at http://lccn.loc.gov/2015047725

∞ *This paper meets the requirements of ANSI/NISO Z39.48-1992*
(Permanence of Paper).

To the memory of my parents,
Daniel J. Sullivan and Helena O'Shea Sullivan,
and to the future of their grandchildren
and great-grandchildren

CONTENTS

ILLUSTRATIONS

ACKNOWLEDGMENTS

Many people helped and supported me while I worked on this book. The editors and readers at the University of Notre Dame Press provided useful suggestions and constructive criticisms. At Rutgers University, Professors Mary Segers and Lisa Hull gave encouragement and a teaching schedule that provided the time I needed to complete the research and writing. My friends MaryAnn McInerney, Elaine Joiner, Gloria Peropat, Jan Shapiro, and Susan St. John Parsons helped me celebrate milestones, attended my lectures, and generously offered suggestions. Paula Derrow and my friends Gretchen Dykstra, Judith C. Tate, and Frank McInerney commented extensively and cogently on the content and style of various drafts. Betsy Selman-Babinecz provided invaluable encouragement and advice throughout the process. I also thank my family, Mary and Jerome Meli, Patricia and John Prael, Jeffrey and Elizabeth Meli, Laura Meli and Nick Moons, Kathryn and Marc Dunkelman, Maureen Meli and Kevin Hennessy, Elizabeth Prael and James Magee, who attended my lectures, listened to my latest thoughts and fears, read early drafts, and responded to requests for comments. Finally, I dedicate this book to the memory of my parents and to the future of their grandchildren and great grandchildren, Tess, Emilia, Cira, Samantha, Helen, and Mae.

INTRODUCTION

This book is a study of the popular fiction written by and for Irish Catholic immigrants to the United States in the middle decades of the nineteenth century. Catholics have always relied on stories, which reach the hearts as well as minds of believers, to explain important truths and to illustrate religious and moral life, as shown in the parables of the Gospels and in the exempla or examples that characterized the sermons of medieval preachers.[1] In resorting to popular novels in the nineteenth century, Catholics were simply continuing that tradition. In England, Cardinals Newman and Wiseman wrote popular novels in these years to reach an audience that might not consult their scholarly works. In America, where Catholic writers began publishing novels in the 1820s, popular fiction became increasingly important as the Catholic population grew rapidly but the official infrastructure of priests, parishes, and schools remained largely undeveloped. Between 1840 and 1870, the number of American Catholics increased from about one million to more than six million, mainly because of Irish immigration. In the ten years after 1845 alone, the Irish doubled the American Catholic population. At the same time, there were only about five hundred priests throughout the country in 1840; the number increased to just over two thousand in 1860 and, indicating the need, approached five thousand by 1875.[2]

1

Irish American writers began to dominate Catholic fiction in 1850, helping to fill the gap caused by the church's weak infrastructure. They directed their fiction to Irish immigrants and their children, clearly assuming that a significant portion of the immigrant population was literate in English and that—in the words of Orestes Brownson, a leading Catholic literary critic and novelist of the time—they demanded "a literature" that addressed "their national tastes and peculiarities."[3]

When I began my research a decade ago, I was interested in the popular fiction as a source of information about the experience of Irish immigrants in the years immediately following the great famine. I hoped that the novels would serve as an archive for a study of the values and social circumstances of people who had so few opportunities to speak for themselves. The Irish American authors who wrote the novels were a professional elite, of course, but they sought readers among the large numbers of more typical immigrants. I assumed that to interest those readers and make it possible for them to engage with the novels, the authors would create characters whose lives mirrored those of the immigrants and their children in important respects. This assumption proved correct in many ways. The novels describe the immigrants' reasons for leaving their Irish homes; their experiences securing employment in America; and their attitudes toward gender roles. Yet, over the course of my research, it became clear that the Irish American writers were part of a tradition of American Catholic—rather than American Irish—popular literature. They used their novels to persuade readers to see themselves as Irish Catholics, a group that linked religion and ethnicity, gave a particular meaning to both aspects of the identity, and emphasized the boundaries that distinguished them from the rest of American society. The novels are best seen as a public record of a conscious effort to define an identity and make it attractive to readers.[4]

To illustrate the role of fiction in shaping Irish Catholic identity, I examined the seven most important Irish Catholic novelists who wrote between 1850 and 1873, focusing on their novels dealing with immigrant life in the United States.[5] (See the selected bibliography for a list of the authors and their novels.) Of the seven novelists, six were men; the one woman, Mary Anne (Madden) Sadlier, was the most prolific and popular. Three of the men—John Roddan, John Boyce, and Hugh Quigley—were priests who attended seminaries in Boston, Ireland, and Rome. The others, Charles James Cannon, Peter McCorry, and John McElgun, as well as Sadlier, were professional writers and journalists. Sadlier was married to James Sadlier of the publishing firm. Five of the writers were Irish immigrants, and two, Roddan and Cannon, were the American-born sons of immigrants. All lived in Boston or New York City except for Quigley, who served in parishes in upstate New York, Minnesota, and Wisconsin.

The Irish American novelists were generally well known in their time. They wrote novels located in Ireland as well as America, and their works were regularly serialized and reviewed in Catholic publications.[6] Roddan edited *The Boston Pilot*; Sadlier was one of the editors of the *New York Tablet*. Sadlier also wrote nonfiction and devotional works, translating some from the French. She received the Laetare medal from the University of Notre Dame in recognition of her contribution to the Catholic community. Cannon and Boyce wrote or adapted plays that were produced on the New York stage. When one of Boyce's novels was produced as a play in New York and London, it starred Tyrone Power and Barney Williams, leading popular actors of the day.[7] Both Boyce and Cannon also lectured frequently in Boston and New York on a variety of historical and literary subjects.[8] When Boyce appeared at the Catholic Institute of Worcester, Massachusetts, he received a "full and respectable attendance," according to the *New York Times*.[9]

The firms that published the Irish Americans were commercial enterprises, owned by Irish American men, who advertised themselves as Catholic publishers and did most of their business with the Church. These firms provided the publishing and distribution systems for writers whose fiction could be described as Catholic. The publishing houses were not officially part of the Church, but they saw themselves as producing works faithful to Catholic teaching. Patrick Donahue, long-time publisher of *The Pilot*—and another recipient of the Laetare medal—announced in 1847 that he was opening a book publishing house to furnish readers "with Catholic books of every style and variety."[10] In addition to books, the houses published missals, devotional pamphlets, and Catholic newspapers, including some that served as the official press of a diocese.

The publishers made every effort to reach a wide audience. They regarded novels as among the most salable items, pricing them among their least expensive products. They also advertised the novels widely in Catholic and Irish American publications. Evidence of sales, printings, translations, and newspaper serials suggests that they had some success. Some of the novels sold thousands of copies, were published in Europe as well as America, and were translated into French or German. Others went through several editions or were reprinted until the end of the century.[11]

Mid-nineteenth-century Irish immigrants did not arrive in America with a ready-made sense of their identity. As Michael Carroll has argued in his *American Catholics in the Protestant Imagination*, the traditional popular Catholicism of holy wells, patterns, and rounding rituals had long been in decline in Ireland, and the devotional revolution in religious practice had not yet taken hold.[12] The immigrants came in small families or as young single adults, largely uneducated about their religion and relatively lax in its practice. Their "loyalty to Catholicism in the New World was by no means automatic," according to Kerby A. Miller in *Emigrants and Exiles*.[13] The Church at the time had good reason to fear that in the competitive religious environment of America, the immigrants would drift away from religion or join a Protestant denomination. In 1836, Bishop John England of Charleston wrote that if there had been "no loss," there would be "five millions of Catholics" in the United States; instead there were "less than one million and a quarter." In 1873, Bishop John L. Spalding of Peoria concluded that despite its considerable efforts, the Church in America had from its first days in the country "lost in numbers far more than we have gained."[14] The immigrants also could have defined themselves in national or political, rather than religious, terms—as Americans, members of the Democratic Party, or Irish nationalists. The authors wrote their fiction to persuade the immigrants to reject these options and to see themselves as Irish Catholic, an identity they presented as the most advantageous, in this life as well as the next.[15]

And, indeed, the immigrants did become Irish Catholic in America during these formative mid-century decades. According to Timothy Meagher, the Church was a "ram-shackle organization in the 1840s in most cities" but slowly managed not only to develop regulations and construct buildings but also to encourage "changes in lay attitudes, knowledge, and devotion" that would transform the institution by 1875.[16] Given the influence of the Irish in church institutions, moreover, the type of Catholicism favored by the Irish became the "gold standard" for all American Catholics, shaping their consciousness and activity until well into the next century.[17]

To forge a sense of peoplehood in their readers, the novelists told stories that gave the immigrants a history, interpreted their present circumstances, and shaped their hopes and expectations for the future. Through their characters and their own interjections, the authors described life in Ireland, defined what it meant to be Irish, and explained why good men and women, married and single, emigrated. They portrayed America's anti-Irish and anti-Catholic hostility as well as the country's guarantees of religious liberty. The authors also addressed the future, evaluating the immigrants' chances to succeed economically and to become loyal, patriotic Americans while at the same time building the institutions that would reflect and preserve their separate culture and society.

In explaining and illustrating what it meant to be Irish Catholic in America, the novelists advanced positions on important issues that continue to provoke debate among scholars. As the characters in the stories confronted difficult conditions in Ireland and struggled to establish an economic foothold in America, they exhibited active initiative or passive endurance and expressed attitudes toward capitalist economic systems and values. As the authors described the appearance, perspectives, and actions of the immigrants, they constructed vivid portraits of race, gender, and class for their readers. The descriptions of the exemplary Catholic woman reflected the lives of poor working-class people, and provided the first alternative in fiction to the reigning domestic ideal of womanhood. The novelists also described, and responded to, American anti-Catholicism, suggesting the role that prejudice played in fostering Irish Catholic group identity. The novelists defined faithful religious practice and took on the controversies of the time about the nature and extent of authority in the Church and, by analogy, in the family and society. They also discussed America's political values—especially religious liberty and separation of church and state—and the political issues of the day, including slavery and the reform movements for abolition and women's rights. In serving these purposes for their immigrant readers, the Irish Americans differed in important ways from the American Catholic novelists who preceded them. Their novels suggest the many ways in which the Irish transformed the popular culture of their church, just as they transformed its membership and institutions.

The chapters that follow consider, first, the origins of Catholic fiction in America, and then, the Irish American novels, which taught the immigrants how to live, survive, and prosper—as Irish Catholics—in their new country. In these chapters I take up the challenge posed by Jay P. Dolan, who argues in his 2008 study *The Irish Americans* that by the end of the nineteenth century, Catholicism, more than any other factor, had come to define the Irish immigrants and their descendants. "How the Church was able to gain such a prominent place in the Irish community," he concludes, "is a remarkable chapter in the history of Irish America."[18] I argue that the Catholic popular fiction of the time suggests some of the reasons why the Church was able to gain its prominent place.

Chapter 1

THE ORIGINS OF AMERICAN CATHOLIC FICTION

In the beginning, Catholic popular fiction in America was not meant for the Irish or even for Catholics. The tradition began in 1829 and gained momentum through the 1840s, as Catholic publishers began to issue novels by American authors. These early works reflected an American Catholic society that had not yet experienced the significant Irish immigration that occurred in the late 1840s. Only one of the prominent novelists at the time was of Irish Catholic ancestry; most were native-born American converts to Catholicism. When the Irish Americans began to dominate Catholic fiction in 1850, they adopted some of the assumptions of their literary predecessors but also introduced new ideas that reflected the ways the Irish changed American Catholic popular culture.

The purpose and audience for the Catholic novel evolved from 1829 to 1850. The early authors aimed their work not primarily at Catholics but at Protestant readers who might be persuaded to convert to the true faith. The first of these early novelists, Charles Constantine Pise, born in Maryland, became a priest, worked in parishes in Washington, DC, and

New York City, and was the first Catholic chaplain of the United States Senate. Besides his three novels, he edited and contributed to Catholic publications and wrote a multivolume history of the Church. Pise's first two novels—*Father Rowland: A North American Tale* and *The Indian Cottage: A Unitarian Story*—were published in 1829 and 1831 respectively by Fielding Lucas Jr., the most prominent Catholic publishing firm of the time. His third novel, *Zenosius; Or, The Pilgrim-Convert*, appeared in 1845, when firms owned by Irish American men were beginning to dominate the field of Catholic publishing. This last novel was published in New York City by Edward Dunigan, the first of the Irish American houses to develop a list of popular fiction.[1] *Father Rowland* and *Zenosius* both had multiple editions and printings; the demand for *Father Rowland* was so great that the first edition was "exhausted," according to the publisher, within two years.[2] Both novels were published in Dublin and London as well as in the United States.

Pise explicated doctrine in his fiction and hoped to persuade Protestants to convert. In *Father Rowland*, he exhorts his readers "to weigh well the reasons which induced" his "most respectable" Protestant female characters "to embrace the Catholic faith: and . . . when once convinced, let human respect be sacrificed, the opinions of the world be immolated, at the shrine of truth, virtue, and Heaven."[3] Pise uses only the very thin plot of a conversion narrative: the wife and daughters of the well-born American Colonel Wolburn are dissatisfied with their Protestant faith and seek the guidance of the local Jesuit priest. The question-and-answer sessions between Father Rowland and the women constitute the heart of the novel. All the reader learns of the women's lives is that they become Catholic.

Pise continues in this vein in *Zenosius*, recounting the conversion of a New England Protestant and his sister to Catholicism. The only concession to plot is the hero's journey to Europe, where he meets people who explain Catholic doctrine and church history.[4]

Gradually, and with the Irish American author Charles Cannon leading the way, Catholic writers began to combine this doctrinal instruction with storytelling—using melodramatic plots and more detailed character descriptions. This model dominated Catholic fiction in the mid-1840s, as it was adopted by the prominent Catholic novelists of the period. One of them, Anna Hanson Dorsey, was the daughter of a United States Navy chaplain and the wife of a judge in Baltimore. She converted to Catholicism as a young adult and published more than forty books over the course of her life. Dorsey was awarded the Laetare medal by the University of Notre Dame and was hailed as a "pioneer of Catholic literature" in her *New York Times* obituary.[5] In the mid-1840s, she published her two-volume *The Sister of Charity* with Edward Dunigan and *The Student of Blenheim Forest* with John Murphy, a Baltimore firm. Both books were still in print at the end of the century.[6]

During that same period, Murphy also published John D. Bryant's two-volume *Pauline Seward: A Tale of Real Life*.[7] Bryant, the son of an Episcopal priest from Philadelphia and a convert to Catholicism, was a physician, poet, and editor as well as a successful novelist. *Pauline Seward* was issued in ten editions over the course of about twenty years.

Like Pise before them, Dorsey and Bryant wrote conversion narratives with a Protestant audience primarily in mind. But they embedded the explications of Catholic doctrine within melodramatic plots in which the characters dealt not only with their families and love interests but also with adventures such as mistaken identities, mysterious disappearances, chance encounters, business reversals, and false accusations. In his preface to *Pauline Seward*, Bryant explains that the "dogmatical portions" of his novel refer "to eternal truths"; though he has tried to "modify" his "sources" "to suit . . . colloquial use."[8] In the preface to her *The Sister of Charity*, Dorsey—who devotes whole chapters to doctrine—says she has "touched lightly on a few doctrinal points," and then cites her sources.[9]

Pise, Bryant, and Dorsey all asserted Catholic truths first and then, as a second priority, defended or explained the doctrines Protestants were most likely to misunderstand. Inevitably, the Protestant characters in their novels come to realize that the Catholic Church is the one true church—and they convert. In Pise's first novel, *Father Rowland*, the mother of the Wolburn family invites Father Rowland to her home to settle the issue of whether the Catholic Church is "the true church." The priest replies: "if there be a true church on earth, it is the Catholic Church."[10] In Dorsey's *The Sister of Charity*, five Protestants convert to Catholicism, including the local Episcopal priest, who announces to his congregation that the "Church of Rome was the only true church."[11]

To support their claims, these authors cited scripture and, in some cases, well-known works of theology and church history. As Pise's Zenosius travels in England, he learns that all Protestant denominations are "innovations" or "novelties" introduced at the time of the Reformation. Bryant's Pauline Seward sees the "unbroken chain" from the apostles to the Catholic Church and concludes that her own Protestant religion is merely "so many distinct sects, having . . . no unity in doctrine . . . and indeed no one bond of union, except, perhaps, that the leaders . . . were all, not apostles, but apostates from the Church of Rome."[12]

Since these authors focused on demonstrating that the Catholic Church was the one true church, they relied on readers to draw the conclusion that church teachings on particular subjects were also true. They did not spend much time dealing with Protestant misperceptions of specific Catholic doctrines such as scriptural interpretation, prayer to images, the sacrament of penance, or the role of the Blessed Virgin Mary. When they addressed these issues, they did not repeat the Protestant criticisms so much as articulate what they saw as the Catholic truths, introducing them through lead characters in the process of abandoning their own mistaken views, responding to the mistaken views of others, or defending Catholicism at public events. In Bryant's *Pauline Seward*, the heroine decides that a lunch party attended by a priest and a bishop is a "good opportunity to disabuse her mind of some lingering prejudices . . . with respect to the use . . . of the sacred Scriptures, in the Catholic Church."[13]

By the latter part of the 1840s, as the American Catholic population increased, authors and publishers began to direct their fiction toward Catholics rather than Protestants. While this new fiction did not ignore a potential Protestant audience, its main goal was to define and strengthen the religious life of Catholic readers. One of the novels, Dorsey's *The Oriental Pearl; Or, The Catholic Emigrants*, was the first to focus on immigrants, in this case, a German family in Washington, DC. Published in 1848 with Murphy, the novel remained in print for twenty years, was also published in Dublin, and was eventually translated into German.[14] Another novel, George Henry Miles's *Loretto; Or, The Choice*, centers around two heroines, a Catholic who has to decide whether to become a nun and a Protestant having doubts about her faith and about her Protestant suitor. Miles's second novel of these years, *The Governess, Or, The Effects of Good Example*, relates the experi-

ences of a Catholic governess in a Protestant family. Miles was a professor of English literature at St. Mary's College in Emmetsburg and another
Maryland-born convert to Catholicism. Both of his novels appeared serially
in Catholic publications and were subsequently published in book form in
Baltimore.[15] Both novels were still in print at the end of the century.

Since they targeted a largely Catholic audience, Dorsey and Miles
downplayed doctrine in their novels. As Miles writes in *The Governess*: "It
is quite unnecessary to record . . . instructions" on doctrine; "we are writing for Catholics, not for Protestants."[16] Miles assumes that his Catholic
readers could and would learn their doctrine from better sources: "our
books of devotion . . . are numerous . . . our catechism is within reach of
the poorest; our treatises on theology, our works of controversy are able
to carry conviction to every man's door."[17] And as the Catholic governess
Mary Lorn tells a minister in Miles's second novel, debates about religion
are not likely to change minds. While Mary can "give a reason [for her
own faith] sufficient for" herself, she could "little expect" the "triumph"
of persuading the minister and so it was "scarcely worth while to" engage
in controversy with him.[18]

Rather than focus on doctrine, Dorsey and Miles tried to describe religious experience, exploring the transformative effects of religious faith
and practice on their characters. When Dorsey's immigrants attend mass,
they experience a "sensation of unalloyed peace." In Miles's novel, the
devout governess and her mother have "never before . . . knelt so fervent,
so thankful, so joyous, so humble, at the mystery of mysteries, at the ban-
quet of redemption."[19] The two authors also hope to inspire readers to
endure adversity and serve as examples for others. Dorsey prays that
"some soul fainting beneath its [life's] cross may find an incentive to encouragement and new hope" in her book's "simple pages." And in his preface to *The Governess*, Miles promises to show "how a good young Catholic . . . without great ability or more than ordinary beauty . . . may recall
many wandering souls to the fold of Christ. . . . [E]very Catholic, however humble his lot . . . may . . . by the force of example, become an humble
missionary in the hands of God."[20] Through the example of her religious
and moral life, not her debating skills, the governess Mary Lorn brings
about the conversion of just about every member of her employer's family,
including the son she eventually marries.

The Importance of Wealth and Status in the Early Catholic Novels

Whether they were portraying Protestants on their way to conversion or faithful Catholic families over many generations, the authors typically created wealthy, well-born American characters. The head of the Protestant Wolburn family in Pise's *Father Rowland* is a former colonel in the Revolutionary War who still communicates with General Washington. Blanche and Cora Leslie, in Dorsey's *The Sister of Charity*, are the daughters of a wealthy Protestant planter in South Carolina; the family lives in a mansion with the lofty name of Elverton Hall. Dorsey marvels that the sister who converts and becomes a nun, a "humble servant of the poor, [is] the scion of one of the oldest and proudest families of Carolina."[21] Similarly, Bryant's Pauline Seward is the daughter of a Protestant businessman whose family "gives a soiree of unusual splendor" and lives with "princely opulence" in "one of the most elegant mansions in the town."[22]

Dissatisfied with their religion, these wealthy Protestant characters search for a true faith and, in the process, initiate the action of the novels. Bryant's Pauline Seward tearfully tells her father that "the world with all its pleasures . . . cannot satisfy this throbbing heart of mine." In Dorsey's *The Student of Blenheim Forest*, the "heart" of the hero, Louis Clavering, is "troubled" from the start.[23]

When these authors came to write primarily for Catholics, they focused their stories on Catholic characters who were not very different from Protestants; the Catholics, too, tended to be wealthy, native-born Americans. In his first novel, *Loretto*, Miles develops his plot around two families: the Catholic Clevelands, whose patriarch owns the estate Loretto and is the "principal man in all the neighborhood," and the Protestant Almy family, headed by a "successful man of business."[24] In Miles's *The Governess*, the heroine Mary Lorn and her mother are American Catholics who were once wealthy, although they have come down in the world since the death of the spendthrift husband and father. Miles emphasizes their excellent background, writing that Mary's education had been "superintended by her mother, until there were few more accomplished persons than she." The mother "was every way equal to the task."[25]

The only exception to this focus on wealthy native-born American characters is Dorsey's family of German immigrants. But the Conradts are not poor. The patriarch of the family, Dorsey writes, had managed to save "a few hundred dollars . . . year after year" in his home country and comes to America intending to buy a farm. Although daughter Marie is temporarily reduced to poverty, Dorsey does not dwell on the poor neighborhood where the young woman lives and works, or on her friends who belong to the same "class" as she, "solely dependent on their own exertions for a support." Rather, the author tends to idealize Marie's temporary poverty, showing how her faith sustains her until, in the end, she and her family prosper and are able to buy their farm.[26]

There are, in fact, very few poor people in these novels, and when they do appear, they are used to make a point about Catholicism rather than about class or social life. Many of these novels, written by southern authors, include slave characters. In *Father Rowland*, and in both of Dorsey's doctrinal novels, the main characters own slaves, as does the Catholic family in Miles's *Loretto*. Pauline Seward's Philadelphia family employs servants, including a freed slave who has opted to stay with his masters. The authors are not interested in describing the lives of these slaves. Instead, they use them to illustrate another, more prominent character's charity or the slaves' simple religious faith. The slave Moses, in Pise's *Father Rowland*, "never lost sight of his religion and his duties" and could answer basic questions about Catholic religious practice.[27]

The Catholic family in Miles's *Loretto* not only owns slaves but also interacts with poor neighbors. The Catholic heroine, Agnes Cleveland, passes "dirty, cramped, dingy hovels" where the inhabitants look "desperate from hunger." Miles's description highlights the heroine's charity rather than the plight of the poor: "By her mere touch, the rubbish around her seemed to lose its chaotic aspect. As we see a gentle, loving woman subduing the ruggedness of poverty by a smile, and reducing all to order, as if by the simple force of her presence, we are reminded of the Eternal Spirit."[28] Equally blithely, Miles suggests that poverty can be a source of happiness, describing the governess Mary Lorn and her mother, who had descended from wealth into poverty, as "happier walking to early mass through the snow—happier stealing home from vespers at dusk—happier at their long prayers . . . than they had even been in the gas-glaring saloons of Mushroom Hill."[29]

Irish people, whether rich or poor, seldom appeared in this early Catholic fiction and never served as main characters. The Catholic authors did not differ from their contemporaries in this respect. Stephen Bolger, in his *The Irish Character in American Fiction, 1830–1860*, found that Irish men and women were never the main characters in the secular popular fiction of the time. Also, like the secular writers, the Catholics described their minor Irish characters as docile, friendly, comical, and childish.[30] They did not, however, use Irish characters to exemplify the outcast, the criminal, and the deviant, as did some secular writers of the time.[31] Catholic writers also used Irish people, as they used other poor characters, to make a point about Catholic life. Bryant's *Pauline Seward* refuses to fire the family's Irish cook despite rumors of an Irish riot in the city. Pauline comments that the woman was "the best servant we have ever had." When told that the family would make arrangements to ensure her safety, the "terrified, but good-hearted Irish" servant is "too much overwhelmed with thankfulness and joy to express her gratitude in words, but the faithful service she gave, both then, and through her after-life, spoke louder than words."[32] In *Loretto*, Miles makes one reference to an Irish husband, "the brawny laborer," and his dying wife. The husband, "whose faith was worthy of the isle that nursed him," insists that his wife see the priest even though the doctor feared the excitement would harm her.[33] And the heroine of Miles's *The Governess* knows "that those good Irish Catholic servants, whom she was passing every minute [on her way to church], would not have missed the Kyrie of early Mass for a month's wages."[34]

The only Irish character treated at length appears in Dorsey's *The Student of Blenheim Forest*. Barney O'Callan (his last name is not given until the final page of the novel) is portrayed with a condescension not seen in the author's description of the German immigrants in *The Oriental Pearl*. Barney's exaggerated accent and exalted expressions are meant to provide comic relief. When the lady of the house approaches him as he begs at her door, he says: "An thin may the angils themselves make ye a bed in hiven, my lady."[35] The German immigrants, by contrast, do not speak with accents. Like slave characters, and unlike the German immigrants, Barney is also a passive recipient of others' charity. He is described as "hopelessly grasping after the bright shadow of prosperity," and living in a "rude shed" with a "deformed and diseased" old Irish woman, in a "sparsely settled and squalid part of the . . . city" where the "miserable, degraded and wretched . . . swarm in their polluted dens."[36] The hero of the novel, Louis

Clavering, and his friends give Barney money, move him and the old woman to a "suitable residence," set him up in business as a fruiterer, and advise him to be "honest, industrious, and . . . attentive to his religious duties." Barney responds to the help he receives "with all the enthusiasm of his warm-hearted nation."[37]

Even when Dorsey speaks of Barney in a more positive tone, she quickly backtracks. In the very same paragraph where she commends him—given his "*self respect*, Barney was in a fair way of becoming a diligent man of business"—she proceeds to describe him as "coarse, though respectable, in his appearance." The only virtues that Barney shares with the Germans in *The Oriental Pearl* are his charitable impulses—"that benevolence and charity which is so conspicuously characteristic among the Irish poor towards each other"—and his "submission to the will of Almighty God." Dorsey offers Barney as a demonstration that "piety, integrity, and virtue meet their reward sometimes even on earth." Even that is a backhanded compliment, since Barney succeeds because of charity rather than his own efforts.[38]

The early writers complemented these portraits of Catholics with accounts of Protestant America—its history, values, and, especially, its attitudes toward Catholics. Here too, the writers displayed some patterns as their views evolved between 1829 and 1850.

Confronting Anti-Catholicism in the Early Catholic Novels

At first, authors minimized the anti-Catholic prejudices simmering in the United States. In his 1829 *Father Rowland*, Pise blames ministers for the prejudice, which he describes as mild and destined to disappear. His strategy: praise Protestants but foster distrust of their leaders. Of the two Wolburn daughters, only one harbors anti-Catholic opinions, and the family patriarch, Colonel Wolburn, who never converts, encourages his wife and daughters to follow their convictions. Pise imbues other Protestants with good character as well, portraying them as possibly deluded but "of the most amiable, benevolent, and pious dispositions." Pise also is optimistic that even the mild anti-Catholicism he describes will eventually dissipate. At one point, Father Rowland hears about a minister's anti-Catholic sermon and marvels that even "in this enlightened and free country, the cant of intolerant England could be carried to such an extreme." Yet he remains confident that the "present generation will think for themselves . . . in religious matters, as they have lately done in civil."[39]

By the mid-1840s, even the most optimistic of the writers begin to acknowledge a more hostile anti-Catholic attitude in the United States. Pise, the native-born Catholic son of an immigrant, eventually becomes the most critical of Protestants. If the dominant tone of his *Father Rowland* is gentle and accommodating, with just a few critical comments along the way, his 1845 *Zenosius* is harsh and critical. Zenosius maintains that Protestant "Editors and Preachers" teach hatred of Catholicism, and their followers accept such teachings because they lack the "courage . . . to . . . triumph over public opinion, and to sacrifice notions and misapprehensions, which were identified with their earliest education and associations." In the preface to *Zenosius*, Pise asks that a "candid reader" not charge him with an "intolerant or . . . illiberal disposition . . . especially when he considers with what little ceremony or regard our Church is branded and condemned by Protestantism."[40]

The converts Bryant and Dorsey also recognize anti-Catholic sentiment and its effects. In *Pauline Seward*, Bryant's heroine comments that everything she has heard of Catholicism has been "hostile to it: . . . its doctrines . . . have . . . been represented . . . as loathsome and superstitious; its sacraments as idolatrous; and its votaries as oppressed and degraded." In contrast to the tolerant Colonel Wolburn in Pise's *Father Rowland*, Pauline Seward's father, Calvin, accepts the views of his Presbyterian ancestors and his minister as a matter of course, without investigating them. He displays "a strong, not to say bitter prejudice in his religious opinions," doubting that salvation can be achieved outside his own church. He joins the "American Protestant Association" and also temporarily disinherits his daughter for converting, although he repents when he later converts himself.[41]

Bryant also brings into his story the anti-Catholic riots that were taking place in Philadelphia in the 1840s. He is the only author in this group to show a connection between anti-Catholicism and the increasing Irish immigrant population. His heroine, Pauline Seward, reports that a band of natives carrying the flag and no popery signs burned down the house of an Irish magistrate as well as a Catholic church, rectory, and school.[42]

Dorsey is the mildest of the writers in her approach to Protestants. In *The Sister of Charity*, the Leslie family exhibits "a certain prejudice, not the less strong than it was vague, against Catholics and their faith," and Mr. Leslie believes Catholicism has "superstitious errors."[43] But even Dorsey grows harsher. In her next novel, *The Student of Blenheim Forest*, one character, a teacher of the hero Louis Clavering, calls the Catholic Church the "Antichrist," and refers to the "overweening priestcraft" and the "ignorance and gloom of the dark ages." In that same novel, Louis's father, Colonel Clavering, displays "a deep-settled opposition to the Church of Rome," insisting that his wife and son abandon their faith, and rejecting his son after he converts.[44] Dorsey is always most vehement when it comes to European Protestants. "There were only two points on which all seemed united," she says: belief in Christ and "hatred towards Catholics." Dorsey is also prepared to criticize American atheists harshly; one such character considers Catholicism to be "vile and idolatrous," and Catholics to behave like "slaves."[45]

Once these writers begin to aim for a Catholic audience in the later 1840s, however, their account of Protestants shifts dramatically. In *The Oriental Pearl*, Dorsey's German immigrants encounter temporary difficulties, but prejudice against Catholic immigrants is not among them. Indeed, the immigrants' expectations that "in this their newly adopted country, all men, however humble, possessed equal rights with the richest and greatest in the land" are realized. In Germany, by contrast, their "good pastor was taken from" them and their "religion, on every occasion, insulted and ridiculed."[46]

Similarly, while Miles recognizes instances of anti-Catholicism in his two novels, he does not make them central to the lives of his characters, because he does not think anti-Catholicism was, or should be, central to a Catholic life. If anything, the America he portrays is dominated by a general indifference to all religion. Even Protestant or lapsed Catholic characters who voice objections to the religion are portrayed as worldly or class-conscious rather than intolerant. In Miles's novels, the Protestant patriarchs will not consider Catholicism, at least initially, because they do not want to risk their economic standing; Catholicism "hurts one in getting along in the world," one successful businessman explains.[47] Characters are also more likely to express social disdain for Catholics than to object to their religious beliefs. In *The Governess*, "a pious communicant of the Established, Transplanted Church of England" comments to a Catholic character that many "resources for consolation invented by the Catholic faith . . . trifled with the dignity of human nature" and were to be expected in an "Italian peasant girl" but not in a sophisticated woman.[48]

To whatever degree these early writers confronted prejudice toward Catholics, their characters suffered very little from it. In some novels, Catholic characters suffer no hardships at all because of their religion. The newly converted Leslie sisters in Dorsey's *The Sister of Charity* and the German immigrants in her *The Oriental Pearl* are good examples. In Miles's novels, the Catholic characters endure occasional attacks on their beliefs, but nothing that materially affects their lives. In *The Governess*, the heroine's Protestant employer promises her "liberty of conscience," and vows that the family will say nothing about Catholicism that would "wound or annoy her." In return, the employer asks that the governess refrain from influencing her young charge in matters of religion, and even then, eventually relents, conceding that any instructions from the governess "must take colour from her own opinions."[49]

At most, prejudice affects Catholic characters in these novels in minimal ways. In Pise's first novel, *Father Rowland*, the worst outcome the newly Catholic Wolburns fear is a possible decline in social standing—the loss of certain friends or potential suitors for the Wolburn sisters. Even more serious effects of anti-Catholicism, which appear in the doctrinal novels of the mid-1840s, tend to be temporary, with Protestants eventually recognizing the error of their ways, whether or not they also choose to convert. The fathers in Dorsey's and Bryant's novels disinherit their children when they become Catholic, but both, in the end, repent.

On the one occasion when anti-Catholicism appears as a social force, in Bryant's *Pauline Seward*, it affects the novel's characters only by happenstance. Calvin Seward's business, which happens to be located in the neighborhood of anti-Catholic riots, is damaged by the mob that also destroyed Catholic churches and homes. Seward, still an active Protestant, blames Catholics for the destruction. But honorable Protestants prevail in the end. The Seward family continues to employ their Irish cook, and after a short time, "peace" is "restored" to the city. "Although deeply rooted prejudices were aroused, there was an evident reaction among the most enlightened citizens, in favour of the persecuted."[50] Calvin Seward is also able to repair his business.

Perhaps most important, the native-born and newly converted Catholics in these novels continue to occupy their prominent places in the society, demonstrating that Catholics and Protestants could, and usually did, interact as neighbors and citizens—and indeed family members—despite their religious differences. The Catholic Cleveland family as well as the converted members of the Wolburn, Leslie, Seward, and Clavering families remain wealthy and powerful, quite able to interact peacefully with their Protestant relatives and neighbors.

The only Irish American among these early Catholic writers, Charles James Cannon, adopted many of these same patterns as he defined his audience and purpose, developed his characters, and confronted anti-Catholicism. Yet at the same time, Cannon always displayed the new perspectives the Irish would bring to American Catholic religious and social life.

Charles James Cannon: The Voice of Irish Catholicism

Cannon was born of Irish immigrants in New York City in 1800 and educated in the city's public schools. He wrote poetry, short stories, plays, and novels, with secular publishers in the 1830s and then with Edward Dunigan and other Catholic firms. His first novel, the two-volume *Oran, the Outcast*, published in 1833, shows that religious faith can promote charity, courage, and self-control, but does not contain any doctrine; the work is meant to appeal to all religious denominations. The title character, Oran, the biracial son of a slave, "early attached" his "heart . . . to the unsinning works of God." He selflessly rescues the poor and helpless until he eventually retires to the "holy silence of the cloister," the cloister reference being the only implication that Oran might be a Catholic.[51]

When Cannon began to write for Catholic houses in the 1840s, he adopted many of his colleagues' assumptions about the audience and purpose of Catholic fiction, but he was always more conflicted than the other writers. Between 1842 and 1845 he wrote *Harry Layden: A Tale; Mora Carmody; Or, Woman's Influence: A Tale;* and *Father Felix: A Tale,* novels that blended storytelling with the explication of Catholic truths.[52] In doing so, he developed the model for a Catholic novel that would eventually be adopted by Bryant and Dorsey—with a difference. Cannon was reluctant to include doctrine in his novels, fearing it would put off both his Catholic audience and the Protestants he still hoped to reach. He tells the readers of *Harry Layden* that he is "not writing a treatise on education, nor a volume of controversial divinity."[53] When Orestes Brownson reviewed *Mora Carmody* in his *Brownson's Quarterly Review*, he complains that "in the parts devoted to the development and defence of the Catholic faith, [Cannon's novel] is quite too brief to be satisfactory, or widely useful."[54] Cannon tried to adapt and included more doctrine in his next novel, *Father Felix*, his most widely circulated work. (It was reissued at least three times within five years, published in London, and translated into French and German.) Yet in his preface to the novel, Cannon still emphasizes that the work is "simply suggestive" and that he is not a "controversialist."[55]

Later in the 1840s, when Catholic writers began to target a Catholic audience and to abandon doctrine, Cannon eagerly followed suit. *Scenes and Characters from the Comedy of Life*, published by Dunigan in 1847, is a collection of loosely connected episodes focused on the same group of characters; Cannon calls the novel "a story—and nothing else. . . . [W]hether it will have a moral or not the reader will determine."[56]

Cannon also followed a typical trajectory in his views of American Protestant society—but again with a difference. In his first writings, in the 1830s, Cannon was even more sanguine about anti-Catholicism than Pise in those years. In *Oran, the Outcast*, published with a secular house, Cannon does not distinguish between Catholics and Protestants at all in terms of morality, courage, or charity. He identifies the opponents of his main characters not by religion but by class; the objects of his satire are rich people with social pretensions.

Cannon's view was different when it came to Ireland, however. "The Beal Fire," a story in his 1833 collection *Facts, Feelings and Fancies* (also issued by a secular publisher), takes place in Ireland, and the author says, in no uncertain terms, that the Irish people's "adherence to the faith of their fathers had often brought upon them the vengeance of a government whose aim for centuries had been the extermination of all the *mere Irish*."[57]

It was not until the mid-1840s that Cannon, like his colleagues, gave greater weight to anti-Catholicism in the United States. Writing now for

Catholic publishers, he blames both ministers and members of Protestant churches for the bigotry, gradually resorting to much harsher language than the other writers. In *Harry Layden*, one Protestant character is described as having "a true Presbyterian hatred of Catholics." The parents of the Protestant hero in *Mora Carmody* had "departed from the strict Calvinist faith of their progenitors, [but] they had lost none of that hatred to Popery, which had characterized their fathers."[58] In *Father Felix*, Cannon describes a man who, though "words of liberality [are] forever on his lips," actually displays "narrow views and most violent prejudices." One Protestant character refers to his "foreman," a man named Reardon, as one of those "foreigners, that are coming among us every day, to take the bread out of our mouths, and, worse than that, a most bigoted papist." "It isn't to be supposed," he continues, "that I, a free-born American, and a Protestant to boot, could submit to his domination." Cannon also refers to "flagitious attacks upon the professors of the Catholic faith, with which the American press has lately teemed."[59]

Cannon is the first of the Catholic novelists to incorporate anti-Catholic riots, which took place in American cities in the 1840s, into his work. The central characters of *Mora Carmody* discover that "a mob, incited to violence by . . . [a] fanatic" has attacked a widow's house because they believe a priest resides there.[60] The mob then goes on to burn the chapel. Like Bryant a few years later, Cannon makes it clear that the riots were directed against Irish Catholics.

Cannon's differences from his colleagues are even more evident as he describes the Catholic population, always using poor and middle-class as well as wealthy people as important characters. In *Harry Layden* and *Scenes and Characters*, he writes about poor young American Catholic men who rise to prosperity by their own efforts. The title character in *Harry Layden* flees a position as a "FACTORY BOY" for a ruthless employer and eventually succeeds in the law profession in New York City.[61] In *Mora Carmody*, a middle-class family takes center stage; and in *Father Felix*, the main character is Paul Fenwick, the wealthy scion of a family who had come to America with Lord Baltimore.

These native-born Catholic characters are just as important in Cannon's novels as the Protestant characters on their way to conversion. The Catholics initiate the action; Harry Layden, Mora Carmody, and Paul Fenwick inspire the love and admiration that motivate the Protestants to explore questions of faith, and they do all or most of whatever teaching Cannon includes in the stories.

Cannon does not identify any of these main characters as Irish until his 1847 *Scenes and Characters*, when he is writing primarily for a Catholic audience. In his earlier work he describes his heroes and heroines, despite their Irish names, as simply American, a literary strategy that may be related to Cannon's own life. In his preface to *Mora Carmody*, Cannon writes that his previous novel "was declared, by a certain sapient editor, to be the production of *an Irish Roman Catholic*." Cannon responds that he is "a little proud, perhaps, of his descent from a people who have suffered more for conscience' sake, during the last three hundred years, than all the other nations of the earth. But he begs to assure the reader, that, instead of being an *Irish* Roman Catholic, he is, what many of the maligners of the faith he professes *are not*, in the best sense of the word, a NATIVE AMERICAN."[62]

But Cannon always includes Irish people as minor characters in his novels, and he treats them with more respect than they receive from the other Catholic writers. He does not use the poor only as examples of piety or as objects for others' charity but describes their social conditions and their courage. In *Oran, the Outcast*, when one wealthy character refers to the "poor" as "dissipated and depraved," his friend takes him to visit some poor families. Some might be poor because of "intemperance," the friend admits, but "there are hundreds of the very poorest among us, whose ideas of right and wrong are as clearly defined as our own, and . . . who act with a more scrupulous regard to them."[63] One Irish immigrant family lives at the end "of a wretched alley" in a room not spacious or comfortable but "perfectly clean." The characters are not idealized; the mother of the family, a "short, stout, middle-aged woman," stands in grief over the corpse of a child and exclaims in strongly accented English: "Och, but this is the sorrowful house." When the visitor recommends that she submit to "the will of Heaven" the woman replies: "Indeed, and I know that well, sir."[64] Although she is resigned and grateful, and although Oran provides for the burial of her child, he does not alter her poverty or make her happy. At another point in this novel, Cannon describes a conflict between a socially pretentious employer and an Irish servant. The employer complains that "the ideas of independence and equality with which the creatures' heads are filled, render them almost useless. O for the good old times, in which servants durst not so much as think, without the leave of their masters and mistresses." The servant, again, is not idealized; she is a "short, stout, sandy-haired, freckle-faced daughter of the 'ould sod'" who speaks ungrammatical English in a pronounced accent. But when another character calls the complaining employer "a sad little aristocrat," Cannon suggests that servants have a right to independence and equality.[65]

In subsequent works, Cannon portrays the Irish poor more favorably. In *Harry Layden*, the Irish immigrant Redmond has to flee Ireland after the "unsuccessful struggle for freedom in Ninety-eight"; his handsome son, Hugh, is a schoolteacher. The Redmonds are educated, politically active people and are on the road to success in America. But Hugh and his convert wife have to leave town when his Catholicism is discovered, and they remain in poverty for the rest of their lives, eventually succumbing to disease. Their daughter too is "forced by the labour of her hands to earn her daily bread." Cannon never blames Hugh or his family for their poverty or shows any of them as resigned, grateful, or happy in their circumstances.[66]

Cannon also portrays less educated, working-class Irish characters in a fairly respectful way in *Harry Layden*. Con Dorrian, from Northern Ireland, earns his wages by cutting roads, living with his wife and children in a "miserable hovel." Still, he rescues and supports the orphaned Harry until the family is "prostrated" by "sickness, that scourge of the poor." Cannon then qualifies his sympathy for the Dorrians, reporting that since "they had been, like most of their kind, as improvident as poor, want was not far behind disease" and the family has to depend for a time on public charity. Nevertheless, Con Dorrian recovers, travels throughout the country to find work, raises his children, and supports the Redmonds' orphaned daughter.[67] Similarly, in *Father Felix*, Cannon describes a poor widow named Dowd, a minor character who lives with her blind son in a boarding house that she also runs. In keeping with some of his earlier work, Cannon describes her in unflattering physical terms, as a woman "without anything remarkable either in figure or face, if we except a look of meek submission to a lot, that had been any thing but a pleasant one." She lives on a street "that could be approached only through a long dark alley" in a "small uncarpeted apartment, meanly furnished, but scrupulously clean." On the other hand, while she may be resigned, she supports herself and her son by managing the boarding house and doing day work: "washing, and . . .

house-cleaning." Although she is illiterate, she owns several books left by her husband and is perfectly capable of explaining Catholic doctrine to her boarder. Unlike Moses in *Father Rowland*, she does not display her learning for the amazement of her Protestant listeners; her teachings ultimately bring about her boarder's conversion.[68]

As mentioned earlier, in *Scenes and Characters*, Irish Catholic characters come to the fore of Cannon's work, and he becomes the first American Catholic writer to make an Irish immigrant and his descendant one of the central figures of a novel. Jack Toland Sr. and his wife come to America "poor and illiterate." They are typical Irish immigrants of the time in Cannon's view; the parishioners of the local priest Father Quigley are "at that time, with few exceptions, both very poor and very illiterate." But Toland always speaks correct English, and a Protestant minister acknowledges that he is "industrious—and—what was a little strange for an Irishman— perfectly sober." This last comment is critical, of course, but since it is the minister speaking, Cannon may intend only to spotlight the prejudices of the Protestant clergy. Toland and his wife make their own way, eventually buying a farm. It is only after his wife dies that Toland shows some weakness, marrying a Protestant woman who ruins him financially, after which he repairs to the tavern for comfort. Cannon is far more generous in his descriptions of Toland's son, Jack, whose character unifies the novel. Jack is educated, dignified, and widely respected. Like Harry Layden, he manages to carve out a successful professional life in New York City, becoming a journalist.[69]

In this portrayal of diverse Catholic characters, Cannon departed from his colleagues of the 1840s and prefigured the works of the Irish Americans who would dominate fiction in the following decades. In his account of anti-Catholicism as well, Cannon differed from his colleagues and set the stage for the next decades.

Like Bryant and Dorsey, Cannon began to confront anti-Catholicism in the 1840s, but unlike his colleagues he described a Protestant hostility that impaired the social and economic lives of Catholics in a lasting way. In *Harry Layden*, the Irish Catholic school teacher Hugh Redmond is fired and driven from the town because of his religion. Hugh's fate is determined not by one or two individuals but "by the spirit of intolerance, which . . . the boasted liberality of the age has not entirely banished from our shores."[70] Cannon does not sugarcoat the impact on the Redmonds, who remain poor and eventually die from disease.

In *Mora Carmody*, Cannon again spotlights the deleterious effects of anti-Catholic prejudice, explaining that Mora's sister had become involved with "miserable fanatics," who displayed "rancorous intolerance towards all who differed from them in matters of religion,—and particularly the idolatrous Romanists." These Protestants converted her, separated her from her family—who were forced to flee their home—and put her on public display. In the end, Mora's sister dies, repentant, of tuberculosis. Her father condemns the treatment of his daughter and also the rioting anti-Catholic mobs for their "malignant spirit of bigotry, which had begun to manifest itself . . . under the guise of patriotism." Unlike his contemporaries, Cannon does not note that Protestants expressed any regret or offered any compensation for the attacks.[71]

In *Father Felix*, anti-Catholicism affects even a wealthy Catholic character whose family has been in America since its founding. When friends of Paul Fenwick nominate him for Congress without his knowledge, "papers of the opposite party came out . . . not against the character or qualifications of the nominee—but against his religion." Fenwick withdraws from the race.[72]

Even as Cannon and the other writers target Catholic readers directly, Cannon's treatment of anti-Catholicism stands out. While Dorsey and Miles now try to illustrate Catholic practice and so eliminate or downplay Protestant hostility, Cannon—presumably seeking Irish Catholic readers with an Irish immigrant and his son as main characters—makes anti-Catholicism even more central to his work. In *Scenes and Characters*, anti-Catholic prejudice against the immigrant Jack Toland Sr. is partly responsible for his decline. His neighbors shun him because he refuses to join them in their "religious exercises"; his second wife treats him badly because she hates Catholics; and as Toland's situation worsens, the local minister rejoices. And Cannon, once again, refers to the riots of the time that destroyed Catholic neighborhoods, with one character commenting that Protestants should do what the people in Philadelphia did, "only on a broader scale."[73]

In this account of anti-Catholicism, Cannon obviously speaks for those with actual experience of prejudice, in Ireland and the United States.

Yet he continues to assume that all Catholics, including the Irish immigrants, want to be full, equal participants in American social and political life, just as he wants to be a full participant in its literary culture. He also assumes that over time most Protestants, guided by American values, will see the justice of the Catholic claims for acceptance and equality. Cannon does not give his main characters, Harry Layden, Mora Carmody, or Paul Fenwick, any ethnic background, despite their Irish names. He identifies them—as he identifies himself—simply as American. Moreover, despite the anti-Catholicism they encounter, Layden, Fenwick, and Jack Toland, the son of an immigrant, develop successful professional careers in the American economy.

In all of his work, Cannon uses the American values of equality and liberty as the basis for his expectations. In the 1830s, he invokes the republican tenets of patriotism—defined as acting for the independence of the country—and of equality. He dedicates his novel *Oran, the Outcast* to James Fenimore Cooper in "respect for the pure republicanism of his principles," and he asks that both employers and poor Irish servants be judged not by their religion or class but by their adherence to these principles. A "grand characteristic of our modern Knickerbockers," he writes, is their "pride of family, and horror of low connections, that is, of those who support themselves by honest industry," even though most of "those at, what is called, the head of *society*, have been placed there by the laudable exertions of their plebeian progenitors." These socially pretentious people are prouder of their ties to "some European *lordling* . . . [or] titled dolt" than to any fighter "for the freedom of our country," he writes scornfully, a sentiment echoed in the heroine's previously noted reference to the servant's mistress as a "sad little aristocrat."[74]

Cannon continues in this vein in his novels for the Catholic publishing houses in the 1840s. In *Harry Layden*, Hugh Redmond Sr. has escaped from Ireland as a political refugee and come to the United States, "where the exile is always sure of a welcome and a home." In *Scenes and Characters*, the American-born Jack Toland Jr. is not downhearted or cowardly when his father is ruined financially. His courage comes, not from his faith or church, but from the "heart . . . [of] a Freeman."[75]

While Cannon's hopes are pinned mainly on the future, he does include a few Protestant characters who act in accordance with American values. His male Catholic characters, after all, are hired for professional jobs by American Protestants. And while bigoted Protestants in his novels do not invariably regret their actions, a few change their minds about Catholics, even while refusing to convert. Cannon concludes *Harry Layden* by informing his readers that the main minister in the novel "still lives; and though the Romanists, as he was wont to call them, are everywhere increasing around him . . . he seems more disposed to attend to his duties as a Christian Minister, than to inveigh against those who are only exercising the right guaranteed to them by our glorious Constitution."[76] In *Scenes and Characters*, the first novel that Cannon writes for a primarily Irish Catholic audience, he includes a broad satire of Protestant ministers but also deals rather kindly with some Protestant characters. In the end, the lead Protestant — a rogue and scam artist who escapes from his Calvinist minister father — reforms, settles down with a wife, and admits that Catholics might have a chance for salvation, all without becoming perfect or converting to Catholicism.[77]

With his greater focus on anti-Catholicism, Cannon also departed from his colleagues in his approach to the Catholic faith. While the other writers asserted that Catholic doctrine and Catholic moral life were superior to all others, Cannon's goal is to defend Catholics from the charges against them. This orientation is part of his demand to be accepted as an American, but it also gives his novels, or, at least, the way faith is portrayed in his novels, a defensive cast not present in other novels of the time. In Cannon's first doctrinal novel, *Harry Layden*, his "purpose" was to say "something in favour of that portion of the Christian family which every dabbler in literature feels himself at liberty to abuse." Rather than go into the details of the teachings, he sums up his point: "Catholicism — the religion of some of the wisest and best men the world has ever known — might have some claim to be considered Christianity." Looking back on this novel a few years later, Cannon writes that the "tale" aims "to show that the professors of the Ancient Faith might be, at least, as good as their neighbors."[78] Cannon's purpose then was not to show that the Catholic Church was the one true church but that it deserved to be accepted as equal.

Cannon remains on the defensive in his most doctrinal works. In *Mora Carmody*, he states that "it has been his wish to show, by texts drawn from the Protestant version of the Bible, that many articles of Catholic doctrine, which have been most misrepresented, are not as unscriptural as they are generally supposed to be." That the Catholic Church is the one true church does not figure in Cannon's fiction until his last, and most obvious, doctrinal work, *Father Felix*, and then only halfway into the book. And even here, where Cannon seeks to "explain" the "true principles of our holy religion," he does not so much assert the truth of his faith as refute false opinions about it; he assumes a Protestant will convert if "the clouds of prejudice that had so long obscured his mind" can be dispelled or if he can be convinced of "the unfairness with which she [the Catholic Church] had been treated."[79]

Cannon serves as a transitional figure between the first generation of Catholic novelists and the Irish Americans who begin publishing in 1850. He suggests the changes that the Irish will bring to Catholic fiction and culture, consistently using poor and middle-class people as central characters in his stories and gradually including Irish immigrants in the mix. When writers begin to seek a Catholic audience, he seeks Irish Catholics in particular and continues to emphasize the pervasive anti-Catholicism in the United States, always portraying a bigotry that seriously affects its victims. As he asks for equality and toleration, Cannon expends more effort defending his faith against its critics than asserting its superiority. Yet Cannon also shares some assumptions with the other early Catholic writers that would distinguish him from his fellow Irish Americans. He does not surrender the hope for a diverse readership and always expects that Catholics, and Irish Catholics in particular, will attain their goal and become an accepted part of American life, placing his faith in republican values and in the influence of some Protestants.

Chapter 2

THE IRISH AMERICANS

Creating a Memory of the Past

Like the authors before them, the Irish American novelists who began publishing Catholic fiction in the 1850s aimed at a Catholic audience—with a difference.[1] This group of writers was more narrowly focused on Irish immigrants and their American-born children, as many of the novels' titles made clear. Hugh Quigley called his first novel *The Cross and the Shamrock; Or, How to Defend the Faith: An Irish-American Catholic Tale of Real Life.* Mary Anne Sadlier's novels included *Con O'Regan; Or, Emigrant Life in the New World.* Boyce entitled his novel *Mary Lee; Or, The Yankee in Ireland.*[2] Some authors were even more specific, reaching out to the most vulnerable Irish immigrants—those who were poor, just arrived in America, or alone. The year 1850 saw the publication of John Roddan's *John O'Brien; Or, The Orphan of Boston* and Sadlier's *Willy Burke; Or, The Irish Orphan in America.*[3] Three of the novels, including Peter McCorry's *The Lost Rosary; Or, Our Irish Girls, Their Trials, Temptations, and Triumphs*, were meant for Irish immigrant single women working as domestic servants.[4]

The authors were unapologetic about their goals. Roddan bluntly states that his book is "written for Catholics. . . . [I]f a Protestant . . . misunderstands it, it is no affair of mine: the book was not written for him."

Roddan does not write for all Catholics, however; he makes no attempt to "appeal to the taste of the literary gentlemen and ladies who are Catholics. I do not mean it for those who have always been wealthy and happy. . . . I speak only to God's poor."[5] Sadlier declares in the novel's preface that *Willy Burke* is for "the young sons of my native land," and a few years later, at the suggestion of Isaac Hecker, the founder of the Paulist Fathers, she writes one of the novels meant for women in domestic service: *Bessy Conway; Or, The Irish Girl in America.* Her purpose: "A sincere and heartfelt desire to benefit these young country-women of mine," "especially that numerous class whose lot it is to hire themselves out for work."[6]

Eventually, some authors began to reach out to Irish immigrants who had entered the middle class. Sadlier is a forerunner of this trend with her 1855 *The Blakes and Flanagans: A Tale Illustrative of Irish Life in the United States,* a novel that sends a clear message that middle-class Irish immigrant parents should send their children to Catholic schools. The work was first serialized in the *American Celt*, and in her preface to the novel Sadlier reports that "it is gratifying to myself to know that the class for whom I intended the work, are in general well pleased with it."[7] Nearly twenty years later, Quigley published *Profit and Loss: A Story of the Life of the Genteel Irish-American,* about the fate of a middle-class Irish immigrant family whose son attends the local public school.[8]

This new focus on the Irish prompted literary critic Orestes Brownson to write in 1859 that a Catholic writer of fiction could

> succeed only by pressing in a national sentiment of some sort to his aid, and that in this country must be a foreign nationality, because comparatively few of our Catholic population have any American sentiments or traditions. He or she who can write a good Irish story may succeed; but he or she who has the misfortune to have no nationality but the English or the American, will find few readers for a purely literary work among Catholics.[9]

Whether or not Brownson was correct, the Irish American authors seem to have found an audience. Mary Anne Sadlier's *The Blakes and Flanagans* reached its "fourth thousand" copies one year after its publication and the "tenth thousand" in another three years. (This novel was also translated

BESSY CONWAY,
OR
THE IRISH GIRL
IN
AMERICA

BY
Mrs. J. Sadlier.

NEW YORK:

D. & J. SADLIER & CO.

Figure 2.1. Title page of Sadlier's very popular novel *Bessy Conway*, written for Irish domestic servants in American cities.

into German.) Anna Sadlier, the daughter of Mary Anne, reported that her mother's novel *Willy Burke* sold seven thousand copies in its first six weeks. Quigley's *The Cross and the Shamrock* merited a second, third, and fourth edition within four years. The novels of Sadlier, Quigley, and Boyce remained in print until the end of the century and were also published in Europe.[10]

The Irish American novelists also broke new ground in their conception of the purposes of Catholic fiction. While Catholic novelists had always presented religious life as an alternative to the life of the material world, the Irish Americans were the first to emphasize the specific dangers inherent in American, as opposed to Irish or European, life. Those dangers included actual plots to lure the immigrants from their faith. The Irish Americans followed their immediate predecessors in downplaying doctrine, but also stepped away from using their novels simply to illustrate an exemplary religious and moral life. Above all, they sought to warn their audience about how easily Irish Catholic immigrants could lose their faith and ethnic identity in America. Their heroes and heroines exhibited the virtues that helped them withstand these dangers and temptations.[11]

Authors feared that the Irish immigrants might be duped, or forced, into apostasy by Protestants who controlled public and charitable institutions, such as foster programs, orphanages, and detention centers. Immigrants might also give up their faith simply to avoid Protestant hostility. Roddan writes *John O'Brien* "to give a faithful account of some of the difficulties which await an unprotected boy in our cities: how traps of all sorts are laid for him — how meanness, and sometimes violence, are resorted to, in order to make him deny the faith of his fathers."[12] In his preface to *The Cross and the Shamrock*, Quigley writes: "Our poor, neglected, and uninstructed brethren [are] in danger," and need to be saved from the "subtle snares" around them, specifically the "odious persecution of servant boys and servant girls, of widows and orphans" because of their religion. The persecution led to the "degradation and apostasy of many Irishmen" because "we are ashamed here of the cross of Christ, when we see it . . . trampled on by heretics and modern pagans" and the "poverty, humiliation, and rags of old Erin . . . scandalize us."[13]

Another major danger was the materialist values of the immigrants' adopted country. Given the prevailing anti-Catholicism, immigrants might think they could succeed by giving up their faith. In *Willy Burke*, Sadlier wants to help young immigrant men "in their arduous struggle with the tempter, whose nefarious design of bearing them from the faith of their fathers is so artfully concealed under every plausible disguise. The most plausible pretence is, that men make their way better in this money-seeking world, by becoming Protestants."[14] Quigley, in both his novels, fears the "scramble for money and pleasures" that might tempt the immigrants to abandon faith and ancestry.[15]

Over time, some authors characterized the American focus on material goods, quite apart from any anti-Catholic prejudice, as a lure that could seduce immigrants and their children into a life devoid of religion. In Sadlier's *Old and New* and McElgun's *Annie Reilly*, newly middle-class women and their American-born daughters value possessions and social status more than their ethnic and religious heritage. In *Annie Reilly*, the Irish American Miss Talbot brags about her accomplishments and acquisitions, admitting that her parents were born in Ireland, but as for her: "*Me* Irish! . . . *I* am no such thing."[16]

In the novels devoted to single women, opportunities for social or sexual freedom were the major temptations—issues that were not a focus for the early Catholic writers with their well-off, protected heroines. In *Bessy Conway*, Sadlier conveys a sense of ever-lurking immorality as she describes the "awful depth of corruption weltering below the surface, and the utter forgetfulness of things spiritual" in American cities, "these great Babylons of the west."[17] In *The Lost Rosary*, McCorry is even more explicit: he tells his young women readers, "Thy virgin modesty will be shocked. . . . Vice will cunningly allure you, with its deformities hidden beneath the garb of wealth."[18]

In the 1871 *Mount Benedict; Or, The Violated Tomb: A Tale of the Charlestown Convent*, McCorry seems to seek a broader audience for his message. For one thing, the title is less explicitly Irish Catholic than those of other novels. And McCorry himself says that he is writing for Protestants, not to enlighten them about Catholic religious beliefs, but to expose and reduce their prejudices. In the midst of his story of Irish immigrants in this novel, he describes the attack on the Charlestown convent, which had occurred nearly forty years earlier, to "put on record the committal of a deed of shame, and horror, in order that its exposure may in the future deter men from the performance of such crimes."[19] Yet despite this intention, McCorry does nothing to appeal to Protestants. He usually writes as though the bigoted and violent attitudes that led to the attack on the convent still characterized Massachusetts and that the necessary change is still to come. "Those were sad days, and their obliteration depends in great measure on the future conduct of the people of Boston and vicinity"; and "even the Puritan State may, in time to come, redeem itself from the foul stain."[20] Moreover, McCorry's Protestant characters tend to be violent hypocrites, with only two exceptions, and both of those characters end up becoming Catholics, one at the beginning of the novel and one at the end. First and foremost, McCorry's account reminds Catholic readers of the ugly truth of Protestant bigotry.

On the surface, Boyce also seems to address a Protestant as well as Irish Catholic audience, though he is less direct about that goal. "Dear Public," he writes, in the opening statement to *Mary Lee; Or, The Yankee in Ireland*, "if you . . . expected . . . a preface . . . according to the ordinary standards . . . you will be entirely disappointed" since he has a "horror for the whole *prolegomena* family—prefaces, prologues, introductions, and explanations."[21] Boyce prefers his themes to emerge in the course of the story. Although the title of his novel is designed to appeal to an Irish American audience, Boyce expressed the wish to reach beyond them, asking American readers in his introductory chapter to accompany him and his Unitarian character Ephraim Weeks on a trip to Ireland and leave their "national prejudices behind." He does not hesitate to spell out those ugly stereotypes: the "Priest and the Bottle" and the "Confessor and the Nun." He asks readers to look at "Ireland . . . face to face with your own honest eyes."[22] Boyce also includes some admirable Protestant characters in the novel, the Anglo-Irish Petershams—a Church of Ireland landowner and magistrate who does not convert, and his sister, Kate, who does.

In general, though, Boyce is harsh in his judgments about Protestant America, targeting its anti-Catholicism and materialism.[23] The point of the novel is to show that the Irish can deflate the pretensions of the American visitor Weeks, at every turn, and also defeat the villains, the Irish Presbyterian Hardwrinkle family, who are connected to American denominations as the Church of Ireland gentry are not. Boyce differed from the other Irish American novelists not in an expectation for Protestant readers, but in his determination to amuse and entertain his Irish immigrant audience—and to assure them that they were equal, if not superior, to their American antagonists. Warning them against America's dangers was a secondary purpose.

Figure 2.2. Title page of Boyce's *Mary Lee* shows hero Ephraim Weeks unable to manage an Irish pony despite his boasts of superior horsemanship. Courtesy of Wright American Fiction Project, Indiana University Libraries.

Cannon, who wrote his last two novels in the 1850s, represents the clearest exception to the pattern established by the Irish Americans as he continued his quest for a diverse audience. In the new decade, as in his 1847 *Scenes and Characters*, he identifies lead characters as Irish immigrants and their children, but his titles suggest his larger goal. He calls his 1855 novel *Bickerton; Or, The Immigrant's Daughter: A Tale*, indicating an immigration theme without the national component.[24] The title of his final novel, the

1859 *Tighe Lyfford: A Novel*, suggests Irishness only by the first name of the title character.[25]

In *Bickerton*, his more typical novel of the decade, Cannon, like Boyce, seeks to entertain (and perhaps enlighten) Irish Catholic readers, not to advise or warn them. Retaining the ambivalent attitude of his earlier works, he expresses hopes for reaching a Protestant audience yet criticizes Protestant society harshly. He writes of the "evils that an intolerant spirit cannot fail to inflict upon a land which the goodness of God and the wisdom of man have combined to render peculiarly prosperous and happy" and refers to actual events that "within a few years past . . . disgraced" this country, including mob attacks on Catholic neighborhoods, churches, and priests. He is not trying to warn Catholics as much as to change Protestant minds. Rather than "frighten the timid, or . . . hold up to the hatred or scorn of other nations the land of his birth," his goal is to "admonish the unthinking."[26]

To appeal to such readers, Cannon includes honorable American Protestants among his novels' prominent characters. Pelatiah Hubbard and his son Fred serve as spokesmen for the argument that Catholics do not threaten America and are entitled to full participation in civic life. Despite harboring some prejudices against Catholics, the older Mr. Hubbard, who has no intention of converting, speaks out for the rights of Catholics to practice their religion, and to form associations, vote, and hold political office. Fair-minded Protestants could identify with characters like these. Moreover, as Cannon's reference to "a land which the goodness of God and the wisdom of man have combined to render peculiarly prosperous and happy" might suggest, he ultimately retains his faith in the benevolent influence of American values.

That Cannon intended his second novel of the decade, *Tighe Lyfford*, for a wider audience is clear. It was published by a secular house, and Cannon asserts in the preface that the work is "a novel, and it is nothing more; . . . [it] was written . . . with the hope of affording an hour's innocent amusement to others."[27] His main characters include Catholics of various ethnic backgrounds, as well as Protestants, and his themes are universal—the importance of moral integrity, especially in professional life. Just as he did in the 1830s, Cannon reserves his satire for the socially pretentious of all faiths.

As they focused their novels on Irish Catholic immigrants, the authors changed the way American Catholics were portrayed in fiction.

Catholic characters now are overwhelmingly Irish, and the wealthy, prominent, native-born Americans who figured in the earlier works have all but disappeared.

A New Catholic Population: Immigrant and Poor, with a Past

Immigration itself becomes the central drama of all but one of the narratives. Typically, the action takes place several decades earlier than the novels' publication date. The plots center on the immigrant experience in America over a period of about twenty years, a time span that allows the newcomers to establish themselves and their children to reach adulthood. Boyce's *Mary Lee* is the single exception; it is not a historical narrative but describes the American character's more or less contemporaneous visit to Ireland.[28]

Although five of the seven Irish American authors were immigrants who came to America in the famine era, from 1844 to 1850, the characters in their novels usually emigrate in earlier years. In novels by Quigley in 1853, and by Sadlier and McCorry in 1861 and 1870, lead characters arrive from Ireland in the 1830s.[29] In three Sadlier novels of the 1860s, the major characters arrive around 1820.[30] In some of the later novels, authors begin to trace the experience of immigrants who come in the early 1840s or '50s.[31] The authors typically bring their characters' lives up to the present, in the narrative or in brief postscripts.

In the course of their stories, the five immigrant authors, but not the native-born Americans Roddan and Cannon, describe life in Ireland, a life defined by a church that shapes social and cultural life to promote the people's happiness. To be Irish in these novels is to be Catholic, a connection Sadlier makes throughout her career. In *Willy Burke*, the wife and mother asks her husband on the night before the family's departure if it wouldn't

> be better to live in poverty here, where we have our chapel an' our priest within a mile of us—an' where we have the comfort of seein' good christians all about us, than to be livin' ever so grand in a strange country, where they say you'd maybe have to travel hundreds o' miles without seein' a priest or an altar?"[32]

In *Confessions of an Apostate*, Sadlier says outright that "Irishmen deserving of the name . . . cherished the memory of the old land as something inseparably connected with religion."[33]

In both his novels, Quigley suggests that his lead immigrant families are an important part of Ireland's historic tie to the Church. In *The Cross and the Shamrock*, the O'Clery children have an uncle in Ireland who is a "vicar general . . . a priest next to the bishop in station." In Quigley's subsequent *Profit and Loss*, the patriarch Michael Mulroony is proud of his "connection, by blood, with . . . his relations who shone in the Church, as bishops and priests, theologians and antiquarians."[34] When the young hero of McElgun's *Annie Reilly* is working in the American oil fields, he remembers Ireland's "quiet plains, gentle mountains and rivers, and green hills with tall chapel-spires peeping over their tops—an emblem of its people's devotion to God and the Catholic Church."[35]

For characters living in Ireland in these novels, the social and cultural world is Catholic. Their antagonists are in the minority, whether they are English, Anglican, or Presbyterian, and whatever control they exercise over the people's economic and political lives, they do not figure at all in their social lives. In Sadlier's *The Blakes and Flanagans*, the immigrant family patriarchs agree that "it's few Protestants we had" in the Irish parish; in fact "there wasn't one within miles of us."[36] When Simon O'Hare, the main character in Sadlier's *Confessions of an Apostate*, first comes to America, it was the first time he has "come in contact with any but those of my own religion."[37] The eldest son of the O'Clery family in Quigley's first novel is from a village in Ireland with only five Protestants: "two *peelers*, the minister and his wife, and the tithe proctor."[38]

Boyce alone portrays free interactions between Catholics and Protestants in Ireland. In *Mary Lee*, the Irish priest Father Brennan interacts easily with the Church of Ireland gentry—the magistrate Captain Tom Petersham (Brennan's "dear friend"), and his sister Kate. Boyce does not equate Irish with Catholic—he clearly regards the Petershams as Irish, just as Kate regards Irish writers like Swift and Moore as her countrymen.[39] Captain Petersham also sympathizes with the novel's nationalist revolutionary character. The implications of the priest's relationships, however, are much more important for Ireland than for America. Boyce's novel, located in Ireland, obviously does not focus on immigrants making their lives in the new world. More important, his Catholic characters in Ireland do not have cooperative relationships with the Irish Presbyterian Hardwrinkles or with the American Unitarian visitor Ephraim Weeks, who represent denominations common in America.

Roddan and Cannon, the two American-born writers, do not describe life in Ireland at all. Cannon speaks only generally of the oppression the immigrants endured. Manus O'Hanlon, the father of the family in *Bickerton*, tells his wife: "we are leaving a ruined home, and a country desolated by the tyranny of man, to find a new home in a new and glorious land." When his wife expresses regret for leaving "behind forever . . . all that one has loved most dearly among the living and the dead," Manus comforts her not with the idea that they might return to Ireland but that they would bring their families out to America some day.[40]

If the first purpose of these authors was to define Irish life by Catholicism, their second was to show that even if the immigrants in their novels were poor in America, they had been accustomed to some prosperity in Ireland. They were not rich like the Catholics in the novels of the previous generation, nor were they prominent public figures, but they had not always been desperately poor either. When the characters come to America as families—as they do in all of the novels published in the 1850s—they tend to have money to finance their trips and to support themselves, at least for a while, in America. Andy Burke, in Sadlier's *Willy Burke*, had been "one of the principal farmers of the district." Arthur O'Clery and his wife in Quigley's *The Cross and the Shamrock* owned two farms in Ireland and came to America with five children and "one thousand pounds, in hard cash, to start with in the new world." The Mulroony family, in Quigley's subsequent novel *Profit and Loss*, had "two hundred acres, at low rent."[41] Although these immigrants resemble Dorsey's German family in the relative prosperity of their past lives, they do not bring enough money to buy their own farms and most of them lose their assets very quickly after they arrive in America.

While most of the immigrants are from farming families, the mother and daughter in Sadlier's *Old and New* are aristocrats; another character in the same novel is a man "brought up to the mercantile business in Dublin" who "came of decent people at home and had a good share of education when he came out, but still he was low enough in cash."[42]

As the Irish immigrant population in the United States changed in the 1860s and '70s, the characters in the novels did, also. Most of the works published during this period centered on single men and women rather than families traveling together.[43] (Sadlier's Con O'Regan and a minor character in Cannon's *Bickerton* are the only examples of married men emigrating alone, intending to send for their wives and children after they have earned some money.) Like the families featured in the novels of the 1850s, the single individuals hail from relatively prosperous farming families who gave them the money to emigrate and to support themselves for a short period thereafter. Typically, the young immigrants had some education as well. Kate and Patrick Crolly, the brother and sister in McCorry's *Mount Benedict*, received the money to make the trip to America from their brother who inherited the family farm. Kate had received a "good education" and had "improved upon" it herself.[44] Simon O'Hare, the eventual apostate in Sadlier's novel, was the younger son of "a small farmer, rather easy in his circumstances" and was educated in a hedge school.[45]

Since their characters had left relatively comfortable circumstances at home, the authors had to account for their decision to emigrate. In most cases, immigrant families and individuals departed because their relatively prosperous lives were threatened, or had been destroyed, by landlords, who were motivated by religious and ethnic hatred. The authors conveyed the tenuous position of even prosperous tenant farmers, but they never blamed the landlords' behavior on economic or political factors. Instead, they laid the blame squarely on religious prejudices that made the landlords greedy and cruel. Authors took pains to reinforce their readers' ethnic and religious identity in their accounts of the difficult, as well as of the idyllic, past.

The motivation for the persecution of the Irish characters is religious, but the results are economic. Unlike the new German landlord in Dorsey's novel, the Irish owners do not prevent Catholics from practicing their religion; they prevent them from making a living. In Sadlier's *Willy Burke*, the once secure Andy Burke tells his wife that "this poor old country's growin' every day worse an' worse. . . . [N]ow, it's just all we can do to pay the landlord and the tithe-proctor, and all the rest. . . . [W]e must go . . . while we have a little money in our hands."[46] In both of his novels, Quigley's characters face economic oppression from landlords motivated by religious hatred. "During the horrors of the general landlord persecution of the Irish Catholics (for it is nothing else than a persecution of Catholics)," the O'Clery family in Quigley's first novel "got notice to quit the homestead of their fathers."[47] In his later *Profit and Loss*, the Mulroony family leaves because a "hard man" inherits the estate. This new landlord is a bishop: not "appointed by Christ" but by "law and the English government, who . . . [has] no care of the people or the poor, but to take their money and oppress them."[48]

All of the authors refer to the bigoted landlords as Protestant, and a few, like Quigley with his bishop, also allude to foreign or English origins. McElgun is alone in suggesting that Irish Catholics too could be among the oppressors. In the preface to his 1873 novel, *Annie Reilly*, he proposes to show that "all the sufferings under which the Irish tenant-farmers . . . still continue to labor, are not entirely owing to the bigotry and rapacity of their foreign and wealthy domestic landlords." Now there is "another class of land-owners . . . who are neither foreign nor wealthy" but manage "to purchase a townland or two . . . and . . . follow strictly the example of their exalted brothers." In the course of his narrative he describes one of the men who evict the Reilly family after buying the townland as an Irish Catholic. But McElgun is not comfortable portraying such a character as a villain; the division among the Irish people in these novels is religion, not class. The landlord in the end actually denies his heritage, insisting that his "forefathers were Normans." He also claims to be a Protestant to obtain lucrative military contracts, but in his travels to Irish Catholic neighborhoods he "always carried a pair of beads . . . and always took care to display them as if by mistake, when making a bargain."[49]

Given these accounts of Irish circumstances, it follows that most of the immigrant characters come to America in search of a better economic future. As Sadlier's Andy Burke explains: "we're only workin' the skin off our bones for them that doesn't thank us, and when the boys and the girls are grown up, what have they before them here but a life of hard labor, an' nothin' for it—that's the worst of it all."[50] The single immigrants might have more complicated motivations for leaving Ireland, but in the end, most come to America to earn money. Sadlier's Bessy Conway and Simon O'Hare mention a "love of change," or a "desire of 'seeing the world,'" but ultimately they seek their "fortune in America" or to be "on the high road to fortune."[51] In McElgun's novel, Annie Reilly's parents advise her to "seek . . . [her] fortune in America" because of the "total absence of any prospect of bettering . . . [her] worldly condition at home."[52] Similarly, in *The Lost Rosary*, McCorry says that many immigrants were ready to "face and to dare hardships of any kind" for the "chance . . . to better their . . . condition" and America had in fact "given to many the means of a better material existence."[53]

The Irish American authors described decisions taken by individuals in specific circumstances; McElgun, in his 1873 *Annie Reilly*, was the first to suggest that emigration had become the pattern of Irish family life. Typically, the family of Annie Reilly had "lived on the land for a hundred years." They were, in the view of the local priest, "the oldest and most respectable family in his parish." The father rented the farm "from a neighboring magnate at an exorbitant rent; but by honesty, perseverance, and skillful management, he never allowed himself to fall into arrears." Then, new landlords—described as "bigots . . . [who] will not leave one Catholic family on the land"—take over and begin evicting the tenants. McElgun's heroine, Annie Reilly, tells her father she "had long known" that she "would have to . . . seek a distant home one day."[54]

There were a few exceptions to this overall tendency to trace emigration to economic oppression caused by religious bigotry. The desire for family unity motivates Patrick Crolly, the young hero of McCorry's *Mount Benedict*, to give his farm to a younger brother who had married a woman they both loved, and then flee to America along with his sister. In *The Lost Rosary*, a main character leaves Ireland because a nephew has stolen something and he is "determined not to remain in the country with . . . [his] name . . . dishonored."[55]

In two novels, some immigrant characters leave Ireland for political reasons. In Boyce's *Mary Lee*, Randall Barry is a revolutionary who flees to America with his heiress wife to escape the law. In McElgun's *Annie Reilly*, the young hero James O'Rourke is falsely accused of planning to steal arms from a local barracks and is forced to flee the country, with money he receives from his father.

None of the immigrant characters in these novels comes to America for religious liberty or the freedom to practice the Catholic religion, again distinguishing the Irish from Dorsey's German immigrants. As the authors portray Irish life, the people have this freedom. Immigrants come because they believe that in America they can practice their religion without suffering economic or political oppression.

Several of the authors speak of the immigrants' search for freedom generally, but they seem to mean economic opportunity, the freedom from landlords and the laws that protect them. In Quigley's first novel, Arthur O'Clery says he wants "to live with his family in 'a free country,' where there were no landlords or tyrants." Another character says that there are two "signs of tyranny" absent in America: "landlords and game laws."[56] The immigrant father Michael Mulroony, in Quigley's later novel, refers to America as "free and open for us all, where there are no landlords, but plenty of land for all the world" and "no bishops or other tyrants that can rob the poor and oppress their tenants."[57]

It is only in Cannon's *Bickerton* that a more general political as opposed to economic liberty is described as the primary motive for coming to America. In that novel, Manus O'Hanlon—driven away by "the scourge of the oppressor"—says, while on a ship to his new country: "already I feel the breath of liberty coming with a welcome to us over the waters, and I shall soon stand a freeman among the free." America was the "Land of Promise" as opposed to the "Island of Sorrow."[58]

While the Irish American authors clearly preferred to focus on comfortably off, although not wealthy, leading characters, they still portrayed a population that faced or actually endured poverty in Ireland, such as McElgun's Reilly family, who after years of prosperity are forced to live with distant relatives after they are evicted. The authors also acknowledged Irish poverty through their minor characters. The immigrant father in Cannon's *Bickerton*, who comes to America with money for the sake of political freedom, describes other immigrants on the ship as "mostly the poorest of the poor, who had parted with everything available, to raise the means necessary to convey them to a land where, as they had been assured, were to be found 'work and bread for all.'"[59] The aristocratic widow in Sadlier's *Old and New* explains to her daughter that the "great majority" of the people in America come "from Old Europe in search of a bare living, denied them at home."[60]

The authors also acknowledged that in America, even those who brought some financial resources with them battled poverty after their arrival. As with the poverty in Ireland, the authors describe the experience in a general way or as a condition that befell their characters at some point after their emigration. In his first novel, Quigley describes the deplorable living and working conditions many Irish encountered in America, writing: "we boast of . . . the number of railroads in operation . . . but the trials, tears, labors, sufferings and injustice which our indifference or avarice has inflicted on those thousands of our fellow-creatures whose hands have built them never occur to our minds or cause us a single regret, while glorying in the advancement of our 'great country.'" Cannon describes the "poor worn labourer, or . . . artisan . . . and the heavy lids of the exhausted needlewoman" and also portrays the northeastern city of Bickerton as actually two cities divided by class as well as religion—one city occupied by the wealthy and the other by "poor and illiterate immigrants . . . the men who dug down the hills . . . drained the marshes . . . and made its streets . . . and the women, who did for the Bickerton*iennes* all that they were too rich, too proud, too delicate, or too lazy to do for themselves." Sadlier's Con O'Regan observes that his "friends and neighbors that are here so many years . . . have so little by them. . . . It's only from hand to mouth with them, and it takes every penny they can make to keep things square."[61]

In another account of poverty in *Bickerton*, Cannon describes an Irish neighborhood, "Little Dublin," as filled with "filthy lanes . . . blind alleys . . . . and "tumble-down" houses. In *Con O'Regan*, Sadlier describes the "comfortless dwellings" of a poor immigrant family who live in a "small, dingy room . . . of a house which was once a private mansion . . . but now . . . sheltering as many families as it contained rooms."[62]

When it came to their major characters, many of the authors show their heroes and heroines living hardscrabble lives in Boston or New York in the first few years after their arrival in America. The authors explain the decline of these families—who had come with some resources—by accidents such as early death, theft, and illness. In Sadlier's *Willy Burke* and Quigley's *The Cross and the Shamrock*, the fathers of the families die during the passage to America, and the survivors quickly use up their resources. In Roddan's *John O'Brien*, the hero's mother dies in childbirth; his prosperous father—cheated by a Protestant business associate—dies later, leaving his son a penniless orphan. In Cannon's novel, a thief steals the families' money just after they arrive in America.

In some cases, accidents befall the immigrants after they have been in their adopted country for some time. A friend and mentor to Roddan's John O'Brien becomes ill, loses his job, and can no longer buy food for his wife and children, who die soon after. A minor male character in Sadlier's *Confessions of an Apostate* earns decent money as a laborer, but when he is injured on the job, his family must depend on the wages of the eldest son; when he dies, they become destitute. In *Con O'Regan*, Sadlier describes an accident of another sort. The directors of a Boston bank invest "in divers speculations on their own separate accounts." As a result, the bank fails, and "thousands of poor people, very many of them Irish . . . were left penniless. . . . How were these poor deluded thousands to obtain redress? They were foreigners, very low down . . . in the scale of social importance, while the robbers, the swindlers, were at its very summit."[63]

The victims received no compensation, and gradually the public forgot about the incident.

The unmarried men and women characters come to America with some money, but they almost always have to work when they arrive.[64] Although they usually do not suffer the accidental losses of money that seem to plague the families in these novels, their lives are not easy. Men do manual labor, often working on gangs that build railroads and canals. McElgun calls the boarding house where James O'Rourke, the lead male character of *Annie Reilly*, resides when he first comes to the city "a New York Menagerie." Single women usually work as domestic servants. The heroine of McElgun's novel works in the palatial home of Mrs. Derby Granville Phillips. The servant's room is a "very miserable apartment . . . the ceiling hardly five feet in height."[65]

While they are certainly willing to portray major and minor characters in America as poor, at least for some years after their arrival, the authors remind readers in various ways that the major characters had once enjoyed more comfortable circumstances. Quigley spends a chapter in *The Cross and the Shamrock* describing the O'Clery family's historical connections to Irish and Catholic heroes, concluding: "that they were not degenerate sons of Erin . . . we trust this history will amply demonstrate." In *Profit and Loss*, Mrs. Mulroony cautions her husband not to emphasize the family's history because their children might have "to earn their bread with hard labor . . . and then it would be hard for them to bear it, when they knew that so few of their forefathers were as low and poor as themselves."[66] The immigrant father in Cannon's *Bickerton* felt "the remonstrances of pride, against seeking his friends in the garb of a common laborer," and an immigrant in *The Lost Rosary* longed for "decent" rather than manual work.[67]

Certain authors are quite explicit about why they emphasize the former prosperity of major characters: as mentioned before, Quigley fears that the "poverty, humiliation, and rags of old Erin . . . scandalize" the immigrants, make them "ashamed of creed and country," and lead to the "apostasy of many."[68] Boyce, who featured the Irish gentry and professional classes in *Mary Lee*, says he is confronting American stereotypes. His American character Ephraim Weeks, like most of his compatriots, thinks that "the Irish *brogue* . . . [is] synonymous with consummate ignorance and absolute barbarism," that the Irish "never could have an idea in their heads above the pick or the spade," and are employed only "on the wharves, [and] on the railroads." As an old Irish woman tells Weeks during his visit to Ireland, "Little as ye think of the Irish abroad . . . there's some o' them at home here'd make ye keep a civil distance, if ye don't keep a civil tongue in yer head."[69]

The Specter of Famine

While the authors are willing to acknowledge poverty, and certainly do not focus their stories on the wealthy, they do not portray their major Irish characters as truly desperate victims. In that light, most of them, including the five born in Ireland—all of whom emigrated between 1844 and 1850—do not directly confront the famine of the late 1840s. Typically, their lead characters arrive in America well before that time, and the authors do not mention the effect of the blight on their characters' lives in later decades. The same holds true for the novels of the 1860s and '70s, which feature characters who leave Ireland in the early 1840s or in the 1850s, like Sadlier's *Con O'Regan* and Quigley's *Profit and Loss*.

At best, most of these novels include a passing comment, or a reference to a bad time that is now over. In Sadlier's 1851 *Alice Riordan*, a novel about immigrants who come to Montreal in the late 1830s, the author describes her characters as "far removed from that squalid wretchedness which, of late years, too often marks the appearance of the Irish emigrant."[70] In Boyce's *Mary Lee*, published in 1860, an old woman in Ireland refers to a "time of need," telling the American visitor, "We're obliged to ye, to be sure, for sendin us over what ye did. . . . [A]n ill it'd be *our common* to forget it, or indeed our childher after us, for that matter."[71] McElgun's *Annie Reilly*, published in 1873 and describing immigrants from the late 1850s, includes one reference to the famine, when an older Irish immigrant asks the main character, a new arrival, if "the people an't starving as they wor when I left there?" The response: It is "not so bad as that now."[72] Quigley adopts another strategy as he uses language evoking the famine to describe the conditions facing the O'Clery family in the 1830s. In his 1853 *The Cross and the Shamrock*, he refers to a cruel Irish landlord who tries to recruit and convert "soupers" during bad times "when 'praties' were dear, and the crops failed."[73]

In only three novels of the period—Sadlier's *Elinor Preston* and *Bessy Conway*, published in 1861, and McCorry's *The Lost Rosary*, published in 1870—do the authors describe the famine in a more detailed way. *The Lost Rosary* is the only novel in which lead characters actually endure the famine and emigrate to flee its effects. Although Sadlier is more willing than most of the other authors to acknowledge the famine, she too never portrays her major characters as victimized by it. Her heroine Elinor Preston mirrors Sadlier's own experience in many ways. Sadlier was the privately educated daughter of a well-off merchant in County Cavan, who came to Montreal in 1844, virtually penniless, after her father suffered business losses and died. Elinor is the privately educated daughter of a well-off Dublin lawyer who stays with her family in Dublin into the late 1840s. The family had remained prosperous during the

> years of commercial depression—that dismal lull which followed the extinction of the great Repeal movement, and ushered in the Famine. It was a time of hopeless, joyless, public despondency; and every family in the kingdom, from high to low, shared more or less in the general depression."[74]

The Prestons do not come upon hard times until the father's death late in 1848, when they discover that he had been deeply in debt. Sadlier does not attribute the father's downfall to the general conditions of the country, however. More than once, she alludes to the fact that Mr. Preston was "one of those good, easy men" with little skill in financial management.[75] Despite the family's changed circumstances, Elinor and her brother George remain in Ireland for another few years. George takes up law; Elinor is supported by wealthy friends. When she journeys to Killarney for a vacation, Elinor describes the beautiful scenery and laments the loss of the abbeys and the Irish aristocracy, but she never mentions the famine or its effects on that part of the country.

In this novel Sadlier offers a unique motivation for her characters' decision to emigrate. Elinor and George, who come to Canada, are motivated, in part, by economics (and, in Elinor's case, by a desire for adventure). But Sadlier also makes it clear that these urban, educated professionals depart for the new world because they do not want to feel ashamed of their reduced circumstances. As George explains it:

> Elinor and I have both to make out our living the best way we can, and . . . we shall do it with more energy and spirit in a new and strange country where nobody knows anything of our antecedents. Here we have—at least my sister has—the galling trammels of aristocratic birth and gentle breeding to operate against her. . . . In a strange country . . . people will take us just as they find us, and we can humble ourselves to almost any employment that may offer a fair chance of success, without having to encounter the hollow pity of pretended friends.[76]

Since Sadlier does not specifically relate the Preston family's difficulties to the famine, she uses only minor characters to illustrate the severe effects of the blight. Elinor, from her first-class berth, observes a poor young woman in steerage who is joining her father in America; she and her mother had supported themselves in Ireland by spinning, weeding, and gathering potatoes for farmers in their neighborhood. Then in the "dismal year of the famine," when these farmers were "reduced to beggary and starvation," the mother and daughter ended up in the poorhouse where "food was hardly sufficient." After the mother dies, the daughter is sent out to service, where she remains for "three or four years" until her father in America sends for her.[77]

If Elinor Preston manages to survive the famine in relatively good economic circumstances, Sadlier's Bessy Conway triumphs over it. Bessy witnesses the consequences of the potato blight when she returns to Ireland seven years after leaving, with enough money saved from her earnings as a domestic servant to rescue her family. She finds "the thatch" in her old homestead "broken in many places, and covered with patches of moss . . . the white walls . . . discolored . . . the small windows . . . disfigured with sundry pieces of board nailed on as substitutes for broken panes, and altogether the house had a desolate, neglected look in painful contrast with its former appearance." "Famine and disease had [also] found their way into that . . . household. . . . [T]he aged father and mother sat . . . watching with distended eyes . . . the family supper, consisting of water and nettles, with a handful or so of oatmeal." Bessy's sister is very ill; and her brothers have "sunken cheeks and hollow eyes." Worse, they are in the process of being evicted by their cruel Protestant landlord when Bessy appears and, with "quite an air of authority," orders the bailiffs to stop the procedure.[78] She not only pays the outstanding rent but buys food for her family and their neighbors.

McCorry is the only author who devotes more attention to the famine than Sadlier. In *The Lost Rosary*, published ten years after *Bessy Conway*, Mary O'Donnell and her cousin Ailey emigrate to America specifically because of the disaster; they are the only lead characters in these novels to do so. Typically, the young women come from a once relatively prosperous family. Mary was educated at "the Old Chapel School" and also had been to boarding school. Then the potato crop showed symptoms of disease, and the "bad times came again and again, until the full storm of the famine of '46 and '47 burst over the land." McCorry implies that all of the families affected by the famine—not only the O'Donnell's—had been comfortably off in earlier years; the blight "left thousands upon thousands, who had never known want in their lives, exposed to the full fury of the desolation that swept over the warm hearths of the affrighted people."[79]

Once Mary's father dies, the young woman, expecting to be evicted, moves with her mother and cousin to a faraway town. When her mother contracts typhus, Mary encounters this scene in the local fever ward: "Stretched on the hard pavement of the street . . . lay some thirty poor creatures, some of them in an advanced stage of fever. . . . Some . . . beds were erected in the open yard, under temporary sheds hastily thrown up to protect the sick from the heat of the sun. . . . The sick . . . lay gasping and moaning, burned with a scorching thirst."[80]

McCorry stands out from the other writers not only in his description of the famine's effects on his main characters but also in his discussion of the political and economic causes of the starvation. "Ireland was under a heavy visitation," he writes, "for that country is under the rule of a foreign power, and the visitation was made by England." In the years of famine, "full-freighted ships, bearing foreign grain, were floating on the ocean, destined for Irish ports. But from these same Irish ports went forth home-grown grain in abundance." Even after a few years of crop failure, "wheat and corn were harvested, not to be eaten, but for sale in the English markets, so that the ever-craving call of rent might be satisfied." McCorry acknowledges that England is not responsible for the loss of the potato crop, "but the effects of the famine arose more from mislegislation, than from any work of nature."[81]

Yet McCorry is loath to appeal directly to Irish nationalism or to stoke a hatred of England: "It is easy to advance proof of this, but such a proceeding would be out of place in a work of this kind," he writes, immediately after his assessment of cause. And while he describes Irish emigrants on board a ship to America as first feeling "hatred" for the "authors of the desolation that afflicted the people," the "spirit of religion battled strongly for possession of the minds of those so afflicted," directing the hatred "from persons to principles of government."[82]

Even in *Elinor Preston* and *The Lost Rosary*, which deal with famine-era immigrants, Sadlier and McCorry take pains to show that not all Irish immigrants are in desperate need. Describing the "steerage" passengers on a ship coming to the United States in 1845, McCorry writes:

> The large majority . . . were Irish . . . of . . . every description of every class of people, . . . some comfortable, others poor; some with cash in their possession, others without a penny; some well provisioned, others without a bite to eat other than the ship's allowance; some, and they were the fewest number, with some prospects before them on landing; others going out on speculation, ready to face and to dare hardships of any kind, rather than submit to those at home, without even a chance throughout life to better their miserable condition.[83]

Ultimately, whatever difficult conditions and circumstances drive their characters, the authors present emigration as an individual moral choice. Their Irish characters are not passive victims of circumstance or compelled by events beyond their control. They emigrate to advance their own interests but also, and this is key, to advance the interests of others as well. The authors do not denigrate activity or extol passivity; they denigrate action motivated solely by selfishness rather than by the Christian ideal of loving others as much as the self. Invariably, their characters are able to serve others *and* themselves.

Justifying Emigration as a Moral Decision

McCorry, in *The Lost Rosary*, describes the unselfish motivations of a large swath of immigrants leaving "fathers and mothers . . . sisters and brothers . . . wives and young families." All "sustained themselves with the thought that, with God's help, before long, they would be able to send the first remittance to cheer the desolate homes they had left forever."[84] When families emigrate together, the decision is made for the sake of the family as a whole. Sadlier's Andy Burke strives to improve his own condition and also to "procure . . . some sort of establishment" for his children. He asks his wife, "where's the prospect for a large family risin' up about us . . . for their sakes we must go."[85]

Single immigrants, too, act for the sake of their families; they leave only with their parents' approval and intend to earn money to help those left behind. Sadlier's Bessy Conway gives her parents "plainly to understand that she would never be happy unless they gave" their consent to her emigration, "and under that pressure the old couple were forced to give in. Very unwillingly they did so." Annie Reilly's parents find her decision to emigrate "painful and distressing," but they are not "sentimental people" and make "no objection."[86] In McCorry's *The Lost Rosary*, Mary O'Donnell and her cousin Ailey initially refuse to accompany their fiancés to America because Mary's father opposes the move; Mary realizes that her departure "would be the death of one or other of" her parents, a "sacrifice" McCorry describes as "noble."[87] Only after helping their parents through the famine and nursing them on their deathbeds do the young women depart for America.

For Sadlier, the only author who credits a desire for adventure as among the motivations of her single émigrés, it is a willingness to help those left behind that legitimizes their decisions. Bessy Conway and the eventual apostate Simon O'Hare, who want to see the world and to make their fortunes, obtain their parents' consent and also resolve to send money back home. Simon is torn between "ambition and the newly awakened desire of 'seeing the world,'" on the one hand, and love for his mother and unwillingness to leave her on the other. Sadlier's inclusion of ambition here does not bode well for the young man's future, but in the meantime, he makes his decision for his mother's sake; as he is reminded by another emigrant, "you'll be able to do more for the ould woman there than you would here, twice over."[88]

In other novels, the unselfish motivations are less complicated. In Sadlier's *Con O'Regan*, Winny, the sister of the title character, works as a domestic servant in Boston; she tells her family in Ireland: "What do I want with money only to make you all comfortable?" McElgun's Annie Reilly informs her family that she will go to America because "I could earn enough there to be of great help to you." Her brother, in turn, also emigrates, joining in the effort to keep their parents "comfortable."[89]

Single men are allowed more selfish motivations only if they are fleeing to save their lives or honor, such as the young men in *Annie Reilly* and *The Lost Rosary*, who escape unjust arrest or family disgrace. Single women are allowed to have purely selfish motivations only if they have no Irish family left at home. The heroines in McCorry's *The Lost Rosary* and Sadlier's *Elinor Preston* emigrate to find their fiancés or to retain their pride only after their parents and other dependent family members are dead.[90]

The authors' emphasis on remittances does not conflict with their message that the Irish have known prosperity because they acknowledge that the once comfortably off families are now threatened with, or have actually fallen upon, hard times. The emphasis on remittances also does not conflict with the authors' determination to show that the Irish families left behind are also moral actors. In Sadlier's novels, the mothers of the single emigrants Simon O'Hare and Bessy Conway do not want their children to emigrate and consent only for the children's sake. Simon's mother is not influenced "by any amount of promise," and especially not by "promises relating to herself." In *Annie Reilly*, too, the parents are sad at the thought of losing their son and daughter but consent because "In that land . . . you will find for yourselves the means we are unable to supply you with here."[91]

The authors' determination to show emigration as an unselfish, moral act may help to explain their reluctance to confront the famine. In the only two novels that depict famine-era immigrants—*Elinor Preston* and *The Lost Rosary*—the single women do not depart until all their dependents have died. (In the other novel that tackles the famine, Bessy Conway does not depart, but returns, at the time of the blight.) The authors, it seems, could not risk showing people leaving their loved ones in the grip of famine, even for some future benefits.

In some of the novels, the authors go further, expressly stating that emigrating for entirely selfish reasons is morally unacceptable. In *The Lost Rosary*, Mary O'Donnell's parents initially disapprove of her fiancé's decision to leave, thinking that he sought only to improve his economic situation. "Seeing as how his circumstances were safe here," Mary's mother says, "he might easily have yielded his desire of America." The parents change their minds only when they realize that the young man is leaving for "motives of honor," namely, to escape a disgrace to his family name. In a reference to another family in the same novel, the author writes that they "might have been enjoying the sweets and comforts of their own country home" but are instead "daybound for a new land" because the wife, an insincere convert to Catholicism, wants to spare her daughters eventual marriage to "some ignorant clodhoppers."[92] The mother's description of Irish men here, like her rejection of her country home, illustrates her selfish materialist motives and undermines any claim to true motherly love.

With this portrayal of the decisions to emigrate, the novels tell readers that their decision to leave their homes is legitimate in the eyes of the Church in America and in Ireland. The only very brief suggestion of Irish clerical opposition to emigration comes in Quigley's first novel, when Mr. Clery, the father of the lead family, "came to America, against the advice of the priest, his brother."[93] Quigley says nothing further about the advice. In the other novels, the local Irish priests attend farewell parties for emigrants, welcome them back on visits to Ireland and, in one novel, happily receive contributions from former parishioners who now live in America.[94]

Legitimating the decision to emigrate may have been especially important for the single women who left their nuclear homes and families.

The leading scholars on the subject, Hasia Diner and Janet Nolan, emphasize the independence and initiative of these Irish women. Diner maintains that they emigrated for the sake of economic independence; Nolan emphasizes their desire to marry and raise a family. Both suggest that the women acted contrary not only to the reigning Protestant domestic ideal but also to the teachings of their church in Ireland.[95] These novels suggest that single women with living parents who emigrate are not ignoring the precepts of the Church—so long as they act for their parents' benefit and with their consent. No exemplary woman character in these novels leaves living parents for self-interested motives alone, whether marriage or economic independence. When the brother of McElgun's Annie Reilly tells her, "I would bet a sovereign, if I had it, that your whole anxiety to get to America is because James O'Rourke [her fiancé] is there," she answers, "you do me wrong there. . . . [M]y whole anxiety is to be able to assist you at home."[96] And no exemplary female character emigrates solely to better her own economic condition; although these women certainly realize they can earn more money in the United States, they mean to use the money to benefit others. Whatever Irish women's actual motivations, their actions are portrayed as legitimate only if they are motivated by a desire to help the families left behind.

With these portraits of their characters' lives in Ireland and immediately after their arrival in America, the authors describe a past life that will help their immigrant readers to survive and prosper, as Irish and Catholic, in the very different circumstances of America. Other than Cannon, who evokes an oppressive past to stoke hopes for freedom, the authors create a memory of a united, harmonious, religious culture and society that provided the Irish people with years of prosperity before being destroyed. The hope now is to restore that past life in a new world.

Chapter 3

AMERICAN
ANTI-CATHOLICISM

The Uses of Prejudice

The immigrant characters in the Irish American novels published from 1850 on encountered an America that was deeply hostile to them. The authors described an anti-Catholic and anti-Irish society that affected the immigrants in every area of their lives. These accounts of American prejudice, however, actually support the conclusions of scholars who argue that the real levels of Protestant hostility at the time cannot fully account for the defensive Irish Catholic culture that developed in America.[1] The novelists did not simply reflect social attitudes. They exaggerated the prejudice and also refused to acknowledge any progress in Protestant-Catholic relations, even when their commentaries and plots suggested otherwise. They emphasized and exaggerated prejudice to serve Catholic purposes, using the theme of unchanging hostility to reinforce their Irish immigrant readers' religious and ethnic identity—their sense of an Irish Catholic "us" as opposed to an American Protestant "them." This Irish Catholic identity consisted in devotion to Catholic religious practices, loyalty to priests, and support for Catholic institutions—including the growing system of schools—that embodied and maintained a separate people. The mid-century novelists adopted Cannon's focus on anti-Catholicism but not his desire that the immigrants be fully integrated into American life, orientations that Cannon retained in his two novels of the 1850s.

American Anti-Catholicism: An Unchanging Force?

The Irish American authors who began publishing in 1850 adopted various strategies to portray an America that seemed permanently anti–Irish Catholic. They did not describe any increase in prejudice from the 1830s to the 1850s, when an active nativist or Know-Nothing movement attacked Catholics for idolatry, subservience to priests, and loyalty to foreign powers.

They also did not describe any decline in these feelings during and after the Civil War, when, most scholars agree, anti-Catholic prejudice waned, as issues of slavery, war, and economic development took center stage. The prejudice against Irish Catholics certainly did not disappear in this later period, but it did not approach the previous levels.[2] The authors also never suggested that American hostility might vary geographically; in their novels, anti-Catholicism was as virulent in Minnesota and Wisconsin as in Philadelphia, Boston, and New York City.

Some authors were blunt about the unwavering Protestant hostility. If anything has changed, they write, it is only the tactics Protestants use to torment Catholics, or the names they give to their various movements. In 1850, Roddan claims that anti-Catholicism has become more dangerous over time, not because it has increased in range or intensity, but because Protestant elites have developed more effective ways of luring Catholics from their faith. Deacon Mills, for example, "did not attack openly. O, no! If he had shown his colors, he would have been less dangerous." Instead, he "labored hard to cultivate in children . . . a taste . . . [that] would be offended by things seen and heard in a church frequented by Irish Catholics."[3] In *The Blakes and Flanagans*, the 1855 novel in which she praises the growing system of Catholic schools, Sadlier writes that the first decades of the century were a time "before Nativism had developed itself into Know Nothingism," names she does not bother to define since both are merely covers for hatred of Catholics.[4]

The Arch Bishop:

OR,

ROMANISM IN THE UNITED STATES.

BY ORVILLA S. BELISLE.

BEAUTIFULLY ILLUSTRATED.

SECOND THOUSAND.

PHILADELPHIA:
PUBLISHED BY WM. WHITE SMITH,
No. 195 CHESTNUT STREET.
1855.

Figure 3.1. Title page of *The Arch Bishop*, one of a group of Know-Nothing novels of the 1850s, which criticized Catholic priests, especially Bishop Hughes, and extolled the Order of United Americans that defended Protestant institutions. Courtesy of Wright American Fiction Project, Indiana University Libraries.

THE CONFESSOR ATTEMPTS TO BURN THE BIBLE.

Figure 3.2. One of the "beautiful illustrations" in *The Arch Bishop* shows a boy rescuing the Bible that a priest—the Confessor—has cast into the flames over the objections of the boy's father. Courtesy of Wright American Fiction Project, Indiana University Libraries.

In the 1860s and '70s, the authors continue to describe a persistent anti-Catholicism. In *Old and New*, published in 1862, Sadlier includes two episodes that suggest different aspects of an unrelenting hostility: two of her characters, Mrs. Bumford and Mrs. Hopington, represent a Protestant charity that takes Irish Catholic children from their families, changes their names, and places them with Protestant farmers in the west, all with the support of "the authorities." The two women visit the Catholic widow Madame Von Weigel, who later tells her daughter that "hatred of Catholicity is at the bottom of all their philanthropic associations." On the same day, a second pair of women, representing the women's rights movement, or the "Bloomer school," also calls at the Von Weigel home. They are anti-Catholic only because they support women's rights and scoff when the widow invokes St. Paul.[5] McCorry shows the persistence of prejudice across time in *Mount Benedict*, published in 1871. He sets the novel at the time of the mob attack on the Charlestown convent nearly forty years before and repeatedly makes the point that the attack should still influence Catholic opinion.

The authors adopted other strategies as well to convey the idea of an unchanging American hostility. By referring to real historical incidents without giving dates, they suggest that the incidents all occurred recently. In *Mount Benedict*, McCorry links the Charlestown attack with other undated events: "Convent wreckings at Philadelphia . . . and attempted wreckings in the north of Ireland," he writes, "are of too recent a date to make us suppose that such evil practices have passed away from our midst for ever" or that they "shall never occur again."[6] Quigley, in his 1873 *Profit and Loss*, describes physical assaults on priests, false charges that priests imprisoned Protestant women in convents, and proposals that "Know-Nothing lodges ought to be revived," all without providing dates. Increasing the sense of overall menace, Quigley also refers to anti-Catholic events in Europe.

> The 'Commune' of Paris have immortalized themselves for what they did to priests and churchmen in our own day. . . . There were men as bad . . . in many countries and many ages in the past. And while the devil is busy . . . there will be such scenes occurring yearly, if not daily, in the world, as we have described without any exaggeration.[7]

Yet the authors also suggest that Protestant America's attitudes toward Catholics are improving, without modifying their overall message of unrelenting hostility. The suggestions come directly—through offhand remarks or more extended commentary—and indirectly, through plots and characters.

Boyce, in his 1860 *Mary Lee*, suggests that Americans have grown accustomed to the Irish. Speaking of America twenty years earlier, he writes: "an Irishman then, in certain sections of the United States, was as great a wonder as a Bengal tiger . . . and he fell so far below the ordinary standard of humanity . . . as to be considered unaccountable to human laws."[8] In Quigley's *Profit and Loss*, a priest makes a speech at the public school castigating various Protestant historians for their biased accounts of European and American history. The priest goes on to say that "now, when the public mind is comparatively unprejudiced, it is disgraceful to leave the people in ignorance of the truth of history."[9]

In more extended commentary, several of the authors suggest that the newer Protestant denominations, such as Unitarians, are less hostile to Irish Catholics than the older Calvinists and Methodists, mainly because they reflect a more secular society. Roddan and Boyce highlight the false teachings of the new denominations, calling them "atheistical," "liberal," or examples of "godless liberalism," but they also indicate that the denominations are more tolerant of Catholics.[10] Rather than welcome this development, the authors see it as another manifestation of Protestant hostility and another danger their readers must avoid. Roddan warns his hero John O'Brien to steer clear of the library societies in Boston, which are dominated by liberal Protestants who allow Catholics to join. Such "mixed societies *always* hurt a Catholic soul," Roddan writes, not because Protestant members abuse Catholics but because the prevailing intention is "not to hurt one another's feelings." "Nothing *really* Catholic . . . . [and] [n]othing *palpably* Protestant is heard." Roddan further warns that Catholics who join these societies, become "Catholics of the very worst sort; that is, l-i-b-e-r-a-l Catholics." Roddan is equally critical of liberal Protestants. They too become "the very *worst* sort of Protestants. I mean liberal Protestants, who, on the whole, rather *like* the Catholic Church."[11]

Boyce makes his opinion of America's newer religions clear in his character Ephraim Weeks, the American who believes in only two religious principles: "the existence of a first cause, and the perfectability of man," the latter to be attained "by reason, science, and experience." Weeks also accepts basic moral rules; he tries "to do about right with every man, and . . . that was religion enough for" him. Although Weeks is not anti-Catholic in any traditional sense and would not interfere with Catholics in the practice of their religion, he is presented as hostile and dangerous in another way. He rejects all religions, "pilgrim and priestly," that "acted like a straight-jacket on the nation, cramping its energies and stinting its growth."[12] Sadlier also comments on the toleration displayed by members of newer denominations but expresses contempt rather than gratitude for such views. The two Protestant women in *Con O'Regan* who, along with their brother, help finance an Irish settlement in the west, attend the services of Rev. Bertram Shillingworth, an "independent preacher." The two women are "firmly persuaded that all mankind, without exception, were destined to be gathered . . . into the garners of the Lord." Such opinions, Sadlier comments, "may appear something like Universalism, but still the good ladies never actually professed that, or any other *ism*, they were merely 'somewhat more charitable than their neighbors.'" They lived according to their principles, "if principles their simple rules of action could be called."[13]

Liberalism, in these novels, is just another form of anti-Catholicism—another menace that Catholics face in Protestant America. More important, as they describe their Catholic characters' lives in Boston, the three authors focus not on liberal Protestants but on crude bigots who abuse Catholics verbally or physically and try to lure them from their faith. Roddan's John O'Brien is mistreated by Protestants while he is dependent on them, as is Boyce's Irish immigrant character, who works as a domestic servant for a family in Boston. In a letter to her aunt in Ireland, the young servant reports that her employer, "who's nothin after all but a shopkeeper's wife," calls her "Paddy girl," "Papist," and "ignorant."[14] Sadlier too does not make the liberalism of her kindly women central to the Boston society that makes life so impossible for her Catholic characters that they have to move out west to an exclusively Irish Catholic settlement.

In addition to these direct references to changes in Protestant views, the authors also suggest the changes in indirect ways. Anti-Catholicism is central to the plots of the novels of the 1850s, which portray American life from the 1830s to the 1850s, a period when anti-Catholicism was actually most intense. In the novels of the 1860s and '70s, this hostility becomes more of a peripheral theme, reflecting a decline in relevance to immigrants' lives. Here again, however, the authors do not actually acknowledge the improvement, but continue to base their recommendations on the assumption of persistent, crude anti-Catholicism.

In the 1850s novels, the centrality of the anti–Irish Catholic theme is evident as the immigrant characters endure verbal abuse, hostile actions, and systematic efforts to convert them in foster care, schools, workplaces, and detention centers. In Quigley's *The Cross and the Shamrock*, an orphan is tortured to death by starvation and neglect when he refuses to eat meat on Friday or attend Protestant prayer services. In Sadlier's two novels of the 1850s, the schools are a major issue. In *Willy Burke*, a wealthy couple willing to pay for the education of the Burke brothers expects them to become Protestants—and they fire the boys' widowed mother when she objects to their plans. The authors also describe physical attacks against Catholics; Roddan and Quigley recount assaults on convents and priests, for example.

The novels after the 1850s are less consistent in their portrayal of prejudice, as the authors adopt more varied themes. In some of the novels—Sadlier's *Confessions of an Apostate* and *Con O'Regan*, McCorry's *Mount Benedict*, and Quigley's *Profit and Loss*—plots are still centered around anti-Catholicism. In Sadlier's *Confessions of an Apostate*, Simon O'Hare becomes an apostate and changes his name, first to Kerrigan, then to Kerr, for the sake of success and the love of a Protestant woman. He lives to regret these decisions, eventually returning to Ireland. In Quigley's *Profit and Loss*, Protestants use camp meetings, "sociables, singing-schools, night spelling-schools sewing-bees, and other lady societies" as well as "such books as . . . *Maria Monk's Disclosure*" to convert the people of the Irish settlement.[15]

Another group of novels of the 1860s and '70s, however, downplays anti-Catholicism, focusing instead on the dangerous attractions of American society, now more willing to accept the immigrants and their children. In these works, America's freedom and materialism, not its hostility, are the main threats to Irish Catholic identity.[16]

In Sadlier's *Bessy Conway*, McCorry's *The Lost Rosary*, and McElgun's *Annie Reilly*—all concerned with single, female immigrant heroines—the danger to the women's Irish Catholicism is America's free social and sexual life. In Sadlier's *Bessy Conway*, three young Irish domestic servants neglect their faith, ultimately coming to a disastrous end because they are interested in "dress," "finery," "Saturday-night dances," and "raffles." The women each marry men they have met at such events; one was a "drunken brute" and another abandoned his wife and child.[17] The temptations for the women come from the social world around them, not from within the households where they work. McCorry and McElgun note the danger of sexual exploitation, but from lodging houses: in *The Lost Rosary*, McCorry's single women face the problem of "low-lodging houses" that are "pitfalls for the innocent and unwary." As an older woman character puts it, immigrant girls—innocent and without money or friends—enter such houses "an,' after a while, become dead lost to every sense o' shame. What is there left them but the streets ever after?"[18]

For young, single male immigrants also, American freedom, rather than prejudice, endangers a good Catholic life. The men are at liberty to engage in vices like fighting and drinking. James O'Rourke, in McElgun's *Annie Reilly*, easily gets work on the docks in New York City and in the oil fields of Pennsylvania; the young Irish immigrant does not experience anti-Catholicism in either place and is readily promoted. But James does note the "reckless" behavior of other men in the oil fields who care only for "drinking, carousing, and fighting." They have "to do hard labor" in their old age because they had spent their money on "whiskey"; "the greater part of them have themselves only to blame for their misery."[19]

For the novels concerned with the newly middle-class or wealthy immigrants, and with the American-born generation—Boyce's *Mary Lee* and Sadlier's *Elinor Preston* and *Old and New*—materialism is the primary threat to Irish Catholic identity. In *Old and New*, Sadlier shows that the greatest danger to her newly well-off immigrants is their love of possessions and social status, not prejudice. While these families do not abandon Catholicism, the wives and daughters, in particular, interpret and practice their faith in decidedly casual ways, arriving late for mass so they can show off their clothes and carriages to their best advantage. The daughters of the families, "our would-be somebody American-Irish Catholics," are also "ashamed of their Irish ancestry" for their own reasons, not because they experience Protestant hostility.[20]

A related theme in the novels of the 1860s and '70s is the Americans' sense that they are superior, as individuals and as a nation, to all other groups, an attitude some of these authors resent just as much as the Americans' previous outright hostility. Boyce's novel *Mary Lee* concerns the various ways in which Irish characters ridicule and humiliate Ephraim Weeks, an American Protestant visitor to Ireland. Weeks believes it is his country's "duty, as a nation, to redeem the world from ignorance" and suggests that his Irish hosts employ "Yankee lecturers. . . . [T]hey'll open your eyes wider than ever they opened before." He is "taken aback by . . . the contemptuous disregard" the Irish show toward "a claim which he thought irresistible all over the world, and especially in poverty-stricken Ireland."[21]

Sadlier, in *Bessy Conway*, adopts the same theme, when a "precise New England woman" speaks to the heroine "with a sort of patronizing air."[22] And in Quigley's *Profit and Loss*, when one character says that Ireland is backward compared with America, an Irish laborer responds that much of the "inventive genius" of Americans is "imitative and borrowed from natives of other countries," though the Irish man allows that Americans had contributed "sewing and knitting machines!"[23]

Over time, the assertions of superiority that irritate the authors come from the children of immigrants, who look down on their Irish parents and ancestors. In the opinion of their immigrant father, the daughters in Sadlier's *Old and New* have the "notion . . . that everything Irish is low and vulgar . . . and nothing's right, or nobody's worth knowing that isn't rale American, or doesn't look American-like."[24] Quigley and McElgun make the same point in their novels of the 1870s. Quigley uses the term "genteel Irish-American" in the subtitle of *Profit and Loss*, summarizing his sardonic message. McElgun, in *Annie Reilly*, introduces Miss Talbot, "a fashionable Irish-American lady" who speaks in accented and incorrect English, "with a voice which sounded so high up in her nose that . . . [the hearer] thought she must be suffering from a severe cold." When she and her husband visit Ireland, they draw "parallels between Ireland and America, to the great disadvantage of the former." The husband notes that the Irish are "darn fools for living in such a country at all."[25] Like Boyce's Ephraim Weeks, McElgun's Irish characters show up a visiting American, except in McElgun's novel, the self-important visitor is not a New England Protestant but an Irish American Catholic.

Despite the shift from the danger of outright prejudice to that of acceptance and assimilation, the authors continue to include at least some episodes of crude anti-Catholicism. However brief the episodes and however marginal to the characters' lives, they remind readers that Americans remain hostile to them. These episodes then serve as the basis for the authors' recommendations.

In Sadlier's *Bessy Conway*, the Irish Catholic cook Bridget is forced to defend confession in a conversation with an African American servant named "Wash." The episode takes up only about two pages of the 316-page book, and the Irish woman wins the exchange easily. In another incident in the novel, involving Bessy's Protestant employer, Mrs. Hibbard, it seems as if the author has simply tacked on the anti-Catholic scene, since the employer's motivations make so little sense in the context of the work. Mrs. Hibbard displays "a want of steadiness . . . and . . . a listless indifference to the affairs of others." On the other hand, she "meant well," was "uniformly kind," and "strongly impressed with a sense of justice." Then, suddenly, at page 205 of the novel, under the influence of the local minister, Mrs. Hibbard wants to save her Catholic help "from the burning," and insists they attend a Protestant prayer service. She fires Bessy, who refuses to attend the service. Sadlier has made her point about Protestant America—and reinforced her recommendation that servants seek Catholic employers—without acknowledging any changes since 1850 when she published *Willy Burke*. In that novel, however, the anti-Catholic actions affect a child, forcing him to leave school, endure accusations that he is a thief, and take a job to support his unemployed mother. The single episode in *Bessy Conway*, by contrast, concerns an adult who immediately finds a better job with a Catholic family.[26]

Similarly, in the preface to *Annie Reilly*, McElgun lists his desire to recount the "fanatical bigotry of some of the mushroom employers . . . [who] take advantage of the dependent station of a Catholic girl, to insult and trample on her most sacred feelings." But while he has made this point, McElgun includes only one relevant episode, which takes up five pages of the 245-page work, and has no impact on the heroine. In the same novel, McElgun's hero James O'Rourke, working in the oil fields, neither witnesses nor experiences prejudice himself, yet he tells a fellow worker that he is a coward "to dread to acknowledge your creed, the creed of your forefathers, because those around you despise religion."[27]

In advancing their message that Irish Catholics should fear and avoid American society, the authors not only exaggerated Protestant prejudice in these ways but also underestimated Catholic power. They were often happy to report significant growth in the Catholic population. Roddan describes his hero's experiences in Worcester in the early 1830s when it had "no Catholic society . . . [and] one Catholic family" and adds that "now" in 1850, when his novel was published, "the Catholic interest is strong there."[28] Authors also focus on the growth of the Catholic population in novels published after 1860. Sadlier's lead character in *Confessions of an Apostate* arrives in Boston around 1815, meets very few Catholics there, and even fewer when he moves to New Haven a few years later. "Catholics, the reader will remember, were but sparely scattered in those days amongst the people of the Puritan city," Sadlier writes.[29] While most of the authors attribute the increase to the growth of Irish immigration, Quigley, in his 1873 *Profit and Loss*, also points to conversions. One of his characters refers to "converts coming in by the hundreds and thousands."[30]

Roddan and Sadlier also note the corresponding growth in Catholic institutions. Writing that Worcester had no Catholic society in John O'Brien's youth, Roddan points out that the city "now . . . [has] a Catholic college . . . and two churches, one of them quite a large and handsome one."[31] In Sadlier's 1855 *The Blakes and Flanagans*, "there were but few Catholic schools . . . perhaps not more than two or three" in New York City at the time she describes. But "the Empire City can now boast of as good Catholic schools as any on the Western continent. . . . New York has now its Jesuit colleges, its Christian schools, its Mt. St. Vincent, and its Sacred Heart, watchwords of hope and joy to generations yet unborn."[32] In her later novel, she notes that "if Bessy Conway were writing" about poverty "now she would have a different story to tell. . . . [T]he deserving poor have found active and devoted friends in the Society of St. Vincent de Paul, now established in every part of the city."[33]

Yet, the authors did not confront the implications of these demographic changes for Catholic influence in society and government. Although the population growth, like the spread of religious liberalism, should make things easier for the immigrants, the authors continue to portray Catholics as a beleaguered group unable to combat the society's hostility toward them. They set their novels in earlier decades when Irish Catholics were still relatively few and marginalized. And though they point to subsequent gains, their messages are rooted in the situation of the immigrants during the previous years. The 1850s novels of Roddan, Quigley, and Sadlier, for example, take place from the 1820s to the early 1840s, well before the growth of the Catholic population they boast about. In his 1853 *The Cross and the Shamrock*, Quigley suggests that as Catholics grew in number, they gained some political power, which they put to good use. After the orphans in the novel are taken by the Protestant poor master and placed in foster homes of his choosing, Quigley declares that such actions would never happen in 1853. "Let it not be said we exaggerate . . . the conduct of the poorhouse officials; and from the improbability of such an instance of injustice and cruelty happening in our day, let not our readers conclude that such a case, and many such cases, happened not in times gone by." In the 1830s, the time frame of the novel,

> the Irish Catholic population of the state was not much more than what that of one county is now. Then an Irish Catholic could not get the office of constable or bailiff; now we have Catholic cabinet ministers, judges, senators, legislators and aldermen. Then the ballot box was sur-

rounded but by a few Irish naturalized citizens. . . . [N]ow the Irish adopted citizen, by the power he exercises in his vote, is solicited by candidates, from a town officer to president; and whoever would attempt to reenact the kidnapping of . . . [the poormaster] and many other officials of his class, in their days of petty power, would be sure to be compelled to retire forever from public life.[34]

Quigley, the only author of the group who explicitly acknowledges that there is political power in numbers, nevertheless uses life in the previous era—when orphans were hounded and even tortured to death by the "Pharaohs of sectarianism" and the aged Father O'Shane "was . . . the sole pastor of the city"—as the basis for his message. The novel, he explains, in his 1853 preface, is meant to help "our poor, neglected, and uninstructed brethren" who were "in danger" from the "trying ordeal of temptation and persecution on account of their religion."[35] This despite his admission that actual conditions had so improved.

In *Profit and Loss*, written twenty years later, Quigley does not even suggest that Catholics are better able to defend or assert themselves. Indeed, as the immigrant father in the novel becomes involved in politics— he is elected a justice of the peace and frequently serves as chair of public meetings—"his earlier religious training was soon obliterated" as his "vanity" was aroused. Rather than seeing his character's new political power as a means to defend his people, Quigley decries the "influence of indifferent, if not evil association."[36] He encourages Catholics to rely on their own institutions, especially schools, and to be wary of Catholic politicians.

Uses of Anti-Catholicism: Fanning the Flames with a Purpose

Why, then, did the authors cling to the vision of an unremitting American hostility toward a weak Irish Catholic population? Undoubtedly, the hostile encounters with Protestants recorded in the novels added tension and conflict to works of fiction that could not rely on romance for these effects. The external hostility also reflected the experience of the immigrants in Ireland and, to some continuing degree, also in America. The fact that prejudice against Irish Catholics had declined did not mean it had disappeared. But the writers did not recount American prejudice simply to reflect the society or to portray the Irish as victims. They described a hostile America and a beleaguered Irish Catholic community to mark the boundaries that separated the immigrants and their children from the rest of America. The attacks against Catholics repeated in the novels were often simply general insults that defined an "us" and a "them." In the novels of the 1850s the anti-Catholic attacks also defined the content of group identity, the "stuff" within the boundary. Irish Catholic characters in these novels were attacked for their religious practices, their attachment to priests, and their loyalty to exclusively Catholic institutions, the elements that defined their identity. The novels of the 1860s and '70s focused mainly on the general insults that served only to emphasize boundaries.[37]

Reinforcing Religious Practice

Unlike the first generation of Catholic writers, Roddan, Quigley, and Sadlier, writing in the 1850s, did not focus on addressing questions about whether the Catholic Church is the one true church. They had far more practical concerns. They advocated prayer, fasting, and reception of the sacraments and used the verbal attacks on Catholics to reinforce those recommendations. Faithful religious practice became a way to distinguish Irish Catholics from others. Protestants in the novels charged that Catholics worshipped images, prayed to the Blessed Virgin more than to God, paid to have their sins forgiven in confession, and followed such superstitious practices as fasting from meat on Friday. In Sadlier's *Willy Burke*, when the widowed mother comes to remind her son to perform his Easter duty, the young man's Protestant employer tells her to come back another time when the boy would have "a few more sins to confess . . . [and] it will be all the same to the priest."[38] In Sadlier and Quigley novels, ministers at Friday night dinner parties scornfully call abstaining from meat on Friday a "puerile folly" or a "foolish" rule that is not appropriate in "this free and Protestant country."[39]

Roddan, Quigley, and Sadlier all responded to these charges. Quigley and Roddan assert that Catholics do not pay for the forgiveness of sins and stress the importance of true sorrow. Roddan, for his part, praises confession for the grace it makes available and says that Protestants, by contrast, have only human means at their disposal and often exhibit "religious insanity."[40] When a Protestant character in Sadlier's *Willy Burke* makes a sarcastic comment about the power of priests to forgive sins, Willy replies that he believes "because the Church believes it, and teaches it to her children."[41]

The authors also answered charges related to abstaining from meat on Friday. Roddan and Quigley invoke the importance of self-denial and the authority of the Church, as does Sadlier.[42] When a dinner party guest asks Edward Flanagan to defend the practice of fasting on "rational grounds" in *The Blakes and Flanagans*, Edward answers: "we Catholics are not accustomed . . . to put forth any *views* on a point of church discipline. We believe and practice, but never presume to discuss the wise teachings of the Church." Edward also ties his religious practice to his ethnic identity; he has, he reflects, "adopted" the "old-fashioned ways and notions" his parents brought from Ireland.[43]

Because the three authors advocated Catholic religious practices in the context of anti-Catholic attacks, they depicted the practices as visible signs of a separate identity. As Ann Taves argued in *The Household of Faith*, the devotions popularized by American clergy helped establish a group consciousness that isolated Catholics from the mainstream.[44] The religious practices as described in the novels were signs not only of difference but also of resistance to a hostile society. Sadlier's Edward Flanagan is quite explicit about this when he says, at the dinner party, "I consider" fasting on Friday as "a public profession of my faith" and "deem it an act of cowardice to shrink from making that profession here or elsewhere."[45]

Not surprisingly, then, Catholic characters who lapsed from faithful practice were succumbing to Protestant pressure and betraying their community. Henry Blake, seeking popularity as a politician in Sadlier's *The Blakes and Flanagans*, expresses disdain for "foolish doctrines" like purgatory, penance, and praying to saints, thereby allying himself "with confession-hating people."[46] More directly, Sadlier's Willy Burke realizes the nature of the school he is attending and concludes that his Protestant employers and teachers want to make him a "turncoat."[47]

In this attention to religious practice, the novelists tended to portray the Catholic faith not as an intellectual commitment or a spiritual quest but as a group of concrete behaviors. As they advocated those behaviors—regular prayer, mass attendance, confession, and fasting—the novelists from 1850 to 1873 encouraged their readers to become what Jay P. Dolan has termed "Mass-and-sacraments Catholics."[48] They did not, however, encourage other practices, such as novenas, devotions to particular saints, parish sodalities, and shrines in the home, suggesting that these aspects of the devotional revolution in America were later developments.

Reinforcing Obedience to Priests

Roddan, Quigley, and Sadlier in their 1850s novels also dealt with specific charges against priests, charges that were more important to them than to the first generation of Catholic novelists. The Irish Americans focused the Protestant attacks not on the priests' designs on American society but on the authority they exercised over Catholics, charging, essentially, that Catholics obeyed the priests rather than the Bible. In Roddan's novel, Protestant characters tell John O'Brien that priests "hoodwinked" their followers and "led [them] by the nose."[49] The priest's claim of authority over Catholics is the consistent focus of the Protestant charges repeated by Sadlier. In her *The Blakes and Flanagans*, Mr. Thompson, the advocate for the public schools, comments that Bishop Hughes "seems to assume too much authority," telling people they "must do so and so." If a minister tried to do the same, he continues, "we would show him that we were the masters, not he."[50]

As was the case with religious practice, the authors associate rejection of priests with "them" and obedience with "us." Any Catholic characters in the novels who question priests' authority are portrayed as under the influence of Protestants or in alliance with them. When Roddan's John O'Brien first goes to confession, he recalls what he has heard about priests in his school and thinks, "what right has *he* to know what I have done."[51] Henry Blake, on his way to join the Masonic Lodge, says the priest "never consults me in his affairs, nor will I go out of my way to consult *him*."[52]

In response to these charges, the authors portrayed priests as ideal characters, the ministers of God and the Church. Sadlier's Mrs. Burke is indignant when she hears the priests "calumniated, and not only them but the divine religion whose ministers they are."[53] When the Protestant Mr. Thompson objects to the bishop's assumption of mastery in *The Blakes and Flanagans*, Edward Flanagan asserts that the bishop "is really our master—our master in the science of salvation, and we Catholics are proud to acknowledge our subjection to such masters."[54]

Even in the 1850s, when these authors included such specific attacks against Catholics, there were certain charges that they, like their predecessors, did not repeat, namely, attacks related to the sexual life of priests and nuns. Boyce comes the closest in his introductory chapter of *Mary Lee*, writing that "the old sets," such as "the 'Priest and the Bottle,'... the 'Confessor and the Nun,' have lost all point ... and are now grown ... stale and flat."[55] The Protestant characters who spark attacks on convents accuse priests of abducting Protestant women but do not describe them as sexually motivated, and only rarely do characters even raise the question of priestly celibacy. In Roddan and Quigley, Protestants simply ask Catholic characters in some amazement why priests are not married; typically, the Catholics dismiss the question.[56]

With the exception of Quigley's *Profit and Loss* and Sadlier's *Confessions of an Apostate* (to a lesser extent), there is almost no mention of specific attacks on Catholic practices and priests in the novels of the 1860s and '70s. McCorry does not include such attacks in either of his novels. Sadlier includes only one brief exchange in *Bessy Conway* concerning confession, and McElgun's Annie Reilly also endures only one attack about reading the Bible and confession.[57]

It is not that these authors have ceased to care about religious practice and obedience. Instead, they choose to illustrate the desired behaviors through faithful Catholic characters and negative behaviors through apostates. This shift also reflects the growth of institutions like churches and schools that can provide the necessary instruction for Catholics. The decline in specific charges and responses also suggests, again, a greater acceptance of Catholicism in the culture. Since Catholics were less likely to face attacks on their practices and priests, they were less in need of advice about how to respond.

Reinforcing Catholic Separation

Besides recounting specific attacks on Catholicism, the Irish Catholic authors starting in 1850 also dealt with general insults that did not merit or receive a response. These attacks were especially likely to link Catholicism with Irish nationality. They were not meant to teach, but simply to portray an American society hostile to a weak Irish Catholic population. The general insults, even more than the specific accusations, showed that Protestants had no genuine fears or concerns about Catholicism; they were just crude bigots. While the novels of the 1850s repeated both specific and general attacks, those of subsequent decades focused on the general, becoming less concerned to reinforce Catholic practice or obedience and more intent on creating the "us" versus "them" world.

In the 1850s, a Protestant man in Roddan's *John O'Brien* criticizes the "low Irish . . . who are as superstitious as they can be." In Sadlier's *Willy Burke*, a public school textbook refers to the Irish people's "obstinate attachment to the debasing doctrines of Popery."[58] In Roddan's novel, Protestants call Bishop Fenwick "the pope of the Paddies" and comment on the "wicked ways" of priests who are always "low Irish," or they would not follow such "a dirty trade." In *The Cross and the Shamrock*, Quigley relates the story of an Irish Catholic immigrant who comes to America with a letter of recommendation from a priest; "the poor fellow . . . little dreamed that a priest's recommendatory paper, instead of a dollar bill, was the worst possible substitute in certain parts of America."[59]

This trend of general insults continues in the later novels. In works by McCorry and Quigley, Protestants call Irish Catholics "benighted" and "idolators." In one episode in Sadlier's *Con O'Regan*, a Protestant employer tells the young hero to "lay aside those shabby garments of yours, and provide yourself with clothes more becoming a civilized land. Frieze and corduroy are unfortunately associated with Popery in the minds of Christian people."[60] In Sadlier's *Confessions of an Apostate*, a Protestant character tells "numberless tales of priestly iniquity, and Jesuitical intrigue." A Catholic character in the novel comments that Protestants would believe anything, "the most nonsensical story any one can invent about priests or nuns, or the Pope, or the like o' that, oh, be dad! it'll go down slick with them."[61]

These continuing references throughout the novels to Protestant hostility and Irish Catholic weakness are meant to create a world in which the immigrants are best advised to rely on their own institutions where they can practice their faith and follow their priests. The authors' treatment of the Catholic schools is a good illustration of this use of prejudice and weakness to suit Catholic purposes. Despite suggesting that public school authorities had tried to accommodate Catholic demands by making the schools neutral rather than Protestant in religion, the authors based their advice to Catholic parents on a portrait of public schools as consistently and crudely anti-Irish and anti-Catholic.

Using Prejudice to Build Support for Catholic Schools

Education in America first became an issue in Catholic fiction with Bryant's 1847 novel *Pauline Seward*, which portrays the public schools as sectarian institutions that force Catholic children to read "Protestant versions" of the Bible. Pauline argues that Catholics are guaranteed the right of conscience, which means they should be able to read their own version of the scriptures in schools.[62] By defining the issue as freedom of conscience, Bryant suggests that Catholics are not asking for anything except toleration and equality.

The schools are an important issue for all the Irish American writers in the 1850s and for Sadlier and Quigley in the succeeding decades. All portray public schools as a major Protestant instrument for luring Catholics from their faith. Roddan, and Sadlier in her first novel, do not distinguish between Protestant Sunday schools and the common or public schools. In their eyes, both systems are Protestant in their teachings and "mixed" in their student bodies. As Roddan puts it in *John O'Brien*: "All the [parental] vigilance in the world will *never* make a mixed school quite safe for a Catholic child." The hero of this novel attends a school characterized only as "Protestant," in which he reads the Bible in class and "learned to love the poor Waldenses, and get quite angry with . . . their idolatrous persecutors . . . and . . . awful Inquisitors."[63] At no point does Roddan consider whether any of the secularizing or "liberal" tendencies he discussed are changing the schools. Sadlier's Willy Burke is given textbooks in which "the religion of Catholics was . . . daubed and blackened, as incidental to the description of Catholic nations" like Ireland. Students "read in the Testament every day" and a "tall, black-lookin' gentleman" often visits the school. Mrs. Burke responds, "Aren't they the sly villains . . . doin' their best to rob you of what's more precious than silver or gold . . . the . . . faith that you got from your father, an' him from his."[64]

Quigley, in his 1853 *The Cross and the Shamrock*, begins to distinguish between schools with a religious affiliation and public schools, but he continues to regard the public system as Protestant and anti-Catholic. The orphaned children of the Irish immigrant characters are placed with Protestant farmers and are expected to attend Sunday school and the common or public school. At first, their foster family decides to ignore the subject of religion. "The change intended to be brought about was to be left to time, conversation, and the influence of common school education to accomplish."[65]

In these novels of the early 1850s, the authors are not proposing a full-time alternative Catholic school system. The novels of Roddan, Sadlier, and Quigley were published in Boston, where bishops were ambivalent about such a system. The three authors suggest different courses of action for Catholic parents. Roddan warns that if they made use of these "Protestant schools . . . parents . . . should make some provision against the danger." Sadlier's Mrs. Burke simply withdraws her son Willy from the schools and sends him to work.[66] Quigley's orphans adopt a third alternative: they "obstinately refused to attend the Sunday school, [and] the meeting house" but they attended the common school, only refusing "to join in the prayer with which school was daily opened."[67]

Sadlier is the first of the authors to present a full-time Catholic school system as the only good alternative to public schools, indicating that she has little faith in the public system. She is also the first of the authors to consider the efforts of the authorities to make the public schools neutral toward religions. She made her case in her most widely circulated work, the 1855 *The Blakes and Flanagans,* which was published in New York, where Bishop Hughes was the most prominent advocate of a full-time Catholic school system. In the novel, the good Catholic Flanagans send their children to St. Peter's school in New York City, while the Blakes send their son and daughter, Henry and Eliza, to the local public school.

In the course of the novel, Sadlier describes the battle in the 1840s over the public schools in the city, quoting Rev. Dr. James R. Bayley's *History of the Catholic Church in New York,* which had been published by Dunigan two years earlier. She comments that Bishop Hughes led the campaign to change the Public School Society, which she calls "exclusively anti-Catholic." The result is the "present Common School system," which, according to her quote from Bayley, is "administered with as much impartiality and fairness as could be expected under the circumstances."[68] Sadlier never deals with the implications of the Catholic assertion of power in the

THE SISTERS SCHOOL.—PAGE III.

Figure 3.3. St. Peter's school in *The Blakes and Flanagans* is all piety and innocence, compared to the intrigue and fighting characteristic of the public school.

political system. Although the bishop does not get what he wants, he forces a change in the school system that is at least intended to respond to Catholic demands. Instead, Sadlier portrays Catholics as a powerless minority whose demands for educational reform are defeated because of anti-Catholic hostility.

She characterizes the bishop's opposition as "the dogged spirit of fanaticism, leagued with infidelity." She is also more begrudging than Bayley in describing the change that has occurred: "this Common School system, objectionable as it still is, is unquestionably an improvement on the system by which it was preceded," she admits, but then stresses only the greater evils of the old order. "What, then, must *it* [the old order] have been?—what a nursery for young Catholics? . . . [who] mounted to fame and honor on the ruins of those religious principles instilled into them in childhood by Catholic mothers."[69]

For Sadlier, as well as Bayley, the new schools still do not meet the needs of Catholics because, according to another quote from Bayley in the novel, they exclude "all religious instruction" and so are "most fatal to the morals and religious principles of our children."[70] But Sadlier does not base her recommendation that Catholic parents avoid the public schools on a portrait of the new secular system as neutral toward religions. She bases her recommendation on a portrait of the schools as anti-Irish and anti-Catholic.

The Blake children in the 1855 novel attend public schools in the 1820s and '30s, when the schools were under the old system, but Sadlier does her best to confuse her readers on this point. She uses the same terms to describe the Public School Society and the newer Common School systems. She and her good Catholic characters, including Father Power, use the terms *Protestant, mixed, ward,* and *common* interchangeably to describe the schools that the Blake children attend and the schools she warns her readers about in 1855.[71]

Sadlier also describes the Blake children's school as incorporating both the newer, more neutral, as well as the older approaches to Catholicism. Miles Blake, the father of the family, sends his children to the "Ward School, because I'd be very ungrateful if I didn't, when the State is so good and so kind as to educate our children without meddling with their religion." But Sadlier and her characters also describe these same schools as

Protestant in their teachings and anti-Catholic in their choice of books and teachers. As a public school boy, Henry Blake fights every day with those who would "vilify his religion, and blacken poor old Ireland!" The teachers, aware that religious prejudice violates school rules, try to hide their own bigotry. Regarding one teacher, Sadlier writes: "It was quite contrary to his principles to *have* an aversion for any Catholic boy; to them he was even smoother and more oily than to anyone else." The same teacher referred to parents who were "I believe, attached to the Romish superstition—I beg pardon, they belong to the Church of Rome."[72]

Writing twenty years later, Quigley follows Sadlier's lead, describing schools as neutral, yet Protestant and anti-Catholic. Mrs. Mulroony, in *Profit and Loss*, opposes her husband's decision to send their son to the public school, warning him about the "danger to his faith at a school where religion, the best branch of education, was omitted if a superstition was not substituted for that essential ingredient in every sound system of instruction." Like Sadlier, Quigley does not consider the school's stated neutrality as an effort by America to accommodate an increasingly powerful Catholic population. Nor, like Sadlier, does he criticize the public schools only as secular or neutral institutions. Instead, he depicts the schools as controlled by Protestants who are obviously hostile to Catholics and wish to convert them, listing the "common State schools" as among the "seven sources from which sectarianism, and especially Methodism, expects to draft the auxiliaries to their legions of deluded followers." At the local public school, "all the teachers were educated in hostility to the Catholic religion," and the principal expresses her hope to convert the young lead character and eventually the whole Irish settlement.[73]

Both Sadlier and Quigley also define "secular" or "neutral" to mean not simply that schools removed religion from the curriculum—with serious consequences for knowledge and morality—but also that they disparaged, ridiculed, and dismissed religion. When Sadlier's Miles Blake defends his decision to send his children to public schools by saying "the school-room is not the place to learn either prayers or catechism; they can be learned in church, or even at home," the Father Power character responds: "If religion be excluded from the school-room, it will be excluded from the mind." One teacher who cannot hide his dislike of Catholics tells his students that "religion is only for men—full grown men . . . the Great

Creator of all things left man to his own free will, in order that he might choose a religion for himself, but he is not in a condition to choose until he reaches man's estate."[74]

For Quigley, once schools eliminate religion from the curriculum they become institutions for "infidels" or heathens. In *Profit and Loss*, a priest warns parents "of the danger of trusting the education of their children to those who have as many religions as there are patches in a quilt, or to those who laugh at all religion." And about the novel's villain, the priest says: "There, in public schools, he learned to despise religion and blaspheme God."[75]

For Sadlier and Quigley, attending public schools is tantamount to abandoning Catholic faith and ethnicity and even becoming hostile toward them. Henry and Eliza Blake leave the Church permanently and marry Protestants. As Eliza lays dying, she calls—too late—for a priest; her husband goes on to marry "a Protestant, of some advanced sect" and brings Eliza's children up in "evangelical religion." Henry becomes a successful lawyer and politician but "inwardly, all went wrong" as "doubt and incredulity" take "possession of that soul whence faith had been so early expelled." Henry's wife is fiercely anti-Catholic, and his sons, Ebenezer and Samuel, who, like their father, attend Columbia College, enter the school "without religion of any kind, saving a sort of predilection in favor of the Baptist sect. . . . [I]t is, therefore, quite probable that they are now to be found in the front ranks of the Know-Nothings, urging on the godless fanaticism of the age, in a crusade against the religion of their fathers and the children of their own race."[76]

In Quigley's novel, the young man who goes to the public school abandons his faith, changes his name from Mulroony to Ronay, and marries a Protestant. He eventually reforms, while in prison. Another young woman in the novel, a "poor victim of a godless and defective education," runs off with a Methodist, who abandons her. She becomes a common school teacher but dies young, still rejecting her mother and the priest, but proud of her "independence." The priest allows her to be buried in an unmarked corner of the Catholic cemetery, as a favor to her faithful mother. The villain of the novel—an apostate, "a notorious libertine," and, in the opinion of the local priest, the "most completely accomplished graduate of godless education that ever issued from the four walls of our godless schools"—fares worst of all, "despised by all his neighbors; shut out from decent society, and . . . a victim of an incurable disease, loathsome to himself and disgusting to society!"[77]

In the twenty years between the novels of Sadlier and Quigley, the only significant change in attitudes toward public education is in terminology. Sadlier uses the term "godless" only at the end of her novel as she warns Catholic parents about the dangers of public schools, while for Quigley, "godless" becomes the preferred term, as in the subtitle of his novel: *A Story of the Life of the Genteel Irish-American, Illustrative of Godless Education*. Both authors, however, are equally determined to recommend Catholic schools not only, or even primarily, because they provide a religious rather than a secular education but because they protect children from the overt and secret anti–Irish Catholicism of the public system.[78] They justify the separate Catholic institutions as a response to a hostility that made engagement impossible rather than as a positive preference for another set of values.

The Irish Catholic authors so focused on anti-Catholicism are a far cry from the first generation of Catholic novelists, who recognized prejudice but did not use it to support recommendations for a separate Catholic life. Charles James Cannon, the only one of the first generation of Catholic novelists with an Irish background, continued to write into the 1850s. He remains a transitional figure, sharing the Irish American's focus on anti-Catholicism but retaining the desire and expectation that Catholics will eventually participate fully in American life.

Cannon's Hopes for Irish Catholics in American Society

Cannon wrote two novels in the 1850s. Only one, the 1855 *Bickerton*, was published by a Catholic house.[79] In this novel, Cannon continues his earlier determination to expose Protestant bigotry. His orphaned heroine is placed in the household of a minister, who changes her name and calls her his daughter. Cannon describes attacks on Bickerton's priests and Irish neighborhoods, and also criticizes some "occurrences," that "within a few years past . . . disgraced" this country. The occurrences—the lectures of the ex-priests "Liehy" and Vastligassi, and the assault on a priest in Maine—actually had occurred recently, in the 1850s.[80]

Yet Cannon still hopes that Catholics will be integrated into American society, a hope illustrated by his treatment of the public schools in *Bickerton*. Like all of his colleagues, Cannon objects to "the schools provided by the state," or "the Public Schools," because they are anti-Catholic institutions, demonstrating the "evils" of "sectarianism" and teaching Catholic students "contempt and hatred of the faith that *their* fathers had suffered so much to preserve."[81] Cannon does not discuss the schools as neutral institutions or criticize them for corrupting the moral development of students. His issue is their anti-Catholicism.

He acknowledges the efforts to develop Catholic schools, although he never indicates whether the goal is a full-time system. He publishes *Bickerton* in New York in 1855 but never mentions the campaign of Bishop Hughes. Instead, Cannon explains that church trustees "made a show of keeping up the schools attached to" the parish churches, but the schools were "so badly supplied with teachers—for men of education and character could not be found to accept them as the miserable pittance they could alone offer—that they were little better than none." The Bickerton priest fights the trustees to gain access to the church revenues, but he has only begun his struggle, and the Catholic schools remain financially weak.[82]

Cannon concentrates on solving the problem of the public schools. He adopts the same stance as Bryant did in 1847, setting forth the principle without the details of implementation. Mr. Hubbard, the honorable Protestant character in *Bickerton*, defends Catholics from the charge that they would exclude the Bible from the schools, assuring his fellow Protestants that Catholics only want to be sure that their children "should not have . . . placed in their hands, as a school book, a version of the Scriptures that is not approved by their Church." To the Protestant Mr. Hubbard, the Catholic position is eminently fair. "For what protestant father . . . would not regard it as an injustice not to be borne, to be compelled not only to send, but to pay for sending his child to a school where the religion of his parents should be rendered, to the mind unable yet to judge for itself, either odious or contemptible?"[83] By making his case through a Protestant character, Cannon indicates that reform of the sectarian public schools is possible and that Catholic schools are not the only good alternative on the table.

And in fact, even before the reform he seeks is implemented, Cannon does not condemn Catholic parents who resort to the public schools, or warn them to make provisions against the danger, as the other Irish Americans had done. Instead, he explains the parents' decisions, writing that the "consequence" of the weak financial condition of the Catholic schools is "that parents, who saw the absolute necessity of education to the future success of their children in life, permitted them to attend the schools provided by the State, and for which they were taxed in proportion of their means."[84] By attempting to persuade Protestants to reform their institutions so that Catholics could participate in them, Cannon differs from the other Irish American authors who used Protestant hostility to help forge Irish Catholic identity, defined primarily by religious practice, loyalty to priests—and support for separate institutions.

Chapter 4

CATHOLICS AND RELIGIOUS LIBERTY

From the beginnings of Catholic fiction in 1829, novelists dealt not only with Protestant objections to Catholic religious beliefs and practices but also with charges that Catholics threatened American institutions because they owed allegiance to a foreign power and would seek to impose their faith on others. Catholic novelists always rejected these charges, maintaining that American Catholics would not use the state or other coercive means to advance their faith. At first, the novelists took the attacks seriously and defended church policy and practice throughout history. The Irish Americans adopted another strategy. They exaggerated the attacks and then dismissed them as ridiculous without further comment.

While the authors rejected the charges against Catholics, they did not explain why the Church would refuse to use coercion to advance the faith, namely, they never clarified whether the refusal reflected principle or capacity. The novels claimed religious liberty for Catholics in America but did not endorse religious liberty as a general right of individual conscience or as a principle that guaranteed equal rights to all religions, even in Catholic countries. Some of the authors communicated their opposition to the idea of a right of conscience; most simply remained silent — suggesting the range of orthodox Catholic opinion at the time.

Yet despite their unwillingness to endorse the principles involved, the writers managed to convey support for the American pattern of church-state relations. Catholic characters in the novels, especially priests, respected the religious liberty of Protestants, intervened in politics—if at all—only to protect the religious liberty of Catholics, and offered no alternative principles of government. In a recent essay introducing a volume about American Catholic history, John T. McGreevy examined the theologian John Courtney Murray's challenge to "traditional Catholic teaching advocating unity of church and state" in the 1950s. McGreevy comments that the "practical wisdom of Murray's approach was self-evident to the overwhelming majority of U.S. Catholics." The novels suggest that influential voices in Catholic popular culture over many decades did much to prepare American Catholics to accept the practical wisdom of Murray's argument that "the U.S. experiment in religious freedom offered a worthy, even superior, alternative."[1]

The novels of Charles Cannon, moreover, suggest that voices in popular culture over many decades also defended the American system on principled as well as practical grounds. Cannon always focused on defending Catholics as good Americans who, as a matter of right, endorsed religious liberty, toleration, and a secular public square.

Supporting Religious Liberty in Practice, If Not in Theory

In their novels from 1829 through the 1840s, the early Catholic writers always denied the charge that Catholics would use the state or other forms of coercion to impose their religion on others. Their main argument: the Church sought only spiritual authority over willing believers. Pise and Dorsey defended church practice throughout history. According to Pise, the Inquisition was established not by the Church but by the state for the sake of "public peace," and the "lay," rather than the "ecclesiastical" judges, inflicted the punishments. When Dorsey discussed the blessings of European Catholic countries, she was careful to explain that the "spiritual and apostolic authority" of the Church was "voluntarily acknowledged."[2]

The early authors also took pains to reassure readers about the positions of the Church in their own time. Bryant writes that Catholics saw the pope only as a "spiritual head"; "politically," they owed "the sovereign Pontiff no civil allegiance." Dorsey occasionally (and gently) ridicules the charges against Catholics. In *The Student of Blenheim Forest*, a recently converted woman reports that many years earlier her now-deceased husband—a deacon in the Presbyterian Church "and a most excellent man"—concluded that the pope "was sending armies disguised as emigrants to lay waste the liberties of our free and happy land." All the Presbyterians in the neighborhood became afraid to go out after dark.[3]

By contrast, in their works directed primarily to Catholics in the late 1840s, authors Dorsey and Miles pay little or no attention to charges related to America, just as they touch only lightly on anti-Catholic charges in general. Dorsey's German immigrants find that America lives up to its ideal of equal rights for all. Miles, on the rare occasion that he mentions such charges, presents them as examples of ignorant bigotry that do not merit defense or substantial argument. When Rev. Mr. Easy in *The Governess* speaks of the "abject superstition and mental servitude of Italy or Spain" or of the Church's "ceaseless war . . . against liberty of thought and action . . . [and its] persecution of innocence," no characters bother to respond at any length.[4]

While these early Catholic writers did what they could to allay Protestant fears, they did not explain why Catholics would not impose their faith on others. In particular, they did not support an individual right of conscience or a religious liberty that applied to people of all faiths. They certainly claim religious liberty for their own people. "Are we not at liberty to act as we please, on the score of religion?" the converted sister asks in Pise's *Father Rowland*. When a friend worries about what people might think of Bryant's Pauline Seward if she went to see a priest, the author laments: "Oh! thou vainglorious, boasting land of freedom! when shall it be that thy devoted children shall enjoy untrammeled liberty of conscience?"[5] But the early authors do not go so far as to endorse the same right for everyone.

Pise and Miles voiced their objections to the idea of freedom of conscience. In Pise's *Father Rowland*, the converted daughter questions advice to follow her own conscience by pointing out that this sentiment could be used to "suit our ease," and for some like the "Deist . . . conscience is silent." Pise adopts a sterner position in *Zenosius*, referring to "the error . . .

that every man hath a right to think and act for himself, with as much freedom in religious, as in worldly, matters." He declares that "the necessity of believing in this [Catholic] church is evident from the fact, that her Divine Founder has made faith the first condition requisite for salvation."[6] Similarly, in Miles's *Loretto*, the heroine laments that she has "seen Catholics almost universally ashamed of the first principles of their faith, and artfully smoothing them over to attract their dissenting brethren." Miles also interjects the comment that "the arguments for Catholicity are scattered thick around us, not only in books, but in every day life; and a physician, whose walks are amongst the lower classes, is surely the last who can put in the plea of invincible ignorance."[7] As for Bryant and Dorsey, the two simply remain silent on the issue of freedom of conscience for all.

These early authors also argue that Catholicism will eventually triumph in America, describing the benefits of religious unity, not diversity. In *Zenosius*, Pise extolls the city of Rome where "all are children of the same Catholic Church—there is no discordancy of feeling, no diversity of opinion . . . [but] a blessed unanimity, which . . . made . . . one harmonious and happy family."[8] Dorsey says that Catholicism brings unity and order across the class system. When a converted cousin of the major Protestant family in her *The Sister of Charity* returns from Europe, he reports that in Catholic areas, "A benign influence seemed to pervade all classes, while the spirit of the religion they professed reconciled each one to the various duties of his state." In Protestant regions, by contrast, the "lower orders . . . acknowledging none but a civil authority, were morose, jealous, and cunning."[9] Bryant ties this argument to political conflicts in America, suggesting that the Protestant principle of "private interpretation" is fueling the sectional crisis. To "this lamentable error," his bishop character in *Pauline Seward* explains, "we may one day have to attribute the dismemberment of this great Republic." With "the Catholic principle" of "AUTHORITY" such a division would never occur. The Church "unites all in unity of action; and preserves alike the crowned head and the majesty of the people; the freeborn and the slave."[10]

The unwillingness to endorse the principle of religious liberty gets lost in the novels, however, as the authors use their characters to show that Catholics will, in fact, conform to the American system. The novels' heroes and heroines—whether born or converted into the Church—tend to be prominent Americans who fight in the country's wars and occupy important positions in society. The fact that such characters are, or become, Catholic demonstrates that Catholicism is a legitimate American phenomenon. In Pise's *Father Rowland*, Colonel Wolburn, the Protestant father whose wife and daughters convert to Catholicism, is a veteran of the Revolutionary War who testifies that "some of the officers of the revolution, brave and good men, were Roman Catholics." Mrs. Wolburn proclaims that General Washington is "as partial to the Catholics as to any denomination."[11] Similarly, the patriarch in Miles's *Loretto* comes from an old American Catholic family and was a colonel in the recent war.

The authors also use their priest characters to show that Catholics will respect the religious liberty of Protestants. Catholic clergy in the novels never act in an authoritative way toward people of other faiths. In the doctrinal works, potential converts always approach priests to seek instruction or reception into the Church; priests never do the approaching. In fact, the priests often advise Protestants to be cautious and to delay a final decision until they are certain, especially if their conversion might disrupt family relationships. When Bryant's Pauline Seward finally seeks out the bishop, he sees her agitation and says: "I can do nothing for you, my child, at present." He simply gives her a book to read, and it is not until many pages, readings, and reflections later that Pauline receives some instruction from the bishop, who still "wisely advised her to exercise caution" to be sure she was not "actuated more by feeling than conviction." Then he gives her another book. The bishop is also mindful that Pauline's father, Calvin, objects to his daughter's conversion and might yet be reconciled to it. Only after much time passes does the bishop finally consent to Pauline's baptism, reflecting "that the Saviour had commanded his disciples to forsake father and mother, and houses and lands."[12]

Priests in these novels never run for public office or occupy public positions. They do not voice hatred of Protestants or take to the public stage to attack them. And though they certainly demonstrate that Protestant beliefs are neither true nor based in scripture, they are never hostile to Protestants themselves. Pise, whose priests in *Zenosius* are harshly critical of Protestant beliefs, explains in his preface that he is dealing with beliefs, not with persons.

These early authors also assign qualities to the priests that are antithetical to any idea of power or authority. Although Pise comments that

Father Rowland has been a priest for twenty years, which would make him middle-aged, most of the priests in subsequent novels are old. The American priest who teaches Zenosius in Pise's later novel is "an aged and exemplary man"; Bryant's bishop is "aged and venerable," and his priest is "old" as well as "worthy." The priest in Miles's *Loretto* is not only "old" but also "diminutive" and "feeble."[13] There are several reasons that might explain the authors' preference for elderly priests. American priests at the time may, in fact, have been old. Age also suggests knowledge and eliminates any implication that these priests would take a romantic interest in the female lead characters of the novels. But depicting the clergy as getting on in years seems mostly a response to Protestant fears of priestly power. Bryant's Pauline Seward disapproves when a Protestant companion engages in "thoughtless ridicule" of a priest, who was "a venerable old man." A Catholic character in *Loretto* chastises a Protestant for criticizing a priest when he is such a feeble old man.[14]

Priests in these novels also display a paternal, gentle, kind nature. The anti-Catholic daughter in Pise's *Father Rowland* believes that Jesuits are "wicked and intriguing," but, seeing Father Rowland's gentleness, she changes her mind. Dorsey's Student notes that the priest's facial expression shows "an ineffable sweetness."[15] More than other male characters, priests are apt to weep along with their followers. When Zenosius, in Pise's final novel, tells the priest of his turmoil, the priest weeps; Bryant's priest is weeping when he comes to offer consolation for a missing child; the priest in Miles's *The Governess* is "easily moved by the sight of sorrow . . . [and] tender-hearted as a child."[16]

While they took pains to show Protestants that priests conformed to America's requirements, the early authors gave the priests various national backgrounds. Pise's Father Rowland was born in Maryland. The minister in the novel, Mr. Dorson, by contrast, is "by birth an Englishman," and "during the revolution, it was very much doubted whether he was not too loyal to his church, not to incur some suspicion of his loyalty to the American government."[17] While Pise seems anxious to assert that the priest is not foreign, Dorsey's priest in *The Sister of Charity* is Italian, and the bishop in Bryant's novel is French. In *The Oriental Pearl*, Dorsey emphasizes the common language that unites the priest and the German immigrants and gives the priest a German last name. She also says that Father Holberg has lived in America for a long time and so is able to advise the immigrants.

When the Irish American novelists took over the field of Catholic fiction, they also tackled the issue of Catholics and America, especially in the novels of the 1850s. In the subsequent decades, the charges that Catholics were somehow un-American appeared much less frequently in the novels, suggesting again a gradual waning of anti-Catholicism and an increasing confidence among Irish Catholics, even if the authors did not directly acknowledge these trends.[18]

When they raised the issue, the Irish Americans followed the path set out by the early writers—though with some differences. They made the attacks so outrageous that they could be dismissed without comment or answer. When Roddan's John O'Brien is in school, he reads "stories about . . . good Christians roasted alive by awful Inquisitors." One of his employers is afraid that in employing John, "Every thing said or done in my house might be reported to the Inquisition." John does not try to defend the Church, but looking back later in life, he says these stories made him "laugh, in spite of my uneasiness and vexation." Quigley and Sadlier repeated even vaguer attacks, also without responding. A Protestant character in Quigley's *The Cross and the Shamrock* tells an immigrant that popery would be the ruin of the country and its institutions. A Protestant employer in Sadlier's *Willy Burke* tells the widowed mother that "popery is not the thing for this age or country."[19] Authors did not record these kinds of attacks to address Protestant concerns but rather to highlight anti-Catholicism and reassure Catholic readers in a general way about the intentions of their church.

The Irish Americans followed the early writers more completely in their treatment of religious liberty and toleration. They, too, did not explain why Catholics would not threaten the American values, or why the charges against them could be dismissed so easily. They claimed religious liberty for American Catholics and stopped there. In the 1850s, Roddan tells his readers that they should not "apologize" for their religion or allow Protestants to attack it, for "we are citizens of a republic where the law makes no distinction between creeds. You have a perfect right to be a Catholic." In his first novel, Quigley says that Protestants who refused to allow Catholics to practice their faith violate the "right to worship according to one's conscience" as well as "that article of the federal constitution that guarantees the right to every citizen to worship God according to the dictates of conscience or individual judgment."[20] In the 1860s and '70s, the novelists devoted little or no attention to asserting Catholics' claim to religious liberty; it is as though in the absence of attack, the assertion is no longer necessary.[21]

Beyond this, the Irish Americans, like their predecessors, either expressed doubts about the idea of freedom of conscience or remained silent on the issue, again indicating the range of orthodox Catholic opinion. The difficulties these authors might have faced had they confronted and tried to respond to the charges about religious liberty for all faiths can be seen from Quigley's brief and confusing treatment of the Madiai case in his 1853 *The Cross and the Shamrock*. The Madiai, a married couple, were convicted and sentenced to prison in Italy in the early 1850s for converting to Protestantism and assembling to worship accordingly, or so their outraged supporters in Europe and America contended. Quigley begins his treatment by suggesting that Protestant nations persecute other religions and Catholic nations do not. In England, "Every sovereign, from Elizabeth down to Victoria, acted the tyrant over the Catholics; and in Sweden, Denmark, Prussia, and the Protestant Swiss cantons, persecution is now a part of the laws of these several states." In the United States, Catholics are "exposed to a persecution such as no Catholic government, king, or despot ever attempted to force on the consciences of their dissenting subjects, not even Queen Mary of England, excepted."

As Quigley continues, however, he asserts that the differences between the Catholic and Protestant countries are, first, that the Catholics adhere to the true faith, and, second, that they are nevertheless forced to attend Protestant services in America, while Protestants like the Madiai in Catholic Italy are not compelled to adopt Catholic beliefs or practices.

> For the so-called persecution by Catholic princes has never been to compel men to adopt a new religion. Protestants in Europe and here attempt to compel the adoption of their false tenets by those who are neither desirous nor willing to adopt them, and who already profess a true religion. This is what makes a vast difference between the persecution your "Madiai" suffer, and this ten times worse persecution which many an otherwise honest and kind-hearted American farmer allows to take place in his family.

Although Quigley's language, and his insertion of the phrase "so-called" in reference to persecution in Catholic countries, might suggest to a typical reader that Catholic countries did not persecute other religions, in the end he takes no position on the principle of religious liberty involved in the Madiai case. He says only that the couple was not forced to adopt or practice Catholicism. He does not deny that they were forbidden to practice their Protestant faith. His main goal is to launch a counterattack on American Protestants, who, he says, have no right to criticize since they are so intolerant of the Catholics in their midst.[22]

Most of the Irish Americans, like their predecessors, remain silent on the principle of religious liberty, but Quigley and Sadlier—like Pise and Miles in the previous generation—communicate their suspicion of the idea. By 1873, Quigley is more straightforward than he had been when discussing the Madiai, as he characterizes the banners that were displayed at the public school assembly. They included "The Bible our religion, the Constitution our Creed" and "Free thoughts, free schools, free religion." The priest asks why they do not add "free love."[23] In one Sadlier novel, Edward Flanagan tries to "repress a smile" as he asks a Protestant man his opinion about the "rule or guide" of conduct. When the man responds, "why, conscience, to be sure," Edward asks what the term means and why "its dictates are not always the same" on such basic questions as infant baptism, number of wives, and eating pork. In another of her works, Sadlier comments on Bessy Conway's refusal to participate in Protestant prayer services, explaining: "It was in vain that the girl excused herself on the score of conscience and obedience to the Church," indicating that the score of conscience was not a sufficient rationale.[24]

Most of the Irish Americans in the early 1850s also resembled Pise and the converts in their expectation that Catholicism would triumph in America and in their preference for religious unity rather than diversity. They stressed the weaknesses of Protestantism and the increasing numbers of Catholic immigrants, whose good example, they believed, would lead to conversions. They also emphasized the advantages America would derive from adhering to Catholicism. In *Willy Burke*, Sadlier writes: the "exiled children of Ireland have a noble part to play over all the earth,— that of spreading the true faith."[25] A character in Quigley's first novel refers to the "divinely decreed result" that the "*institutions* of heresy and sectarianism" were "doomed to fall before the irresistible and unerring progress of Catholicity." Quigley, echoing Bryant, has this to say about religious and political unity: "There can never be a real union among the States," he writes, "till the minds of people, north and south, are united in faith and sentiment." In a footnote added to a post–Civil War edition of the novel, the editor writes: "the late war and its horrors, undoubtedly brought about by sectarian fanaticism prove that the predictions of the author of this book were true."[26] As they extolled the advantages of religious unity, the Irish American authors, like their predecessors, failed to address how any religious minorities might be treated in a Catholic America.

After the early 1850s, the Irish Americans no longer referred to this "certain decline of the institutions of sectarianism," to again cite Quigley. They no longer expect the country's conversion, despite the rise in the Catholic population and its institutions. In his final novel, however, Quigley again shows his seeming lack of concern about Protestant views when his priest character makes extensive claims about the Catholic contribution to American history. In his speech at the public school assembly, the priest says: "If there be any country in the world that ought to be called a *Catholic Country*, it is America; for it was discovered not only by a Catholic admiral and sailors, but the inspiration and design of the discovery was a pious Catholic enterprise, having for its end the spread and glory of the Catholic Church. In that sense, the country is Catholic, whatever the people may be."[27]

Despite their reticence on the matter of principle, the Irish Americans, like their predecessors, convey to readers that Catholics will conform to American requirements. Since they make Irish immigrants the central figures in their work, they cannot use the sheer fact of American birth to show that Catholics are patriotic citizens. But they do refer to the role that Catholics have played in defending America in wartime. In his *Mary Lee*, Boyce asks his immigrant readers to remember that America continues "to hate and spurn" them despite the "blood you shed in her battles." And Robert Murray, the American-born son of an Irish immigrant in Sadlier's *Old and New*, says that he loves both Ireland and America: "both are equally dear to my heart, and for either I am willing to shed my blood."[28]

The Irish Americans also show their priest characters respecting the religious liberty of Protestant Americans. They convey this message although their priests differ in some important ways from those in the earlier novels. Most of their priests are Irish immigrants who care for the immigrant population, and they are robust rather than elderly men. The authors reserve old age for priests of the past, such as those left behind in Ireland—like "the most paternal and the best-natured of all old priests" in Sadlier's *Confessions of an Apostate*—or the French priests who once dominated in the United States. Irish priests in America who are engaged in deliberation and recommendation rather than action, such as Sadlier's unnamed "ecclesiastics" at the Buffalo Convention for colonization, are also described as "venerable in years."[29]

The clergymen who care for the immigrants in America, however, such as Bishops Cheverus and Fenwick, are not described as either old or venerable. In Sadlier's *The Blakes and Flanagans*, Father Power is a "mighty man in his generation" and is replaced by the even mightier Bishop Hughes.[30] Sometimes, in the 1850s, the Irish priest characters are shown to replace priests who retire or die. The first of Quigley's priests, Father O'Shane, is an "aged gentleman" with a cane, who ultimately dies, but Father Ugo is "a young gentleman" and "a robust, brave-looking man." At the novel's end, he is still "living, and battling for the faith."[31] In Sadlier's *Bessy Conway*, Father Daly comes to America with the immigrants, remains in New York for more than seven years, then goes on to minister to the Plains Indians.[32] The authors do not describe the priests as young, which might connote inexperience and also raise issues about their relationships with women. They simply do not depict them as elderly.

Over time, priests in novels by the Irish Americans also become less prone to weeping than priests in the earlier works. In their first novels, Sadlier and Quigley, like their predecessors, depict priests as easily moved to tears. In *Willy Burke*, when the old priest meets the widow and her children, "the tear of pity trickled unheeded down his cheek." Even the priest's younger replacement "wiped away an obtrusive tear" when Willy tells him about giving so much of his inheritance to charity.[33] After the early 1850s, priests either do not cry at all, or only do so at extraordinary moments. Certainly, historical figures who appear in the novels, like Bishops Cheverus or Hughes or Father Power, are not weepy. The closest Bishop Fenwick comes to tears is in McCorry's novel, when he is told about the burning of the convent, and "his sorrow became almost overwhelming." In *Bessy Conway*, Father Daly makes "an effort to restrain his tears" and takes "the old woman's hand tenderly" while telling her that her son has died, but this is the closest the priest comes to crying, and no tears are actually shed. In Quigley's *Profit and Loss*, the only time a priest sheds tears is when he nearly raises a woman from the dead.[34]

Yet the Irish American authors, like those before them, are bent on showing that the priests act in accordance with American values. They are concerned with their immigrant congregations and deal with Protestants only when the religious lives of Catholics and willing converts are at stake. In Roddan's *John O'Brien*, when the Protestant employer accuses the bishop of invading her family altar, the bishop is merely trying to ensure that John can attend Catholic services and is not forced to attend Protestant ones. When Quigley's priest in *Profit and Loss* is asked to speak at the public school assembly, he is reluctant to go "among such a bigoted set." He finally agrees, saying: "If there are some of my people there, sure enough, I ought to look after them. That is my duty."[35]

Priests in the Irish American novels, like those in the earlier works, also do not run for office or take political positions. The only exception is *The Blakes and Flanagans*, in which Sadlier recounts the role of Bishop Hughes in the schools controversy and calls him "the great champion of Catholicity" and "the head of the Catholic party."[36] Even so, Sadlier is extremely vague about the bishop's political goals and never mentions the issue of public funding for Catholic schools, emphasizing instead the fight for freedom of education, or the freedom to establish a separate educational system.

Given the authors' response to the charges against Catholics and their description of priests and other Catholic characters, the overwhelming message of the novels is that Catholics will respect religious liberty and the existing relations between church and state in America. The Irish American writers, in particular, communicate to immigrant readers that—however persecuted they might be and however fearful, suspicious, and separate they remained—they will not do anything to endanger the American system. The authors certainly do not support principles contrary to the American ones. When they mention countries that show an enviable unity in religion, they specify that the unity is voluntary; they do not defend any Catholic nation that imposes faith on its citizens. When they expect the eventual triumph of Catholicism in America, they never suggest that it will come about by force or even by electoral victories but only by population changes and voluntary conversions. And they base their claims for Catholic rights on grounds of religious liberty and not on the rights of the Church as representative of the true faith.

Cannon: A Voice for the Future

The only Catholic writer who stands out from his colleagues on this issue of religious freedom is Cannon. Throughout his career, he gives greater prominence to charges that Catholics are un-American than any other writer and, in the end, is the only Catholic writer of the time to make the defense of Catholics as good Americans central to his fiction. In responding to the charges, Cannon is also the only one of the writers to endorse the American ideas of freedom, toleration, and separation of church and state.

In his early novel *Mora Carmody*, the first discussion of Catholic doctrine comes when the Protestant hero and the Catholic heroine encounter a clergyman speaking about the "enemies of civil and religious liberty— of our glorious Constitution and of the Bible—the emissaries of Rome." In *Father Felix*, where the author is supposedly focusing on conversions and where the novel's central characters, the Fenwicks, are wealthy established Catholics, the main Protestant character's first response to Paul Fenwick is to pity him as a "pliant tool of a crafty priesthood . . . sinking into the vassal of a foreign despot." In *Scenes and Characters*, written for a Catholic audience, the only specific charges against Catholics that Cannon includes are about America.[37] In his two novels of the 1850s, Cannon continues to focus on these charges; the tension in *Bickerton* stems from the group of nativists who preach of "the danger to which the State was exposed from the encroachments of the Church . . . to which those . . . foreigners . . . belong."[38]

Cannon resembles his colleagues in some of his responses, even if he uses harsher or more direct language. In *Mora Carmody* his heroine reminds critics that the pope is the spiritual head of the Church and nothing more; for his role "as a temporal prince they [American Catholics] care no more for the Pope than for the Great Mogul." Cannon also focuses his novels around characters like Mora Carmody, a native-born American, or the Fenwicks in *Father Felix*, whose family has been in Maryland since the founding of the colony. His *Scenes and Characters* and his two novels of the 1850s feature Irish immigrants but are centered on their American-born sons and daughters, who have the hearts of free people. Cannon also emphasizes the role of Catholics in American history. In *Father Felix*, a good character points out that "in our revolutionary struggle, the few Catholics among us were neither the least active nor the least efficient of the friends of American Independence, and nothing then was said or thought of their allegiance to a foreign power inimical to our liberties."[39]

Cannon's priest characters are also typical in many respects. In his early novels, priests tend to be old; Father Felix is an "old gentleman" and an "old man."[40] But as he addresses an Irish immigrant audience, priests like Father Quigley in *Scenes and Characters* and Father Eldridge in *Bickerton* are middle-aged. Whatever their age, the priests are "gentle, cheerful, benevolent," although not as weepy as priests in the other novels.[41] Above all, the priests never act to undermine religious liberty. They never approach Protestants except to offer help. Father Felix promises a home and job to a Protestant alcoholic if he stops drinking, never mentioning conversion, and Father Eldridge "meddled in no man's affairs, nor would he suffer any man to meddle in his."[42]

Cannon uses the priests' ethnic background for some different purposes, however: Father Quigley is the first Irish immigrant priest important to the stories, and Father Eldridge is the first to represent Cannon's hopes for a union of Irish and American, Protestant and Catholic. He was born in the United States; "he was not a foreign emissary, nor even a foreigner by birth, but a native of the soil." He was partly "of Puritan blood" since his father was a Protestant from New England, and partly Irish since his mother was a Catholic from Ireland. As Cannon describes it, the priest combines the best elements of both traditions: "the strong common sense and unflagging energy of the one, united with the warm imagination and earnest, religious feelings of the other."[43]

Cannon's response to the attacks on Catholics becomes unique when he starts to explain why Catholics will not impose their faith; his answer is that Catholics support religious liberty. He not only claims religious liberty for Catholics—in *Harry Layden*, he writes that Catholics were "only

exercising the right guaranteed to them by our glorious Constitution—
the right of worshipping God in the manner they deem most acceptable
to Him"—but also claims the same right for others.[44] In *Mora Carmody*,
when the heroine is confronted with charges about "bloody Mary" and
the "churchmen who were her principal advisors," she responds: "I deny
that persecution has ever been a *principle* of the Catholic Church." Mora
does not deny that "many princes and persons in power, claiming to be
members of the Catholic Church, some of them even wearing the sacer-
dotal robes, have indulged in the un-Christian practice of persecuting such
as differed from them in matters of faith." She admits that such persons
did not seem to know that "error is never dangerous, while reason is left
free to combat it," but reminds her accuser that Catholic countries "have
grown wiser . . . and now in Catholic France and in Belgium all religions
are tolerated. . . . Protestant governments, however, have not kept pace
with their Catholic neighbours," and inflict various degrees of restrictions
and punishments on Catholics. In *Father Felix*, Cannon claims that Catholics brought religious liberty and rights of conscience to America. He
asserts that "Lord Baltimore . . . was the first, among legislators, who recognized the inalienable right of man, to worship God according to the dictates of conscience."[45]

Cannon gives his most extensive defense of religious liberty in the
1855 *Bickerton*. In the text of the novel, he gives the official church position
in a long citation from the American bishops' recent pastoral letter from
the first provincial council of Cincinnati. The honorable Protestant Fred
Hubbard reads the letter aloud in the course of a conversation. The bishops state the Catholic position that has informed the views of the other
Catholic novelists—they claim religious liberty for Catholics as they pray
that "Providence would perpetuate to us all, and to our children . . . the
glorious boon of equal rights and equal protection." Although the bishops
do not directly comment on the general principle of religious freedom or
toleration, their reservations are implied when they connect liberty to the
true faith. They write: "to the lover of freedom she [the Church] proposes
as a model a higher and nobler liberty—the liberty of the glory of the
children of God. She proclaims . . . the truth shall make you free . . . where
the spirit of the Lord is there is liberty."[46]

Cannon goes beyond the bishops and endorses American values
through a long letter Fred Hubbard writes to decline a position in the na-

tivist party. Fred describes himself as a "lover of my race and of my country" and cites a writer who is "as staunch a Protestant and as true an American as the best among you." His father agrees with his son's letter simply as an American: "he that would not subscribe to the sentiments you have there embodied, is no American at heart," he tells his son.[47]

Neither Fred Hubbard in his letter nor Cannon as author echoes, or comments further on, the bishop's reservations. Fred declares himself a "friend of religious freedom" and "freedom of conscience," citing colonial legislation, the Declaration of Independence, and the Constitution to show that the principle is part of the American tradition. He makes his claim not only for the rights of Catholics but for the religious liberty of all groups. Once Americans begin "proscribing" people "for their religious opinions," he writes, they would not stop with Catholics. "The jealousy of religious bigotry is a thing which grows with what it feeds upon." Americans would come to proscribe many groups, he predicts, bringing "sectarian jealousy" and "warfare . . . amongst the different Christian sects." Fred argues, instead, for a continuation of the traditional policy, which is to "tolerate all religions and leave each church free to pursue its mission in its own way."[48]

Fred Hubbard also defends Catholics from the charge that they would alter the relations between church and state, echoing the position taken by Catholic novelists since Pise. He points out that "Catholics deny that they owe allegiance to any foreign power, or that any is claimed of them by the Pope, beyond what is due to him as the head of their church in spirituals." Fred also quotes the pastoral letter, in which the bishops write of rendering to Caesar and to God and affirm that "the power of the Sovereign Pontiffs . . . is spiritual in its objects and in its sphere of action." However, Fred also cites the bishops' assertion that the Church "wishes her just rights to be protected" and that she is "occasionally forced into conflict with worldly passions and interests . . . in defence of her heaven-born rights and privileges." In the passages that Fred quotes, the bishops do not define the realms of God and Caesar, or specify the rights and privileges of the Church, but clearly maintain the church's prerogative to intervene in the public square in defense of her interests. The bishops also assert the traditional Catholic position that if the Church should lose in such conflicts, she will continue to teach "patience."[49]

As he does with the principle of religious liberty, Cannon uses Fred Hubbard to go further than the bishops in supporting the American principle of church-state separation. In his letter rejecting the nativist offer, Fred says nothing at all about the just rights and privileges that the Church would defend, maintaining simply that the Church seeks only a spiritual jurisdiction over her members. He also maintains that Catholics and Protestants have the same position when it comes to church-state relationships. The "Catholic of the present day," he writes, "no more admits the supremacy of the Church in temporal matters than the Protestant—their difference is in regard to spiritual concerns." Fred continues to equate the positions of Catholics and Protestants when he gets more specific about the issue of separation, defining the issue as a matter of religion and politics rather than church and state. He does not speak of the Church at all. Instead, he maintains that it is not church rights that define the limits of temporal power but the laws of God that bind all Christians. Both Catholics and Protestants believe, he writes, "that the allegiance which they owe to God is higher than any obligation to man; and that in a conflict between human and divine laws, you must serve God rather than man."[50]

To maintain the necessary separation, Fred urges restraint on the state. Conflicts would arise only if "the civil government undertakes to legislate upon religious subjects, and to draw spiritual matters under a temporal jurisdiction, instead of keeping them apart . . . as has been our practice heretofore in the administration of civil affairs."[51] With this discussion, Cannon comes closer than any of the other authors to advocating a secular public square in which the state stays clear of religious subjects. Yet even Cannon, when he included the bishops' statement that the Church would intervene in political contests in defense of its interests, does not endorse a complete church withdrawal from politics.

Speaking through the Hubbards, Cannon makes his case for religious liberty, toleration, and church-state separation on grounds of America's values and its interests. More than the other Irish Americans, he argues that Protestant Americans should not merely accept or tolerate Catholics but incorporate them fully into America's political—and eventually cultural and social—life. He also goes further than the other Irish Americans in arguing that this assimilation is the immigrants' goal.

In his letter, Fred Hubbard asserts that America should accept religious diversity and base its unity on the shared role of citizen. "Will not a Catholic who agrees with you on all the political issues, and differs from you in religion, make you a better legislative representative than a Protestant who agrees with you in religion, but differs from you on all matters of political principle?" Fred asks. This is the reverse of the argument advanced by those Catholic authors who claimed that religious unity would eliminate political divisions; here, political unity would make religious differences irrelevant to public life. Old Mr. Hubbard declares that such political unity would eventually bring cultural and social unity: "No matter where a man may have been born, the moment he declares his intention to become a citizen of this republic, he ceases to be a foreigner." Over time, Mr. Hubbard concludes, the immigrants' "children, if not themselves, are as thoroughly American as the best of us."[52]

For his part, Fred argues that religious liberty, toleration, and separation are all policies that would advance America's interests. In a more negative sense, a nativist policy would alienate the immigrants. The Catholic might "become indifferent and perhaps hostile to the government, which has treated him as an alien and as a member of an inferior caste of society." More positively, toleration and acceptance would "widen the basis upon which our government stands, and increase the number of those who are bound to it by the ties of sympathy and interest."[53]

The issue is America's interests for the future as well. In making this case, Cannon went much further than the other authors in expressing his preference for the American system. For Fred Hubbard, a nativist policy would not diminish the number of immigrants, but it would deteriorate their quality. Nativist policies would "shut out men of fortune and education" who emigrate "because they prefer our institutions, and desire to incorporate themselves into the great body of American society, to share its privileges and partake of its destiny." Fred concludes that the important question is whether "we make them [the immigrants] friends or enemies? It has been our ancient policy to cultivate their friendship. Why not continue to pursue it?"[54] Fred recognizes that the American effort to incorporate a wide diversity of groups — including not only Catholics but the approximately "twenty-two hundred thousand foreigners" in the country — was "quite a new experiment in the conduct of society, and has not been tried except in those cases where one portion has actually subjugated the other." "Incidental evils" inevitable in such great changes would have to be met, but "this new element ought to be assimilated with the great body of American society, as far as it can be done."[55]

In his final novel, *Tighe Lyfford*, from a secular publisher, Cannon makes an even more extensive case for liberty in all its forms, claiming the Catholic Church as its main advocate. He says that the Catholic—like the American—has "a heritage of freedom," appealing "to the history even of our own land, and to the acknowledged intelligence of the Catholics of the United States." He praised the "clear mental vision . . . scholarship . . . logical mind . . . legal acumen . . . and . . . intellectual grasp" of eminent Catholic men, including bishops and the pope. More generally, he concludes that the Church has created a world where "Liberty" was "always sure of a welcome and a home."[56]

Cannon also communicated his support for American values by what he did *not* say. Unlike the other Catholic writers, he never voiced triumphal sentiments, and he assumed that American society would be religiously diverse. In fact, he seemed to comment ironically on both the Catholic hope for widespread conversions and the Protestant fears of a Catholic takeover. In *Bickerton*, he cites a newspaper article reporting that Fred Hubbard had married the Catholic heroine and converted during their honeymoon trip to Rome. The paper advised its Protestant readers to "let your young men take heed how they marry lovely Catholic wives. . . . There is more danger to their protestantism in the experiment than they are aware of."[57]

Cannon's treatment of American values throughout his career reflects his unique position in this group. He was the only Irish American among the first generation of Catholic writers and the only lay American-born author among the Irish Americans. Unlike the immigrant authors, he placed great value on being American, and, unlike the native-born converts, he could not take that status for granted. As a result, he is the most concerned about Protestant charges that Catholics threaten America and the most determined to assert that Catholics, and Irish Catholics, are good Americans in their values and actions. He is not the precursor of the Irish Americans who immediately follow him—most of whom are immigrants—but rather of the American-born generations that come later.

Continuity in the Catholic Position on Church-State Relations

Cannon goes further than his colleagues in support of American values, but there is still general agreement among the Catholic writers that the

Church would not do anything to threaten the American pattern of civic and political life. This consistency provides some evidence against the conclusions of the political scientists Philip Hamburger and Tracy Fessenden about the origins and implications of the American idea of church-state separation.[58] Both scholars argue that in the mid-nineteenth century, the principle of separation acquired more importance and a more rigid meaning than it had earlier in American history, tracing the change to the rise in anti-Catholicism that accompanied the significant increase in the American Catholic population. The increasing rigidity was intended to keep the Catholic Church and its clergy out of politics.

Both Hamburger and Fessenden argue that, in response, the Church withdrew from political participation, though neither provides much evidence on this point.[59] They are more interested in examining the reasons for the withdrawal and the implications for the contemporary relevance of church-state separation. Hamburger maintains that the elaboration of separation in such an anti-Catholic context intimidated the Church and continues to have a chilling effect on American churches, if not on religious individuals, to this day. Fessenden argues, on the contrary, that Catholics responded to the anti-Catholicism at the root of separation by more fully endorsing a secular public square to guarantee Catholics equality as citizens. The Catholic response, in her view, illustrates the value of the principle and challenges Hamburger's conclusion that its origins are suspicious in nature.

The Catholic novels, especially those by the Irish Americans, support the idea that the mid-nineteenth-century discussions of separation were grounded in anti-Catholicism. Protestants in the Irish American novels complain of the political ambitions of popes and priests, though they never mention the ministers running for public office, serving on political boards, or running charities and reformatories funded by the government. But the novels also provide no evidence of Catholic Church withdrawal from 1829 to 1873. On the contrary, they suggest a church always anxious to assert its interest in spiritual matters and its passivity in political life. Bryant in 1847 and Sadlier in 1855 were equally loath to acknowledge that Catholics or their clergy actually used political power to advance church interests on the subject of education. And Catholic authors before 1847 never even suggested a political position on the public schools. If there was any change over time, it was toward assertiveness rather than timidity. The earlier writers—native-born Americans all—pointedly defend church history, while the Irish Americans are less interested in appeasing critics, limiting their comments to the intentions of American Catholics at the time. In addition, the Irish Americans are far more willing than their predecessors simply to ridicule Protestant charges as unworthy of response.

On the other hand, the novels also provide no evidence of a church adopting the idea of a secular public square. Cannon goes furthest in this direction, yet he includes the bishops' statement that the Church reserves the right to interfere in politics when necessary. The novels, in short, suggest continuity in the nineteenth-century tradition of a politically passive church conforming to the principle of church-state separation.

Chapter 5

THE ANTI-PROTESTANT
NOVEL

Catholic novelists did not just respond to charges against Catholics, they also attacked their accusers. While scholars have analyzed the anti-Catholic popular literature of nineteenth-century America — showing that the literature served cultural functions for Protestants — they have not given the same attention to the anti-Protestant components of the literature produced by Catholics.[1] This literature too served functions for its audience. Both the early Catholic writers and the Irish Americans used their attacks to show that Protestants, not Catholics, violated religious liberty and separation of church and state, a response that proved particularly useful for writers who could not endorse these values directly. Catholic writers also used their criticisms of Protestants to uphold the celibate priesthood and, more generally, the ideas about authority that ensured order and unity among Catholics.

Although these attacks were present in Catholic fiction from the start, the Irish Americans made them more central to the novels and expressed them in harsh language and crude satire or caricature of specific Protestant denominations and their ministers. Their portraits of ministers illustrate the style of the Irish Americans' attacks. In the 1850s, ministers in the novels were the powerful but ignorant leaders of anti-Catholicism, men who did not deserve the authority they wielded. In later decades, ministers appeared as weak, ridiculous figures, who were dominated by their female congregants. The Irish Americans also expanded the attacks to cover many aspects of Protestant society, becoming the first to write anti-Protestant novels, or at least parts of novels, to match the anti-Catholic fiction of the time.

While some of the Irish Americans used these traditional criticisms simply to amuse their readers, the more authoritarian writers expressed the fears that lay beneath the attacks. They were concerned that American Catholics, influenced by the Protestant ideas of individual freedom, would reject the authority of priests, parents, and employers, bringing conflict and disorder to religious, family, and social life. Essentially these writers feared that Catholic faith and culture could not survive in a society committed to individual autonomy, and they responded with a combination of anger and disdain.

The first generation of Catholic writers usually confined themselves to making the standard Catholic arguments against the Protestant religion—it was not the true faith, as witnessed by its recent origin and its internal divisions. When they went beyond debating points, the early authors focused on ministers, painting them as uninformed about religion and bigoted against Catholics, despite their supposed attachment to religious liberty. The portraits of ministers highlighted the advantages of priests and supported their claims to authority over Catholics. Pise contrasts Father Rowland, who invokes invincible ignorance to reassure Protestants, with the Reverend Dr. Dorson, who is "bitterly averse . . . to the *popish sect*, as he sneeringly denominated the Catholic religion."[2] In Bryant's novel, ministers give "bitter sermons against the Catholics," call on their followers "to emulate them in their unholy work," and secretly welcome the anti-Catholic riots.[3] In the late 1840s, ministers came to represent the religious indifference of American society. In Miles's *The Governess*, the minister's name is Mr. Easy, which—as opposed to Bryant's Dr. Bogus—conveys a lack of conviction rather than a commitment to Protestantism.

The early authors also portray ministers as ignorant compared to learned priests. Since ministers do not represent the true faith, they cannot defend their beliefs. When the anti-Catholic Wolburn daughter in Pise's novel repeats Father Rowland's arguments to Dr. Dorson, "answer the argument he could not: he sought only how to evade it most dexterously," and then tells the young woman not to be "too curious."[4] Miles continues in the same vein. A young man who observes the governess discussing the infallibility of the Church with Mr. Easy is "amazed at . . . her perfect comprehension of the points" as she "foiled the minister."[5]

The Protestant clergy are also depicted as caring primarily about themselves and their own families, illustrating the advantages of a celibate priesthood. Father Rowland's house, suitable for one person, "was small, but comfortable and neat. He possessed a competency: he asked no more." The minister, Dr. Dorson, by contrast, lives in "a large comfortable mansion" with a farm.[6] Twenty years later, Miles notes the difference between the priest's house and the "lovely residence" of Dr. Wright, the Episcopalian, and his family.[7] The ministers' family obligations interfere with their duties. In *Father Rowland*, the minister's chief concerns are "to take care of his children, preach a sermon, and calumniate the Catholics."[8] Dorsey continues with what has become the standard illustration of ministers' deathbed behavior: When a "clergyman of the most fashionable church in the metropolis" entered the room of a sick child, he first spoke "to the physician, and, after ascertaining—very prudently, for he had a large family of his own—that the disease . . . was not contagious," he approached the child and his family.[9]

The early Catholic writers also showed ministers actively trying to prevent followers from converting to Catholicism and, in this way, exercising the type of authority Protestants typically attributed to priests. Turning the tables on their accusers, especially on charges related to America, became standard practice in Catholic fiction. In *Father Rowland*, the minister writes to the Wolburn daughter's future in-laws in an effort to prevent her conversion. The father in Dorsey's *The Student of Blenheim Forest* tries to prevent his son's conversion by insisting that he have a series of conversations and a year's travel with the Episcopal bishop. More rarely in these novels, the ministers tried to persuade Catholics to become Protestant. In Miles's novel, the Protestant employer and her minister attempt to talk the Catholic governess out of her convictions and persuade her to join the family at services.[10]

The early authors do not, however, extend their criticism of ministers to personal qualities. The minister in *Father Rowland*, Dr. Dorson, is "a tall, spare . . . person with a bald head, and a stern, sanctimonious countenance," but Pise also admits that he is "yet not undignified."[11] Bryant and Dorsey are more generous. Dorsey's Student rejects the proffered counsel of the Episcopal bishop "with all due deference to his intelligence, piety, his simple and unostentatious manners and gentlemanly and dignified bearing."[12] Miles admits that Rev. Easy, apart from his inability to defend his faith and his vague anti-Catholic statements, is "really a kind hearted man."[13]

In the mid-1840s, when anti-Catholicism becomes a more significant feature of the doctrinal novels, Pise and Bryant extend their criticism of ministers to the members of the Protestant churches. They continue to focus on the Protestant refusal to acknowledge the true faith and their bigotry against Catholics. Pise tells Protestants, "investigate, and you will believe." If they do not investigate, it is because they lack the "courage . . . to overcome human respect, to triumph over public opinion, and to sacrifice notions and misapprehensions . . . identified with their earliest education and associations."[14] The Protestants in Bryant also are not seen as blameless. They are all too ready to believe false rumors about an Irish Catholic riot when their "deeply rooted prejudices" are aroused, although their better nature prevails in the end.[15]

Apart from these mildly insulting characterizations of ministers and people, the Catholic writers in this formative period did not generally embody their criticisms in Protestant characters. In *Zenosius*, while Pise is harsher than Bryant, Dorsey, or Miles, he criticizes Protestants mostly for their teachings and practices, without introducing characters to bring these to life. He refers to Protestants as "Sectarians" who are not only in error but also in a "labyrinth," or in "chains," "captivity," and "meshes." Because they lack "supernatural virtues," even if Protestants practice works of mercy such as feeding the hungry, they act from "worldly motives."[16] Yet in his preface, Pise takes pains to defend himself against charges of being "severe on Protestants," maintaining that he has "nothing to do" "with their persons, and, if you choose, their sincerity"; the issue is "their errors and schism."[17] Since there are no important Protestant characters in his novel apart from Zenosius and his sister, who seek and eventually find the true faith, Pise remains true to his statement that he does not attack Protestant persons. The early authors also confine their criticism to Protestant religious life; they do not criticize Protestant society generally.

Irish American Authors Develop the Anti-Protestant Novel

In the 1840s, Cannon gradually becomes more willing than his contemporaries to use satire or caricature to attack Protestants for many aspects of their religion and culture. His first works, for secular houses, do not invoke anti-Catholicism or attack bigots, but this changes when he begins to write for Catholic publishers.[18] He now displays the harsher side of his attachment to America, as admiration and longing for acceptance are accompanied by hurt at rejection and angry retaliation.

In *Father Felix*, the Reverend Mr. Carver is a "schoolmaster of the 'universal Yankee nation,'" whose only skill is his "rude, but powerful eloquence." While the early authors pointed out the ministers' concerns for their own families, Cannon portrays the ministers as selfish in all areas of life. The Reverent Carver is "essentially worldly at heart," interested in women for their money and willing to inveigle property from his adherents.[19] In the same novel, Cannon extends his reach beyond ministers and uses harsh language to satirize Protestant divisions and practices. He describes a Methodist as having "all the enthusiasm, and much of the straitness and illiberality, of the sect," and calls a woman a "Presbyterian, or rather, a member of that portion of the Church of Many Names known as the Dutch Reformed." "Millerism" is a "malady . . . of the mind . . . [a] wild and terrible heresy . . . [founded by] a miserable fanatic, or most audacious knave."[20] Among Protestant religious practices, camp meetings are a favorite target. In *Harry Layden*, Cannon devotes a chapter to a Protestant camp meeting that he calls "mummery" and "a cover for works of abomination."[21]

In his 1847 *Scenes and Characters*, where an Irish immigrant and his son are central characters for the first time, Cannon's main purpose is the satire of Protestants. He writes, in effect, the first anti-Protestant Catholic novel. He sums up his goal in his description of the Irish American hero's newspaper columns: "their satire was keen, but never personal . . . [they exhibited] eloquence . . . [but] not . . . one line of mere declamation."[22] Cannon's own satire, however, is often cruder than that, and quite personal. Protestant ministers, with names like Rev. Hazadiah Sprowl, Elder Croak, and Brother Dawdling, are unprincipled hypocrites motivated by self-interest. A Brother Hoover, who has deserted his wife and daughter, is a "universal dealer" who proclaims "himself the great leader in some wonderful movement, that had for its ostensible object the elevation of the masses, but in reality his own glorification." Brother Hoover ends up with the Mormons in California and becomes a leading figure and "a warm advocate for the 'spiritual wife' system." Cannon also uses the ministers to return the Protestant charges that Catholics violate American values. The "liberal Dr. Trim" hails "as brethren" "everyone who had the remotest pretention to the Christian name . . . all except the poor Catholics, to whom he denied even the possibility of salvation." Cannon also refers to an "association of visionaries, made up, principally, of half-mad ministers, the representatives of a thousand and one denominations of Christians" who want to convert Catholics, including the pope.[23]

Cannon continues to portray the divisions among Protestants in insulting language. He calls an Episcopalian "so extremely 'low' that it was hard to distinguish him from the sectaries," including Presbyterians, Baptists, Methodists (New Light or Old Light), Quakers, and all of their subdivisions. He also satirizes Protestant religious practices. A minister opens a meeting with "a prayer . . . plentifully interlarded with 'Ohs' and 'Ahs,' in which he addressed the Almighty in a tone of greater familiarity than he would have ventured to use in speaking to a 'fellow worm' who might . . . 'be clothed in a little brief authority.'"[24]

Cannon's treatment of Protestants was undoubtedly satisfying to readers more accustomed to being the targets of attack. In *The Dublin Review*, published in London, one reviewer wrote that Cannon's novel had no "purpose, unless the very laudable one of quizzing the American field preachers, temperance preachers, etc., of whom a motley and amusing group has been collected."[25]

Nevertheless, Cannon's willingness to insult Protestants to amuse readers was at odds in many ways with his aspirations to change Protestant attitudes and his hopes that eventually Catholics would fully integrate into American social and political life. Yet ultimately, he sought to achieve both goals. His satire, after all, is directed mainly against Protestants who attack Catholics for threatening American values even as they themselves violate those values. Cannon also continues to include at least a few sympathetic Protestant characters. The main Protestant in *Scenes and Characters*—the minister's son who runs away from his father—is not portrayed as evil but as a rogue, a "scapegrace," or "foolish boy." The young man voices some of the novel's criticisms of Protestants, saying that his father exercises "unnecessary severity," and regards God as an "inexorable tyrant" intent on "vengeance." He also is not anti-Catholic in any way, in the end admitting that if all Catholics were like some of those in the novel, there was a chance they could be saved. It is in describing the fate of the young man that Cannon comes closest to his stated ideal of satire cited above: "keen but never personal . . . [with] eloquence . . . not . . . mere declamation." The minister offers his son two jobs—"a clerkship in the Treasury Department, or a Secretaryship to the Board of Foreign Missions." The son chooses the church job because government employment is "unstable," but there is always money to be made from the board "as long as those two great classes in the 'religious world' exist—Knaves and Fools." The young man also eventually marries the woman with whom he has eloped, and she takes a job with the "Moral Reform Society."[26]

Starting in 1850, the other Irish American authors picked up where Cannon left off in their willingness to satirize or caricature Protestants on a wide range of issues. Cannon also continued on this path in his 1855 novel *Bickerton* but not in his 1859 *Tighe Lyfford*, which was published by a secular house. While all of these authors were more willing to attack Protestants than their predecessors, there were differences among them. Roddan most closely resembles the early writers in his preference for intellectual arguments about doctrines and mild criticisms of people. Boyce's characterization of Ephraim Weeks, the American who is so easily bested in his encounters with the Irish, comes closest to genuine satire that could amuse rather than wound. Quigley is the most extreme, in his willingness to attack Protestant persons and beliefs both directly and through crude satire. Despite the differences, all of the Irish American authors in the end rely on blunt and defensive caricatures that undoubtedly appealed to readers accustomed to being attacked but also deepened the gulf between Catholics and other Americans.

In their novels of the 1850s, Irish American writers continued to portray ministers as the powerful leaders of anti-Catholicism in America. When Quigley and Sadlier use Friday night dinner parties as the occasion to defend fasting, they make sure that ministers are present to launch the attacks. Ministers also influence the larger public. In Roddan's *John O'Brien,*

"Some New York ministers of the gospel induced . . . Maria Monk" to become "a wholesale liar."[27] Roddan is mild compared with Quigley, who says that Catholic domestic servants are "forced to hear the disgusting ranting or ludicrous prayer of any imposter who may take on himself the office of preacher."[28]

Ministers in the novels continue to act contrary to their stated American values. They participate in public life and do all they can to prevent their own followers from seeking truth elsewhere. In Quigley's first novel, "the six sectarian teachers of the village" try to stop a priest from attending the deathbed of a Protestant seeking to become Catholic, and then, when he dies, insist on presiding at his funeral.[29] Above all, ministers lead deliberate plots to take Catholics—children and adults—away from their own faith and convert them, an emphasis that was new in Catholic fiction at the time. All of the authors in the 1850s portray ministers as using their power in charitable and public institutions to accomplish this goal. In novels by Roddan, Quigley, and Cannon, ministers influence foster care decisions, and Quigley's preacher is also the elected poormaster and a local council member who uses the schoolhouse for his religious services.[30]

The Irish Americans also depict ministers as ignorant about the Church. Roddan most closely resembles his predecessors with his emphasis on the ministers' intellectual failures. "The crowd of ministers," he writes, "are commonly as ignorant of the real nature of the Church as their people are."[31] Cannon and Quigley are harsher, as they illustrate the ministers' ignorance. "It was occasionally whispered about" that Cannon's Rev. Scroggs of *Bickerton*—the "most fashionable preacher of the day"—"had once been a shoemaker in a distant city." Scroggs and his family occupy an "imposing residence" alongside a man who sold "a medicine warranted to cure every known and every unknown disease." The two are "celebrated quacks, but in different lines."[32] Quigley refers to the "low cunning of unprincipled parsons, who, from being peddlers, and poor, shiftless mechanics, without any proper discipline or preparation," move to the "less laborious trade of preaching."[33]

This preaching is the only skill the Irish Americans allow to ministers. In her first novel, Sadlier describes the "ranting Methodist preacher," and in *Confessions of an Apostate*, the minister speaks "in first-rate style, as to quantity." One of Quigley's ministers is as "impure as Caligula, as cruel as

Nero or Calvin himself, and as violent as Luther or John Knox," but still he was "the most popular, well supported, and *respected* minister in the whole state" because he "was a good preacher, an eloquent expounder of the word, a smart man; that was enough."[34]

Like Cannon did in the 1840s, the Irish American authors portray ministers as motivated by selfish interests in money, status, or power in all aspects of their lives, greatly expanding the earlier Catholic writers' criticisms and using more insulting language to do so. Roddan, the most restrained of the group, remarks that "preaching is the *trade* of . . . ministers. . . . You seldom, if ever, see them called from a rich congregation to a poor one." Similarly in Sadlier, the minister Mr. Mortimer wants to convert Peter Burke and display him at a bible meeting because it would make his "collection . . . a first rate one."[35]

The self-interest of the Protestant ministers is an important theme in Cannon's and Quigley's novels, and both create exaggerated accounts of this behavior. In Quigley's work, "the teachers of the stuff which they call by that noble name" of religion "procured" the preacher the office of poormaster "as a reward for his hypocrisy." Quigley's ministers also preach for whatever denomination pays them, shifting viewpoints to advance their interests. A Presbyterian minister goes from a proslavery to an antislavery church because it provides him with a better living.[36]

Some of the authors encapsulate their caricatures in the ministers' allegorical names and physical appearance. Cannon describes Mr. Scroggs as "short and stout, . . . [with] coarse hair, . . . staring whitey-blue eyes, . . . flabby, colourless cheeks, . . . capacious mouth, and . . . perpetual bile on the tip of the nose."[37] Quigley's preacher/poormaster, Von Stingey, is "of the middle size, of thin, cadaverous appearance, short neck, snake head, with lank, sandy hair, nose flat and simex-like, small eyes."[38] Other ministers in Quigley's novel are named Prying, Gulmore, Cashman, and Boorman.

The authors go beyond criticizing ministers to attack the Protestant laypeople who follow them. In the 1850s novels, it is Protestants, not Catholics, who are superstitious, easily duped, and prone to mass hysteria. For Roddan, the ministers who encourage Maria Monk have not only "lined their pockets" but also "enjoyed the supreme satisfaction of sitting in their arm-chairs, and laughing to think how they had gulled their dearly-beloved brethren and sisters!" Roddan also tells Protestants: "*you* are slaves to your preachers." Quigley marvels that Protestants "submit themselves blindly and without control to the guidance" of such ministers.[39] Given this behavior, Protestants are clearly hypocrites when they proclaim their love of American liberty or attack Catholics as a threat to the country. For Quigley in 1853, "Protestant sects . . . with the word *liberty* ever on their lips . . . all play the tyrant in their own way."[40] In *Bickerton*, Cannon writes that the nativists would "destroy liberty of conscience itself by . . . persecuting these men [Catholics] for opinion's sake."[41]

Cannon's insulting characterizations of Protestants in *Bickerton* are, again, at odds with his stated hopes for Catholic integration in society. As he does earlier, he tries to resolve this conflict by emphasizing that the nativists are violating their own American values and by including honorable Protestants like the Hubbards among his main characters.

The Protestant ministers portrayed in these novels are clearly not legitimate leaders; they are ignorant, bigoted, and selfish men who preside over dupes—all in contrast, of course, to the educated, tolerant, devoted priests to be discussed in chapter 7. Yet, however much these authors of the 1850s resort to caricature, it is clear that the Protestant ministers in the novels exercise real power over the Catholic characters, who are targets of conversion plots especially in their dependent positions as foster children or servants. In the subsequent decades, the balance between fear and ridicule shifts. Ministers still personify American anti-Catholicism—showing that Protestants, not Catholics, violate American values—and continue to be motivated by ignorance and selfishness.[42] But as anti-Catholicism becomes a less prominent theme in these novels, ministers play a less important role, no longer affecting the lives of Catholics or even of Protestants. They are weak ridiculous figures without any authority, legitimate or not, and they illustrate the ultimate effects of Protestant values.

In some of these later novels, ministers are shown as the prisoners rather than the authors of prevailing opinion as they try but fail to control public actions. Deacon Samuels in Sadlier's *Confessions of an Apostate* is a slave to public opinion. He tells Simon, the lead Irish immigrant character, to practice his faith only in private because if the people of New Haven knew that the deacon had hired a Catholic, his position in the community would be undermined. In Boyce's novel, American ministers are simply seen as products of American culture: hustlers and speculators who enter and leave ignoble or humble occupations, such as fishmonger or lumber salesman, in search of the main chance. At most, the ministers are more to be blamed than others given the supposedly religious nature of their profession.[43] The minister briefly described in Sadlier's *Con O'Regan* lacks influence because he has no religious opinions to advance. Dr. Shillingworth "preached 'on his own hook' . . . [at] Jefferson street Church, thus designated in lieu of any doctrinal appellation." And of course his name indicates his real motive.[44]

Increasingly, the ministers are shown as more and more ridiculous in their motivations, behavior, and weakness. They certainly have no influence over Catholics, and they also do not merit or receive the respect of their Protestant congregations. A preacher in Sadlier's *Confessions of an Apostate* marries the bigoted Aunt Olive. He had been a shoe salesman but was now in another "line . . . Preaching." Sadlier associates the preacher with the sensual pleasures of food as Aunt Olive lures him into marriage by cooking him large meals. At one point, when he grew uncharacteristically quiet, the women at the table "ascribed [it] to the fullness of the spirit waking within him." In fact, however, he is deciding to marry Olive because she bakes "good dough-nuts." Simon O'Hare, now Simon Kerr, the lead character of the novel, calls the preacher "the good-natured man of grease."[45]

Rev. Dr. Brassman in McElgun's *Annie Reilly* has a "very peculiar" head with "eyes large and watery . . . and forehead surprisingly high and narrow" and a name that points to his habit of shouting his sermons. He seeks to "make a name here on earth," not the "poverty and humility" of the apostles. He knows that "Gospel preaching" will not bring multitudes to hear him, so he gives "other and more entertaining information" in his very long sermons.[46] The main minister in Quigley's *Profit and Loss* runs for public office and supports the activities of escaped nuns. He is called Redtop and is a "tall, lank young man . . . of a melancholy aspect. . . . His eyes were small and . . . he had enormous ears . . . [and a] hoarse, chronic cough." He is "an insurance agent" and traveling salesman as well as a preacher, and he would give it all up if only he could obtain a government office. He adopts whatever political or religious stance will help him attract adherents and contributions but is never elected to anything.[47]

This increasing tendency to portray ministers as powerless, ridiculous figures can be seen in the way the Irish American authors treat relationships between ministers and Protestant women. Throughout the twenty-five-year period of Irish American fiction discussed here, women are second only to ministers as representatives of their church and its anti-Catholicism.

Relationships between the ministers and women are also used to illustrate the ministers' selfish interests, the authors often showing the ministers seeking marriage to satisfy materialistic desires. Cannon's minister Scroggs marries Mrs. Frump, who abandons her husband, because she "made a voluntary offer to him of herself and all that she possessed," and the minister does not yet realize "the brilliant future that was before him."[48] Sadlier describes Rev. Joel McClashen in *Bessy Conway* as interested in conversions, "although there were not wanting some uncharitable persons . . . who shrewdly surmised that the rich . . . widow [Bessy's employer] was personally of more importance than the convert in the Rev. Joel's estimation."[49]

The ministers in these novels are interested in women who are attractive as well as wealthy, although the authors never acknowledge any love matches. Instead, the ministers' interests mire them in petty ordinary life rather than in religious obligations. In Quigley's *The Cross and the Shamrock*, Protestant women attend "donation parties, and *quilting matches* at young ministers' houses," write "epistles on love to young preachers," and are jealous if a preacher marries someone else.[50] The "poor" Baptist minister Ebenezer Sookes in McCorry's *The Lost Rosary* is at first interested in the widowed mother he employs as housekeeper, then runs off with her daughter, after which the abandoned mother files a breach of promise suit.[51]

Except for Roddan's *John O'Brien*, all of the novels of the 1850s show that relationships with Protestant women involve the ministers in sexual sin and even crime. In *Willy Burke*, Sadlier implies an improper relationship in one scene as the minister, Mr. Mortimer, speaks to Mrs. Watkins, the married employer:

> If *you* will try your powers of persuasion, dear, and lovely, and bewitching as you are, he [Peter Burke] cannot . . . refuse. Do sweet friend!— and the minister's voice assumed a softer tone—do, and you will bind Frederick Mortimer by yet another chain.[52]

The part-time preacher/poormaster in Quigley's first novel ends up "in disgrace with many of his church-going brethren" because "a negro girl, who was put under this *religious* man's care by the abolitionists . . . had just given birth to a young mulatto child in his house"—a child, Quigley adds, who looked like the preacher.[53]

Quigley and Roddan are the only authors in the 1850s to hint that the ministers are subordinate to women, though, to be more specific, Quigley implies some mutual influence between the ministers and Amanda Prying, the main Protestant woman in his first novel. Amanda seeks the ministers' praise and is desperate to capture one of them for a husband. Yet she also exerts her influence; she persuades one minister to steal the orphan's letters from the post office, and Quigley refers to her at one point as "the female parson."[54] Roddan means to address all Protestants when he says that ministers are "in bondage" to the "*caprices*" of their congregations. But his specific example concerns "old maids" or "spinsters" in the congregation of a young handsome minister who vie with "the *young* maids," leading to "a schism" and the minister's dismissal.[55] Ministers' subordination to women was not the main point of either Quigley or Roddan, however. Certainly Deacon Mills and Rev. Willis at the detention center, who exert such terrible influence in the life of Roddan's John O'Brien, and the preacher Von Stingey and the Reverend Gilman, who ruin the lives of Quigley's orphans, are not led by any woman. Sadlier and Cannon never even hint that women control the ministers. Cannon's Scroggs was a "tyrant" to his wife, who had dominated her first husband but now "acknowledged a master."[56]

In the novels of the 1860s and '70s, the theme of sexual impropriety almost disappears from the fiction. In her five novels in these years, Sadlier includes only one incident of sexual misconduct as she describes the advances the colporteur Jacques la Rue made to Elinor Preston.[57] Even Quigley becomes less extreme: in his final novel, he refers to an "instance of modern 'progress'" when a Protestant church council approves the elder's decision to leave his wife.[58] The dominant theme now is that ministers are dominated by the women in their lives, a theme that corresponds with the increasingly prevalent idea that Protestant ministers, as a whole, are ridiculous figures who lack all authority. The authors now present the Protestant church and society as a group of self-seeking but weak or "unmanly" ministers manipulated by women who usurp their functions.

McCorry undermines his minister's pretentions to power by demonstrating his subservience to his mother. "It is unnecessary perhaps to observe," McCorry writes, "that the Rev. Alvah Morton was in complete subjection to the orders and dictates of his respected mother." He was "induced" to place the inflammatory statements against the convent in the newspapers, for example, "by the instigation of his pious mother."[59]

Even the ministers who play lesser roles in the novels are dominated by the women in their lives. In Sadlier's *Confessions of an Apostate*, the preacher and former shoe salesman is manipulated into marriage to Aunt Olive because of his weakness for food. In McCorry's *The Lost Rosary*, the minister Ebenezer Sookes "knew very little of the world" and displayed "a softness" of character, as well as a "nervous temperament." "The greater part of his congregation consisted of aged spinsters, who managed to make their pliable pastor much more like a good-natured sheep, than one used to taking charge." The women explain that in their advocacy of women's rights, they seek "nothing but equality; and, after all, to be only equal to the likes of him."[60] Redtop, the minister in Quigley's *Profit and Loss*, wants to marry the principal of the public school, who is also part of the group planning to convert the residents of Irish Corners. The minister is desperate to obtain her favor, follows her lead on all issues, and is "nearly beside himself" with jealousy when she pays attention to others, or seems to reject him in any way. He visits a spiritualist for advice on how to win her, threatens to kill himself, and waits for years after she marries someone else.[61]

Sadlier's *Old and New* represents the culmination of this trend, as one of the ministers is actually a woman, the Reverend Julietta Fireproof, B. A., an advocate of women's rights. While Quigley in his first novel calls Amanda Prying "the female parson" because of her influence, Sadlier makes the minister actually—or almost—a woman. The reverend and her female companion are "nondescript animals attired in a fashion half masculine, half feminine, but rather inclining to the former." They wear "rakish-looking hats . . . Turkish trowsers and stout buckskins." The reverend is a "tall Amazon" or "uncommonly tall with a dark face and a lowering brow" who speaks in "loud, emphatic tones."[62] Sadlier's portrait of this female minister who looks and speaks like a man suggests that the role of minister is so "unmanly" that even a woman can do it. The portrait also seems like a culmination of the misogyny that characterizes the authors' portraits of Protestant women in general.

Like Cannon's works of the 1840s, these later anti-Protestant novels went beyond the caricatures of ministers to attack Protestant structures, doctrines, and practices with insulting language. A common theme was that the Protestant commitment to individual liberty, which has undermined the authority of ministers, has also fractured the Protestant community. In *John O'Brien*, Roddan says that "ministers *will* be ambitious. Dr. Boggs will be uneasy because Dr. Coggs has got a hundred men, women, and children on the anxious seat, while he has only got sixty." The novel's lead character works for one family in which each member belongs to a different denomination.[63] And the minister in Sadlier's *Bessy Conway* is named McClashen.

Cannon and Quigley are, as always, harsher. Cannon lists the Bickerton denominations as the "High Church Simmer and Low Church Trimmer, and old School Blinker and New School Skinker, and Primitive Higgins, and Wesleyan Spriggins, and Whitfieldian Wiggins, and Trinitarian Riddle, and Unitarian Twiddle, and Universalist Diddle, and Free Will Douser, and Close-Communion Souser, etc., etc."[64] Quigley, for his part, refers to the "incredible and contradictory creeds" and lists "Nothingarian" Protestants as well as "unbaptized Quakers, groaning Methodists, blaspheming Presbyterians, faithless Universalists and Unitarians, and humbug spiritual rappers." One Presbyterian "during his long life . . . had changed his creed no less than nine times." His "transformations and metamorphoses . . . [were] like Jupiter of old."[65]

Although the authors do not spare any Protestant denominations, they seemed to target Calvinists/Presbyterians, Methodists, and the newer Spiritualists, Mormons, and Millenarians.[66] Boyce makes his opinion of Presbyterians clear in his portrayal of the Irish bigot Robert Hardwrinkle, who comes from "a very grave and orderly family," whose "religion . . . had withered them up."[67] Protestant dreariness is a favorite theme of Sadlier. The main character in *Confessions of an Apostate* reflects that for "Puritans," that "over-strained and misapplied 'religion,'" the Sabbath is "ever a dreary day—dull, and cold, and cheerless. . . . In fact, cheerfulness (not to say mirth) is prohibited on the evangelical Sabbath."[68]

Nearly all the authors ridicule Methodists. Roddan says that "the Methodist stirs up the whole *animal*, and tries to make him be good on the same grounds that urge a persecuted dog." In Boyce, the Irish Anglican magistrate refers to a "canting, Methodist class-leader" and says that Methodists would "first reduce you down with psalm singing, till you're as flat as dish water and as weak as a wendle straw, and then finish you off with mock piety, private scandal, and weak tea." For Quigley, Methodism "has neither method nor order. It is called a church, though it has neither a fixed creed nor decent hierarchy. It is called a religion, and yet it neither binds nor unites men to their Creator, nor to one another."[69]

Most of the authors are also particularly critical of Millenarians and Mormons. They offer these denominations as egregious examples of what happens when people reject the authority of the true church. Roddan speaks of the "fanatics who arise up so often" in America. Some of the Protestants who flock to such movements, Roddan says, are "driven . . . incurably insane. . . . . Talk of superstition! People who live in glass houses ought not to throw stones."[70] Quigley says that "If they [Protestants] have produced Mormons, Transcendentalists, Universalists, and spiritual rappers, in the nineteenth century, what monsters would they not have produced in the ninth."[71] Cannon remains particularly hard on Mormons. In the 1840s the minister in *Scenes and Characters* ended up with the Mormons; in 1855, Mr. Scroggs of *Bickerton* finally goes to Salt Lake, where "he bids fair to rival the renowned Brigham Young, not alone in his popularity as a preacher of Joe Smith's gospel, but in the number of his wives."[72]

The Protestant beliefs and religious practices that might substitute for church or clerical authority were also subject to particularly harsh scrutiny. Quigley attacks the Protestant reliance on the scriptures. In his first novel, he says that "the Mormons, spiritual rappers, and Transcendentalists explode the Bible altogether," and in his subsequent work, he calls all Protestants "Bible-mongers."[73] Sadlier is sarcastic about the Protestant idea of the spirit. When Bessy Conway's employer pressures her and the other servants to attend prayer services, they "could not possibly unravel the mystery unless on the supposition that their mistress had turned Quaker and was moved by the spirit to move *them*." But the servants soon realize that their boss is under the influence of the minister McClashen, "who had moved her directly, let the spiritual agency be as it might."[74] Quigley ridicules the Protestant method of prayer, referring to Methodists as "that sect whose principal devotion consists in loud groans and hysterical gestures" and describing their hymns as "discordant chanting of Methodist melody by such ludicrous hymns as" the one he reproduces.[75]

In the 1850s, authors also focused on the revivals and camp meetings associated with the Great Awakening. Cannon divides the Protestants of

Bickerton into those who go to "the splendid churches . . . [with] well-dressed Christians in luxurious pews" and the "poor conventicles, where piety, run mad, makes known its fervour by violent contortions and meaningless vociferations."[76] Quigley ties the practices to sexual transgressions— essentially using them as the Protestants use the convent narratives. The Catholic Church, he says, has never "sanctioned" "a *camp meeting . . .* authorized her ministers to *feel 'for the change of heart'* in young ladies . . . or to raise funds by the abominable practices of the 'donation parties' for the support of her institutions. And mind, these scandals the sectarian churches sanction . . . by day as well as by night."[77] But after 1860, Quigley is the only author to make Protestant revivals an important theme, calling them "a paradise of the animal passions."[78]

While they attacked Protestants for their fragmentation, the authors also claimed that all the denominations were false religions and so were essentially the same. Even the authors who took the time to provide details about Protestant divisions also indicated that the differences were superficial. Roddan gives the competing ministers similar names, Dr. Boggs and Dr. Coggs, and also suggests that Protestants themselves do not take their differences seriously. They rent their churches to other denominations and also hire their preachers. "It is a fine state of things, when a Calvinistic congregation sit and sleep comfortably under a Unitarian. They agree to pay his salary, if he will promise not to hurt their feelings by saying in the pulpit that Christ is not God." To Roddan, this—and not the faith of the Catholics—"is idolatry . . . publicly practiced . . . and unreproved."[79] Quigley goes further: in his final novel, he calls all Protestants "deluded"; "the motives and objects which delude . . . are different, but the delusion and discomfiture of the victims of all these errors of the human mind are the same substantially."[80]

The authors also communicate the essential sameness of Protestant denominations by using generic labels. Sadlier calls the state of Connecticut "perhaps, the most Puritanical in the Union," adding that the children educated by the bigoted Aunt Olive would grow up with minds "of puritanical ice." McCorry calls Massachusetts "the Puritan State" and the bigoted Mrs. Morton "that most angelic piece of Puritanical humanity."[81] Authors also use variants of the term "evangelical." Sadlier says Aunt Olive has "evangelical virtues," McCorry calls the ministers behind the

Charlestown attack "evangelicals of a like type," and Quigley refers to Protestants as "male and female evangelizers."[82]

To show that differences among Protestants essentially do not matter, the authors also make a point of displaying their ignorance about the denomination of a Protestant character. Sadlier describes the son of Henry Blake going off to Columbia College "without religion of any kind, saving a sort of predilection in favor of the Baptist sect."[83] Other authors conflate denominations. The supposedly Baptist minister Sookes in McCorry is also "a Methodist, [and] a Revivalist," and Cecilia Morton, the still to be converted character in *Mount Benedict*, is "an Episcopalian Methodist." Quigley says that one of his characters was baptized in the "Methodist Episcopal Church (as it is called)."[84]

Another related charge that gained prominence over time was that Protestants had no firm beliefs or principles at all. For Roddan, "atheism" had become "the fashionable *religion* in Boston." Boyce portrays his American character Weeks as a type of Unitarian, who believes in God only as first cause. Dr. Shillingworth, the independent preacher in Sadlier's novel, has no "doctrinal appellation"; he and his followers are "not addicted to any particular notion of religion." McCorry also implies that his minister Sookes has no religious beliefs: in addition to being a Methodist and Revivalist, he is an "earnest worker in the field of missionary labor, provided said field consists in gliding here and there to nice little evening parties, shaking hands . . . with ladies."[85]

To these authors, Protestantism is so deficient that it does not qualify as a branch of Christianity or even as a religion. Roddan concludes not only that atheism is becoming the religion of Boston but also that "Protestantism . . . was in the beginning little better than atheism dressed in a few Christian garments," which have now been cast off. He advises readers confronted by a Protestant to "attack his so-called religion; make him *prove* that it is true," suggesting that Protestantism does not deserve the designation.[86] The other authors also went beyond accusing Protestants of adopting "false" religions, or descending from a "motley group of proud, soul-destroying heresiarchs."[87] They refuse to grant Protestants the status of Christians. Quigley refers to Protestants as "modern pagans," telling them: "ye call yourselves Christians, though Universalists, Methodists, Quakers, Shakers, and Muggletonians, and other such titles, are your proper names."[88] The good Protestant women in Sadlier's *Con O'Regan* have no particular religious beliefs, in Sadlier's view, but simply live in accordance with some basic moral principles "if principles their simple rules of action could be called."[89] When the young Protestant Cecilia Morton in McCorry's novel tells a nun in the convent of Mount Benedict that she is a fellow Christian, the nun responds: "Yes, yes; no doubt, child, according to your own fancy—or, excuse me, according—well; yes, dear, you are a Christian of the Episcopalian Methodists."[90]

The authors typically do not even refer to Protestant denominations or houses of worship as churches but as "sects" or "conventicles."[91] Sadlier also uses the term "meeting-house," as when the backsliding Peter Burke refuses to enter the "Wesleyan Methodist meeting-house," indicating that "the last tattered remnant of shame still clung around him." Henry Blake leads his Protestant bride "to the altar . . . that is, to the altar of the world, represented by the communion-table in her own meeting-house."[92] Quigley refers to the Protestants' "spurious churches" and to "Protestant Christian churches, falsely so called." In his last novel, he uses terms like "piebald churches" and "shabby sects."[93]

Obviously the Irish American authors did not publish these attacks, which reflected long-standing Catholic criticisms of the Protestant Reformation, to persuade Protestants to change their minds. Apart from praising the Church and its clergy for the unity and order they provided, the authors intended to amuse Catholic readers and to make them aggressors for a change rather than victims. The more authoritarian of the Irish American authors—Roddan, Sadlier, and Quigley—also expressed the fear beneath the attacks more directly, and it was not fear of Protestant bigotry. These authors were concerned that the Church could not survive in a society committed to the American Protestant idea of liberty, where individuals rejected authority not only in religious but also in family and social life.

Anti-Protestant Novels Reflect Catholic Fears and Purposes

However careful Catholic authors were in considering liberty of conscience for Protestants, they clearly did not support religious liberty or freedom of conscience for individual Catholics. The more authoritarian writers were explicit. When authors like Quigley and Sadlier occasionally expressed some disdain for ideas of religious liberty, their disdain did not reflect hopes to impose their faith on Protestants but rather fear that Catholics might assert such liberty against the Church. In their accounts of anti-Catholicism, these more authoritarian writers emphasized the attacks on the authority priests exercised over Catholics, tracing them to the concept of individual liberty. In Quigley's *Profit and Loss*, the apostate professor tells the Catholic father that "if a priest would have the audacious presumption to dictate to me, a free American, to what school I should go, I should at once have a petition drafted in the fairest calligraphy . . . and have him removed at once." When the father decides to send his son to the public school, the professor calls him "liberal and free by . . . not being a slave to priests."[94]

When the American-born children of the immigrants begin to abandon their faith, they invariably also espouse these false "American" and "Protestant" views of liberty. At his first confession, Roddan's John O'Brien questions the priest's right to know what he has done. In Sadlier's *The Blakes and Flanagans*, the adult Henry Blake opposes the bishop's campaign for the schools and says: "I feel . . . that I have crossed the Rubicon, [and] declared myself a free man, as far as the priests are concerned."[95]

In *Profit and Loss*, Quigley draws a contrast between American liberty and the true liberty found in the Catholic Church, which entails faithfulness to priests and religious practice. The young American-born lead character Patrick Mulroony abandons his faith and achieves his worldly goals: he changes his name, graduates from the academy, and gains "a County superintendency of education worth $900 a year . . . the name of being a smart man in the community . . . [and] a few academy prizes." For Quigley, "If ever any man . . . could say that he was his own master, and had his own way, free to think and act as he pleased," that was Patrick. Yet the young man comes to realize that he is "far from being happy." He loses his mother's love, and then, through a series of events, he also loses his property and his Protestant wife. Finally, he loses the liberty he so values when he is sentenced to jail, and it is only in prison that he returns to his faith, concluding: "though within these walls, I am free . . . from the chains . . . around . . . my captive heart." Indeed, his statement, "*I am free*," followed by his original name, are his last words in the novel.[96]

These Irish American authors also conveyed their suspicion of American ideas of liberty, autonomy, or independence when they considered relationships in the family and workplace.

Sadlier associates "liberty" with an arrogant self-assertion that could manifest itself in both trivial and important matters. In *Old and New*, a woman selling cleaning products door-to-door, "entirely self-possessed . . . [and with] spurious pretensions," insists that a servant usher her into the Von Weigel parlor. The aristocratic daughter of the house comments about "American 'institootions'" such as "lady-peddlars" who could call on anyone, even "the President's wife."[97] On more significant issues, some of Sadlier's immigrant characters, after spending a few years in America, begin to neglect or disobey their Irish parents. In *Confessions of an Apostate*, as Simon begins to withdraw from his faith, he only "glanced . . . impatiently over" his Irish mother's letters, with their "maternal admonitions." He also behaves in a disrespectful way to an Irish schoolmaster in Boston, making a "show of independence" as he "snapped" at the old man for inquiring about his religious practice.[98]

These authors were especially concerned about the children of the immigrants, who might claim liberty or independence from their parents as part of the process of adopting an American identity. Sadlier's Peter Burke, when summoned by his mother, replies, "I'll go to see my mother when it answers me," because he is "following the bent of his own inclinations, and thus giving a proof of what he considered independence." Peter is influenced along this path by his Protestant employer, who advises him: "do not suffer her [his mother] to carry your reason captive. Learn to think for yourself."[99]

To show that this dangerous idea of liberty is not only Protestant but American, Sadlier gives characters who espouse liberty over authority American accents, wherever they happen to have been born. (Sadlier is the least American of the Irish American writers. She immigrated first to Canada, not to the United States, and returned to Canada at the end of her life. Alone among the authors, she also sent many of her lead characters back to Ireland at the end of her stories.) Sadlier's characters display an American accent by using words such as "ain't" or "real" and by mispronouncing words such as "been." This accented speech usually also violates the rules of grammar, a not-so-subtle way of expressing the author's opinion of people with such views. The more traditional characters speak without such accents, again, regardless of birthplace.

In *Con O'Regan*, for example, Sadlier indicts Boston for its systemic bigotry but also for its effect on the immigrants' children. One father explains that his son Patsey, who had "a will of his own," had "got some Yankee notions of independence into his head." Patsey's behavior improves markedly after the family's move to the western settlement, an improvement evidenced in his accent.

In Boston:

Patsey: "Ha! ha! . . . then I'm real glad I wasn't born in Ireland. Boys a'nt treated so here. There a'nt any whipping allowed here, you know, and I often heard boys say that if Irish Paddies had their way they'd give their children awful usage."

(at a later point, complaining about his father): "He needn't have used me so!—it a'nt any wonder that folks talk so of Irish Paddies!—they're real mean."

In the western settlement:

Patsey (still needing to improve his grammar but without the American accent): "I like the country far better than the town. Father never lets me do any work that I'm not able for, and I like to help him with whatever he's at."

Con O'Regan (the recent Irish immigrant): "And what about Jake Hampton and all the others? . . . wouldn't you like to see them again? I thought you meant to go back to them as you got the chance!"

Patsey: "Oh! I hadn't any sense then. . . . I don't want to see any of them fellows now. . . . if you'd only hear the wicked talk that they used to have, and how they'd curse and swear—and there wasn't one of them Irish—not one."[100]

Of all the authors, Quigley comes closest to Sadlier, especially in his final novel *Profit and Loss*, in which the immigrant father Michael Mulroony expresses a desire for his son to attend the public school called the American Academy. There, the boy would acquire the "real *refined Yankee nasal* accent" and the associations that would help him to succeed. The pious wife and mother of the family opposes the "Yankee school" because it would endanger her son's faith as well as his obedience and respect for his parents. And, indeed, after the son and a neighbor, Nellie, attend the school, they lose their faith and treat their parents badly. Nellie "lost the natural love and respect which every rational animal, and almost every animal of the lower creation, generally entertain for their parents," because she has been "so flattered" by those "roaring Methodists . . . for her *independence* and *enlightenment.*"[101]

In *Old and New*, Sadlier suggests that America produces families in which the parents don't even bother to assert their authority in the first place. The newly rich Mrs. Gallagher only laughs when her daughters make fun of her accent. She later accompanies her daughters when they get married without their father's knowledge. Mr. Gallagher, Sadlier makes clear, does not assert authority or any "salutary severity" in his family. He seeks only to keep the peace and in the end wishes that he had not given his daughters "so much of the tether as I did."[102]

Sadlier also feared that single women immigrants would be dangerously influenced by American values of liberty and independence, expressing her concerns about economic, as well as religious and family life. In *Bessy Conway*, the Irish immigrant object lessons, Sally and Bridget, come to very bad ends because they pursue a social and sexual life. Underlying this behavior is their assertion of American liberty against the authority of church, parents, and employers.

Once again, Sadlier uses the servants' accents to indicate their new, dangerous American values, as in this conversation among Bessy, Sally, and Bridget after Sally has been asked by her employer to give up her evening off to take care of a sick child:

Sally: "Now, Bessy a'in't this too bad?—Ain't it?"

Bridget: "I say it's *mean.*"

Bessy Conway: "What is it?"

Sally: "Here am I dressed to go out, and Mrs. Hibbard sends down word that I can't go this evening. . . . I a'nt so green that folks can treat me so."

Bessy: "But, dear me! . . . why didn't you ask leave to go out *before* you dressed? . . . Don't you know Miss Lizzy is very sick, and the poor child doesn't like to be left alone?"

Sally: "Well! it a'nt any matter about that, I'm going out."
Bridget: "I would, if I was you. . . . I'd let them see that I'd have my
   rights."[103]

American values, for these authors, also have disastrous consequences
for political life. In many of the novels, the Protestant denominations with
their minimal creeds are shown as more interested in social and political
causes than in religion, and their causes are for greater liberty. In a list of
"manias" that "within the last few years, have sprung from the sectarian
systems," Quigley, in his first novel, lists not only spiritual rappers, Mor-
monism, and gold hunting, but also woman's rights.[104] In his subsequent
Profit and Loss, the public school principal and her minister are avid supporters of women's rights. Sadlier also suggests that commitment to contemporary social movements, especially women's rights and abolition, is
taking precedence over religion among the newer types of Protestantism.
When the aristocratic widow Von Weigel quotes St. Paul to Rev. Julietta
Fireproof, the women's rights advocate scoffs: "A fig for your great Doctor of the Gentiles . . . whom nobody minds now-a-days." The reverend
lectures on women's rights as well as "on Physiology and Animal Magnetism and Bi-ology. . . . Spiritualism and Negro Slavery." The minister
Sookes in McCorry's *The Lost Rosary* is "an advocate of women's rights."
McCorry castigates the women's rights movement as a threat to moral and
social authority, "calculated to destroy virtue . . . to raze society to its foundations."[105]

In drawing out the implications of their attacks on Protestants, the
three authoritarian writers do not speak for all of their colleagues. Some
Irish American voices are more positive about American liberty, if not
in church affairs, at least in family and society. When McCorry advises domestic servants in *The Lost Rosary* that "A disposition for spending time
idly, although the spare hours properly belong to us, and not to our employers, is too often the gateway to ruin, and should always be carefully
avoided," he implies that servants might at least choose the activities with
which to fill their spare hours, as opposed to Sadlier, who believes servants
must obey employer demands even on their days off. On another occasion
in this novel, McCorry indicates that America is superior to Ireland in bal-
ancing authority and independence in the workplace. One of the young

male immigrants working on a farm in America writes home to Ireland that his master is "never called master, but just . . . boss." The boss did not watch his workers so closely as the master at home but "leaves a good deal to one's own decency an' that's just where he shows himself a wise man."[106] The young man prefers the American way and also concludes that people work much harder for bosses than for masters.

Boyce sees even more advantages in the American approach to social life. The most serious anti-Catholic character in his novel is the Irish Presbyterian Hardwrinkle, hardly a champion of liberty, rather than the American Ephraim Weeks. Boyce also conveys his appreciation for the idea that each man can pursue his own good and allow others to do the same. His American character, Ephraim Weeks, adopts a tolerant "live-and-let-live" attitude and so is not envious or resentful. Weeks is "pleased to see every one thrive" and simply assumes that each man seeks his own interests and is ready to make "sharp bargains," "taking advantage of his neighbor in speculations." Weeks adopts this "all fair in war" attitude even when he loses a battle in trade or romance. When he realizes that the revolutionary Randall Barry is his "rival" in love and has been imprisoned for treason, Weeks continues to admire him: "I don't think the less of him for that," he says. "He's a fine, spirited, gallant-looking young fellow. . . . Let every man have a fair chance." The American view of liberty is not Boyce's ideal—he prefers the aristocratic societies of Ireland and Europe, in which each person knows his place. Yet the Americans are at least better than the Irish Presbyterians. The pious Hardwrinkle, who criticizes Weeks for his opinions about individual freedom, is portrayed as a hypocrite, a bigot who aims to impose his views on others, and a "mercenary man" "envious of his neighbors' prosperity."[107] The Americans, whatever their deficiencies, are not hypocrites.

Cannon typically is the most interesting of the authors. He enthusiastically repeats the standard criticisms of Protestants with vituperative language and crude caricatures. Yet, although the point of the attacks is the defense of church and clerical authority, his main goal is to amuse his readers rather than to warn them against the idea of liberty. Contrary to the implications of the attacks, he defends religious liberty (as discussed in chapter 4) and also supports characters who assert their liberty in family and social life.

As he did on the issues of religious liberty, Cannon cites the position of the bishops' pastoral letter on liberty in general, then uses his Protestant characters to express more complete support for the American values. In the passages Fred Hubbard reads from the pastoral letter, the bishops state their concerns about the idea of individual liberty. The Church exhorts "her children to temper freedom with the proper control of unruly passion," teaching Catholics that "while they love true liberty, they must curb passion, cherish law and order, and respect authority." Cannon, however, does not follow up on this idea. On the contrary, old Mr. Hubbard, one of the Protestant spokesmen for toleration of Catholics, endorses a general liberty of thought, saying that Americans should not "attempt to arrest the spread of popery" by coercion but should "meet it openly, with the weapons of truth and reason."[108]

Cannon also communicates his support for American liberty through his characters. Approaching the shores of America, the Irish immigrant in *Bickerton* tells his wife, "already I feel the breath of liberty coming with a welcome to us over the waters, and I shall soon stand a freeman among the free." Cannon also supports the immigrant's daughter, who treats her oppressive foster parents in a "haughty, cold and positively cruel" way as she becomes uniformly "taciturn, sarcastic, or defiant" in their presence. The minister Scroggs in this same novel violates the norms of liberty not only in his bigotry but also in his treatment of his family and associates. Cannon calls Scroggs a "tyrant" to his wife and refers to him as "his Protestant Popeship."[109]

As discussed in the previous chapter, Cannon makes an even more extensive case for liberty in his final novel, *Tighe Lyfford*, claiming the Catholic Church as its main advocate. He says that the Catholic—like the American—has "a heritage of freedom," appealing "to the history even of our own land, and to the acknowledged intelligence of the Catholics of the United States." He praises the "clear mental vision, . . . scholarship, . . . logical mind, . . . legal acumen, . . . and . . . intellectual grasp" of eminent Catholic men, including bishops and the pope. More generally, he concludes that the Church has created a world where "Liberty" is "always sure of a welcome and a home."[110]

With his attraction to American values, Cannon was clearly not willing to emulate Sadlier and draw out the implications of his attacks on

Protestants. He meant simply to amuse his readers by embellishing standard Catholic criticisms. And his work, like all of the anti-Protestant novels, undoubtedly appealed to the Irish Catholic reading public, who could enjoy seeing their Protestant accusers attacked and ridiculed. But it can also be argued that the novels, including those of Cannon, reflect an unfortunate and inflammatory "reverse prejudice."[111] The attacks also convey the defensiveness of a people who fear their faith and culture cannot survive in a diverse country committed to ideas of individual liberty and autonomy.

Chapter 6

THE CHURCH AS FAMILY

Catholic novelists did not simply defend Catholics or attack Protestants in return. They offered the good life made possible by membership in the Catholic Church as the alternative to American Protestant society. The first generation of writers portrayed the Church primarily as an institution that taught theological and moral doctrines and administered sacraments. The Irish Americans, starting with Cannon's work in the late 1840s, depicted the Church mainly as a community, a people bound together by a shared ethnicity and by bonds of love and trust among the members, and between them and their priest leaders. The Church was the immigrants' inheritance from the home they had left behind and their only home and family in their new country. This link between faith and ethnicity undoubtedly met the readers' basic desire to belong and strengthened their identity as Catholics, at least in the shorter run, but it also associated church membership with youth and separated the Irish immigrants not only from Protestants but also from other Catholics.

The ideal of community did not mean total agreement. Catholic novels always reflected some of the conflicts within the Church of the day, in particular the debates about authority and nurturance generated by the writings of militant Catholic Orestes Brownson. All of the authors criticized Protestants for rejecting church authority, but they disagreed about the nature and extent of that authority over Catholics. As on the question of parents and employers, Boyce and Cannon were more liberal voices; Roddan, Quigley, and Sadlier were authoritarian.

Irish American authors also conveyed, however carefully, their differences with official church policy on particular issues, with some advocating a more flexible church and others seeking greater firmness. In addition to Cannon, who advanced unorthodox positions on religious liberty and church-state relations, authors differed from their bishops on such issues as Catholic schools, emigration, colonization, and revolutionary Irish nationalism. The range of views demonstrates that Catholic popular fiction accommodated a variety of perspectives on church authority, contrary to the conclusions of Brownson—and more recently of David Reynolds in *Faith in Fiction*—that popular literature inevitably had a liberalizing influence on American religious life.[1]

The Church in the Early Catholic Novels: Teaching and Inspiring Individuals

As described in chapter 1, the first generation of Catholic writers began with doctrinal novels centered on the intellectual search of individual Protestants for the one true church. Pise, Bryant, Dorsey, and Cannon all emphasized basic Catholic theology primarily for the benefit of Protestants interested in conversion. As the Wolburn daughter in Pise's novel *Father Rowland* tells her father at the end of her studies, "I am quite convinced of the truth of the Catholic religion."[2] In tracing the path of a Protestant character to conviction and conversion, these early authors emphasized a church that met the individual, primarily intellectual, needs of those who subscribed to it.

That changed in the late 1840s when the early writers began to assume their readers were Catholic and made Catholics, not Protestants, the lead characters in the novels. They presented the Church primarily as the source of sacraments, prayer, and other rituals that met the emotional, rather than the intellectual, needs of individuals. Membership in the Church transformed people, inspired their moral conduct, and strengthened and consoled them in times of adversity. Both Dorsey and Miles, for example, show that the grace received through the Church motivates people to serve a higher end and to lead a moral life. Agnes Cleveland, the young Catholic heroine of Miles's *Loretto*, is tempted to abandon the convent for the pleasures of social life and has to rely on grace, rather than her own strength, to maintain her commitment. Ellen Almy, the young Protestant woman in the novel, stops caring about fashion, balls, and social life after her conversion and devotes herself to charity.[3] In Miles's other novel, the Catholic mother of the governess says that "her religion . . . was her only consolation." When she lost her husband and her wealth, she remembered, there was "nothing to shield me from despair and ruin, but the sacraments which the Catholic Church alone can bestow."[4]

In her account of the German immigrants, Dorsey hints at another conception of the Church: as a people bound together by ethnic background and heritage. After coming to Washington, DC, the immigrant Conradt family enter a Catholic church, recognize it as a familiar institution, and "feel at home." The father comments that although they all think about their "distant home . . . this holy temple is the Christian's faderland!" An older German immigrant tells new arrivals that "a great many of our countrymen form . . . [the] large congregation" of the church.[5]

Dorsey does not develop this idea, however, continuing to emphasize the traditional functions the Church serves for individuals. She describes her heroine Marie Conradt's troubles to provide encouragement and hope to readers, and indeed, Marie develops "a heart strong in its faith in God," not given to "bewailing senselessly . . . and indulging in the luxurious sentimentality of grief in supine idleness." The Conradt family does not live in a German neighborhood or associate with other Germans. In fact, the men of the family travel west in search of their own farm. In addition, the immigrants are not subject to anti-Catholic or anti-foreign sentiment in America. The Church is their home or fatherland, but so is American society in general. And, as always in Dorsey's work, America is shown as superior to Europe because it allows immigrants to freely practice their faith. Even the Church itself, familiar as it is to these immigrants, is portrayed as better in America than in Europe. The priest in the German town compares unfavorably to Father Holberg in America. The adopted son of the family describes his former German pastor as "extremely severe towards me; he spared me neither in the pulpit nor in the public streets." Father Holberg was all benevolent kindness.[6]

In their discussions of the Church, these early writers conveyed varying messages about church authority. At first, they downplayed claims over Protestants and Catholics, mainly to appease Protestant opinion. In *Father Rowland*, Pise invokes invincible ignorance to assure Protestants that they, too, can be saved. After she became a Catholic, Mrs. Wolburn, the wife and mother of the family, responds to some Protestant friends who assume that she now regards them as "all to be lost. Oh, what a cruel, cruel belief!" Mrs. Wolburn replies: "I have no such convictions." Her daughter reminds the company that, according to Father Rowland, "a heretic is one who impugns the known truth." Mrs. Wolburn continues: "surely we cannot believe that our good protestant friends come under this denomination. . . . *You* certainly do not oppose the *known* truth—what *we* know to be the truth, you have been taught to regard as error." Pise even suggests that it is Protestants, not Catholics, who take a more rigorous view of salvation, describing Colonel Wolburn, a member of the Church of England, as "one of those liberal charitable men, who think that even *Catholics* may be saved."[7]

Cannon, in his 1844 *Mora Carmody*, also downplays church authority, appealing to invincible ignorance to convince Protestants that they need not be members of the Catholic Church to attain salvation. Before his conversion, the hero of the novel asks the Catholic Mora if she believes "all Protestants are beyond the reach of mercy?" She responds: "Heaven forbid! I have been taught to believe that thousands, who have never borne the name of *Catholic* on earth, will find a place in the heaven of the elect of God." Like Pise, Cannon defines a heretic as "One *that impugns the known truth*."[8]

Another feature of the early novels is that Protestants convert to Catholicism only after their own reason and logic have been satisfied. Father Rowland tells one of the Wolburn sisters to become a new member of the Church only "through pure conviction," to which she answers, "never shall I act otherwise, than from conviction, dearest sir."[9] Priests in these novels do not assert any more authority over Catholics than over converting Protestants. In fact, by portraying priests as elderly and sentimental types, the authors do what they can to undermine their connection with authority.

In the mid- and later 1840s, as the Catholic writers portray a more pervasive anti-Catholicism in society and begin to direct their novels to Catholics, they conveyed different conceptions of the Church. Pise and

Miles adopt the more authoritarian position advanced by Orestes Brownson. In *Zenosius*, Pise declares the "necessity of believing in this [Catholic] church," never mentioning invincible ignorance. Miles dismisses the idea altogether: "The arguments for Catholicity are scattered thick around us," he writes, "not only in books, but in every day life."[10] Pise and Miles also stress that Catholics are obliged to obey the Church. When Zenosius asks, "what, then, is the best reply a Catholic can make, when asked why he believes as he does," the answer is "because the Church, the infallible interpreter of the Word of God, has taught it, and demands my assent." A priest advises Zenosius to exhibit "docile submission to the Catholic faith" and adopt "the yoke of authority . . . which . . . requires that the pride of man should stoop."[11] For Miles, when a Protestant character in *The Governess* says that she reads and interprets the Bible herself, the Catholic mother replies, "Are you infallible?" The freethinking doctor in *Loretto* rejects the priest's offer of instruction and begins to read books of theology, "still considering *himself* the infallible interpreter."[12]

By contrast, as Bryant, Dorsey, and Cannon give greater emphasis to anti-Catholicism, they stop repeating the earlier assurances that Protestants will be saved, but they do not follow the authoritarians. The three authors simply remain silent on the whole question of authority, heresy, and salvation, just as they remained silent on the principle of religious liberty, as seen in chapter 4.

This shift in thinking toward Protestants and salvation between the 1830s and later 1840s suggests that David Reynolds's argument—that religious fiction in the nineteenth century tended to foster unity across religious denominations by emphasizing a shared Christian morality—needs to be qualified. Catholic writers, in fact, moved in the opposite direction. At first they tended to adopt views that blurred the distinction between Catholics and Protestants. That changed in the subsequent years when the authors viewed anti-Catholicism as a more serious threat.

The Church in the Irish American Novels:
An Enveloping Community

In her novel on the German immigrants and in his 1847 *Scenes and Characters*, Dorsey and Cannon make brief or oblique references to an ethnic bond uniting a congregation. In doing so, they begin to suggest the idea of the Church primarily as a people, an idea that will be developed by the Irish Americans in the succeeding decades. Cannon's description in *Scenes and Characters* recalls—albeit in greatly modified form—the portrait of the Church in his 1835 story "The Beal Fire," which takes place in Ireland in the eighteenth century. The lead character is Father Egan, who speaks for a people. He "laboured . . . untiringly to effect . . . the regeneration of his country." Interestingly, the priest defines the people as Irish rather than Catholic. In a speech to assembled rebels he says: "let us, then, forget that religious distinctions have ever existed among us; let us, as children of the same family join in driving from our shores those who have come amongst us with the avowed purpose of dividing to conquer . . . and prove to the world that *Irishmen can be united*."[13]

In *Scenes and Characters*, Cannon reinterprets this concept of a priest and people for a "Catholic" novel. His lead characters, the Toland family, are Irish Catholic immigrants with an American-born son. The priest character in the novel has the obviously Irish name of Quigley, and, as discussed in chapter 4, he comes from another "home," one he shares with his congregation. Cannon only hints at the priest's home, however, saying that Father Quigley serves a people who are "at that time, with few exceptions, both very poor and very illiterate"—the same terms Cannon uses to describe the Tolands when they first arrive from Ireland. Cannon also describes the priest in the same terms that bigots in his novels use to insult Irish immigrants: he is "coarse-featured" and "uncouth."[14] While "Beal Fire" suggests a people bound by nationalism despite religious differences, *Scenes and Characters*, despite the reticence about the priest's ethnic identity, suggests a church in which ethnic ties among the people and the priests support the bonds of religion.

In the 1850s Cannon and the other Irish American writers developed this view of the Church as a community united by a shared legacy from home, the "faith," "religion," or "creed" of their "fathers" or "ancestors."[15] In Quigley's *The Cross and the Shamrock*, the family, robbed soon after they arrive in America, are left with only the crucifix they had brought with them. In Cannon's *Bickerton*, the only thing the orphaned girl retains from her parents is the prayer book they had brought from Ireland. She clings to this possession and is able to remain "a Catholic at heart" through her long years in Protestant foster care.[16] Of course, this church provides doctrine and liturgy, but the emphasis for the Irish Americans is that the Church is a people bound together by ethnicity and history, who then also share doctrine and practice.

Unlike Dorsey, who suggests that the Church in America is superior to the one left behind, the Irish Americans advise their readers to remain faithful to their inheritance. Quigley aims to "impress" upon the immigrant "the honor and advantage of defense and fidelity to the Cross and the Shamrock, and . . . give him two ideas that will come to his aid in most of his actions through life." For McCorry, in *The Lost Rosary*, the "only hope" for Irish immigrant girls is to "be true to the old father, and the old mother . . . the Old Chapel and its humble Cross."[17]

In associating Catholicism with Ireland, the authors tie religion to their readers' memories of youth and innocent happiness, increasing the appeal of the faith but also coupling lay members and children. Sadlier does this throughout her novels. In *Old and New*, a good Catholic character comments on weddings in Ireland, where all was "fun and . . . harmless merriment. . . . [T]he only rivalry . . . was to see who'd . . . get the most countenance from his reverence at the head of the dinner-table, where he sat in state with the bride on one side and the groom on the other." When a priest in McCorry's *Mount Benedict* asks the Irish immigrant Patrick Crolly to assist at mass, the young man recalls how he had done the same in his "boyhood days," when "he was happy, and blessed in the possession of both parents."[18]

The authors urge the American-born generation to adopt the same attitude. In Sadlier's *The Blakes and Flanagans*, the Catholic school teacher says that if parents keep "the traditions of our race constantly before their children," there will be no "demoralization . . . [or] backslidings from the faith." Sadlier's Robert Murray in *Old and New*, who had never seen Ireland, regards it as a land with "many claims on the love and honor of its children—and *their* children." Ireland, he says, is "the cradle of my race, the grave of my fathers, the most faithful of Christian nations."[19]

The Church in America is not only a legacy from an idealized past but also the only home and family most of the immigrants have in their current lives. In the novels of the 1850s, most lead characters, female and male, are orphaned very shortly after their arrival in America; the Church and its priests are their only home and parents. As Paul O'Clery, the eldest orphaned son in Quigley's novel, says to his younger brother: "you have no parents here but one, the Catholic Church; and if you obey not her counsels and precepts, you will not be rewarded by Christ."[20] In later novels, the major characters are often single men and women whose parents, if they are alive, remain in Ireland. These characters, too, have no home in the traditional sense. Certainly, the domestic servants do not find a home within the households of their employers. Nineteenth-century observers noted that Irish domestic servants were "at home once more" in a Catholic Church: "It is the atmosphere of the sweet old land that breathes about them; they have there the shadow of home . . . strangers in a strange land, the church is father and mother, home and country too!"[21] The novelists at once illustrate and forge this association. Sadlier's Winny O'Regan, a domestic servant in Boston, "turned away with a sickening sense of despondency" from the post office when letters from her mother did not arrive. "Gathering her woolen shawl around her, she retraced her steps toward her present dwelling—*home* it was not."[22]

Single male characters are in a similar predicament. They live in lodging houses in the cities or at campsites while they labor on canals and railroads. McElgun, for example, describes the horrible lodging house in which his lead character lived when he first arrived in New York.[23]

Even families in their own residences find their true home in the community of the Church. The only Irish American novels between 1850 and 1875 that feature intact nuclear families in America are Sadlier's *The Blakes and Flanagans* and Quigley's *Profit and Loss*—at least, in this latter novel, before the husband died. In both cases, parents, or especially wives and mothers, are essentially brokers who bring their families to the Church. As Sadlier writes about the Flanagans, religion and the Church are "the sun of their solar system, giving life and warmth to themselves and all around them."[24] In Quigley's novel, the good Catholic wife is willing to move to the farm in Minnesota only after her husband assures her that it is near a settlement called "Irish Corners," which is "exclusively Irish," and includes a large church with a "nice little priest" who is Irish, and "several flourishing schools, taught by men of their own race and religion."[25] This account of the woman's motivations highlights the differences between the view of the Church in Irish American novels and the view in Dorsey's work, where the German immigrants search for their own farm in the west.

In accordance with the idea of legacy, the authors present the Catholic Church in America as the same sort of nurturing community the immigrants experienced in Ireland. Though the characters in these novels cannot exactly reproduce the environment Miles Blake and Tim Flanagan recall in Sadlier's novel—where "there wasn't one [Protestant] within miles of us"—and though they interact with others economically to some minimal extent, they live their emotional, social, and cultural lives solely among Catholics, and Irish Catholics in particular.[26] There is almost no interaction between Irish Catholics and the rest of the American population, including Protestants and even Catholics of other backgrounds. With the exception of Cannon, who, like the authors before him, is interested in Catholic integration into American society, the community idealized by these authors is Irish as well as Catholic.

In Roddan's novel, John O'Brien's father, on his deathbed, tells his son to associate, as much as possible, only with good Catholics, without specifying ethnicity. But by the end of the novel, John has married the daughter of an Irish Catholic immigrant and counts among his friends only boys he had met in the Catholic school in the Irish neighborhood.[27] In McCorry's *The Lost Rosary*, the single women heroines, Mary and Ailey O'Donnell, live in an exclusively Irish Catholic society, residing in a lodging house that two older Irish women had established so that "neither son nor daughter of the ould country will ever have cause to complain." The young women also socialize with an older Irish Catholic couple they meet while strolling through the Catholic graveyard. Any encounters with non-Irish Catholics tend to be unfortunate; one man who makes inappropriate overtures to one of the heroines at her job is identified only as a "Scotchman."[28]

If Sadlier's good characters manage to find a home in America, even temporarily, they find it in Irish Catholic society. When Bessy Conway obtains a position as servant to an Irish woman and is able to associate with one good Irish Catholic fellow servant, she is "as happy as she could be, away from home." In one of Sadlier's more optimistic passages in this novel, Bessy, in a letter home to her parents, reports that when she went to church in New York, "I'd forget sometimes that it wasn't at home in Ardfinnan. I was with Father Ryan there in his robes before me and the people of our own parish kneeling about me."[29]

Sadlier's ideal is exemplified in *Con O'Regan*, in her account of the western settlement, where her characters live in a community of Irish immigrants; the settlers plant shamrocks, and St. Patrick's Day "was as well celebrated as Father Doran's means would permit." Sadlier concludes that the children of the settlers are "brought up in the same pure, moral atmosphere, and under the same healthy influences that had changed the little Yankee rowdy into a genuine Irish boy, full of the traditional virtues of his people."[30]

These authors, essentially, reaffirm the connection between ethnicity and religion that they developed in their descriptions of America's hostility to the Irish immigrants. Characters like the Flanagans, the Von Weigels, Annie Reilly, and the heroines of *The Lost Rosary*, who remain Catholic, also remain proud of their ethnic heritage. Those who surrender one aspect of their identity ultimately surrender the other as well. In Sadlier's *The Blakes and Flanagans*, Henry and Eliza Blake reject their faith and disparage their Irish heritage. As a boy, Henry resents attending a St. Patrick's Day celebration, and as an adult politician, he cynically courts Irish voters by pretending to be interested in Irish nationalism. Simon O'Hare in Sadlier's novel becomes an apostate and, eventually, a Protestant; Patrick Mulroony, the son in Quigley's *Profit and Loss*, stops practicing his faith. Both men marry Protestants outside the Church and also change their names, to Kerr and Ronay, to hide their ancestry.

The authors' treatment of marriage illustrates their attitude and approach to Catholic interaction with other groups. For the first generation of Catholic writers, the heroes and heroines, if they married, chose Catholics, which usually meant American Protestants who had recently converted to Catholicism. In novels by Bryant, Dorsey, and Miles, the Protestant heroines convert, then refuse to marry their Protestant suitors until they, too, eventually convert. If Catholic characters in the novels marry (and do not enter the priesthood or convent), they also usually unite with recently converted Protestants. Mary Lorn, the Catholic governess in Miles's novel, marries the Protestant son of her employer after his conversion; in Cannon's novels, the Catholics in *Harry Layden* and *Father Felix* also wed newly converted Protestants. (Mora Carmody refuses to marry her Protestant suitor because he is not a Catholic. By the time he converts, she has entered the convent.)

Cannon is the only author in the early period of the 1830s and '40s who gives an ethnic background to some of his important characters. He does not, however, make this an important consideration in their marriages.

The Irish-born Hugh Redmond in *Harry Layden* marries an Anglo-Saxon American Protestant convert, and Jack Toland Jr., the immigrant's son in *Scenes and Characters*, marries a woman from an old American family whose father had converted in his youth. Cannon's marriages, like those of his colleagues, symbolize the union of Catholics—in his case, Irish immigrants—to American Protestants. The conversions indicate eventual Catholic triumph, of course, but nevertheless illustrate the importance of interactions between groups, even if only to make conversions possible.

In her first novel in 1850, Sadlier continues this tradition. At the end of the book, a sister of Willy Burke marries a young man who has converted to Catholicism. After 1850, neither Sadlier nor any of the other authors—again, except for Cannon—uses marriage to symbolize such unions between American Catholics and Protestants. McCorry comes closest in *Mount Benedict*. At the novel's end, the Irish immigrant Patrick Crolly marries Cecilia, the wealthy orphaned niece and ward of Alvah Morton Sr. Cecilia was raised as a Protestant but, influenced by the example of Kate, Patrick's sister, who works as Cecilia's companion, she converts before meeting Patrick. McCorry is clearly ambivalent with this outcome, however, hinting that Alvah Morton had once been a Catholic and is also Irish, implying that his niece comes from the same background. At the beginning of the novel, Morton tells Cecilia that he does not want to hire Kate because she is "Irish . . . and worse. . . . Worse! reiterated Cecilia, Being Irish cannot be a great fault, dear uncle, seeing that you yourself— Hush!," Morton replies, closing the topic. Later, Morton accuses his fanatically Protestant wife of having spoiled their plans, "just as sure as my name's Alvah Morton." His wife replies, "Of course, dear. But it so happens that your name ain't Alvah Morton, and, therefore, I ain't spoiled" the plan.[31]

Cannon in his 1855 novel, *Bickerton*, is the major exception to the overall pattern, continuing the earlier tradition of applauding marriages between Irish immigrants and American Protestants. He is also the first of the Catholic authors to approve of a marriage with a Protestant who has not (or not yet) converted.[32] The immigrant's daughter in the novel marries Fred Hubbard, who rescued her from the anti-Catholic mob and is the spokesman, with his father, for Catholics against the nativists. At the time of the marriage, Fred agrees to raise their children Catholic but does not wish to convert, though he does, after the marriage. Father Eldridge, the Bickerton priest, born in the United States of a Protestant father and an Irish Catholic mother, also illustrates the potential for relationships between American Catholics and Protestants. Cannon never indicated whether the priest's father had converted.

The overwhelming majority of the heroes and heroines of Irish American novels after 1850 not only refuse to marry Protestants, even converted ones, they also do not marry Catholics from other immigrant groups. Whenever the authors refer to such groups, they do not present them as desirable partners. The only marriage between ordinary Irish and German Catholic immigrants occurs in Sadlier's *Old and New*, where minor characters, the servants in the Von Weigel household, are a married couple — Betty, from Ireland, and her husband Jan, a German Catholic. Sadlier does not criticize the union but, through his accent and actions, she shows the German, Jan, to be stupid. He is "a thick-set, sour-looking German" who does not understand when a visitor to the Von Weigel house uses the French phrase "mon ami" and responds: "No *mon-amee* live here." Jan also tells a visiting dressmaker, who wants to deliver a package to the Von Weigels: "Der deyvil! no, you shan't. . . . I go up myself mit it. . . . *I tell you dat now.*" The Irish Betty is not the equal of the Von Weigels, of course. As befitting a minor character of the working class in a Sadlier novel, she has an Irish accent and violates rules of grammar. But her understanding and her speech are far superior to those of her husband. In a conversation with the newly rich Mr. Hackett, she asks, "So you tell me you weren't at the wedding Mr. Hackett? . . . You done just what you ought to do . . . it's *too good* for them you'd be . . . the conceit of them people and the airs they put on them is past the common!"[33] Clearly, the servant couple is not a model or a symbol of a desired unity for Sadlier's immigrant readers.

It is not until the 1870s that the authors begin to refer more frequently to other immigrant groups, and they do not convey appreciation. Quigley, in *Profit and Loss*, which takes place in the Midwest, mentions Norwegian girls — without specifying their religion — who had been corrupted by the novel's villain. McElgun describes passengers on board the ship to New York, including "Germans, black and greasy, [who] lay in heaps together. . . . [T]heir hands and faces were so dirty, and their old rags smelled so disgustingly, that we pity any company in a close room who would have a German amongst them." There are also "a few garrulous and excitable Frenchmen . . . talking loudly; Italian organ-grinders and beggars . . . and two or three swarthy Spaniards."[34]

That Irish American authors do not applaud marriages of their immigrant characters with Protestants or with members of other Catholic immigrant groups does not mean they reject all intermarriages. Sadlier, for instance, welcomes unions between Irish Catholics and southern American Catholics. She considers this group the closest America has to an aristocracy, and by implication she supports their conservative political positions. (Sadlier was married to James Sadlier of the publishing family; they were the only northern publishers accused of harboring pro-Southern sentiments even during the Civil War.)[35] In *Willy Burke*, Sadlier's 1850 novel, a second Burke daughter marries a "wealthy planter from the South," who is connected with the Catholic partner in the firm where Willy works.[36] Sadlier provides the same happy ending for Robert Murray, the American son of an Irish immigrant, in her 1861 *Old and New*. The Murrays are upper middle class, not aristocrats, and, in Sadlier's view, show that people can be examples of taste, "each in their own degree." Robert represents the best that most Irish immigrants in America can aspire to. He is in love with Bertha, the daughter of Madame Von Weigel, but she refuses him. He eventually marries the daughter of a wealthy Southern planter who also has some political connections — to Europe, not America, but still in the right direction. The young woman is of French ancestry, from an "old Vendean family — connected by blood with the great Larochejacquelin, the hero of the Vendee!" — and the symbol of Catholic and Royalist counterrevolution. The American aristocrats are superior to their countrymen but not equal to the Irish or Europeans. Robert acknowledges that his wife was "not *Bertha* — nobody ever was or can be like Bertha."[37]

The authors' general reluctance to countenance interfaith marriages applies to characters who come to America, not to those who remain in Ireland. Centering their hopes for union between religious groups in their old not their new country, several authors are prepared to allow Catholics in Ireland to marry Protestants, including some who have not converted. McCorry is explicit about the differences between Ireland and America, expressing his great fear of American society. He advises "Irish girls" in

The Lost Rosary to "Choose poverty, rather than run the risk of marriage with one that professes not your faith. . . . Under any circumstances, a mixed marriage is an unmixed evil," but such a marriage "in America . . . is worse, a thousand-fold" than it would be in Ireland because the women here are "removed from the holy influences of home, and the care of those who are dear to" them. One year later, writing in *Mount Benedict*, McCorry suggests again that a mixed marriage is not completely evil, as long as it occurs in a Catholic society like Ireland. He speaks of the

> joy experienced by an Irish wife, in the full and unexpected conversion of her husband. Mixed marriages are doubtless often a great scandal, and entail great misery as the penalty due to such unions. . . . Neverthe-less, there are many instances where the virtue and religious practices of a good Irish wife have resulted in the conversion of the husband. . . . [G]reat good often springs from that which at first sight often-times appears to be incurably bad.[38]

Sadlier and Boyce also use interfaith marriages to illustrate their hopes for reconciliation between Protestants and Catholics in Ireland. In Sadlier's case, the unions represent the potential for Catholics to unite with the Anglo-Irish aristocracy. In *Bessy Conway*, the heroine remains in America for seven years, where she consistently resists the overtures of a wealthy Irish Protestant aristocrat and landlord, who follows her to New York. She refuses him because he is not a Catholic and because she also sus-pects his motives, given the class differences between them. At the end of the novel, however, Bessy returns to Ireland, rescues her family, sees that the aristocrat has converted, and agrees to marry him in Ireland, where the couple remains.

It is in *Old and New*, however, that Sadlier most clearly expresses her acceptance of interfaith marriages involving aristocrats in Ireland. Madame Von Weigel is an Irish Protestant raised in a castle. As her Irish servant Betty says, Madame is "Irish to the back-bone, for all she comes of some high-up Prodestan family . . . and herself was one, too, till long after she married the old Ritter." The Old Ritter (a title of nobility in German-speaking areas) is Mr. Von Weigel, "a noble fine Catholic." The two meet and live the first years of their marriage in Ireland. Sadlier's point, of course, is that the Europeans—German and Irish—represent a single aristocratic class with aristocratic values and manners. The Von Weigel mother and daughter, for example, often converse in French and read books in German. But the Irish are still shown as superior: Sadlier describes Mr. Von Weigel as "marked by the strong peculiarities of his race . . . with a certain solidity of look that approached to heaviness, indicating his Teutonic origin. Still it was a handsome face expressive of good, rather than great qualities." Bertha Von Weigel, the daughter of the family, has a "deep, calm earnestness . . . from her German ancestors" but from the Irish, she inherited "a beautiful face" with "the light of genius playing over all."[39] Despite the disparities, Sadlier allows her aristocratic characters to marry Protestants, a liberty she never grants to immigrant Catholics in America. Madame Von Weigel does not become a Catholic until "long after" her marriage, and the union of aristocrats continues with the Von Weigel's daughter, Bertha, who marries the Irish Protestant aristocrat Edgar Montague (though not before he converts to Catholicism). The couple remains in Ireland after their marriage.[40]

Boyce also includes a marriage between an important Irish character and a Protestant who has not converted. His union also represents a hope for Ireland rather than America, but his focus is not aristocracy but nationalism. At the end of *Mary Lee* the priest marries the title character and the Irish Protestant revolutionary Randall Barry just before they flee to America. Barry remains a Protestant, and Boyce merely suggests this may change when he describes the young man's love for church ceremonies and the powerful example that Mary Lee will exert.[41]

In their conflicting feelings between the hope for union—whether for the sake of conversions, aristocracy, or nationalism—and the fear that Catholics would be lost to the Church, the Irish Americans were willing to choose the risk for Ireland but not for America. Overwhelmingly, good characters in the novels living in America marry fellow Irish Catholics. John O'Brien, the Flanagans and O'Regans, Annie Reilly, the good daughter of the new rich in *Old and New*, and the heroines of McCorry's *The Lost Rosary* all wed Irish immigrants or their children. Since Boyce's interfaith couple did not come to America until the last pages of the novel, Cannon was the only author who used marriages in America to symbolize integration of Catholics and Protestants there.

The Church as Nurturing Comfort and Authority

The Irish American authors present the Irish Catholics as a unified community, but, like their predecessors, their work reflects the ongoing debate at the time about church authority, sparked by the essays of Orestes Brownson. As their attacks on Protestants indicate, the Irish Americans rejected their opponents' views of liberty and authority but did not put forward a consistent alternative. The differences among the authors on church authority follow the pattern set in their treatment of family and social life. For Roddan, Quigley, and Sadlier, the Church is primarily an authoritative source of rules, while Boyce and Cannon emphasize its nurturing comfort.[42]

Roddan, who worked with Brownson on the *Edinburgh Review*, is best able to articulate the authoritarian vision of the Church. Like Pise in *Zenosius*, he presents the Church as an infallible institution with doctrines and rules that people must obey if they are to be saved. Writing in 1850, Roddan does not ascribe infallibility to the pope but to the "teaching Church, which is made up of bishops in communion with Rome." He agrees with Brownson that those who die "out of the one true Church . . . will be damned eternally," allowing one qualification: "no one can say that *you* will be lost forever, because no one can foresee whether you will persist in your rebellion to the last." Roddan objects to "l-i-b-e-r-a-l" or "silly sentimental Catholics" who quarrel with this idea, and he traces their mistaken views to a habit of mixing in Protestant societies, where they compromise their views to avoid hurting Protestant feelings.[43]

Roddan is also clear that religious truth must be the standard of judgment in all fields, including popular literature. Mixed library societies, he writes, "pursue *literary* objects. Now, the Protestant has no suspicion that philosophy and the other sciences, political and natural, are truly dependent upon theology. . . . There is *no* science that cannot be . . . used by the agents of the devil for the ruin of souls." He also advises Catholics to "be very careful about your reading. While you read only such books and *papers* as the Church allows, you are safe."[44]

Quigley and Sadlier also stress church authority, though they do not use the term "infallible" or devote much attention to articulating the grounds of the Church's claim. They simply assert her authority as the true church necessary to salvation. In *The Cross and the Shamrock*, Quigley's hero, Paul O'Clery, says that he is "bound to obey" the Church "particularly when I have the promise of Christ that she can never err." Sadlier's Mrs. Burke adopts the same stance in response to a criticism about reading the Bible: "I believe what the Church proposes to me, an' I'm sure there's no other safe guide on earth."[45]

Quigley and Sadlier also agree with Roddan when it comes to the relationship between religion and other subjects. Sadlier's Father Power tells Miles Blake, who is sending his children to public schools, that "religion . . . must be ever present with your children; it must regulate and control their studies . . . words . . . [and] actions, that is, if you wish them to grow up Christians; if you are content to make them heathens or infidels, then you are quite right to do as you are doing."[46]

The two authors do not entirely ignore the Church's role as nurturer. But their comments in this direction conflict with the overall message of their novels and have a decidedly tacked-on feeling. Quigley's priest in *The Cross and the Shamrock* comments: "O, how cold, selfish, and intolerable would life be, if the Catholic church was not present, on all occasions, with the graces, blessings, and consolations of Christ!"[47] Yet even in this, his milder novel, these comments about the Church were made only at the point of death. Sadlier, too, makes occasional reference to an alternative view of the Church, but when she does, they conflict with her main message even more starkly. In *The Blakes and Flanagans* and *Confessions of an Apostate*, Sadlier traces the miserable fates of the lead characters who abandon their heritage. Yet she also says that Henry Blake has the wrong attitude about his faith: "to him religion wore the lowering aspect of a stern monitor, a severe mistress—he knew her not as the gentle soother of human woe—the one sweet drop in life's bitter cup. . . . [H]e never knew the sweetness of religion." Yet in the same section of the novel, Sadlier concludes that Catholic parents who send children to public schools "are more inhuman than the heathens of China and of Madagascar who destroy their helpless infants . . . [and should] consider that they are . . . bound, under pain of deadly sin, to transmit it [the faith] to their children pure and undefiled." Similarly, the lead character in *Confessions*, Simon O'Hare, reflects that his children, raised as Protestants, miss the "all-consoling trust in the kindly intercession of the Saints." Yet Simon suffers even more than

Henry Blake does, losing his wife and all of his children except for the one who becomes a violent nativist.[48]

Of all the authors, Boyce most clearly articulates the alternative view of the Church as primarily a source of comfort and inspiration. Through his spokesman Father Brennan, the Irish priest, Boyce, objects to the authoritarian vision articulated by Dr. Henshaw, a character based on Brownson. Henshaw, in the view of Boyce (and his priest character), sees church "doctrine under its severest aspect. Her dogmas and anathemas were the only signs of her divine power he could discover. . . . The consequence was, that he regarded her only in her coercive capacity. . . . [He] became a very despot in religion." Father Brennan also says that Henshaw misrepresents "the true tone and spirit of Catholicity" and presents "the church in a repulsive attitude."[49]

Boyce and his priest maintain that the way to appeal to Catholics and Protestants alike is to "exhibit the church under her most alluring and attractive form." "In an age such as this," Father Brennan says, it is necessary to "convert hearts." When the priest is asked how he persuaded the Anglican heroine Kate Petersham to convert to Catholicism, he replies, "not by dosing her with dogmas, anathemas, and philosophy"; he "merely pointed out to her the beauties of our holy religion, and sent her down to" a good Catholic character "to see them illustrated." Boyce's Catholic characters never explain their conduct as a matter of obedience to church rules.[50]

In accord with his view of the Church, Boyce also adopts a gentler approach to Protestants and salvation. Dr. Henshaw articulates the authoritarian view, calling Protestantism "a chronic disease." He tells Protestants: "You have no faith at all, and you let your morals take care o' themselves." "If you die out o' the Kaatholic church, you'll be lost." Henshaw is "finally" willing "to consign . . . [Protestants] to perdition, as enemies of the Catholic church." The priest clearly rejects Henshaw's position but does not exactly propose the opposite view that all can be saved. Instead, he urges mercy and understanding rather than severity. Of Henshaw, the priest says he is "without the least pity for those who had grown up in the midst of hereditary prejudices against Catholicity, or compassion for those who would willingly have embraced it, if they could only be made to see their error, he consigned all beyond the pale of the church—all, without exception—to unutterable destruction. . . . [H]is heart was that of a pagan philosopher—as cold and unfeeling as a stone."[51]

Boyce also challenges the all-pervasive relevance of Catholic doctrine. Henshaw judges everything, including literature, by the standards of Catholic truth, objecting to the writings of the Protestant Jonathan Swift because of the "moral sentiments" he expresses. He also disdains Catholics like Thomas Moore as "an immoral man and a bad Kaatholic." Through Father Brennan, Boyce—whose novels, incidentally, had been criticized by Brownson—objects to Henshaw's "inveterate habit of intruding . . . [his] faith into everything." The priest concludes that Henshaw "never should attempt to criticize" works of literature; they are "entirely out of the sphere of his taste and acquirements."[52]

Henshaw, in turn, accuses the priest of "making an apology for the severity of Catholic deescipline, and the conservatism of Catholic doctrine," turning Catholicism into "namby-pambyism," and changing the "old Katholeecity" to "syllabub and water gruel."[53] In his review of Boyce's novel, Orestes Brownson makes the same point. He was well aware that with his Dr. Henshaw character, Boyce wanted to "rebuke" Brownson for "insisting on the doctrine that, out of the church there is no salvation." Brownson, in turn, accuses Boyce of adopting "the false liberalism some Catholics affect." Brownson also defends his practice of bringing "in his Catholic faith and morals" in reviews of "purely literary works." "A Catholic reviewer," he asserts, "has the right, if he sees fit, to review any book under the point of view of Catholic faith and morals, and no other . . . for no man, certainly no Catholic, has the right to hold or teach, to publish or practice any thing not in accordance with the dogmas and morals of the church." All Catholics must be "firm and uncompromising" and not "hesitate to impress . . . on anyone we converse with on the subject, that salvation is attainable in our church, and not elsewhere."[54]

Boyce's view of the Church seems to correspond to his vision of an ideal organic society in which people know and accept their place, leaders preside over willing subjects, and relationships are governed by mutual respect and affection. In Catholic Europe, he comments, "each grade in the community had its own legitimate trades and occupations," but in America, life was "a universal scramble, in which every body snatched at what came handiest."[55] In an organic community, Henshaw's (and Brownson's) ideas of command and obligation to obey—and of constitutions and rights—are out of place. Boyce develops his conception with reference to the Church in Ireland and acknowledges that American society is, and will continue to be, governed by quite different precepts. If a church exemplifying his principles develops in America, it will stand apart from the rest of the society.

Cannon, always more interested than Boyce in praising American values, also offers a more nurturing vision of the Church, although he is less interested than Boyce in church affairs and more concerned with social and political life. He expresses his vision of the Church partly by what he does not say. He never refers to the Church as infallible or suggests that obedience is necessary for salvation. He does not express worry about the ultimate fate of old Mr. Hubbard or the priest's father, who remain Protestants. When he shows good Catholics leading lives faithful to Catholic practice or to Catholic teachings, he does not add that they are obliged to do so or that, in doing so, they are obeying the commands of the one true church on pain of eternal damnation. Moreover, Cannon does not offer Catholicism as the standard measure for all subjects. He objects to public schools only because they are anti-Catholic, not because they attempt to study some subjects without reference to religion.

Cannon expresses his views more positively in his description of the convent, which he, like many authors, uses to symbolize the Church. He is concerned to show that the convent is a place of peace, harmony, and genuine family feeling, an institution quite in accord with American values. After the immigrant's orphaned daughter in his *Bickerton* is rescued from her Protestant foster family, she lives in a convent, writing in her diary that she is "a changed creature, for am I not FREE?" The young woman calls the convent "a safe and pleasant home," with "all . . . modern improvements." She finds the nuns to be a "pleasant . . . set of ladies . . . and some of them quite young and really pretty and . . . utterly without cant."[56] McCorry, too, portrays Mount Benedict as a place of beauty and peace that convinces the Catholic Kate Crolly to become a nun and the Protestant Cecilia Morton to convert.

Contrast these with Sadlier's portrayal of the Irish convent at Cabra in *Elinor Preston*. Cabra is a "vision of perfect beauty" but also "of exquisite neatness" with "well-kept grounds . . . all in perfect keeping." Sadlier also

Figure 6.1. The heroines of McCorry's novel *Mount Benedict* gaze longingly back at the convent after their first visit. Courtesy of Wright American Fiction Project, Indiana University Libraries.

uses the Jesuit seminary to symbolize the Church. The seminary at Clongowes is the Church militant and defensive. The Jesuits were known to "resist from age to age the unceasing attacks of the enemy of souls." The seminary is an "imposing edifice," a "stronghold of faith, held for Christ."[57]

Orestes Brownson criticized Cannon and Boyce for their nurturing vision of the Church. Although he acknowledged that Cannon had "labored long and industriously to promote in our Catholic population a taste for polite literature, and to contribute what he could to create for us such a literature," Brownson concludes that "in all the works we have read of the author, we miss the stern moralist. . . . [I]n his moral lessons he is very often not only defective but wrong. He writes as a man who has earnest Catholic faith combined with the moral notions of philanthropists, sentimentalists, and Transcendentalists." For Brownson, Catholic writers were "required not to contradict" the faith and "to avoid favoring the Protestant cant against it," rules that Cannon violates when, for example, he cast "slurs on the Inquisition" in one of his plays."[58]

This range of opinions about church authority suggests another qualification to Reynolds's argument that nineteenth-century popular literature inevitably promoted a less authoritarian view of religious institutions. For Catholics, if not for Protestants, popular literature from 1829 through 1873 was compatible with a rigid as well as an accommodating approach to church authority. The authoritarian voices of Pise, Miles, and Sadlier were not necessarily typical, but neither were the milder, liberalizing views of Boyce and Cannon.

Agreement—and Disagreement—with Church Teachings

Apart from questions of authority, the Irish American authors touched on other controversies within the Church. On some of the issues, they clearly sided with their bishops. In *Bessy Conway*, in a conversation between Irish and American priests, Sadlier reproduces the controversy between Bishop Hughes and Orestes Brownson about the relative merits of foreign, that is, Irish, as opposed to American, clergy. She criticizes the American priest for his worldliness, and the Irish Father Daly character extolls the priests from Ireland. She ends the scene on a note of reconciliation, however, as the priests resume their friendly relationship. Sadlier also clarifies that their differences, in any case, were about "certain matters, not of faith."[59]

Cannon and Sadlier also tackle the conflict between the clergy and lay trustees. In novels published in New York in 1855, both authors support the clergy against laymen, presenting the trustees as selfish and incompetent. Sadlier, but not Cannon, also emphasizes the obligation of Catholics to obey the priests.[60]

On issues of education and marriage, Sadlier also sides with the official church but can be even more uncompromising than the bishops in her arguments and positions. In *The Blakes and Flanagans*, Sadlier's priest characters speak for the Church, and Sadlier, as author, without indicating any divergence, takes a harder, firmer line toward the public schools and Catholic parents. The fictional Father Power is more forceful in opposing the public schools than Dr. Bayley is in the passages Sadlier cites from his book. Bayley points to the lack of religious and moral instruction, while Father Power also objects to "the companionship of Protestant children," concluding that those who attend public schools "are with very few exceptions, growing up, without fear of God or man, despising their parents in their hearts." Sadlier herself allows for no exceptions. In her own commentary and in that of the good Catholic Tim Flanagan, she consistently employs extreme arguments. Although she writes that she had "carefully avoided all exaggeration or undue coloring in this simple tale . . . [but] merely strung together a number of . . . incidents . . . growing out of the effects of good or bad education," Henry and Eliza Blake after attending the public schools abandon their faith, lead immoral lives, reject their Irish heritage, and consistently abuse and neglect their parents, who endure a "cheerless old age."[61]

In her own voice, Sadlier also adopts a fiercer stance toward Catholic parents than did Dr. Bayley or her Father Power character. In the final paragraph of the novel, Sadlier quotes Bayley who writes that "we must, above all things," give "the rising generation . . . a good Catholic education. In our present position, the school-house has become second in importance only to the House of God itself." Father Power is also clear about the obligation of parents. He says, "I must insist" when he tells Miles Blake to remove his children from the common schools and send them to St. Peters. As Tim Flanagan points out, however, Father Power "never laid his commands on" Miles Blake, "for he doesn't like to go so far if he can help it."[62] This presumably means that the priest did not order Blake under pain of deadly sin, denial of the sacraments, or excommunication. And, in fact, the Church did not take such a hard-line stance at the time.

But Sadlier is uncharacteristically vague when Miles Blake brings up the alternative to Catholic schools — that he and his wife teach their children religion at home and send them to catechism classes as well as to mass every Sunday. Tim Flanagan does not condemn the idea outright but only answers that Blake's action is "all right, as far as it goes, but do all Catholic parents do the same? . . . [O]r do they all get as good teachings at home, and see as good examples before them?" (Quigley, who also takes a firmer stand toward Catholic parents than his priest characters, is equally vague in *Profit and Loss*. When the father of the family suggests to his wife that they teach their son at home and send him to the priest's catechism classes, his wife replies that the priest could not even fill up his classes.)[63]

Sadlier, in her vagueness, seems to suggest that such supplementary systems, if implemented, might make public education acceptable. But this is not her message. She predicts dire ends, in the next life as well as in this one, for parents who choose the public schools, accusing them of "unaccountable folly" and, as previously noted, of being "more inhuman than the heathens of China and of Madagascar," and of courting "deadly sin." Tim Flanagan also believes that the priest should have issued a command to Miles Blake. When Miles objects that "the Bishop goes too far—he objects to every system of education that leaves out religion—I suppose he'll be for getting up Catholic schools all over and commanding the people to send their children to no other!" Flanagan responds, "isn't it just what he ought to do?"[64]

Sadlier and her good lay characters also take a firmer stance against interfaith marriages than do the priests in her novels, who voice the official church position. Her Father Power clearly disapproves of the Blake marriages: "grave, and even sad, was the face of the good priest" as he "duly performed" the marriage of Henry—in his residence rather than in the church. Father Power leaves Eliza's ceremony to the assistant pastor. Yet the priest agrees to the marriages after the Protestant parties vow not to interfere with their spouses' religion and to raise their children as Catholic. As for Sadlier herself, she writes that "such marriages are contracted in direct opposition to the teachings of his [God's] Church."[65]

In *Old and New*, Sadlier voices her disappointment with an insufficiently firm clergy on still another issue. Strongly critical of the Irish Americans who disparage or reject their ethnic heritage, she "would earnestly beg of all intelligent Irish parents, teachers, and, above all, priests, to set their faces against these ridiculous airs, and repress, by every means in their power, the growth of a sentiment so unjust to an old and noble nation."[66]

The Irish American authors were not always on the same side as the official church. On some issues, they acknowledge the conflict with bishops, ostensibly support the clerical views, but continue to suggest their opposition. On the question of how Irish Catholics should respond to provocation, McCorry, in *Mount Benedict*, shows the bishop and priest characters urging followers to refrain from violence before, during, and after the attack on the Charlestown convent. The Irish immigrant Patrick Crolly argues against them, saying that it is "a disgrace to stand idly by and see the danger increasing, without going forth and making an attempt in some way to confront that crowd." According to the author, if the priest "had judged himself by the heart" as the young man "had just done, he would necessarily have arrived at the same conclusion." In the end, Crolly complies: "it is not for me, Father, to dispute with you on such matters, knowing that you are the better judge of such things . . . and believing, as I do, that you are fully competent to understand the whole situation."

In his own comments, however, McCorry expresses his continuing resistance, pointing out that the bishop and priest are mistaken in their assessments. "Bishop Fenwick could not bring himself to believe that anything worse than a turbulent ebullition of mis-directed feeling was then possible." Similarly, "the good priest" hears an initial, erroneous report that the crowd has dispersed, and feels reassured that "his judgment had been properly formed." McCorry quickly excuses the bishop—"judging matters by the same standard as the Bishop, most men would have been of the same opinion"—but he nevertheless has made his point. McCorry also says,

> Viewed calmly at the present day, one cannot help admiring the super-excellent wisdom of the good Bishop Fenwick, while on the other hand we can scarcely help wishing that the bonds of restraint had been burst asunder for the purpose of teaching the bigots of Charlestown that America, originally the home of the Red man, is as free to the Irish race as to any colony of Dutch, or English Cromwellians.[67]

More typically, these authors express their views without openly disagreeing with the clergy. As seen in chapter 4, Cannon gives the bishops' official view of religious liberty and church-state relations and then, without acknowledging any differences, proceeds to express his own more unqualified support for American values through his Protestant characters. Similarly, Sadlier's determination to be more fiercely authoritarian than the Church (and more deeply suspicious of America than her own bishops) sometimes brought her to unorthodox positions. She never acknowledges her departures from official church positions, but in her later novels, where she sends all of her major characters back to Ireland or to a western settlement, she takes a stand against emigration that is not supported by the bishops. In her preface to *Bessy Conway*, she writes: "some may say that I have drawn too gloomy a picture. Such persons know little about it. . . . [T]he fathers and mothers who suffer their young daughters to come out unprotected to America in search of *imaginary* goods, would rather see them laid in their graves than lose sight of them, did they know the dangers which beset their path in the New World." Bessy herself tells Irish women whose daughters were thinking of emigrating to "keep your girls at home."[68] Sadlier deals with the conflict by keeping her priest characters in Ireland and America silent on the question of emigration.

She adopts another strategy to express unorthodox views while avoiding direct confrontation with her bishops on the issue of colonization. In *Con O'Regan*, she advances her support for the movement, calling it "one of the best-conceived plans ever brought before the American-Irish for the permanent advantage of their newly-arrived compatriots." In the novel, she ignores the debate among the American bishops, and the opposition of Bishop Hughes of New York. Rather than keep her priests silent, as she did on the subject of emigration, she simply includes only priests who support, or do not oppose, the colonization scheme. She praises "the high-souled generosity, the noble disinterestedness and the entire devotedness" of the movement's initial supporters, stressing that "some of them [were] ecclesiastics, venerable in years and in high repute for wisdom and virtue." In the novel, the priest in Boston tells Con O'Regan that he "might make . . . [himself] quite easy with regard to the clergy and the churches, for that if there's not a priest or a church in every settlement, there soon would, he was sure." Father Doran, the Irish priest in the settlement, tells Con that it was "just such men as you we want to found new colonies in these magnificent regions: men who will hand down to their children the Christian virtues and the Christian faith pure and unsullied as they came to them from their pious ancestors."[69]

Sadlier published this work not under Bishop Hughes in New York but in Boston, as a serial in the newspaper *The American Celt*, at the time of the 1856 conference supporting the colonization plan. T. D. McGee, the editor of the paper, supported colonization. The novel was not issued again until it appeared serially in the Sadlier firm's newspaper, the *New York Tablet*, in 1863—the last year of Bishop Hughes's life. It was not published in book form until 1864, after the bishop's death. By these years, Sadlier acknowledged, the colonization movement had failed "for want of public encouragement." She published the book in hope that "a day may come when" colonization "will be eagerly adopted," but even if that day "should . . . not come," the book would record a noble effort.[70]

Irish nationalism was a particularly vexing issue for many of these authors. Some avoided any conflict with church positions by advocating only the type of constitutional nationalism supported by the church hierarchy. In *Elinor Preston*, Sadlier endorses Daniel O'Connell's repeal association, which is saved from "revolutionary excess" because "of the hold which religion has on all the feelings and faculties of the people." Religious beliefs, in fact, were "the elements of which Irish nationality is composed."[71] In her later *Old and New*, Sadlier continues to oppose the revolutionary nationalists, associating them with other European movements. She describes a Mr. McFustian, an "illustrious patriot" out from Ireland who, in the opinion of one observer, "hasn't done much . . . but he has made a great noise, and that's all the same now-a-days." He is allied with the English Chartists, Kossuth in Hungary, and also with Smith O'Brien, who was a leader of Young Ireland in 1848. Sadlier calls all of these revolutionary ideas "hobbies" and the men who espouse them "hobby-riders."[72] But Sadlier now includes the repealers in her general contempt for politicians, writing that Henry Blake, now a Tammany leader, has also become a repealer who would "rail against British tyranny, etc." because it helped to "secure . . . votes" from *"our Irish citizens."* Sadlier comments: "of those who headed the Repeal movement in America, it is morally certain that some were actuated by just such motives."[73]

McElgun also avoids conflict with positions taken by the church hierarchy. The priest character in his 1873 *Annie Reilly* is so saddened at the eviction of Irish tenants that he "resolved to join the National Association," the group formed in the 1860s under the auspices of the Archbishop of Dublin as a moderate Catholic alternative to the revolutionary nationalists.[74]

Some of the authors had a more difficult time as they navigated the tensions between their support for revolutionary nationalism and the opposition of most Catholic bishops in Ireland and America.[75] At issue were questions about the use of violent methods and the union of Catholics and Protestants on grounds of nation despite differences in religion. Cannon, the Irish American, was the only author to express unqualified support for revolutionary nationalism, and he expressed the support through a priest character. But he developed this position in an early work—the story "The Beal Fire"—published by a secular, not a Catholic, house. In eighteenth-century Ireland, Cannon writes, Father Egan, "the last of a once powerful" Catholic family, supported a nationalist rising, using violent methods. When a nationalist woman vows to him that "Peace never can come to my dwelling, father . . . until the freedom of my country is restored," he responds: "And that, with Heaven's blessing, soon may be." Having heard "that the long-threatened blow will soon be struck that restores us to our rights," the priest is urging that all Irishmen regardless of religion begin "co-operating with those who are ready to hazard all for their country's salvation." He stipulates only that the action be taken in the name of "justice" not "vengeance." In this story, Cannon expresses his typical admiration for American values. Many years earlier, Father Egan had been a missionary priest in the American Colonies and witnessed how "the great work of American independence was accomplished." It was at that time that he began to hope, and work, for the "regeneration of his country."[76]

Writing for Catholic houses in succeeding decades, neither Cannon nor the other Irish Americans would ever be so forthright again, either about resorting to arms or the union of Protestants and Catholics. But three of the writers born in Ireland had nationalist backgrounds. McCorry edited *The Irish People*, a weekly journal that served as the official organ of the Fenian Brotherhood in New York City in the late 1860s and early '70s. Quigley had to be ordained in Rome rather than Ireland because, while a student at Maynooth, he refused to take the required oath of allegiance to the British government. He also joined the Young Ireland movement and came to New York after the 1848 Irish rising. Boyce, too, was involved in the Young Ireland movement and, while still in Ireland, published in its newspaper, the *Nation*. These authors, as well as Cannon, managed to convey their sympathy for the movement, but, to conform to official church positions, they did not mention organizations or leaders.

McCorry, Quigley, and Cannon kept their Irish and American priest characters silent and advanced their views through lay characters or their own interjections. McCorry was the most circumspect. In his own voice, he blames English misgovernment for the effects of the famine. He says, however, that further discussion of the causes and responses "would be out of place in a work of this kind."[77] McCorry does not find it out of place to discuss other issues, such as the women's rights movement, where he clearly agreed with the positions taken by his bishops. But it may be that McCorry's defense of a forceful response to the convent burning of forty years earlier, perpetrated by those he refers to as "English Cromwellians," actually expresses his opinion about responses to more recent injustices.

The other authors praise the revolutionaries of the previous era without referring to more recent uprisings. Cannon, in 1842, says that the father of the Irish immigrant Hugh Redmond took part "with his countrymen in their unsuccessful struggle for freedom in Ninety-eight." Cannon continues to refer to this rising, rather than to the more recent events of 1848, in his story "The Devil's Chimney," published in 1855. In it, the father of the American-born hero has "bravely, but unsuccessfully, struggled for the restoration of her [Ireland's] rights, in the disastrous year of NINETY-EIGHT."[78] In Quigley's *Profit and Loss*, published in 1873, after the risings of the 1860s, the lead family had "forefathers" who partook in the national struggles against the English invaders "under O'Neil, O'Rorke, or O'Moore" and "against Cromwell; 'Dutch Billy,' and every other invader . . . down to the rebellion of 98."[79]

Another strategy used by these authors was to support the revolutionary nationalist movement in general but lament that it could not be successful at the present time, leaving open hope for a future. In Cannon's *Bickerton*, the Irish immigrant on board the ship to America addresses Ireland: "could I, by pouring out my blood upon the altar of thy freedom, give thee thy true rank among the nations, right gladly would I. . . . [B]ut what, alas! can one arm, however strong, one heart, however devoted, do for a country so long down-trodden."[80]

Boyce is the most courageous on the issue as he expresses approval for a contemporary Irish revolutionary nationalism that united Catholics and Protestants, in a novel published by a Catholic house, and implies that his priest character also approves. The heroic revolutionary, the Protestant Randall Barry, was prepared to use physical force. "The young outlaw was no lover of war or bloodshed for the gratification they afforded him, but reluctantly adopted as a last and desperate resource for retrieving the fallen fortunes of his country." Barry also would use violence only "in broad daylight . . . not assassin-like, in the dark . . . [and] in a fair field and open fight." He gains the support of the Anglican gentry, in the character of Captain Petersham, the local magistrate, and of the American Ephraim

Weeks but not of the Irish Presbyterian Hardwrinkle or the American Puritan convert Dr. Henshaw. On the issue of Ireland's fight for independence, Boyce again expresses some affection for American values. Weeks, the "grandson of an old revolutionist of seventy-six," says, "It's full time . . . the people got rid of . . . these darned old tyrannical governments."[81]

Boyce does not describe Barry as a member of any organization, nor does he follow his activities after his flight to America. He also distinguishes him from other revolutionaries. Barry was "without a trace of the socialist or the red republican." Yet Barry's intentions are clear. He hoped "that God, in his own good time, would inspire the young men of the land to rise once more—not as wranglers and brawlers—not as mercenary anarchists and sordid demagogues, but like Spartan brothers, to do, and dare, and die for their country's weal . . . true to right, to justice, and to honor!"[82]

Boyce's priest character is not as forthright on this subject as on the nature of the Church, but he communicates his support for the revolutionary just the same. He agrees when others praise the young man's character, and expresses hope that he will escape after the Presbyterian turned him in to the authorities.[83] Boyce may have been referring to his own position on Irish nationalism as much as to his views about the Church when he indicates that his priest character had gotten into trouble with the bishop. Dr. Henshaw comments that what the priest said "is not all gospel I suspect," and other characters respond, "nor his preaching either, if what his bishop says be true . . . a very serious charge, indeed . . . and no doubt reason enough for it too."[84]

These controversies about the nature and extent of authority and about such specific issues as education, assimilation, and nationalism continued to pose challenges to the Church in succeeding decades. Many of the arguments repeated in the novels arose later in the century during the "Americanist" controversy and have continued into our own day. Perhaps a greater challenge in the long run came from the equation of religion and ethnicity that the novels fostered. As the authors saw it, each aspect of the Irish Catholic's group identity strengthened the other. The Irish shared a race, as the novels defined it, as well as a home and history that distinguished them from all others. As Catholicism was tied to this ethnicity, it was rooted in the same factors. While the novels and the Catholic publishing houses were mainly focused on strengthening their readers' religious attachment, in the process, they also strengthened their ethnic identity. As Timothy Meagher has argued, "an ethnic group . . . is a historical phenomenon" and ethnic identification waxes and wanes.[85] An important reason why Irish ethnic identity took hold and endured in the United States among the immigrants and their descendants was its connection to Catholicism and its network of established institutions.

The equation of religion and ethnicity, however, also eventually threatened the Church. As the immigrants and their descendants identified as Irish Catholic, and not simply as Catholic, they had some difficulty accepting other immigrant groups, such as the Italians, who arrived later. The authors also did not confront the implications of any waning of ethnic identification over time. Those who raised the subject, like Sadlier and McElgun, simply lamented the development and exhorted the American-born generation to continue to identify with Ireland. But tying religion to ethnicity meant that, in the twentieth century, as ethnic consciousness weakened among the descendants of the immigrants, religious commitments could weaken as well.

Chapter 7

THE MATERNAL PRIEST

During his journey to Ireland in the summer of 1835, Alexis de Tocqueville observed "an unbelievable union between the Irish clergy and the Catholic population" of the country. The clergy, he wrote, "have the same instincts, the same interests, the same passions as the people." One of the priests Tocqueville interviewed noted: "the people love me . . . and they have reason . . . for I myself love them. . . . Every man considers me in some way as one of his brothers, the eldest in the family."[1] The Irish American novelists transferred this relationship between priests and their people to America, though their priest characters were "fathers," more than elder brothers. They were also fathers who exhibited the traditional qualities of mothers, acting primarily as caretakers and rescuers for the poor and vulnerable. Only in the few novels that portrayed middle-class Irish immigrants were the priests mainly teachers or advisors, the role they performed for the earlier generation of Catholic writers during the 1830s and '40s.

Whatever their conception of the primary role of priests, or of the Church for that matter, Irish American authors described priests as loving figures, endorsing the idea that clerical leadership was legitimate because it was directed to the people's material and spiritual welfare, exercised in a loving and forgiving manner, and followed willingly or not at all. In the end, even Sadlier and Quigley, the Irish Americans who shared the most authoritarian view of the Church, did their best to preserve priests as figures to be loved. They illustrated the limits of the priests' authority and relied on others—lay teachers and, above all, women as wives and mothers—to monitor behavior and enforce church rules. This conception of devoted priests, so appealing to Irish Catholic readers, was also a response to Protestant charges that priests were tyrants who represented the conflict between the internal structure of the Church and American ideas of democracy.

The Priest in the Early Catholic Novels: Teacher and Advisor

The first generation of Catholic writers made laymen and women, not priests, the central characters of their fiction. The only exception: Pise, who was himself a priest. In all of the novels, priests said mass and administered the sacraments, but these were not the roles that defined them. In the doctrinal novels, the priests were primarily teachers. In Pise's first novel, Father Rowland conducts the question-and-answer sessions that lead the Wolburn women to convert. In Pise's later novel, Zenosius seeks out a priest in every country he visits to serve as his "devoted instructor."[2] In the doctrinal novels of Bryant and Dorsey, priests serve the same role but to a less significant extent, since the Protestants in these novels typically convert because of their own readings and reflections. Bryant's Pauline Seward is persuaded by her "almost daily theological researches" before she approaches a priest—one-third of the way into the novel. She does not receive any instruction until two-thirds of the way into the work. Similarly, Dorsey's hero in *The Student of Blenheim Forest*, convinced by his readings, declares himself a Catholic and is disinherited by his father before he meets the priest or receives any instruction from him. Priests in Bryant and Dorsey were also not the only teachers. One of Pauline Seward's friends is instructed by a Catholic woman, "educated an Episcopalian, but now a Catholic . . . [and] remarkably intelligent, and well informed."[3]

In these doctrinal novels, the priests interact with wealthy Protestants seeking the truth. The authors tell readers that the priests are also "benefactor" to the poor, "father" to the orphan, and the type of men who "watched, tended, and administered day and night to . . . [the] wants" of patients in the hospital.[4] But the central characters of these novels do not require such help. In Pise's novel, the renowned English scholar, Rev. Dr. Lingard, is on his way to visit the poor and sick when Zenosius waylays him. Dr. Lingard then proceeds to explain the history of the Church in England over many pages.[5] Even when these authors describe poor characters, they do not always include a helping priest. In Dorsey's *The Student of Blenheim Forest*, the Irishman Barney O'Callan receives money and help in starting a business from wealthy lay Catholics.

Priests, if anything, are less important in Cannon's early fiction than in the other novels of the 1840s. In his first doctrinal works, priests do not teach the inquiring Protestants. In *Harry Layden*, the Irish American schoolteacher Hugh Redmond instructs his fiancée; in *Mora Carmody*, the heroine instructs her love interest. Only in *Father Felix*, Cannon's most orthodox novel, does the priest take the lead in explaining the Catholic faith to the wealthy Protestants, and he is not their only teacher—Father Felix himself traces his conversion not to any priest but to his readings and to discussions with an educated layman.[6]

If Cannon's priests are typical in the secondary roles they play, they are unique in their priorities. They may not teach, but they do help Catholics and others in their material and spiritual lives, a role that reflects Cannon's relatively minimal interest in communicating doctrine and his willingness to include poor, vulnerable people among his characters. In *Harry Layden*, the priest is not part of the instruction of the Protestant character but appears at the start of the story at the bedside of Harry's dying mother, then again later to help rescue the orphaned daughter of the Redmonds. Even when the priest is the primary transmitter of doctrine, as in *Father Felix*, he appears first to find a job, home, and temperance society for the alcoholic, an important subordinate character. And Cannon does not overstate the priest's helping role. When the Protestant hero of *Father Felix* is falsely accused of a crime, the priest concentrates on his spiritual welfare; it is the Catholic lawyer who proves him not guilty. In *Harry Layden*, an Irishman named Con Dorrian, not a priest, rescues the title character.[7]

As the writers begin to center their novels on Catholic characters in the later 1840s, moving away from communicating doctrine, they continue to assign priests secondary roles but alter their priorities. Dorsey shows

Father Holberg advising the German immigrants, "which from his long residence and experience in this country, he was well qualified to do." The priest also approves the men's plans to travel west and offers consolation to the young woman, Marie, who is left behind in the city, when she is poor and feels abandoned. Dorsey also follows Cannon in showing the priest helping the immigrants: he watches over Marie and tries to locate the money that her father left for her. Yet despite the priest's greater importance in this novel than in Dorsey's previous works, he cannot do much for Marie and is not her only helper. The father of the family leaves the money for her care with a wealthy merchant, not with the priest, and Father Holberg does not locate the money.[8]

In both of Miles's novels, the priests serve primarily as confessors in the broadest sense. When Agnes Cleveland, the Catholic heroine of *Loretto*, wants to accompany her Protestant cousin to the city for a few months, she and her mother consult the priest. In *The Governess*, the Catholic heroine Mary Lorn seeks out the priest for advice about accepting money from her employer and about remaining in his employment when she is not able to teach from Catholic books.[9]

In Cannon's *Scenes and Characters*, also written for a Catholic audience, the priest Father Quigley makes only a few appearances. He says mass on the Irish immigrant Jack Toland's farm since the family lives in an isolated area, among Protestants, and also visits Jack's deathbed. Priests play no role in the life of the novel's main character, Toland's son, however. In a brief description of Father Quigley, Cannon again emphasizes the priest's role in serving the poor, in this case focusing on spiritual rather than material needs. The priest "had devoted himself to the ministry with the pure intention of doing his Master's service, by attending to the spiritual wants of the poor in the household of faith."[10]

The early writers emphasize characteristics of the priests that correspond with their primary roles. In the doctrinal novels, authors focus on the intellectual abilities appropriate to teachers, which also speaks to Protestant claims that Catholics do not value intellectual life. Pise's Father Rowland, although born in Maryland, was educated at Jesuit seminaries in England and Liege with "great and virtuous men." In *The Student of Blenheim Forest*, Dorsey's priest has a "well-furnished library," and "*could* awe when necessity required it" because he was "highly gifted and polished" with a "superior intellect." Miles combines the priests' learning with their wisdom and holiness, qualities appropriate for advisors. He refers to the clerical leaders of the Church as "the gifted and the great, whose genius has placed them in conspicuous stations."[11] For all of the authors, the priests' intellectual achievements distinguish them from ministers, who—as described in a previous chapter—could not even defend their own faith.

Along the same lines, the priests in these early novels also display sophisticated manners that make them desirable companions in the best society. Father Borgia in Dorsey's *The Sister of Charity* comes from an Italian family of "high birth. . . . [T]he blood of royalty itself courses through his veins." Pise is more interested in manners. Father Rowland, whose "education [was] refined, as well in the sciences of the sanctuary, as in the formalities of high life . . . was not wanting in the civilities of life, but happily combined the gentleman with the priest."[12]

These early authors also recognize the priests' unselfish devotion to others and illustrate this virtue in similar ways. Priests live in "humble" residences and tend to the sick without regard for their own safety, though the authors give this selfless quality only secondary importance as befits the priests' secondary role as helpers. The priests illustrate their selflessness in conduct offstage or in interactions with minor characters. On the other hand, when Dorsey writes about the German immigrants, she follows Cannon in emphasizing the priest's role as caregiver and so makes selfless devotion, rather than learning, the most important feature of Father Holberg's character. The most she says about the Redemptorist priest in terms of his education or manners is that he displays "the friendly and social qualities of every day life." Much more important is that in "loving the poor," Father Holberg helps those who need him.[13]

Compared with the other writers of his day, Cannon makes more modest claims for priests' virtues. The title character of *Mora Carmody* suggests that her Protestant suitor seek a priest, "one capable of instructing you which I, unfortunately, am not." This is relatively mild praise, and the hero, in any case, prefers Mora's instruction. In his last doctrinal novel, Cannon lists "learning" among Father Felix's qualities, along with "piety, and untiring charity," but does not elaborate further. And he does not attribute any particular intellectual background or ability to the Irish priest in *Scenes and Characters*. In fact, Cannon seems to criticize his colleagues for their descriptions of priests' learning and manners. He says that Father Quigley is a fair specimen of the priests of his church. . . . With little of the gentleman in his appearance, and less in his manner, to conciliate those into whose company he might be thrown, and with no knowledge of the literature or politics of the day to render his conversation pleasing to a chance acquaintance, he was not one to be sought as a companion by the refined or the trifling, who differed from him in religion; and those of his own faith were not likely to rub off the rust which he had brought with him from home, being at that time, with few exceptions, both very poor and very illiterate.[14]

More important, Cannon differs from his colleagues because he always makes selfless devotion the dominant virtue of his priests and shows, rather than tells, his readers how the priests exhibit this quality. In *Harry Layden*, the priest's "active charity" saves abandoned orphans. In *Scenes and Characters*, Father Quigley comes to the deathbed of Jack Toland, even though he has just returned after an absence of several days "during which he had travelled some hundreds of miles in the discharge of his duties."[15] Cannon's portrait of Father Quigley's "rust" and lack of polish may seem insulting both to the Irish priest and to his congregation but it can also be interpreted as what Cannon views as the most vital qualities of a true priest.

For the most part, these priests in the early novels—who serve as teachers, counselors, and helpers, and exhibit learning, wisdom, and charity—are not presented as authority figures. They do not tell Catholics what to do, nor do they sanction them in any way for noncompliance. The authors also assign traits to priests—passivity, age, and sentimentality—that are the antithesis of power. Dorsey, for one, describes Father Holberg in America as kindly, and is critical of an authoritarian priest the immigrant Conradt family has left behind in Germany: Henrich, the adopted son of the family, complains that his German pastor criticized him "in the pulpit . . . [and] in the public streets." Dorsey suggests that this public humiliation was not effective. As Henrich reports, his "evil propensities strengthened in proportion to the degree of coercion which was used towards" him, concluding that the German pastor "seemed not to understand the tact and nicety of managing a temperament like mine."[16]

Pise and Miles advocate a more authoritarian view of the Church, but only Miles imbues his priests with that quality. In Pise, priests assert the authority of the Church but do not claim it for themselves. They interact with the Protestant Zenosius on his way to conversion, seeking only to teach and persuade.

Miles, in contrast, centers his novels on Catholics and shows priests asserting authority over them. He makes it clear that instruction is the provenance of priests alone. When the Protestant doctor in *Loretto* becomes interested in Catholicism, he considers reading the Church Fathers. The priest asks him if he wants to study for the priesthood, and, when the answer is negative, the priest says that a "little catechism would be better."[17] Priests in both of Miles's novels also exert authority in their primary role as advisors. Whenever Catholic characters are in doubt about what to do, they seek out priests and intend to follow their advice without question. Unlike Dorsey, who merely tells her readers that the priest approved the immigrants' plan to travel west, but not that the immigrants needed his approval, Miles's Catholic characters seek the priest's consent before they take action. In *Loretto*, when Agnes Cleveland wants to accompany her Protestant cousin Ellen Almy to live in the city, her mother says she will leave the decision to her daughter and her confessor. The mother's "own reasoning failed to satisfy her," Miles comments, and she wants "advice . . . from those who were commissioned to instruct." The mother then tells the priest: "I leave the matter entirely with you." Miles makes his position on authority explicit when the Protestant doctor accuses the priest character of "heartless tyranny" in persuading his now converted fiancée to refuse to marry him. The priest answers, "I claim a right to advise in all these cases, and hold myself accountable to God alone."[18] Miles's works point up the absence of similarly authoritative priests in the other novels of the time.

Yet even Miles qualifies priestly authority—and even undermines it at times. As noted in chapter 4, he describes the priest in *Loretto* as old, feeble, and diminutive. In addition, after the governess Mary Lorn determines that she will follow whatever direction the priest gives, Miles (as author) interjects that her resolve reflects "a determination dictated by her own judgment and feeling, and matured without advice."[19] Essentially, Mary resolves that she will obey her confessor, whatever he decides, on the basis of her own reason and conscience.

The portraits of priests in early Catholic novels show that despite their criticisms of Protestants for rejecting church authority—and despite the willingness of some to emphasize the Church as the source of rules and sanctions—the writers were reluctant to show the priests as authority figures. Even Pise and Miles did not embody their vision of an authoritative church in priest characters. The preference for loving priests who are followed willingly or not at all is partly a response to Protestant attacks on priestly power, as authors show that authority within the Church is not totally incompatible with American ideas of legitimate leadership. The preference is also a way to appeal to Catholics, to portray priests as men who deserve their love and loyalty.

The Priest in the Irish American Novels: Rescuer and Spokesman

Like their predecessors, the Irish Americans who began writing in 1850 did not typically make priests the lead characters in their novels. (The only exception was Boyce, one of the priest-novelists.) The Irish Americans also follow Cannon in making their priests primarily helpers or spokesmen. But they stress, more than Cannon did, the key role priests play in the lives of the immigrants. McElgun illustrates this in his 1873 novel, *Annie Reilly*, describing the apartment (in a "neat-looking brick house") of a working-class immigrant couple, Terence and Bridget McManus, who had made a good life in America.

> Over the wooden mantel-piece hung a handsome engraving of Archbishop Hughes, side by side with another of St. Patrick, and on the opposite wall hung a picture of Killarney Lakes. Several other pictures, some of Irish clergy, some of American, were fastened round the walls, all very tastefully arranged.[20]

The priests in these Irish American novels have no rivals or equals. More clearly than ever before, they are the loving "fathers" who take care of their community. In the 1850s, Cannon, too, gives greater importance to priests, in this case following, rather than leading, the other Irish Americans.

The authors who portray Catholic life in Ireland convey to readers that the priests perform their usual functions—they say mass, administer the sacraments, and give catechism classes and sermons. Above all, however, priests provide help to their people in times of trouble, or serve as spokesmen for their interests. The priests teach as well, but their teaching role is entirely secondary. Sadlier's widow Burke recalls the Irish priest who "couldn't put a bit or sup in his own mouth an' know that anybody wanted it." When the father of the O'Donnell family in McCorry's novel becomes ill during the famine, his daughter Mary suggests calling the local priest even before the doctor because the priest "is known to be very skillful." When the priest arrives, he diagnoses the problem and comforts the family, although his own "heart was buried in grief . . . for those present." In McElgun's novel, the mother of the Reilly family takes ill, just as the Reillys are being evicted. The priest responds to the family's call for help and "looked with a serious, troubled face" at the "desolated" cottage and "sighed heavily." He tends to the mother until she is out of danger, and "soothed so much . . . [her] anguish . . . that it almost made her forget her desolation." The priest drives the family to their new home and leaves them "with as sad a heart as those he had parted from."[21]

The priests in Ireland also speak for the interests of their people. In his first novel, Quigley's O'Clery family must emigrate because the father's brother, a prominent priest, had written letters to the newspapers "about the cruelty of the [new] landlord . . . and on that account, and because the priest took part with the poor,—as they always do, God bless 'em!—the landlord came down on" the family.[22]

The priests in Ireland do not do much teaching, mostly because there are no doubters or backsliders to instruct. No priest in Ireland resembled the German pastor in Dorsey's novel, who rebukes his parishioner in private and public. The other professionals who appear in Irish scenes are teachers—the priests' subordinate allies—and doctors, who join the priests at deathbeds. In Sadlier's *Willy Burke*, the priest and teacher come to the going-away party for the family, and the teacher quotes the priest as he tells the family to remember their faith and their country.[23]

The American Catholic community in these novels recreated the one left behind in Ireland not only with its ethnic base and all-encompassing cultural and social life but also with its Irish priest leaders. Although the authors occasionally mention the French priests who had played an important role in America's past, or historical figures like Bishops Fenwick or Cheverus, the great majority of their priest characters are Irish. Some, such as Roddan's Bishop Fitzpatrick and Sadlier and McElgun's Bishop Hughes, are not identified as Irish but clearly are. Other priests are given obviously Irish names such as Quigley's Father O'Shane, who comes to the dying widow in *The Cross and the Shamrock*; McElgun's Father Fitzsimons, who gives reading material to the Irish immigrant working on the railroads; and McCorry's Father Byrne, who assists Bishop Fenwick during the crisis at Mount Benedict. Whenever Sadlier's characters make a home in America, their priests are specifically identified as Irish. Father Fitzherbert, in *Willy Burke*, is from Ireland, retired there, and is replaced by Father O'Hara. Sadlier's priest to the Irish settlement in *Con O'Regan* is also Irish, as is Father Power, another historical figure, who appears in *The Blakes and Flanagans* and gives the Flanagan son Irish literature and who "loved the boy for his Irish heart, for he himself . . . still fondly cherished the memory of his own dear land."[24] Quigley makes some allowance for an American contribution when he says that the priest in his last novel was from Ireland, where he received his "preliminary education and virtuous training," but emphasizes that he is also "an American priest, having completed his ecclesiastical studies, and received ordination in a well-known seminary in Maryland."[25]

Roddan and Cannon, in the 1850s, take a different tack from their Irish-born colleagues. Roddan, who placed his novel in the 1820s and '30s, does not comment on the ethnicity of his priests. Cannon typically uses his priest in *Bickerton* to integrate Irish and American identities, giving him a New England Protestant father and an Irish Catholic mother. Cannon's final novel, *Tighe Lyfford*, published with a secular house, includes the only example in the Irish American novels of a non-Irish priest who plays an important role in the lives of immigrants and their children: his name is Rivas, he is said to have "an imperfect command of English," and he solves the crime at the heart of the novel, rescuing the kidnapped victim. Beyond that, Cannon does not specify the priest's ethnic background.[26]

In the Irish American novels, priests assume the role of "father" to those who so often had no parent in their new country. When the orphaned John O'Brien in Roddan's novel goes to speak to Bishop Fenwick, the bishop says, "tell me just as if I were your own father; as indeed I am." In Sadlier's *Willy Burke*, the widow calls the priests "the fathers o' the poor."[27] Most of the novels, whether they advance a nurturing or authoritarian view of the Church, interpret "father" to mean nurturing caretaker devoted to the welfare of others, qualities traditionally assigned to mothers. In the more authoritarian works of Roddan, the priest's main role in the orphan's life is to find him a job with a Catholic employer and a residence with a Catholic family. Sadlier's Mrs. Burke, on her deathbed, tells the priest that she "wanted to see your reverence a'n the children here, so that I might give them up to your care before I leave this world." She tells the children that the priest will "watch over you, for God's sake,— poor, lonesome creatures that ye'll be." When she realizes that the priest had found a home for her daughters and jobs for her sons, she thanks him for his "truly paternal care of her children," saying "sure, your reverence has done for them what I couldn't do—a poor, lone woman like me, that nobody here knew."[28]

Despite their divergent views of the Church, both Quigley's and Cannon's priests perform the same caretaking function, but their role is usurped for some years by Protestant-controlled institutions. The dying widow in Quigley, like Mrs. Burke, gives her children over to the care of the priest, telling her son to go with his brothers and sisters "to the priest, telling him not to forget that I gave ye all up to his care." After the widow's death, the priest—who had been on the road for days and "suffered terribly" from frostbite—tries his best to "provide for . . . [the] poor orphans," but they are spirited away.[29] In Cannon's novel, the orphaned girl is also taken to a Protestant foster family and does not encounter Father Eldridge until she is nearly eighteen years old. The priest turns out to be the young woman's only relative and could become her legal guardian. He tells her she has not only finally "found such a friend as my priestly character obliges me to be to all, but your nearest relation." He will "provide a home for her . . . and then, in . . . [his] character of relation and natural guardian . . . make a formal demand for her."[30]

As the centrality of orphans fades in the novels of the 1860s and '70s, the priests continue to serve primarily as helpers or rescuers for the poor and for young single immigrants. In McCorry, the priest reunites the Crolly brother and sister and finds homes with Catholic families for those who need them. In McElgun's novel, a priest encourages and gives books to James O'Rourke, who is working in the oil fields, and waits for him to arrive before starting mass.[31]

The authors are careful, however, to circumscribe the role of priests as helpers to the young single women in America. In the three novels focused on this group, the authors do not show priests in America interacting with, helping, or advising the heroines. The Church still represents home and family, but the authors do not symbolize that attachment in a relationship between the women and a priest.[32] In McElgun's novel, for example, the priest gives books and encouragement to James O'Rourke in the oil fields (as mentioned above), but no priest interacts with Annie Reilly, the heroine. In Ireland, by contrast, where the women are living with families and surrounded by a Catholic culture, they interact freely with priests, both before they emigrate and after they return. When Annie Reilly is reunited with her family on a visit from America, she has several conversations alone with the priest.

Several of the authors tie the priests' selfless devotion to the shortage of clergy in America, particularly in novels set in the 1820s and '30s. Quigley's Father O'Shane, in *The Cross and the Shamrock*, was "the sole pastor of the city . . . in those days." Cannon refers to "priests, who, few in number, were already worn down by their excessive labours."[33] Invariably, the authors emphasize the priests' willingness to extend themselves out of love, not mere duty. Father O'Shane is "tender hearted" in his pity for the poor, and Cannon describes Father Eldridge as "a person who, but for the unusual benignity of his countenance, would have passed among ordinary men for an ordinary man." The loving priests share their people's emotions: when the priest in *Mount Benedict* realizes what had happened to the convent, he is "heart-broken."[34]

Unlike their predecessors, however, the Irish American authors do not stress the priests' poverty or humble living conditions. Indeed, most do not mention their living situations at all. While Father John Brennan, Boyce's priest in Ireland, refers to himself as "poor," and lives in a "humble edifice," he also has a servant. The abandoned orphans in Quigley's novel write to their uncle, the rector in Ireland, expecting that he could send money to them.[35] Cannon's Father Eldridge in *Bickerton* also has money: the immigrant's daughter says that the priest "whose fortune is ample, wishes to settle upon me what will provide handsomely for all my wants." And in a reversal of the comparisons between priests and ministers that appeared in the novels of the 1840s, Quigley, in *The Cross and the Shamrock*, refers to "parsons, who have scarcely enough to eat, and who envy the priest the comparative independence which the liberality and true Catholic charity of his flock enable him to maintain."[36]

When these novels that focus on priests as rescuers mention educational or intellectual abilities at all, they give them minimal importance, often using the credential to illustrate the priest's piety rather than his learning. In *Bessy Conway*, Sadlier introduces Father Daly as a "gentleman . . . who sat much alone, generally reading . . . in a . . . black book," as observers note "the grave and somewhat pensive countenance of this studious personage." The reader learns nothing of Father Daly's education, but does find out that he took the old woman's hand "very kindly."[37]

Priests in the Irish American novels are leaders of the community and, in this respect also, differ from the priests in the early Catholic novels. They speak for the people's interests, continuing a role described by Cannon in his early story "The Beal Fire," though without the nationalist implications. Quigley's priest is "not the man to wink at the cruel treatment to which . . . his poor fellow-men and fellow-Christians were submitted." Rather, "there is no man daring enough to speak a word in favor of the cruelly-oppressed railroad man, except an odd priest here and there." In Sadlier's novel, Bishop Hughes leads the Catholic party in the fight for "freedom of education"; Sadlier does not mention any other political leaders advocating for this cause. In McCorry's *Mount Benedict*, the Irish turn to the bishop and his priests to lead them before, during, and after the attack on the convent. Sadlier's ideal is, again, stated very clearly in her portrayal of the western settlement, where one of the original settlers says that "when we have a good priest and a good schoolmaster, we'll have all we want." At a party, the priest "took possession of the seat of honor," "thus gracefully assuming a command which he well knew was most pleasing to his host and hostess."[38]

In their descriptions of priests whose leadership compels them to take a more public role, the Irish American authors give intellectual and educational credentials more or less the same value as virtues associated with selfless charity. Roddan's John O'Brien recalls that Bishop Fenwick "looked . . . pleasantly" at him and spoke "in . . . a mild way," but also notes the bishop's well-stocked library, and thought "what a very learned man he must be."[39] The lead character in Sadlier's *Confessions of an Apostate*

observes "the great and good Bishop" Cheverus, "ubiquitous in his ex-
haustless charity," while a Protestant woman in the novel describes him as
a "most uncommon larned man," and Sadlier herself says that all of Boston admired the bishop, "even . . . the fastidious and 'exclusive' *literati* of
the self-styled 'Athens of America.'" In *Con O'Regan*, Sadlier comments
that "the hundred gentlemen, some of them ecclesiastics" who assembled
at the convention for colonization were "in high repute for wisdom and
virtue."[40] Father Ugo in Quigley's *The Cross and the Shamrock*, who represents the railroad men before the employers, is "highly educated," a "Rev.
Dr." who impressed one of the Protestant characters as "a well-read, intelligent fellow."[41]

Even when they elaborate on the priests' intellectual credentials, the
Irish Americans, like Cannon in the 1840s, are not interested in the priests'
"gentlemanly" qualities, never mentioning, for instance, the aristocratic
backgrounds or manners of the bishops. Neither do they show bishops
or priests attending elegant dinner parties, except on rare occasions when
their presence is required in the performance of duty.[42] Quigley's point
in describing the conduct of Father Ugo, who speaks for the men on the
railroads, is not to show the priest as equal to elegant Americans but to
demonstrate that Americans are not so elegant after all. The priest is "accustomed in Europe, where he was chaplain to Lord C___d, to the most
aristocratic society," yet he had "unaffected manners, bordering on plain-
ness." Given his experience in Europe, Father Ugo had "contempt for the
mushroom aristocratic imitations that he witnessed in America," referring
to "'the monkey aristocracy' of the new world."[43]

The Irish American Priest as Teacher and the Question of Authority

As rescuers of the poor and vulnerable, priests in the Irish American novels
are certainly portrayed as loving figures. In their secondary role as teachers,
also, priests behave in a manner meant to elicit the love of their followers;
they teach through persuasion, not command. In promoting temperance,
Cannon's Father Eldridge does not resort to "wordy declamation, or de-
nunciations from the pulpit." Rather, he goes "to every family" in his congregation and appeals to their "religious feelings, and, what was even more

powerful in most, their national pride." At the time of the convent burning, McCorry's priests use "peaceful persuasion" to convince the Irish immigrants not to confront the crowd, and after the event, the bishop "convened meetings, and implored of his hearers to forgive the crimes of those who had injured them."[44]

Roddan, Quigley, and Sadlier, despite their more authoritarian concept of the Church, also show priests relying on loving persuasion rather than command as they fulfill their secondary roles as teacher. The harshest priest that Roddan would allow hears John O'Brien's first confession. The young man is frightened and unfamiliar with the process, and the priest tells him "sharply" what to do, since "I cannot wait all day." He then "lost his patience" and tells John to go home. Roddan is implicitly critical of the priest's conduct since the young man does not return to confession for six years.[45]

In most of their novels, Sadlier and Quigley also downplay the priests' authority. In *Willy Burke*, Sadlier describes the priest as "mild, benignant. . . . His eyes . . . had nothing stern in their look." In *Confessions of an Apostate*, Bishop Cheverus speaks to Simon O'Hare with "affectionate remonstrances" after a long period in which he had not attended mass or the sacraments. Similarly, in Quigley's *The Cross and the Shamrock*, Father Ugo gives a sermon to the railroad men, referring to the men's failings, and telling them to "guard against drunkenness and faction fights." For the most part, however, he expresses only sympathy for the harsh circumstances in which the men live and work. "You, poor fellows," he says, "have to work hard . . . [and] are exposed to dangers from accidents, and frequently from the influence of evil-advising men."[46]

In only three Irish American novels—Boyce's *Mary Lee*, Sadlier's *The Blakes and Flanagans*, and Quigley's *Profit and Loss*—are the priests primarily teachers, and they deal with middle-class, wealthy, or professional people in Ireland (in Boyce's novel) and America (in Sadlier and Quigley). Since these priests are teachers rather than rescuers, the authors must directly confront the issue of their authority. In the three novels, as in those where priests are public leaders, authors give more weight than is typical to the priests' intellectual or educational credentials. Boyce's priest, Father Brennan—who argues with Dr. Henshaw about the nature of the Church—meets Henshaw when they are both students at Oxford. In

Sadlier's novel, Father Power is a doctor of divinity "endowed with a strong and piercing intellect; a giant in the arena of controversy, [and] a powerful and eloquent preacher," while Bishop Hughes displays "indomitable energy and singular prudence . . . [as well as a] penetrating eye." In Quigley's final novel, Father John is a "good classical scholar" and a "learned man . . . of vast experience."[47]

Boyce's priest exemplifies the beloved figure who leads by example. Father Brennan embodies Boyce's view of the Church as attractive and alluring as opposed to the authoritarian Dr. Henshaw. The priest helps the poor and vulnerable but interacts mainly with his social equals, the Church of Ireland gentry, Catholic professionals, and Dr. Henshaw. He is known as "Father John," behaves "familiarly" in the homes of his parishioners with whom he engages in "good-natured" banter, and is a "dear friend" both of the magistrate, a member of the Church of Ireland, and of the doctor, a Catholic—the word "friend" in both cases implying an equal, not a rescuer.[48] Dr. Henshaw is a former Presbyterian, which suggests that his rigid views are Calvinist in origin. He is called "doctor," does not engage easily with people, has an "air of self-complacency," and is "quite conscious of his mental powers, and . . . personal importance." When first introduced, he is in a small boat with the priest and the boatman, who are engaged in lively and familiar conversation. Henshaw remains "absorbed" in his book and speaks in a "deep, gruff voice" to the boatman, "growling out his dissatisfaction at being disturbed."[49]

Boyce's Father John seldom engages in disputes and is never shown chastising a follower. But when Henshaw is introduced to the Anglican Kate Petersham, he bows "stiffly," raises his "spectacles to look at her in detail," and almost immediately engages her in a dispute about Jonathan Swift. The priest is accepting and compassionate, while Henshaw is judgmental and humorless. When the heroine of the novel says she likes riding and sailing, Henshaw says, "not very feminine, I should think," as his "eyes dilated into what he intended for a smile." Henshaw also finds "unpardonable" the heroine's "fool-hardiness" in attempting a risky jump on her horse; Father John only prays that she will make it.[50]

Boyce's priest also accepts that others, Catholics as well as Protestants, might disagree with him on important issues. In a conversation with a man in his congregation, the priest regrets that the young revolutionary

Randall Barry has been "imprudent" in remaining in the area to be near his love interest, the Catholic Mary Lee. The man responds: "Hush, hush! Father John! nonsense! Say no more about that. Love's a thing you're not competent to speak of, you know. It's out of your line altogether." In the course of the disagreement, the man calls the priest "Mr. Brennan." The Church of Ireland magistrate rejects Father John's advice outright. When in the course of a trial, the priest tells the magistrate, "you must take another time and place to rebuke" the Presbyterian villain of the novel, the magistrate replies in an "indignant" tone, "No sir, I shall not. . . . This is the proper time and place to rebuke him."[51] Dr. Henshaw, on the other hand, resents disagreement. When Kate Petersham argues with him about Swift, Henshaw asks, "have you read much" and "do you study what you read?" On other occasions, he is "full of indignation at Kate's presumptuous boldness" and "went even so far at last as to rebuke her harshly for her familiarity." While the priest is loved and admired by all, Henshaw is disliked and rejected. He leaves the country never to return, complaining that Ireland has not even "the ghost" left of its "old Katholeecity."[52]

The other two novels in which the priests serve primarily as teachers — Sadlier's *The Blakes and Flanagans* and Quigley's *Profit and Loss* — provide the only instances in which the Irish American authors with an authoritarian vision of the Church embody that vision in their priest characters, at least to some degree. Sadlier calls Father Power "a mighty man in his generation — in the early day when his services were most required" and before "a mightier than he descended into the arena where the School question was being agitated." She also says that Father Power is "as much beloved as . . . feared, and respected," adding "feared" to the usual catalogue of virtues. Similarly, a good Catholic in Quigley's novel declares, "Catholics all love their priests, and fear them as well."[53]

While the priest in Boyce is called Father John, Sadlier makes it clear that calling the priest "Father" rather than "Dr." is as familiar as her Catholics could get. He is "a doctor of divinity, but the people amongst whom he labored like better to call him Father Power — a thing very common amongst the Irish, who, with their characteristic and most filial attachment to their clergy, merge all honorary titles in the patriarchal one of *Father*." The title here means father as authority, and since Father Power — unlike the priests in Miles's two novels — interacts with Catholics who resist him, he must clearly assert his authority. He orders Mr. Blake to remove his children from the public schools, using the words "I must insist." Father Power also criticizes the parents' conduct, telling Blake that he has "no one to blame but yourself" for his son's bad behavior. When Mrs. Blake informs him that her daughter intends to marry a Protestant, he replies that he does not expect that his "admonitions would have any good effect," and concludes the interview quickly, saying "I can do nothing for you. . . . [I]f you permit your daughter to marry . . . you must all take the consequences of your own rashness—shall I say presumption? These are harsh words . . . but they are just what conscience and duty both dictate."[54]

Quigley's priest is also a commanding figure, speaking "curtly" to Patrick, the son of the Mulroony family who is questioning his faith, and telling other priests that Patrick is "conceited and impudent." Patrick, in turn, tells his mother that the priest is "entirely too sharp, too much of a critic, and altogether too harsh," reporting, "he snapped at me . . . rebuking me openly, and on other occasions, he has, I am told, censured me severely." The priest is even harsher toward the villain of the novel, a former Catholic, now a Methodist preacher and professor at the public school. The priest tells the professor "sternly" to "Shut up, sirrah . . . how dare you address yourself to me, or even come in the presence of any decent people! I do not want to have any conversation with such a renegade as you! . . . [I]f you interrupt me a second time, I shall rise and leave this house, if you are not kicked out of it."[55]

In both novels, the uniquely authoritarian quality of the priests is heightened by threats of faithful Catholics to report the bad behavior of backsliders. Mrs. Blake, the wife and mother; the good Catholic Tim Flanagan; and the old apple woman all tell Father Power about Miles and Henry Blake. In Quigley's novel, Mrs. Mulroony threatens her husband: "Believe me, the priest shall hear of your conduct if you send him to that school." Mr. Mulroony is at first "alarmed at the fear of having his conduct exposed to the parish priest." Another mother in the same novel tells her daughter, Nellie, who had attended the public school and is criticizing Catholicism: "I'll tell the priest on you."[56] The priests in the novels of Sadlier and Quigley preside over a system of authority that includes parents and teachers, and extends to private, social, and public life.

Sadlier also emphasizes the priests' superiority over Catholic laypeople in her accounts of the priests who will serve the American Church in the future. The American-born sons studying for the priesthood in *The Blakes and Flanagans*, including one of the Flanagans, are "studious" and are the only faithful Catholics in the novel to go to university. The other Flanagan son, Edward, who serves as Sadlier's spokesperson in the novel and is slated to take over the family business, is "not of a very studious turn" and received only "a good solid mercantile education." As his father maintains, "that is all he wants . . . he knows quite enough to work his way decently through the world."[57]

To some degree, the differences between the priests in Sadlier and Quigley and the more nurturing priests in the other novels of the time center around the grounds on which readers are asked to accept the priests' authority. Cannon, as much as Sadlier and Quigley, points with some pride to the influence that his more nurturing priests have over their followers. He explains the fighting and drinking of men on the labor gangs partly by the absence of priests, "who had exercised over them a salutary authority, based upon the truest kindness."[58] There is a difference, however, between basing authority on obligation and fear of penalty and basing it on love and gratitude. Only in the latter case is obedience grounded in the views and feelings of followers, which can be affected by the behavior of priests. Retaining love and gratitude, as well as obedience, may require some accommodation on the part of the authority. As Machiavelli said, the prince who rules by love is dependent on his followers, while he who rules by fear depends only on himself.

The significance of the grounds used to justify authority can be seen in the different approaches of Cannon and Sadlier to the controversy surrounding lay trustees. As shown in the previous chapter, both authors support the clergy against the laymen. Cannon, however, bases his argument on the assertion that the trustees are concerned with advancing their own interests. They "seemed to think of nothing but how they could make most for themselves out of the power with which they were invested." They made poor use of church revenues, which came "out of the small savings of labouring men and servant maids," and, as a result, Catholics had to contribute even more to the support of the church and schools, "until many of these poor people left themselves without a dollar for their own necessities." The priests, on the other hand, act selflessly for the people's welfare, using the revenues for schools and for teachers' salaries. Cannon essentially conditions priests' authority on their behavior. In principle, if they don't act in the people's interests, obedience might be withdrawn.

Sadlier also portrays the more authoritarian Father Power as concerned for his congregation as compared with the selfish and incompetent trustees, but emphasizes the obligation of Catholics to obey the priests. In her view, the trustees are in error not only for their management of church revenues but also because they "held fast by their delegated authority in opposition to the priests." Once Miles Blake and the other trustees were "'deck'd in a little brief authority,' they began to wax great in their own estimation, and to think themselves quite equal, if not superior, to the priests." As a result, "the majority of them were ranged against the priest in the temporal order, and in the spiritual they were hardly one whit more docile or obedient."[59] There is no correlation here between the obedience of the followers and the actions of the authority.

In some cases, the various priests take different positions on controversial issues, indicating that their differences reflect substance as well as emphasis and tone. The nurturing priests are sometimes willing to accommodate the preferences of their followers; the authoritarian priests in Sadlier and Quigley are not. Cannon applauds priests who recognize the people's love of festivals in their teaching. Father Eldridge in *Bickerton* is a "judicious reformer" who does not condemn the festivals or seek to destroy "habits, not evil in themselves, which had become a second nature, or the abrogation of customs to which, because they had come from 'home,' they [the people] now clung with the tenacity of the heart to a first love." The priest is willing to "let" the people "enjoy themselves in their own way," and in the end, the people "enjoyed, without fear of the priest, their frequent gatherings." Cannon also concludes that with this accommodation the priest is more effective than the "over-zealous cure" and other clergy who inveigh against superstitious practices, "to very little purpose, we are afraid."[60]

On the issue of public schools, Cannon's discussion leaves Catholic readers with hope that the public school system might become less sectarian and more acceptable to Catholics. His priest never tells, advises, or commands Catholic parents to send their children to the Catholic schools.

As a narrator, Cannon also expresses some understanding of the emotional and financial needs of Catholic parents who choose the public schools, as opposed to Sadlier's Father Power, who says "I must insist" as he orders Miles Blake to remove his children from the public schools.[61]

The nurturing and authoritarian priests also react differently to interfaith marriages. Boyce's priest marries the Protestant felon Randall Barry and the Catholic Mary Lee without comment before they escape to America. Boyce does not refer to the priest imposing or asking for any conditions at all, seeming to rely, instead, on the influence of example and the beauties of the Catholic faith.[62] Cannon's nurturing priest—himself a product of an interfaith marriage—also willingly marries the immigrant's daughter to the Protestant Fred Hubbard but on the condition that Fred promise to raise their children Catholic and to respect his wife's religious practice. The young man agrees but says: "further than this I cannot promise." The priest replies: "And further than this I do not ask you to promise," that is, he does not require conversion, although eventually, after his marriage, the young man becomes a Catholic.[63] Cannon in no way suggests that the priest regrets the interfaith marriage or gives the couple anything but a full church wedding.

In contrast, Sadlier's more authoritarian Father Power agrees to the marriages of the two Blake children after the Protestant parties agree to the same conditions about interference and raising children, but he clearly disapproves, as mentioned in chapter 6, and performs the ceremony for Henry in the rectory, not in the church. The priest also predicts that sorrow will come to the Blake parents as they reap the "consequences" of their own "rashness" in sending children to the public schools.[64] Sadlier seems to know that the Protestant spouses will not live up to their promises, as indeed they do not.

Despite this stress on the priests' authority, Sadlier and Quigley do not depart completely from their colleagues. They assert that good Catholics fear as well as love their priests, but ultimately, it is the love they strive to preserve. Moreover, they are more concerned with preserving love than is Miles, the earlier Catholic writer with the authoritarian conception of the Church and priest. For one thing, whenever the priests in the two Irish American novels assert their authority, they do not succeed in changing behavior. The fathers of the Blake and Mulroony families decide to send their children to the public schools despite the priests' objections. In Quigley, the priest even has "great trouble to get all the children to attend" his classes at the church, and the resistors do not change their behavior even after others report them to the priest. In Quigley's novel, Nellie tells her faithful mother: "I don't care, old woman . . . if you . . . tell the priest, and bishop too." The priests' authority is limited on public issues as well. In Sadlier, Father Power's directions to trustees are "set at naught," and Bishop Hughes's campaign against the Public School society did not bring the results he wanted.[65]

When the priests face resistance, moreover, they take very little action. The response of Quigley's priest to the young backslider Patrick Mulroony is to "warn him of his danger . . . frequently," and, when that does not produce results, the priest "made up . . . [his] mind never again to speak on the subject to him."[66] Unlike Dorsey's German pastor, priests do not condemn people from the pulpit or in public. Instead, they give up, sigh in sad resignation, and remain ready to forgive. Any negative consequences that occur as a result of the people's bad behaviors do not arise from sanctions imposed by the priests. In a somewhat oblique reference to the limits of Father Power's authority, the Catholic school teacher in Sadlier's novel comments that Miles Blake "surely . . . wouldn't stand against" the priest's "advice," and the good Catholic Tim Flanagan replies that he has seen the priest advising him before to no avail. Flanagan then continues: "of course, his reverence never laid his commands on him, for he doesn't like to go so far if he can help it." Father Power never lays his commands on anyone. Instead, when his advice is rejected, he—like the priest in Quigley—departs "with a heavy sigh" and a prayer, or simply "in sorrow."[67]

Finally, the priests do their best for backsliders, in life and after death. Father Power comforts the Blake parents in their miserable old age. Quigley's priest "mitigate[s] the grief of the disconsolate parents and sympathizing relatives" of the public school teacher and "allowed her a place of internment in that corner of the cemetery reserved for strangers and stillborn infants," where her mother could tend her grave.[68]

The only instance in the two novels (and thus in all the Irish American novels of the period) when a priest seems to have taken action against a resisting Catholic is an implication that the priest may have excommunicated the villain of Quigley's novel, the apostate professor at the public school. Even then, Quigley is not explicit that the action has actually been taken by the priest. The Catholic mother warns her daughter, Nellie, that the "priest excommunicated" the professor "for a horrible crime," related to "his cruel treatment of the poor Norwegian girl whom he ruined." But another Catholic character tells the professor that, as "a Mason," he cannot continue as a "member of a Church that excommunicates you and your society," which suggests the action was automatic.[69]

Even these most authoritarian priests, moreover, are sometimes compelled to accede to the wishes of their resisting followers. Father Power has no choice but to allow the marriages of the Blake children, for example. In the end, even Sadlier seems to have given up on the efficacy of coercive or commanding authority. In *Con O'Regan*, the hero tries to break up a drunken fight, telling one of the participants, a man named Tom, that he will inform the priest about his conduct. The threat "only served to increase . . . [Tom's] rage," and he responded: "Let him [the priest] mind his own business. He a'nt in Ireland now, I guess!"[70]

Sadlier and Quigley are more comfortable presenting the priests as victims—even victims of fellow Catholics—than as commanding figures able to compel obedience. If the priests in their two novels do not rely on love, they still rely more on guilt than fear. Sadlier's Father Power, who fails with the resisters, has to deal with "all the harassing cares of his ministry," and he dies "a martyr to the iniquitous system of lay-trustees." In Quigley's novel, the mother speaks of the priest as "almost a martyr in the holy cause of Christ."[71]

These authors who emphasize an authoritarian church yet seek to preserve the nurturing priests did more than show real limits to the priests' power. They also insulate the priests from the authoritarian church by assigning to others the tasks of defending the priests' authority, monitoring the behavior of Catholics, and imposing sanctions for disobedience.

In Roddan, Sadlier, and Quigley, most of the claims for the authority of church and priests come by way of interjections from the authors themselves, or comments from good characters, not in the voice of the priests. Roddan as author asserts that the bishop is the representative of the infallible church. A Catholic teacher, not the priest, tells John O'Brien to ask the bishop for advice and "do just what he says." In Sadlier's novel, it is Willy Burke, not the priest, who upbraids his brother for taking a position with a Protestant family "without consultin' any one—even Father Fitzherbert."[72]

Even in the novels with the two most authoritarian priests, *The Blakes and Flanagans* and *Profit and Loss*, the claims of authority are made by others far more often and insistently than by the priests. In Sadlier's novel, Edward Flanagan, not a priest, proudly acknowledges his "subjection" to such "masters" as the bishop. The good Tim Flanagan judges that "no man who rebels against his clergy will ever prosper in this world or the next." It is Sadlier the author, not Father Power, who associates Henry Blake with the "confession-hating people," and it is Tim Flanagan who criticizes Henry for having "a Protestant heart—if he hadn't he could never have the face to come out openly against the Bishop as he does." Finally, Sadlier (as author) and the good Catholic Flanagans take a stronger stand than the priest on the interfaith marriages of the Blakes. Father Power, after all, performs the ceremonies, but Sadlier interjects that the marriages are "in direct opposition" to church teachings, and the Flanagans refuse to allow their daughters to attend the weddings.[73]

Sadlier and Quigley, but not Roddan, also assign the role of monitor and enforcer of rules and regulations to other characters, who represent the authority of the Church. The priests remain nurturers, comforters, or at least martyrs. While these other characters might threaten to tell the priests about the actions of resisters, their own actions are more severe and, in the end, more efficacious than those of the priests. Sadlier uses the lay Catholic teacher as well as the wife and mother as her primary monitors and enforcers; Quigley uses only the wife and mother.

Lay teachers in Sadlier's novels often wield authority on behalf of priests. In *Bessy Conway*, the priest in Ireland is the "good old pastor" with his "paternal kindness," and Father Daly, in America, is always "kindly," but the old schoolmaster is "the crossest and roughest, yet kindest, withal, that ever wielded "the rod of empire" in village school." In *Confessions of an Apostate*, where priests are nurturing figures, the teacher at the night school, an Irishman, repeatedly warns the lead character Simon about his behavior, writing about it to his mother and the bishop. Simon resents "the pertinacity with which he [the teacher] interested himself in my affairs" and regards it as "altogether intolerable." The teacher's "continual *surveil-*

lance, he reports, "haunted me like a spirit." Even Father Power, Sadlier's most authoritarian priest, is no match for the Irishman who teaches the Flanagan boys at St. Peter's school. Mr. Lanigan is "strict," an "autocrat," and an "old-fashioned Catholic teacher" who knows "how to administer the birch, when necessary . . . when all other remedies failed." When a boy questions him in class, Lanigan responds: "never dare . . . to give your own opinion contrary to mine, or insist that you are right when I have pronounced you wrong." Neither Father Power nor any other priest in a Sadlier novel ever administers corporal punishment or orders anyone not to contradict him.[74]

Sadlier and Quigley rely primarily on wives and mothers to enforce compliance with church rules and regulations. If husbands and fathers ever play a similar role—a rare event—they do not act alone but in alliance with their wives. When Mary, the domestic servant in Sadlier's *Bessy Conway*, marries her worthless husband against the advice of the priest, her father tells her "never to darken his door again"; her mother says that Mary had "made her own bed."[75]

But even more than the priests or the men in their lives, wives and mothers represent the authoritarian church and can be hard and unloving. In Sadlier's *Confessions of an Apostate*, the lead character, Simon, receives a letter from his brother saying that the local priest is sad and disbelieving about his apostasy; he "can hardly believe it yet that you'd fall away from the true faith." Simon's mother is much harsher, her letters indicating, according to Simon, that she "had cast me from her heart" and grown "cold and strange." And when Simon's mother discovers that he has actually become a Protestant, she communicates through his brother that she never wants to speak to him again. "The enemy of God can be no child of hers," Simon's brother writes, and, in any case, the mother would not live long after "the crush that she got when she heard of your turnin'." The decisive factor in Simon's return to the fold is a dream, in which his now-deceased mother comes to him, points to a "fiery cross," and warns in a "sepulchral voice . . . by that cross you shall be judged. . . . Do penance, or you perish miserably." Even with repentance, Simon's mother declares, he will have to pay for his sins: "for a sign and in punishment of your apostasy, your idols of flesh shall be broken and destroyed." Soon after, Simon's wife and all but one of his children die.[76]

In Quigley's *Profit and Loss* also, the priest asserts more authority than is typical, yet the role of monitor and enforcer is played by the Mulroony family's wife and mother. She, not the priest, repeatedly warns her husband about the dire consequences of sending their son Patrick to the public school. She also chastises her son more often than the priest does. When Patrick is injured and is taken to the home of a Protestant teacher at the public school, it is his mother who wants him removed from that home "even if he died on the way." The priest, by contrast, examines the young man and "after having made a diagnosis unfavorable to the removal, he prevailed on his mother, for the present at least, to leave him where he was."[77]

The Importance of the Priest to the Irish Catholic Community

In the end, priests in these novels never succeed in compelling obedience, but they care for the spiritual and material welfare of their people, who therefore love and follow them. Catholic popular literature, which proved compatible with varying views of the Church, had a more uniform effect on conceptions of legitimate leadership, confirming David Reynolds's thesis in this respect. In popular culture, whether Protestant or Catholic, leaders deserved allegiance because they served their followers and treated them with loving kindness. Like the early Catholic writers, the Irish Americans used their characters to respond to Protestant charges that priests were tyrants who manipulated or controlled people to advance their own power. But even more than their predecessors, they reflected and strengthened their Catholic readers' loyalty to the priests and attachment to the community they represented.

The priests' importance in these novels can also be seen in the effects of their absence. In Sadlier's novels of the 1860s, priests play an unusually minor role in the life of the characters in America. In these works, Sadlier also becomes the only Irish American writer to show that immigrants are not able to establish satisfactory Catholic lives in the northeastern American cities. Her characters either return to Ireland or establish settlements in the west.[78] Sadlier signals the characters' lack of community by showing them—faithful Catholics all—living without relationships with priests, her point being not that the immigrants left the cities *because* they could not find a priest to love and follow but because they disliked American culture and, in one novel, also because they suffered discrimination in economic and social life. The absence of ties to a priest is a symbol of the larger lack of a community or home.[79]

In *Confessions of an Apostate* and *Bessy Conway*, the main characters return to Ireland. In the former, the lead character, Simon O'Hare rejects the chance for community in America for many years. Even when he returns to the Church in guilt and misery, Simon has no relationship with any particular priest. He is never shown interacting with the unnamed mission priest who restores him to the Church, or with another unnamed priest to whom he gives a large donation to build the first church in New Haven. Once Simon returns to Ireland, however, his life is centered not only on his faith but also on a priest, with a name. "The only one whom he visited was the parish priest, and with him many of his hours were spent," Sadlier reports. Bessy Conway also returns to Ireland, but hers is a happy ending. The absence of a relationship with a priest in her life in America reflects her status as a single woman and her ultimate rejection of life in her new country. She practices her faith but has no personal connection to the priest, Father Daly, who is never alone with her and never directs any help or advice specifically to her. Bessy's lack of community is reflected in her remark that in America she has "not one but myself and God's good Providence" to protect her. Once she returns to Ireland, Bessy reestablishes her community, reporting on her conversation with Father Ryan about visiting historic abbeys.[80]

In *Con O'Regan*, her novel in favor of colonization, Sadlier's characters reject life in Boston for the Irish settlement in the west. The priests in this novel are important only in Ireland and in the settlement, not in Boston. No priest plays a significant or ongoing role in the lives of the faithful Catholic Con and Winny O'Regan during all their years in the city. Sadlier makes one reference to a priest visiting Winny in the hospital, and to another when Con seeks his opinion on the move out west. That is all. In the settlement, by contrast, the priest, Father Doran, is "the greatest man . . . for years and years," seconded by the teacher he hired.[81]

These accounts of the importance and functions of priest characters in the Irish American novels show the lengths to which authors went to reproduce and justify the ties between priests and people that Tocqueville observed in Ireland. Priests in these novels are easy to love, certainly as rescuers but also as teachers, since even the most authoritarian of the writers is prepared to sacrifice the priests' power to preserve him as a figure who merits the loyalty of his followers. The Irish American Catholic community in these novels was united, first, by a common ethnicity and history and, second, by a shared and loving tie to their priest leaders.

Chapter 8

A WOMAN'S PLACE

Making the Communal Home

In the Irish American novels, women were the priests' main allies in building and maintaining the Catholic community. The authors offered a view of women that encouraged them to assume this role. They constructed an ideal woman who mirrored the circumstances of Irish immigrants and their daughters, offering the first alternative to the reigning nineteenth-century definition of women, the cult of domesticity.[1] The domestic ideal, promulgated in popular literature by Protestants and by the first generation of Catholic novelists, portrayed women as wives and mothers in middle-class homes, transmitting religious and moral values to their families.[2] The Irish Catholic construction showed women emigrating on their own, working for wages whether they were single or married, remaining unmarried for long periods, and heading their own households. This construction limited women in some ways, but it also legitimized the immigrants' lives, offered options for the future, and gave them power in their families and communities, sometimes even in opposition to traditional patriarchal norms.

Nineteenth-century Catholic popular fiction was written by men and women, most typically by men. The first generation of novelists generally agreed on the domestic ideal for Catholic women. The Irish Americans

189

basically agreed on the alternative vision. Anna Dorsey, in the first generation of Catholic writers, and Mary Anne Sadlier, in the second, shared the
same ideal of women as the male authors. The scholarship on the role of
women in popular fiction has concentrated on the domestic ideal, and it
usually includes only women writers, linking popular, sentimental, and domestic literature—however these terms are defined—with women authors. The scholars who have analyzed the construction of women in
Catholic fiction have also focused on Sadlier.[3] But many allegiances in addition to gender shaped the authors' work. In the Catholic context, at
least, the most important allegiances, the ties that defined the writers, were
the institutional objectives of the Church, the value systems of the changing Catholic audience, and the sense of fiction's purposes, all of which
Dorsey and Sadlier shared with their male colleagues.[4]

Women in the Early Catholic Novels: Fulfilling the Domestic Ideal

The ideal woman in the Catholic novels published from 1829 through the
1840s was similar in class, marital status, and occupation to the women
portrayed in the Protestant literature of domesticity. She was a wife and
mother in an upper-middle-class home who shaped the moral and spiritual lives of her husband and children.[5] For the single woman, the task was
to develop the moral character that would make it possible for her to
choose a good man with whom to build a home and family.

The first generation of Catholic writers usually made young single
women their lead characters. The focus on women reflected the belief, expressed by Orestes Brownson, that women were "the inveterate novel"
reader.[6] Whether Protestant or Catholic, the women tended to be well-off,
native-born Americans living in their own homes with both parents or,
more often, with a widowed parent, usually a father. The central drama in
the novels was essentially the same as the drama in domestic fiction. The
heroine takes time to develop her character and then selects a good man to
marry, often after rejecting an unworthy suitor preferred by her parent.

The distinguishing characteristic of the Catholic novels was that the
process of developing a character involved cultivating the true faith. The
Protestant heroines in these novels find the Church, often over the objec-

tions of a parent, and the Catholic heroines deepen their faith as they meet some challenge, such as a decline into poverty. As for a good man, that meant a Protestant who had converted, or a Catholic who had become more serious about his faith. The Protestant Pauline Seward is disowned by her father when she becomes a Catholic. She rejects two suitors, a non-practicing Catholic and the Protestant man whom she loves. By the end of the second volume, her father has relented, the young Protestant man has converted, and Pauline has happily agreed to marry him. The other Catholic element in the novels—and a departure from the domestic ideal—is that some good women become nuns. In Dorsey's *The Sister of Charity* and in Miles's *Loretto*, heroines enter the convent.

While the lead characters in these novels were usually single women, there were some exceptions. Pise's *Zenosius* and Dorsey's *The Student of Blenheim Forest* feature single men, Protestants, who seek the truth, convert, and become priests. Cannon was the most important exception during these years, focusing on men and assigning even key women characters to a subordinate role. In only one of his five novels of the 1830s and '40s, *Mora Carmody*, is the lead character a woman. Still, Cannon followed the same pattern as his colleagues in making the women well-off, native-born Americans. The Protestants, like the women in *Father Felix*, seek the true faith and a good Catholic man to marry. The Catholics, like Mora Carmody, endure adversity and then marry a good Catholic man or enter the convent. Mora Carmody refuses to marry the Protestant narrator because he is not a Catholic, then enters the convent before he is able to convert.

When married women appear in these early Catholic novels, they reside in their own homes with husbands and children. The central characters in Pise's first novel are the Protestant Mrs. Wolburn and her unmarried daughters, who live on an estate with their husband and father. Colonel Wolburn is head of the family and supports the women's interest in Catholicism. In Dorsey's *The Student of Blenheim Forest*, the mother of the Clavering family, who has a "lineage . . . ancient and respectable" from a Catholic "noble house" in England, has given up her Catholicism to marry her husband, and lives with him and their son Louis, the student of the title, on their estate.[7]

In these early years, widows were important characters only in the two novels of Miles. Even then, the widow Mrs. Cleveland in *Loretto* is not the head of her family; she lives with her daughter Agnes on the estate owned by her brother. In contrast, the mother in *The Governess*, as Miles writes, "stood without one earthly protector" and is the only important woman in the early Catholic novels to fill this position.[8]

In accordance with the domestic ideal, none of the well-off single or married women in these novels works outside the home, other than participating in charities. While the young German immigrant Marie Conradt in Dorsey's novel has money, she too does not work but tends to two or three bedridden people the priest has placed in her care. The two wealthy heroines of Cannon's *Father Felix*, one a Catholic and one a Protestant, are not involved in "mere ladies' work — the frittering away of precious hours, upon the embroidery, perhaps, of some article of no manner of use when finished — but such work as women can always do, who have any regard to the comfort of those around them, or the wants of the poor."[9]

Among the poor, some women do work, particularly those who have descended into poverty from better circumstances — like the German immigrant in Dorsey and the mother and daughter in Miles's *The Governess*. They regard working as an unfortunate necessity and a trial from God, which usually does not afford them economic independence or improvement. The young German immigrant earns "small sums . . . time after time by sewing and netting" and eventually by "fine washing and clear starching." Still, she cannot pay the rent, and just as she is about to pawn a family treasure, her father and the young man return and rescue her. The mother of the governess, Mary Lorn, in Miles's novel, who takes in sewing until her health declines, is resigned to her poverty without "the hope or wish to rise." Mary herself accepts the job as governess with a Protestant family, and is unique in the novels because she succeeds in earning a living for herself and her mother.[10] Miles is clear, however, that in education and background, Mary is of the same class as the Protestant family for whom she works. Her mother is deeply afraid that Mary will be treated "like a hireling." In addition, the father of the Protestant family has, since his youth, been in love with Mary's mother. In other words, Mary may be the governess but she is not living in the home of strangers of a different educational or economic background. At several points, Miles remarks that the Lorn mother and daughter feel awkward about their new class position; the governess reflects on "the moat which wealth digs between itself and poverty."[11]

Women in these novels who have always been poor tend not to work. In some cases they are too old, such as the deformed woman supported by the Irishman Barney in Dorsey's *The Student of Blenheim Forest*. But the younger poor women living in the cottages near Loretto also do not work. Their circumstances improve only when the heroine, Agnes Cleveland, acts on their behalf. Irish characters are the exception. The casual references to working poor women throughout these novels usually involve Irish women, such as the Seward family's cook in Bryant's novel and the domestic servants that the governess and her mother encounter on their way to mass.

Because he included the poor and the Irish among his minor characters, Cannon was more likely than the other authors to refer to women who work. He comments briefly on an Irish domestic servant in *Oran, the Outcast*, and in *Harry Layden*, after the Irish Hugh Redmond is fired from his teaching position, his wife goes to work making shirts as piecework. Neither she nor her husband is successful. After being raised in an orphanage, their daughter, Mary, also works. When the hero encounters her, Mary is being harassed in the streets and explains that she is "forced by the labour of her hands to earn her daily bread," and so is subject to such treatment. The widowed Mrs. Dowd in *Father Felix* runs a boarding house and also does housework. She supports herself and her son and is the most successful poor working woman in these novels.

The early Catholic writers, to a surprising extent, also mirror Protestant domestic fiction in linking women and religion with the family home rather than the Church. The single Protestant heroines conduct their readings and research in their own homes. They go to church and encounter a priest only when they are far along in the process of conversion. In Pise, where the priest plays an unusually large role, Father Rowland still comes to the Wolburn home to instruct the women, staying overnight to complete the process.

Of course, heroines who are already Catholic go to mass and receive the sacraments in church. In that sense, their religious lives are centered outside the home. Agnes Cleveland, the heroine of Miles's *Loretto*, is more involved with church institutions than others, since she attended boarding school in a Catholic convent, and she and her mother often consult the priest. Even in this novel, however, the mother is the main force in her daughter's religious life, supporting her interest in becoming a nun against the doubts of the priest and opposition of her uncle, who owns the estate. Other Catholic heroines rely even less on church institutions. Cannon's Mora Carmody faces the difficulties of anti-Catholicism, instructs her Protestant suitor in the truths of her faith, and rejects his proposal of marriage in and around her own home without recourse to a church or priest. Catholic mothers also usually take care of the religious education of their children at home. The mother in Dorsey's *The Student of Blenheim Forest* builds an oratorio on her estate, where she keeps the Catholic books her own mother had given her. She helps guide her son to Catholicism in this oratorio and, in the process, revives her own faith. Miles, in *The Governess*, says that Mary Lorn's education has been "superintended by her mother."[12]

Women in the Irish American Novels: An Alternative Ideal

In contrast to the women in this early fiction, Irish American heroines vary in age, marital status, class, and occupation. Some are single women, young and old; others are married wives and mothers; many are widows. Some have come to America with husbands and children, some on their own, and some are the American-born daughters of immigrants. Most are laywomen; a few are nuns. Most are poor or working class, but a few are middle class or wealthy. Whatever the class or marital status, some are employed and some are not. The women also reside in many different types of residences. This variety of heroines, some of whom flouted the domestic ideal, matched the circumstances of Irish immigrant women and also represented legitimate options for them.

Single Women: Options for Emigration, Work, and Marriage

Like those of Cannon in the previous decades, the Irish American novels of the 1850s are centered on young men rather than young women. Roddan's *John O'Brien*, Sadlier's *Willy Burke*, and Quigley's *The Cross and the Shamrock* trace the lives of their young heroes and include women as sisters, playing minor roles, or as widowed mothers, who are more important. Sadlier's *The Blakes and Flanagans* features two married couples who illustrate good and bad lives. Among the American-born generation, the novel focuses on the sons, Edward Flanagan and Henry Blake. In Cannon's *Bick-*

erton, a young woman, the immigrant's daughter, is the central character, but in his subsequent *Tighe Lyfford*, men take on the more important roles. Only in the 1860s do single women become the focus of Irish American novels, reflecting changing patterns of immigration. Although women outnumbered men among immigrants from the poorest parts of Ireland even in the 1850s, in the succeeding years they began to outnumber men among the immigrants as a whole. Increasing portions of the women, moreover, were unmarried and between the ages of fifteen and thirty-five.[13]

The single women immigrants in the novels who come to America leave their Irish homes and parents behind. They are not like Dorsey's German heroine, who emigrates with her father.[14] The authors seem aware that their young female characters represent a departure from traditional views of women. For that reason, they make it clear that the women are not totally alone. They emigrate only with their parents' consent and often with their financial help. Employers may also help: Bessy Conway's passage is paid for by her new employer as well as by her parents.

Moreover, though they are without their parents, the young women often come with brothers, cousins, or employers. Kate Crolly, the heroine of McCorry's *Mount Benedict*, as well as Sadlier's Elinor Preston come with older brothers; Bessy Conway comes with her employer and with cousins and friends; the two young women in *The Lost Rosary* who emigrate together were cousins and hoped to meet their Irish fiancés already in America. In *Annie Reilly*, the heroine emigrates by herself but plans to stay with an older couple from her village who had emigrated twenty years earlier. This novel, published in 1873, is the first in which an earlier generation of immigrants is available to provide assistance. Sadlier's Winny O'Regan is the only heroine in these novels who seems to have come to the United States without companions anywhere.

The authors sometimes express their ambivalence about young women characters who emigrate without traditional "protectors." Bessy Conway, in Sadlier's novel, advises Irish mothers that "America is a bad place for young girls to go to, unless they have their father, or brothers, or somebody to look after them." An old Irish woman in McCorry's *The Lost Rosary* says, "God look on them that haven't the firm hand to guide them."[15]

Yet despite the ambivalence, Sadlier and McCorry show their heroines thriving, without fathers, brothers, or other guides to protect them. Bessy Conway's first employer ends up returning to Europe, and from then on, Bessy chooses any mentors she may require. Her cousin, Ned Finigan, who had promised Bessy's father that "he would look after her," becomes a saloon keeper and an alcoholic. Accordingly, when the Irish mothers on the receiving end of Bessy's advice ask about her support system in America, Bessy replies that she had "not one" person to rely on but only "myself and God's good Providence."[16] Kate Crolly in McCorry's *Mount Benedict* emigrates with her brother, but the two are separated immediately after their arrival. In McCorry's *The Lost Rosary*, the two O'Donnell cousins, who come with each other, do not find their fiancés for many years and still manage to do very well in America. Sadlier's Winny O'Regan establishes herself in Boston without help and then, years later, provides protection to her brother. Despite the authors' protestations, the novels show that young women can manage quite well without protectors, male or female.

The novels offered options to the Irish Catholic single women regarding work as well as emigration. Heroines work and—unlike most of the poor women in the earlier Catholic novels—they succeed in achieving economic independence. They are employed as domestic servants, with a few exceptions: one ends up "in the work-room of a tailoring establishment"; another is an "overseer in a dry goods concern, where some fifty girls were employed at slop work"; and a third works as saleswoman in a shoe store. There are also the apple sellers, referred to as apple women.[17] Most exemplary characters in these other positions eventually move on to domestic service. A few of the single women immigrant characters—those who arrive with some education—do not start at the bottom of the ladder. Kate Crolly in *Mount Benedict* finds work as a companion, rather than a maid or cook.[18] All of these women earn sufficient wages to support themselves and to send money to those they left behind.

Very few single immigrants in these novels are in the better-off classes, but one who is—Bertha Von Weigel in Sadlier's *Old and New*—does not work, except for charities. But unlike their predecessors, the Irish American novelists extol work; they do not present it as an unwelcome necessity or a trial from God. Rather McCorry, in *The Lost Rosary*, talks about the "trial" of "enforced idleness" and the "love of work in itself."[19]

In contrast to the immigrants, the young single women born or raised in America occupy a greater variety of class positions and have more choices regarding work. Those who are poor work; the elder Conlon daughter in Cannon's final novel, *Tighe Lyfford*, is a domestic servant. But daughters born in America who are middle class may or may not work. Sadlier never mentions the Flanagan daughters working, for example, and the well-educated daughter of the upper-middle-class Murrays, in her *Old and New*, sponsors charities, following the example of her aristocratic mentor.[20] But some of these daughters do work for wages even if they have other means, a departure from previous Catholic fiction. When the wealthy Protestant woman in Sadlier's novel offers to provide for the Burke daughters, Willy Burke replies, "I want them to get their decent trade learned, so that they'll be able to do for themselves; and I'd rather a thousand times see them working hard with Mrs. Williams [the Catholic woman with the straw bonnet business] . . . than to have them sitting up in idleness with Mrs. Watkins and the other 'rich lady.'" The immigrants' daughters in Roddan's *John O'Brien* and Cannon's *Bickerton* also work, as teachers. In Cannon's novel, the young woman insists on working despite the priest's offer of support; she would not "waste the time and talents—whatever they are—that God has given me, in unproductive idleness."[21]

The Irish American authors also offer their single women characters options about marriage. This is another departure from the cult of domesticity fiction, whether Protestant or Catholic, that typically centers on a woman's efforts to develop her moral or religious character, marry a good man of her own choosing, and begin to make a religious home and family. Only one lead character in the Irish American fiction resembles these earlier heroines, in terms of class and options. Sadlier's aristocratic Bertha Von Weigel in *Old and New* is wealthy and lives with a parent—in this case, her mother—in a New York City mansion. Bertha is pursued by an Anglo-Irish aristocrat, has doubts about the young man's character, sees his reform, marries him, and lives the rest of her life in Ireland. She is often alone with the young man and is not warned about associating with him. The narrative arc for Bertha—who faces no challenges to her identity or moral character except her attachment to the young man—focuses on her relationship.

With this exception, the Irish American writers use the conventions of romance to make another point—that, as Sadlier puts it, "it's only religion that can make people really happy, even in this world."[22] The romance of these novels concerns the drama of immigration from a Catholic to a Protestant country, which requires the heroine to maintain her Catholic identity against all obstacles, and to play a part in saving her original family and building a new community.[23] In addition, the Irish immigrant heroine, unlike her counterparts in domestic fiction, does not undergo a series of trials to develop or strengthen her character. Instead, these heroines are formed by their earlier life in Ireland; the struggle is to maintain the values they have been taught.

As the authors well knew, however, readers expected traditional happy endings for their heroines. *Alice Riordan*, which Sadlier first published in serial form in a newspaper, concerns a single woman who, in this case, emigrates with her blind father to Canada. Over the course of the story, Alice rejects two marriage proposals and, at the story's end, remains pious, happily employed, charitable to the poor, and devoted to her father. As Alice says, "I am happy, father. . . . Happy with you—happy in performing the part which God assigned to me! Oh, indeed, I am as happy as I can expect to be here below." The first edition of the book simply reproduced the plot of the serial, but three years later, Sadlier explained, she added "another chapter to the original work, as a sort of magic glass, whereby those who were so anxious to know 'what became of Alice?' can have a peep into the privacy of her after-life."[24] In this chapter, Sadlier reports, without much ado, that Alice has married a respectable man, though still ends the novel with the happy death of her good and pious father.

Sadlier and later authors continue in this vein in their novels about single women in America: their plots do not concern the women's development of character on the path to a good husband but instead deal with their steadfastness and ability to maintain good character in the face of prejudice and temptations. Bessy Conway's experience as a domestic servant is quite different from the experience of the governess in Miles's novel. Bessy has no mother in the neighborhood and must endure a Protestant employer who fires her because she refuses to participate in evening prayers, as well as fellow servants and immigrants who tempt her with "dancing saloons." She has no problems with the secret longings of Protestant householders or with the love of their sons, nor is she particularly conscious of the "moat" that divides the classes. In fact, she is delighted to secure a position as servant to the Irish Catholic Mrs. Delaney. The only heroines in the novels who actually improve their characters are those who convert to Catholicism, such as Cecilia Morton, the Protestant ward in McCorry's *Mount Benedict*, who learns to be less proud and selfish. Bessy Conway's experience is also quite different from that of the aristocratic Bertha Von Weigel in Sadlier's other novel. Like Bertha, Bessy is pursued by an Anglo-Irish aristocrat, has doubts about the young man's character, sees his reform, marries him, and lives the rest of her life in Ireland. Unlike Bertha, however, Bessie is warned never to associate with the young man and confronts many challenges to her identity and moral character apart from her attachment to him. The narrative arc for Bessy does not focus on her relationship; the drama in her life concerns her triumph over the temptations of America and, finally, over the famine itself. There is some suspense about Bessy Conway's courtship, but it pales in comparison to the tension generated by her encounters with American life as she struggles to survive as a Catholic woman.

Most of the authors follow the path Sadlier adopted in *Alice Riordan* and *Bessy Conway*. They try to satisfy the romantic interests of their readers by adding at least a brief account of a heroine's marriage to a good man at the novel's end (after making the point that she had successfully maintained her Catholicism). Sadlier adopts this strategy in *Con O'Regan*: the hero's sister Winny retains her Irish Catholic identity in Boston despite hard menial work, a hostile Protestant employer, and sexual advances from a Protestant doctor, before moving out west. She is "well and happy" and, in fact, "thought at first it was all a dream," as she lived in the exclusively Irish community surrounded by her brother and their Boston friends, all under the leadership of the priest. Then, on page 393 of the 405-page novel, at a community get-together, the priest teases her briefly and affectionately about a young man named Thady Landrigan, and Winny blushes in response. Thady Landrigan never appears in the novel, but five pages later, in the novel's concluding chapter, Sadlier tells readers that Winny has married the young man in the local church. As in *Alice Riordan*, Sadlier seems to resent having to include marriage as a part of Winny's happiness, describing it in as little detail as possible. In her scant, two-page account of the wedding—mostly given over to the point that Winny's brother, mother-in-law, and friends all endorse the union—Sadlier is parsimonious in her praise of the young man. He had "inherited" the "careless, happy temperament" of his mother, so that "it was seldom indeed that Thady *did* think, and that day [of his wedding] he thought less than ever."[25]

The heroines of McCorry and McElgun must also first survive famine and/or eviction in Ireland, harrowing journeys, and the various challenges of life in America, maintaining their faith and virtue and achieving economic independence, before marriage is presented as a possibility. The immigrants accidentally reencounter men they had known in Ireland. On page 238 of the 245-page *Annie Reilly*, the heroine is attending mass when the young man, who happens to be there, notices her. The various couples tend to marry within days of these chance encounters, sparing the authors from having to provide any details about courtship.[26]

The authors adopt the same practice in discussing the American-born daughters of the immigrants, informing their readers at the novels' ends that the young women have married. In *Bickerton*, Cannon's heroine retains her attachment to Irish Catholicism through her long years in Protestant foster care until she is rescued by the priest and finds refuge and peace in the convent. At the end, she marries Fred Hubbard, the man who rescued her, and the convent, from the mob. In the final sections of *The Blakes and Flanagans*, Sadlier also informs her readers that the Flanagan daughters marry good Irish Catholic men, though she doesn't name or describe them.

Although the compromise arrangement allowing for the eventual marriage of the younger women was adopted in most of the novels, there were some in which heroines or minor female characters were not married by the final chapter. Through these characters, the authors introduced permanently single women—who were not nuns—into the Catholic ideal. The lead female character in Boyce's *Mary Lee* is Kate Petersham, an Anglo-Irish aristocrat. Kate is a beautiful and intelligent woman who remains single from the novel's beginning to its end without any commentary whatsoever from anyone on her status. In his review of the novel, Orestes Brownson, with his very traditional view of women, writes that Kate "is a glorious creature, full of life and mischief, tender and affectionate . . . but the author has judged wisely not to marry her; for a young lady who prides herself on sailing a boat, or riding a steeplechase . . . is not precisely the woman a quiet man would take for his wife."[27]

Women characters also remain unmarried in some Sadlier novels. Elinor Preston in Canada is single until her death, rejecting one tempting

ANNIE REILLY.

Figure 8.1. McElgun portrays Annie Reilly in church on the morning that she and James O'Rourke meet by chance. Courtesy of Wright American Fiction Project, Indiana University Libraries.

marriage proposal because the young man is a Protestant. In *Old and New*, the upper-middle-class Alice Murray—who is focused on her charities—as well as several daughters of the new rich families also remain unmarried. One of the new rich daughters decides to care for her father, who plans to "leave her what would keep her independent all her days, and then she'd be sure to have plenty of friends and a choice of homes every day of her life." Another daughter takes employment with the Von Weigels in Ireland, where she develops a more robust character than she had formed within her own family.[28]

The authors tended to downplay marriage as a component of the good life not only in their stories of single women but also in their accounts of Irish Catholic wives, especially in America.

Mothers: Wives, Widows, and Others

In Ireland, wife characters are usually shown with living husbands. When the single immigrants reflect on their earlier lives, they typically speak of two parents; any deaths tend to happen when the children are at least teenagers. Similarly, the married women who emigrate come with their husbands and children. But in America, only one novel from 1850 to 1873 places a faithful Catholic family, with two living parents, at the center of the plot: Sadlier's *The Blakes and Flanagans*. One other novel, Quigley's *Profit and Loss*, features an intact nuclear family for some years in America, but then the father dies and the widowed mother takes over. Minor characters in traditional nuclear families appear in most of the novels, but here the authors do not need to explicate relationships between husbands and wives.[29]

The Irish American authors do not depart significantly from their Catholic predecessors in depicting so few intact nuclear families in their novels. The difference is that the Irish Americans write about families headed by widows rather than widowers—in both of Quigley's novels, in much of Sadlier, and in Cannon's final work. The elderly childless women in the novels, such as the apple woman Biddy in *Mount Benedict*, are also widows.

Many other women in the Irish American novels share an uncertain marital status, meaning that the authors fail to mention a husband, living or dead. In *Willy Burke*, the priest finds the well-off Mrs. Williams to raise the deceased widow's daughters. According to the priest, Mrs. Williams is a "worthy woman who carries on the straw-bonnet business pretty extensively" and "has no children of her own." Sadlier never mentions a Mr. Williams. Mrs. Malcolm, another character in *Willy Burke*, is an "old Scotch housekeeper" in the boarding house where Willy and his brother live after their mother's death. Sadlier never mentions a Mr. Malcolm or any children. McCorry in *The Lost Rosary* includes two "old" Irish immigrant women who establish a boarding house in New York City. One is Mrs. McGlone, whose title indicates that she is married, but McCorry never mentions a husband or children. The other is Moll Hanley; here, the absence of a "Mrs." suggests Moll is single. Some of the apple women who appear in the novels are also of uncertain status.[30] This focus on mature women without husbands will have implications for the Irish American authors' depictions of work and discussions of the women's communal functions.

On the subject of work, poor married women in the novels are employed, even if they have husbands and young children. In *Willy Burke*, Sadlier indicates that the wife of a sick husband has taken over the superintendent duties in the tenement apartment where the Burkes live; in *Con O'Regan*, she refers briefly to a poor couple—a man who works and his wife who takes in washing—in order to save money.[31] Among the poor widows, Mrs. Burke in Sadlier's novel and Mrs. Conlon in Cannon's *Tighe Lyfford* take in housework by the day in their own homes or work in the homes of their employers. In Sadlier's *Con O'Regan*, another widow with children takes in boarders. The homes of these poor women, then, are also places of work.[32]

But well-off wives with living husbands actually referred to in the stories do not work—and are the major exception to the tendency of Irish American authors to portray working women. Among major characters, these married women include Sadlier's Mrs. Blake and Mrs. Flanagan, and Mrs. Mulroony in Quigley's *Profit and Loss*. They do not work. Neither do minor characters, including Mrs. Delaney—who employs Bessy Conway—and the wives of the successful Irish immigrant storeowners, mechanics, and longshoremen in *Old and New*, *The Lost Rosary*, and *Annie Reilly*. Sadlier praises the newly rich Mrs. Gallagher in *Old and New*, who is "willing to work" with her husband both at the start of his business and after he is ruined, thereby "laying the foundations of their prosperity."[33] But Mrs. Gallagher does not work in the years of her husband's success. No author describes a woman like Sadlier herself, who had a middle-class life with a living husband and six children as well as a career as a writer, translator, and publisher. Perhaps Sadlier thought of herself as working for the family business. Well-off women who were specifically identified as widows, such as Madame Von Weigel in Sadlier's *Old and New*, Mrs. Mulroony in the later sections of Quigley's *Profit and Loss*, and the baroness in Cannon's *Tighe Lyfford*, also do not work.

In this view that better-off women, including wives with husbands mentioned in the stories as well as widows, do not work, the Irish Americans resembled those who explicated the ideal of domesticity. For the Irish Americans, however, this view is not as much of a limit to their women characters. Very few of the heroines are in these categories, and the authors are quite willing to portray better-off middle-aged and older women who work—they simply ignore the issue of husbands. These working women include Mrs. Williams, who owns the straw bonnet business; Mrs. Malcolm, the housekeeper of the boarding house where the Burke brothers reside; the two women in McCorry's novel, who establish the lodging house; and Else Curley, the old woman in Boyce's novel, who runs her small farm. McCorry describes the character Moll Hanley as "a romping good worker," and simply ignores the issue of her marital status.[34] Colleen McDannell, in her analysis of the nineteenth-century idea of a Catholic home, concludes that when Irish American writers want interesting female characters, they ignore the women's husbands, thus evading the problem of paternal authority.[35] Interesting female characters in these novels include women who work even if they do not have to.

As in their treatment of single women, the authors do not present work as a painful necessity or a comedown, either for poor or better-off women. Biddy, the apple woman in McCorry's *Mount Benedict*, explains that in earlier years she had a good job but then lost it, and concludes: "there's no disgrace in following up any daicent employment, and so I just . . . commenced a little trade."[36] Through work, the women support themselves as well as their families and associates.

On the related question of whether, in the end, the wife and mother who did not work outside the home represented the ideal woman, the

Irish Americans sent a message that distinguished them from the writers of domestic fiction. To some degree, they advanced the view that marriage was the ideal state, based on the ultimate fate of most, even if not all, of the single heroines. Yet at the same time, they gave such fleeting descriptions of the single heroines' encounters with men and featured so few women with living husbands that one cannot come away from the novels with the idea that a woman making a home for husband and children represented their vision of the ideal life. Such a woman is not a symbol the Catholic group could rally around.

As this discussion of single and married women suggests, nuns were not particularly important characters in the Irish American novels. While the earlier Catholic novelists loved to send single and widowed heroines into the convent, the Irish Americans did not. Among major characters, only Kate Crolly in *Mount Benedict* is an exception—she enters the convent after being reunited with her brother.[37] This change may reflect Orestes Brownson's complaints about the plots of the early writers. It also reflects the economic circumstances of the immigrants, who needed to earn money for themselves and their Irish families and would not have the dowries required by the convents of the time.

While several novelists refer briefly to professed nuns, only Sadlier, in *The Blakes and Flanagans*, and McCorry, in *Mount Benedict*, include nuns among their characters. In both cases, the nuns play minor roles but are the most accomplished women in the novels, both before and after they enter the convent. Nuns are in fact the only women in any of the novels who are praised for professional accomplishments. Sadlier describes the "excellent understanding... strong and vigorous mind... seconded by all the advantages of education" of the superior of St. Peter's school. Of the nun's aristocratic background, she writes: "her family ... [was] one of the first in her native county." The superior of McCorry's *Mount Benedict* "received the greater part of her highly polished education on the continent of Europe, was a ripe scholar in modern languages," and had "a well-trained, scholarly mind." Both Sadlier and McCorry also emphasize the nuns' authority: McCorry comments on the superior's "grave responsibilities," including superintending the nuns, the novices, seventy to eighty pupils, and "teachers and servants for in-door and out-door work."[38] Through these portraits of nuns, the Irish Catholic writers created educated professional women in responsible positions, women who were much less likely to appear in the Protestant domestic fiction of the time.

The prevalence of Irish American households headed by women in these novels was, to some extent, simply a reflection of reality. Scholars have commented on the large proportion of such households among the famine-era immigrants.[39] But the preference for women unaccompanied by husbands also allowed the authors to include in their plots adult women who worked and achieved independence in economic and social life. It also made it easier for them to advance the view that women were the main allies of the priests in building the Catholic community.

The Ideal Catholic Woman:
Acting for Others and Building the Community

All of these heroines—the immigrants and the American-born, with their varied marital, class, and employment situations—could fulfill the Catholic ideal because, like all Christians, they were motivated by the desire to benefit others as well as themselves, and because, as women, they directed this motivation to serving the Catholic community. It is in this last respect that the good Catholic woman departed so significantly from the domestic ideal.

Just as good women emigrated for unselfish reasons, they also worked for the sake of others, typically in service occupations. In Sadlier's *Bessy Conway*, Bessy's employer notes her selfless attitude, advising her to "cherish those unselfish dispositions and think more of others than of yourself."[40]

Mothers in these novels also showed selfless devotion to their children. The newly bereaved father in Cannon's *Bickerton* teaches his daughter "how good, how patient, how loving, how forgetful of self" her mother "had always been." Other good women act as mothers in a broader sense: Sadlier's *Willy Burke* says that Mrs. Williams, of the straw bonnet business, has been "a mother to" his sisters. Mrs. Malcolm, the housekeeper in the novel, looks after the young man, defending him when he is falsely accused of theft.[41]

Indeed, many of the women characters extended their care beyond their immediate circle. The wealthy baroness in Cannon's *Tighe Lyfford* provides housing for the poor residents of her community as part of her charitable activities. In McCorry's *The Lost Rosary*, Moll Hanley and Mrs. McGlone establish a lodging house for Irish immigrants. Nuns illustrate an even higher level of selfless devotion than other good women. Sadlier says that the superior of the Catholic school devotes herself "to Him in the service of his creatures," caring for the poor and destitute like a "ministering angel." Despite her accomplishments, the selfless nun does not seek any public acclaim. "Had she been a Protestant . . . she might have taken the lead at public meetings, edited a daily newspaper . . . delivered public lectures, and written huge volumes on metaphysics or philosophy."[42]

In comparison, the old women in the novels seem to have some leeway in their actions and motivations, though in the end, they, too, exhibit the typical characteristics of good women. Boyce's Else Curley smokes, curses, and keeps a gun. McCorry's "gruff" Moll Hanley also smokes, drinks, and stays late at parties. In one incident, Moll went to a job site and "roared" her objections to an overseer who had struck an employee.[43] The old women also occasionally resist the requirements of selflessness. In McCorry's *Mount Benedict*, Biddy the apple woman rejects the heroine Kate's advice to refrain from counterattack: "it's well I'm not as good as you, for then I couldn't gratify my ould spite at them." Biddy also gives voice to McCorry's own suppressed attitude toward the mob that attacked the convent. She "was . . . up in arms, and everywhere . . . rousing her countrymen to a sense of their duty" and was "well nigh being the cause of retaliatory measures on the part of the outraged Irish."[44]

But the old women, too, serve others, at times standing in as examples of simple piety much like the slaves in the earlier Catholic novels. The apple woman Biddy in *Mount Benedict* tells the proud Cecilia Morton that one of the nuns had been a great singer but never mentions it. McCorry responds: "unconscious Biddy, what a teacher thou wert without knowing it!"[45] But Biddy also does "all in her power to assist the nuns in their flight." When she loses her apples in the effort, she responds, "What matter?" explaining that "it's a good work in which I'm engaged." McCorry's Moll Hanley, who establishes the boarding house and defends its residents, acts as if she were "the appointed guardian of her sex in all America." Her "kindly disposed nature . . . [and] warm and generous heart . . . made Moll . . . a perfect woman."[46]

This unselfishness simply fulfilled the Christian ideal, which, in a sense, was gender neutral. Men also emigrated for the sake of others and, as will be seen in the next chapter, tried to succeed for the sake of others as well. But the authors placed greater emphasis on the unselfishness of women, unless the men were priests. McCorry, in *The Lost Rosary*, applauds Irish women for their "self-abnegation" (a term he never applies to men), as well as their willingness "to make any and every sacrifice" in fulfilling their duties to others. In contrast, when he praises a young male immigrant who leaves his friend in the city to pursue a job, he writes: "Quite right. . . . True friendship is valuable and pleasant, but must not be indulged in at the expense of the great battle of life."[47]

In the working world, also, the men in these novels pursue a variety of careers as clerks, laborers, soldiers, or stockbrokers—but are seen as serving others simply because they are working to support their families. Good women, on the other hand, serve others both by supporting the family and, usually, by taking up service occupations. Mrs. Williams, owner of the straw bonnet business in Sadlier's *Willy Burke*, is unique in not being in service, though her business is still centered on the world of women. Nuns, although praised for their intellectual and professional attainments, were invariably in teaching or nursing.

Authors also refer specifically to women when they applaud particular selfless acts. Roddan comments that "the Boston Irish Catholic young women, who do the work in families, or otherwise labor hard for their bread . . . have built every church in Boston. . . . Their monument is a church in every quarter of the city." Con O'Regan, in Sadlier's novel, tells his sister Winny: "I'm afeard it's what you left yourself bare and naked to send home money! and I suppose it's often the same story might be told of them that sends home money to Ireland." Sadlier then comments in a footnote: "Con's surmise was perfectly correct. . . . We have all of us known numerous instances of poor servant girls sending home several pounds in the course of a couple of years, from an average wage of *five dollars* a month."[48]

Women's selfless motivations were directed primarily to building and maintaining the Catholic community. Both women and men made the Church home, but maintaining that home was primarily the task of women. Unlike the women who exemplified the domestic ideal, Catholic women were not anchored in nuclear families and homes, even if they had them; they were anchored in the larger religious community. The novelists of this period made little effort to describe the homes of the immigrants; at most they called them neat and tidy. Only the wealthy Von Weigels in Sadlier's *Old and New* tried to reproduce the fixtures of a church in their home, "fitting up" one room in their mansion "as an oratory."[49]

Irish American authors also portrayed good women, rather than men, as emotionally attached to their communities. Though in rare instances, a married woman character initiated the emigration of her family, in most cases, women were shown as reluctant to leave friends and neighbors united in a local church under the leadership of the priest.[50] In novels by Sadlier and Cannon, Irish wives questioned the decision to emigrate and their husbands reminded them of the economic realities or, in Cannon, the chance for freedom. In Quigley's *Profit and Loss*, the husband expresses regret at leaving Ireland but not because of the loss of community. Instead, he tells his wife, "it will break my heart to leave this place where I labored so long and made so many improvements in vain." Typically, any married woman who expresses interest in emigrating—even for the sake of her family—is not to be admired. Mrs. Clarkson, the insincere convert in McCorry's *The Lost Rosary*, leaves a good home rather than see her daughters marry "some ignorant clodhoppers."[51]

Whatever their regrets, good women act to reestablish these communities in America. Single women seek to maintain loyalty to the Church, by their example and teaching. Winny O'Regan in Sadlier's novel finds her newly arrived brother a job and a respectable boarding house in which to live, and advises him about church teachings. She tells him that "dances . . . were forbidden by the clergy at home, an' it's ten times worse they are here." Bessy Conway suggests that her fellow servants obey their employer and fulfill their religious obligations. After Bessy returns from mass one morning, she asks Bridget, the cook, if she had been to mass. Bridget says no and Bessy replies: "why didn't you get up and go to 6 o'clock Mass . . . you'd have been back at seven, and have plenty of time to do your work." Bessy also refuses, on behalf of all the servants, to participate in the Protestant prayer services, telling her employer: "*we're* all Catholics, ma'am, and we can't join in your prayers."[52]

The task of the women who are mothers, or act as such, is to maintain the community by making sure that the young and vulnerable learn and follow church teachings. Even when fathers are present, mothers are responsible for their children's religious upbringing. In *Confessions of an*

Apostate, Sadlier equates mother and religion: Simon O'Hare's teacher in America tells the young man that his mother, who writes to the teacher, "says you're beginning to neglect *her*, and that that's a sure sign that you're neglecting your God." Sadlier also describes Simon's early life in Ireland as though only his mother was involved—even though his father was alive until the boy was sixteen. The only reference to his father in Simon's account of his religious upbringing is when he recalls the "simple joy of our parents" when he and his brother and sister made their first communion.[53]

In fulfilling this task, Irish Catholic mothers in the novels certainly teach their children prayers at home. But since church teachings are seen as best transmitted by the Church itself, the mother's task is to bring the young to the Church and its institutions. The Church, not the mother in the home, is primarily responsible for shaping character and imparting religious and moral truths. This distinction between home and church, putting religious function squarely in the hands of the latter, distinguishes the Irish American novels from both the Protestant and early Catholic literature of domesticity.[54]

In *Confessions of an Apostate*, Sadlier portrays the life of a mother in Ireland. The lead character Simon O'Hare recalls the "devotional assemblies in the . . . chapel" and that "it was there my mother took me by the hand on Sunday and holiday mornings to hear Mass, followed by a colloquial discourse from his reverence Father Brannigan." Simon also remembers that when he asked his mother, who "was not much versed in hagiography," what the saints used to do, she advised him to "ask Father Brannigan."[55]

In America, also, mothers must see to their children's religious upbringing, and the authors emphasize the importance of the Church and its schools even more strongly. That is obviously the case in families headed by widows or by women whose husbands never appear in the story, but, just as in Ireland, mothers tend to assume this role even when a husband is mentioned. Quigley, in *Profit and Loss*, treats the father of backsliding Nellie just as Sadlier treats the Irish father of Simon O'Hare. Nellie is always confronted, chastised, and, at one point, rescued solely by her mother. As Quigley writes, Nellie, after her rescue, came again "beneath the maternal roof." The reader hears of a husband and father only when Quigley refers to Nellie's "parents."[56]

For the mothers in these novels, the first priority is to instill faithfulness to the Church in their children. The widowed Mrs. Mulroony, in Quigley's *Profit and Loss*, is not impressed when her son wins prize money at the public school, noting only that he is neglecting his religious obligations. She rates his Catholicism even above his life, insisting that he be removed from a Protestant house even though he has been seriously injured. Fortunately, the priest arrives to dissuade her.[57] The idea that a woman's task is to bring her children to the Church for their formation is symbolized by the actions of the widowed Mrs. Burke and Mrs. O'Clery in the first novels of Sadlier and Quigley. They bring their children to the church for services and lessons and then, on their respective deathbeds, turn the children over to the priest. Sadlier and Quigley are also clear that religious education is best left to the Church, not to parents or mothers in the home, when they argue that children should attend Catholic schools. The message of their two novels is that parents who choose the public schools and give religious instruction at home are following a dangerous path even when the home efforts are supplemented by the priest's Sunday school. The import of this attitude can be seen in the convert Orestes Brownson's criticism of Sadlier's *The Blakes and Flanagans*, which, he says, gives too much emphasis to the influence of the Catholic schools rather than the "home and the family" in the moral development of children.[58]

The women who functioned as mother substitutes in these novels serve the same function in their working lives. Mrs. Williams of the straw bonnet business makes sure the Burke daughters go to church for mass and religious education. Mrs. McGlone and Moll Hanley, in *The Lost Rosary*, not only establish the boarding house for young immigrants but also accompany the boarders to church and advise the young women that they should "never forget the ould faith nor the ould shamrock."[59]

The sole responsibility for transmitting loyalty to the Church can easily be assumed by these women because they do not have living husbands actually present in the novels. That is not the case for the relatively few women whose husbands appear in the stories. In Sadlier's *The Blakes and Flanagans* and Quigley's *Profit and Loss* (before the husband died), the men make the important decisions—including about the education of children—which suggests that these authors consider patriarchy to be the norm in family life. Sadlier and Quigley, as well as other authors, also comment about the importance of patriarchy. Sadlier's Madame Von Weigel, for example, quotes St. Paul that wives should obey their husbands.[60]

It is easy for Sadlier and Quigley to adopt this position when a husband and wife agree with church teachings. Mrs. Flanagan, for example, simply supports her husband. On the subject of Catholic schools, "it was well known that, with all her mildness, she was, on this point, to the full as inflexible as" he.[61] When husbands and wives are not in agreement, however, the authors confront the tensions that might arise between a woman's function and the norms of patriarchy. In the Sadlier and Quigley novels, Mr. Blake and Mr. Mulroony opt for the public schools despite their wives' preference for the Catholic system. Both authors resolve the tension in favor of the women's function, thereby undermining the patriarchal norms.

In Sadlier's novel, Mrs. Blake is not happy about her husband Miles's decision and believes that priests are the "better judges . . . of what was right to be done." When Father Power insists that Miles remove his son from the school, Mrs. Blake makes it clear that she and her husband engaged in many "a hard tussle" on the topic. Here, Sadlier undermines patriarchy by showing that it was the husband who made the wrong decision on the matter, then goes further by holding Mrs. Blake equally responsible because she followed her husband's lead. When Mrs. Blake comes to Father Power about the marriage of her daughter to a Protestant, the priest—seeing the marriage as the result of the daughter's attendance at public schools—says: "you must all take the consequences of your own rashness—shall I say presumption." In an author commentary, Sadlier writes that in later life, "conscience was lashing both [Blake] husband and wife; they could not but see in their present desolation, the effect of past imprudence, . . . rashness and presumption," as though Mrs. Blake as well as her husband had permitted the children to go to the public school.[62]

Sadlier is prepared to blame Mrs. Blake for being too submissive to her husband, as when she agrees with him despite her own preferences, saying, "[W]ell, well, Miles, you know best. . . . [W]hat pleases you, pleases me." At another point, when Miles and Tim Flanagan ask her opinion, Mrs. Blake "had no mind to 'bother herself' with such debates. 'Just talk it out yourselves,' said she, 'you're the best judges; as for me I don't know much about it.'" Tim later complains to his wife: "I know she's at bottom, as much against sending the children to the Ward School as you or I, but she hasn't the pluck in her to say so. She's *so* submissive and *so* willing to leave it all in Miles's hands, just as if she hadn't as good a right to the children as he has!"[63] The import of Sadlier's account is that Mrs. Blake should have fought to fulfill her function even though she would have violated the patriarchal tradition.

Quigley's wife in *Profit and Loss* does just that—and fares much better at the author's hands. Mrs. Mulroony forcefully and consistently maintains that her son should attend the Catholic school, arguing with both her husband and the public school professor, and threatening to tell the priest about her husband's intentions. Quigley clearly endorses Mrs. Mulroony's efforts. She is the better partner and should have prevailed. She wants only "to please God and to keep herself and her children free from the contamination of the world." Her husband, by contrast, is vain; his "highest ambition was to be somebody; to hold office; to excel; to have the applause of his fellow-men."[64]

In the end, Sadlier and Quigley avoid taking a direct stand on authority within the family. In their specific recommendations, they urge "parents"—not fathers or mothers—to send children to Catholic schools.[65] Yet this refusal to take a stand undermines patriarchy by assigning equal responsibility to men and women; the parent in the right—the one in accord with the teachings of the Church—should make the key decisions. And in their novels, that parent was most often the mother. The tension that can arise in nuclear families when husbands and wives disagree in such important matters helps to explain why the authors, who seem to subscribe to patriarchal norms, prefer to deal with women characters who head their households.

The Matriarchal Lay Society and the Alliance with Priests

Women's community-building function, which gives them power in their relationships with husbands, also serves them well as they interact with guardians, employers, associates, and friends. In the Irish American novels, women characters are often more adamant and less willing to please than men. Mrs. Mulroony, in Quigley's novel, tells the professor advocating for the public school that his arguments are "balderdash" and a "lie" and calls him "a brainless half fool." Her husband is upset at her "roughness" toward the professor and apologizes to him.[66] The women in these novels also oppose ill treatment wherever they encounter it. Mrs. Malcolm, the housekeeper, challenges Willy Burke's employers when they falsely accused him of theft. Moll Hanley, in McCorry's *The Lost Rosary*, says she will "stand up for the . . . rights" of any worker who is "badly used." Cannon applauds the women who "threw stones and brickbats, and every missile they could most easily command" at the mob assailing their neighborhood. The authors also criticize women who do not stand up for their beliefs. Sadlier, who stresses obedience more than the other authors, always draws the line at principle. She criticizes Mrs. Blake and also characterizes a non-ideal domestic servant as "one of those good-natured, harmless persons . . . [with] no fixed principles."[67] By contrast, women who defend principles and not simply their own interests are universally praised.

Women often exert their power or influence by persuasion and example. The mothers in Cannon's novels, and in the first novels of Sadlier and Quigley, are nurturing, loving figures. Kate Crolly's influence over the ward Cecilia Morton in *Mount Benedict* is exerted through good example. But women also make use of any sanctions available to them. Single women like Bessy Conway and Bertha Von Weigel reject potential suitors and colleagues who are not loyal to the Church and Irish identity. In Sadlier's *Confessions of an Apostate*, Simon O'Hare is angry when the wife of his friend severs the men's relationship after she learns that Simon has stopped going to church.

The most serious sanctions are reserved for mothers who reject children, of all ages, for any apostasy. These are the women who save the priest from a monitoring or punishing role. The Irish mother of Simon O'Hare in Sadlier's novel refuses to correspond with her son after he adopts the religion of his Protestant wife. Mrs. Mulroony, in Quigley's novel, refuses contact with her son in the years when he abandons the Church. Her son reflects about his "saintly mother, who left me in disgust and took with her all my luck."[68]

When acting to ensure that their children follow church teaching, and when punishing them for not doing so, these women can be harsh and unloving. Mothers who indulge their children are sometimes criticized. In Roddan's novel, John O'Brien, still a child, wants to eat too much fruit; his mother tries bribery, and when this does not work, she gives in and the boy gets sick. When his father finds out, he says, "Foolish mother!" As for John, he realizes "*I could have my own way with mother*." Sadlier, for her part, criticizes the Blakes for their "over-indulgence" of their "frail" daughter Eliza, whom they "humored." The author refers to them as "doting" and says they love their children "not wisely, but too well." On the other hand, the authors never criticize mothers for harshness. Mrs. Flanagan is a "careful and affectionate mother," as though affectionate without the qualifier is a matter for suspicion. The apostate Simon O'Hare's image of his mother is illustrated in the dream where she predicts—without pity or grief—the destruction of his life. The authors praise priests and nuns rather than mothers for traditional "motherly" qualities. Sadlier describes one young nun as a "kind teacher," who spoke "mildly" and called a student "my dear child." Mrs. Flanagan does not speak to her children in this way.[69]

These good women who act to maintain the Catholic community— specifically the middle-aged and older women who can act as mothers— are connected to the priests by motivation and function, in a mutually supportive relationship. Like priests, they devote themselves to caring for others without regard to their own interests. The women defend the priests against critics. When the young man in Quigley's *Profit and Loss* complains to his mother that the priest has treated him harshly, the mother says that "perhaps" he "deserved" the "rebuke." Women also remind their spouses and children about the priests' teachings, and Mrs. Mulroony, in Quigley's novel, prefers the Catholic school for her son because "the priest will have him under his control."[70]

Women also turn to the priests for advice, as men do not. When the Blakes have questions about the marriages of their son and daughter, it is Mrs. Blake who goes to see Father Power. Mr. Gallagher, in Sadlier's *Old and New*, never consults the priest about his fashion-loving wife and daughters. And it is women, more than men, who tell the priest about others' bad behavior. Wives report husbands (never the reverse); and mothers, not fathers, tell on children. It is dying women, like the widows Burke and O'Clery, rather than dying men, like the widowed father in Roddan, who turn children over to the care of the priest. The father in Roddan simply tells his son to associate only with good Catholics.[71]

Yet the relationship between priests and women is mutual; priests also provide women with defense and support. In Boyce's novel, the priest defends the heroine Kate Petersham in her argument with Dr. Henshaw. In Sadlier, the priest regards Mrs. Burke, this "unlearned, simple woman . . . [as] a pattern of true and unassuming piety!" A priest praises the apple woman in McCorry's *Mount Benedict* for her "gallant conduct." In his final novel, Quigley says that Mrs. Mulroony's "very superior mind, and unassuming piety, made all her acquaintances, not excepting the priest . . . to regard her opinions, judgments and presentiments as something partaking of the nature of predictions."[72]

The priests provide more tangible support to women as well. When serving primarily as rescuer and friend, the priests' efforts are mostly on behalf of women, like the widowed Mrs. Burke, Mrs. O'Clery, and Mrs. Mulroony in Sadlier and Quigley novels. In Quigley's *Profit and Loss*, the priest comes to the backsliding Patrick Mulroony when he is injured, explaining, "I am really sorry for his good mother, but for the lad himself I have not much sympathy." In the same novel the priest also comes to the dying young woman Nellie at her mother's request. In Ireland also, the priests focus on women. In McElgun's *Annie Reilly*, the priest is summoned to the sick mother during the eviction and provides comfort and rescue. But in McCorry's *The Lost Rosary*, when the father is dying during the famine, the priest comforts the grieving wife and daughters.[73]

The alliance does not, of course, make women the equal of priests. But Catholic women share this subordination with Catholic laymen and might be considered to have the better position. Several scholars, moreover, have found that over time, women's independent responsibility to maintain the faith led them to challenge bishops and priests.[74]

With this conception of the Catholic woman, the Irish American authors contributed to the "feminization" of religious life in nineteenth-century America. The Catholic contribution to this development has not received much attention from current scholars.[75] It preoccupied Orestes Brownson at the time, however. He argued that Catholic novelists were imitating American Protestant popular culture by positing the Church as a nurturing comforter rather than a stern uncompromising authority and teaching a creedless piety to replace robust dogma. He also objected to the novelists' assumption that women were both morally superior to men and the natural allies of the clergy. Brownson blamed women who were the writers and readers of popular literature but also male authors who, he wrote, acted like women to be popular.[76]

The novels do not support Brownson's accusations of anti-institutional bias. For the Irish Americans, the religious community was centered in the Church and priests, not in homes and families. Some of the authors also retain the idea of the Church—if not the priests—as a source of command and authority. In addition, although the Irish American novels do not focus on teaching doctrine, they make it clear—especially when they defend Catholics against Protestant charges—that the Church teaches doctrine as well as morality.

Nevertheless the novels do suggest a process of "feminization" in other ways. The association of priests with the feminine selfless caretaking qualities challenged contemporary definitions of gender and distinguished priests from other men, Catholic and Protestant, who were involved in making a living to support themselves and their families.[77] The novels also made women—far more than laymen—the most important members of the Church and the main allies of the priests in advancing its interests. The Catholic Church had some of the same reasons as Protestants to engage in this process of feminization. The Church was organizing itself in a new country where it did not control economic life and had to be careful about asserting itself in politics.[78] It could more easily advance its interests by seeking an alliance with women to influence or control family and social life.

For immigrant women and their daughters, the Irish Catholic ideal had its limitations. As in the reigning cult of domesticity, exemplary women were depicted as selfless rather than assertive or ambitious. Perhaps more uniquely, the emphasis on women's community-building function in alliance with priests could undermine their relationships with husbands and introduce a coldness and harshness into family life. This was especially true in the novels of Sadlier and Quigley, but they were also the authors who gave married couples a central role in the novels. The Irish Catholic ideal, like the cult of domesticity, also removed women from politics and from some aspects of economic life. Women worked and achieved economic independence but, as will be seen in the next chapter, they did not seek upward mobility by dint of their own efforts. Upward mobility and politics were the province of men.

But the Irish Catholic ideal also offered many advantages to women. Unlike the cult of domesticity, it was an ideal that could be met by women in all social classes. Scholars have not paid sufficient attention to the important role that Irish American novels played in the mid-nineteenth-century decades, before the Irish had established a sizeable middle class. The novels serve as a counter-discourse in terms of class as well as religion, articulating an ideal that imbued the life and circumstances of working-class women with meaning. Scholars have tended to argue that poor immigrant women could live only against the standard of the middle-class domestic ideal, struggling to achieve it and longing for the country and society from which they had emigrated.[79] But in these novels, a poor or working-class woman, whose home was a tenement apartment where she raised children and worked for wages, met the ideal just as much as a middle-class woman who did not work ouside her well-appointed home.

The Irish Catholic ideal also supported women's independence. Good women could emigrate without parents or husband, choose to remain unmarried, and work to support themselves and to help others. The authors' willingness to ignore the men in the lives of well-off married women made work an option even for them. The ideal also assigned a crucial function to women within their communities. If it did not give women the autonomous base that the home provided to middle-class Protestant women, it did give them an important role in a wider community, a community organized around the most important institution in their world. This role gave women status and power in their relationships, including with husbands.

Chapter 9

CATHOLICS AND
ECONOMIC SUCCESS

Just as they did with women, the Irish American authors made poor and working-class men central characters in their stories. The heroes may have known some prosperity in Ireland, but they were poor at least during their first years in America. To accommodate these working-class heroes, the Irish Americans adopted a standard "young man makes good" model, tailored to suit Catholic purposes. To some extent the experiences of men mirrored those of women. Men found their first jobs, as manual laborers, relatively easily, supporting the view of those scholars who doubt the prevalence of "No Irish Need Apply" signs. The men, like the women, did not passively accept their circumstances but cultivated the virtues of hard work, thrift, and self-discipline to get ahead. To accomplish their Catholic purposes, the authors showed that the men, like the women, overcame prejudice and were able to succeed without abandoning their heritage or yielding to America's materialist values.

Yet the definition of success in these novels varied by gender. Immigrant women succeeded as domestic servants, but men moved into middle-class occupations. Except for Cannon, the authors also showed that good men achieved this upward mobility within a Catholic economic niche, as owners or partners of their own establishments, without integrating into the mainstream economy. Much as the Irish American authors used the conventions of romance for women, they used a rags-to-riches saga for men to illustrate their more important point—that Irish immigrants could retain their group identity and also make it in their new country by developing separate economic enclaves, and resisting structural as well as cultural assimilation.

Although the Catholic authors sometimes criticized the values of a capitalist economic order, they did not advocate any organized efforts for change and in many ways reproduced that order within the separate Catholic niche. The economic advice they offered to readers, however, also suggests some conflicts of interest between religious and economic elites within the immigrant community rather than a unified effort to promote a bourgeois culture.

Achieving—and Defining—Success in America

Besides showing that good, practicing Catholic men and women could make it in America, the authors used events in their characters' lives to illuminate the qualities that could lead to this success—qualities mostly shared by men and women in both the working and middle classes. Successful male and female characters in the novels did not passively accept their circumstances but worked hard and skillfully, saving money largely because they did not spend their earnings on drink or entertainment. These may be considered middle-class virtues, but the authors might ask in response why hard work and self-discipline are not useful qualities for all classes.

Bessy Conway is employed from the day she arrives in America until the day she leaves; Annie Reilly places an ad in the paper seeking a situation "the second day after her arrival in New York." When she quits this first job, her only regret is that she is now "idle."[1] Successful male characters— Tim Flanagan in Sadlier's novel, the store owner Mr. O'Meara in *The Lost Rosary*, the older mechanic Patrick Sweeny, and the young hero James O'Rourke in *Annie Reilly*—succeed by "persevering industry" as well as "ability." Simon O'Hare, the apostate in Sadlier's novel, says that he is "steady and assiduous in the discharge of my duty to my employers," however much he might neglect his religion.[2]

Good men and women also seldom ask for, or take, time off. McElgun's Annie Reilly "worked very hard" on a Sunday to complete all her tasks before going to church. James O'Rourke is, "of all the men in the [oil] fields, . . . the most attentive to his business, and never . . . idled away a moment."[3] By contrast, characters in these novels who do not work skillfully inevitably fare badly. In *Bessy Conway*, Sally is fired for neglecting her work, and Mary is "dead tired . . . after being at a dance the night before." Many men in the oil fields in *Annie Reilly* waste their time and money on liquor and fighting.[4]

The authors' emphasis on the qualities necessary for success does not blind them to the role of fortune or luck. In several places, Sadlier refers to "the blind goddess" or "the capricious jade!" that brings economic success to some and not to others. In *Tighe Lyfford*, Cannon describes two Irish immigrants who had been in America for many years; one "remained a poor man . . . the other, by a lucky speculation, early became the owner of a considerable property, which in a few years, amounted to . . . a handsome independence."[5] But the authors do not rely on luck to explain their characters' success. Even when magical interventions occur—Willy Burke receives a substantial inheritance from his employer, and starts his own firm; a minor character in *Bessy Conway*, who works in a shoe repair shop, uses an inheritance from an old woman he has cared for to buy the shop for himself— they are the result of previous hard work and good behavior.

While work, skill, and discipline were considered necessary for all working people in these novels, there were some differences in the qualities required by men and women, indicating that the authors defined success differently for the two groups. The lead male characters invariably find some way to get an education. Priests offer Willy Burke the use of a library, after enrolling him in evening school, and, in *Annie Reilly*, give books to James O'Rourke in the oil fields. Simon O'Hare, in *Confessions of an Apostate*, realizes that if he is "to rise in the world . . . it must be by knowledge and skill, not by labor," and so he goes to night school.[6] The authors seem to assume that education is the only distinct requirement for a middle-class occupation; they do not stress entrepreneurship, initiative, or risk taking.

In contrast, women immigrant characters are never offered books or access to libraries and are not encouraged to spend their evenings at school. Even Annie Reilly—whose teacher in Ireland calls her "the best scholar . . . at his school, and so smart in every way"—does not continue her schooling in America or move beyond work in domestic service. The skills that immigrant women acquire, "smartness," "neatness," "order," "mildness and good sense," make them better servants, nothing else.[7]

In some novels, men and women also differed in their attitudes to employers. Boyce and Quigley briefly endorse obedience, and Sadlier, typically, makes it a central factor in her novels. The three authors praise obedience only when it does not involve matters of religious or moral principle. They also tend to praise the quality in characters with working-class, not higher-level, occupations, and particularly in female domestic servants. At one point, Boyce suggests that Irish domestic servants have a reputation for being disrespectful to their American employers. During an exchange over a domestic servant's letter to Ireland from Boston, the American visitor Ephraim Weeks tells an Irish woman that "some of your girls are pretty spunky."[8] This confirms the conclusion of Margaret Lynch-Brennan, who argues in her article on nineteenth-century Irish domestic servants that differences in social codes separated the immigrant women from their American employers. "In contrast to the ideal of the submissive woman . . . in the cult of domesticity, culture in peasant Ireland permitted women to be verbally assertive. . . . [P]opular American literature was rife with stories of the assertive Bridget."[9]

Boyce dissuaded the women from this behavior because it threatened their continuing employment. After Weeks comments about the spunkiness of the Irish American domestic servants, the Irish woman replies: "I don't doubt it, sir . . . and may be there's plenty of them desarves to be turned out of doors too for their impudence. But can't all that be done without casting up their religion and their priest to them?"[10] Boyce did not seem to have similar concerns about male employees. Quigley gives the virtue of obedience greater prominence. In his first novel, a priest in confession tells a domestic servant, who had argued with her employer, "to be obedient to those even who are not amiable nor kind; to serve them for God's sake." Quigley also lauds obedience in a male employee in his final novel, albeit one who behaves much more egregiously, striking an employer who has withheld his wages and made anti-Catholic remarks. The laborer says he will go to confession for striking "a fellow-creature; and besides, my employer whom I ought to obey and love."[11]

Sadlier emphasizes obedience to employers for her working-class characters and for women domestic servants especially. She does not mention obedience when she describes the working life of the immigrant on the stock exchange or Elinor Preston, who works as a companion and teacher. But the Protestant employer in *Con O'Regan* defends the working-class immigrants in Boston because the "great majority of them are . . . honest, submissive to their employers, and able and willing to undertake the hardest work." In *Bessy Conway*, an Irish immigrant working as a servant explains: "I engage to do people's work for them, and sure it isn't to please myself . . . so whatever way they want it done, it's all the same to . . . [me]. . . . I always feel as if I was serving God when I'm serving them." By contrast, the characters who serve as object lessons in the novel resent and refuse employers' requests and suffer accordingly.[12]

In matters of obedience, Boyce, Quigley, and Sadlier echoed the advice of Protestant employers, but they did not speak for all of their Irish American contemporaries. The immigrant's daughter in Cannon's *Bickerton* refuses to obey or to be respectful toward her Protestant foster family on matters both secular and religious. McCorry, in *The Lost Rosary*, not only says that domestic servants are entitled to their time off but also praises the older and younger immigrant women who "stand up for the . . . rights" of a worker "badly used" by an overseer.[13] And even Boyce, Quigley, and Sadlier counsel women to retain and defend their faith, ethnicity, and moral principles, regardless of employer demands.

Another distinction between working women and men concerned the relevance of faithful Catholicism to economic success. In their treatment of men, authors were clear that good behavior did not always bring success and bad behavior did not always bring failure. Some good Catholics—even if always minor characters—exhibit the virtues of hard work and discipline but are not upwardly mobile. Patrick Scanlon in Cannon's *Bickerton*, a "mere laborer" who manages to bring his entire family to America, and the longshoreman Terence McManus in McElgun's *Annie Reilly* remain in working-class occupations. Other exemplary minor characters, including a construction worker in Sadlier's *Confessions of an Apostate*, lose their jobs and become destitute because of accidents, illness, or other circumstances beyond their control. By contrast, some of the backsliders, such as Sadlier's Miles and Henry Blake and Quigley's Mr. Mulroony and his son, rise to the middle class.

It is different for women. Faithful Catholicism may not guarantee their success, but backsliding always brings failure—and permanent failure. The single working women in Sadlier's and McCorry's novels who abandon their faith for the sake of a social or sexual life always come to a very bad end. The lodging-house keeper in McCorry tells of a young immigrant domestic servant who "went out o' nights; then to them low dancin' saloons . . . then she began to thieve," at which point she was fired from her job and "went as a bar-maid into a low den, an' before ten weeks . . . [she] was a public strumpet on the streets."[14] The only woman in the novels who is ambitious for education and a higher occupation is the character Nellie, in Quigley's *Profit and Loss*, who rejects the Church, runs off with a Protestant, and dies young. Compare her fate with the Patrick Mulroony character in the same novel, who suffers for his apostasy, including spending some years in jail, but ultimately reforms and becomes a wealthy contractor.

The only male characters whose fates compare somewhat to those of faithless single women are Sadlier's, and they drink excessively. For Sadlier, drinking was a surer predictor of failure for men than apostasy; she allows only a few, like one of the working-class men in *Con O'Regan*, to reform and prosper. Ned Finigan, the immigrant saloon keeper in *Bessy Conway*, ruins his business and dies of alcoholism. In *The Blakes and Flanagans*, a minor character goes to public schools, frequents engine houses, theaters, and taverns, and eventually dies after a drunken fight.

As the different qualities required of men and women indicate, the definition of success in these novels varies by gender. Women characters, as shown in the previous chapter, typically attain economic independence through work as domestic servants. They do not leave the occupation or improve their class position during their working lives. In fact, McCorry presents domestic service as a sign of upward mobility for women who begin by working in factories or selling apples in the street. For servants, economic success means receiving higher wages for additional work, assuming less onerous domestic tasks, or finding better employers. Sadlier's Bessy Conway agrees to take on a second domestic job for additional wages "to increase my little store." Winny O'Regan moves from "coarser and . . . harder" housework to sewing and dressmaking as a reward for her hard work and loyalty.[15]

The few better-educated women, such as Sadlier's Elinor Preston or Kate Crolly in McCorry's *Mount Benedict*, begin as companions to their employers, and in some respects they are able to improve their positions.

Elinor Preston becomes a teacher in a small Catholic school in a remote French Canadian village. Kate Crolly enters the convent. Yet these women are not after economic advancement, nor do they regard their change in occupation in this light: Elinor wants only a peaceful retirement in the country among Catholics. The two women are not offered as models of economic success; that role is played by the successful domestic servants.

The differences in the economic lives of women and men are illustrated in Sadlier's account of her purposes in two novels. She wrote *Bessy Conway* to "point out to *Irish Girls in America* . . . the true and never-failing path to success in this world, and happiness in the next"; the path in this world was to "win respect and inspire confidence on the part of their employers." In other words, the goal of these women should be to retain their employment as domestic servants. She wrote *Willy Burke* to show "the young sons" of her "native land" that if they emulated her hero, they would "soon become wealthy, esteemed, and respected," because "a man may be a good Catholic . . . and yet obtain both wealth and honor even here below."[16] The difference can also be seen in the authors' comments on women who yearned to move from working- to middle-class occupations. Quigley consigns the ambitious Nellie to an early death, but McCorry praises a wife — who had made an independent living as a domestic servant before her marriage — for "the admirable manner in which she seconded her husband's efforts to get on in the world."[17] While women achieve economic independence, they move up in the world only through their husbands.

When it comes to the American-born daughters of the immigrants, however, the authors send a more mixed message about upward mobility. In Quigley's final novel, Nellie illustrates the danger of ambition as she ruins her life by seeking an education and job within the public school system. In Roddan and Cannon, the American-born writers, the immigrants' daughters fare somewhat better; they become teachers. In *John O'Brien*, the sixteen-year-old daughter (who will become John's wife) is earning "her living by teaching, drawing and music . . . [in] the houses of wealthy persons." The young woman in Cannon's *Bickerton* says that she will support herself "by teaching," without specifying the school system. By being vague, Cannon proves more willing than the other Irish American novelists to show a young woman entering the public school system, a mainstream economic institution that many Irish American women actually entered on their path to upward mobility. Roddan's young woman is a private tutor (and Sadlier's Elinor Preston teaches in the school established by the priest). But in contrast to their treatment of men, neither Roddan nor Cannon expresses any particular pride in the women's achievements. Cannon seems impressed only with his character's determination to support herself. And in his final novel, *Tighe Lyfford*, Cannon criticizes women's interest in reaching for better occupations. The daughter of a poor family who works as a domestic servant laments that her younger sister is too proud to enter the same occupation. The servant criticizes her sister because "the contempt with which servant girls are spoken of, by the silly young men and sillier young women of her acquaintance, has made her, like many others, look down upon the whole of a useful class of females."[18] Both authors indicate that the daughters have been upwardly mobile compared with their mothers but do not go so far as to suggest that ambition is a virtue that women should cultivate.

The trajectories, if not the starting points, were different for men. The authors were fairly realistic about the men's initial employment opportunities. Their characters usually begin in manual labor, as workers on canals, oil fields, or docks; porters in warehouses; salesmen in stores; or apprentices in a skilled trade or on a farm. Only the educated men, unlike the educated women, start in middle-class occupations. Elinor Preston's brother is a commissioned British army officer in Canada and India. Randall Murray, in *Old and New*—who was "brought up to the mercantile business in Dublin" and "to be sure . . . came of decent people at home and had a good share of education when he came out"—was a trader on the stock exchange.[19]

If most of the immigrant male characters begin in unskilled, working-class jobs, it is only the minor characters who remain in these situations. Even they, like the women domestic servants, manage to do well enough over time to support themselves and their families. In Cannon's *Bickerton*, an older man named Patrick Scanlon earns enough money "as a mere labourer" to support his own family and to bring his parents and all of his siblings to America. McElgun's hero James O'Rourke, in *Annie Reilly*, coming to America by way of Liverpool, notes the difference between "the miserable appearance of the English working-men" and the appearance of a fellow Irish immigrant in America, Terence McManus, who is a long-shoreman. It is clear from the American's hands "that he belonged to the working-class," but his clothes are "clean" and he lives with his wife in an apartment in a "neat-looking brick house," where James is entertained in "a tidily furnished room of comfortable dimensions."[20]

The major male characters in the novels move on to better occupations. If a male immigrant arrives in America at the start of the story, he has invariably improved his income and status by the end; if the character has been in the country for a number of years as the novel opens, he has already acquired a better position.

The authors are quite prepared to praise men who strive for this type of success, once again praising active effort, not resignation or acceptance. McCorry, in *The Lost Rosary*, seconds his young hero's decision to leave the city and his friend in pursuit of a good job. He also readily understands the desire of the older established immigrant, Mr. O'Meara, who says that in his earlier life he had taken "menial employment, but his spirit yearned for decent work."[21] Sadlier objects to parents who "complain of so much time being lost in Catholic schools in teaching and learning the Christian doctrine," but she also points out that religion lessons take up only "about a quarter of an hour" of the day at St. Peter's, where boys received a "sound business education." Sadlier is also quite prepared to criticize characters who do not make an effort to succeed. Ned Finigan, the future saloon owner in *Bessy Conway*, is "well disposed to take the world easy . . . while awaiting for 'something to turn up.'"[22]

As the authors described the upward mobility of their male characters, they made little effort to be realistic; rather, they advocated certain occupational paths for the immigrants. The most common pattern in the novels is for male characters to eventually own a business. In Sadlier's novels, Willy Burke eventually owns a trading firm; Tim Flanagan establishes a leather dressing business, through which he and his family attain a life of "ease and comfort" and amass "a considerable sum of money."[23] An immigrant friend of the Flanagans—a minor character in the story—begins as a cooper; another male immigrant in *Bessy Conway* starts off in a shoe repair shop; both end up owning their own establishments. The new rich in *Old and New* own butcher, bakery, and grocery stores. In McCorry and McElgun, older immigrants, including Mr. O'Meara (who had yearned for decent work), also end up owning their own businesses—a store and a mechanic's shop. And major characters in three of the novels purchase their own farms.[24] Just as the authors failed to note the potential of public school teaching for women, they also failed to note some occupations that Irish men in America actually entered, such as saloon ownership and politics, fearing they led to excessive drinking, challenges to clerical leadership, and integration into the larger society.

Male characters also rise from laborers to clerks, then to partners in a firm, a second occupational pattern. Again, they own the business, but in common with a few others. A street orphan in Sadlier's *Bessy Conway*, and James O'Rourke, the hero of McElgun's *Annie Reilly*, who begin as newsboy and laborer in the oil fields, respectively, follow this path. In the latter novel, James appears at the end as a "richly-clad, wealthy-looking gentleman," demonstrating that his "upright life was receiving its reward even here." James is "on the high-road to fortune, if he had not already reached its golden gates."[25]

Cannon is the first of the Irish Americans to portray the economic lives of the American-born sons of immigrants. In his novels of the 1840s, the heroes of *Harry Layden* and *Scenes and Characters* rise from poverty to become lawyers and journalists for mainstream firms and newspapers. Cannon continues to show his male characters as part of the American economy in his novels of the 1850s: in *Tighe Lyfford*, an immigrant's son becomes a lawyer. Cannon's interest in seeing the sons merge into the American economy is unique among the Irish American novelists. Most male characters followed the paths forged by their fathers; the Flanagan sons join the family's leather dressing business; Patrick Mulroony, the son in Quigley's *Profit and Loss*, becomes an independent contractor after his reformation; and Roddan's John O'Brien, who begins as an apprentice tradesman, goes on to become a clerk and partner in a firm.

The Irish American authors clearly were not interested in using their novels to staff the Church. Just as most women characters did not become nuns, most men did not become priests. Quigley was the exception: Paul O'Clery, the hero of his first novel, is the only major male character, of either the immigrant or the American-born generation, who becomes a priest. Quigley is also the only author to directly recommend the priesthood to his readers, and he recommended it as a path to upward mobility:

Behold, . . . how the church . . . encourages the promotion of the humblest of her children. . . . How many scores of young men might be now shining lamps in God's sanctuary, instead of being degraded to the level of the drudges of the earth and the slaves of the world, if they only took as their model Paul O'Clery, the orphan boy![26]

Despite protestations to the contrary, the Irish American authors also clearly did not show male characters to be content with poverty or only moderate success. Examples of protestations abound. Boyce criticizes his American visitor Ephraim Weeks, who "despised" "the man who contented himself with a competence and a quiet life at home," and McCorry commented in *The Lost Rosary* that success is "always best when moderate and unaccompanied with too strong a desire, lest its companions in virtue should suffer by its exaltation." Quigley's priest tells the men on the railroads that the Church teaches men "to be content with a competency."[27]

Yet in all of these novels, including those by McCorry and Quigley, the main male characters strive for and achieve much more than a competency. Sadlier, in *The Blakes and Flanagans*, is a good example of the authors' actual message. At first, she seems to present the good son, Edward Flanagan, who joins his father in the leather dressing business, as less educated and less prominent than the worldly politician Henry Blake. Edward receives "a good solid mercantile education," which, in his father's eyes, is "quite enough to work his way decently through the world." Henry Blake, on the other hand, goes to Columbia College and becomes a lawyer. Yet Edward does more than work his way decently through the world. He shares in the economic comfort of the family business, and he marries the only daughter of a wealthy Irish immigrant, who, at his death, leaves Edward "his whole fortune, amounting to thirty thousand dollars."[28] In the end, Edward is richer as well as happier than Henry, even in this life. Whenever a Sadlier character expresses regret about his path to wealth or status, he has abandoned his faith. So it is the apostate Simon O'Hare, and not Edward Flanagan, who says at the end of his confessions: "Would that I had never taken into my head the foolish notion of rising in the world. Had I been contented in the lowly sphere wherein I was born . . . I might now be cheerful and happy."[29]

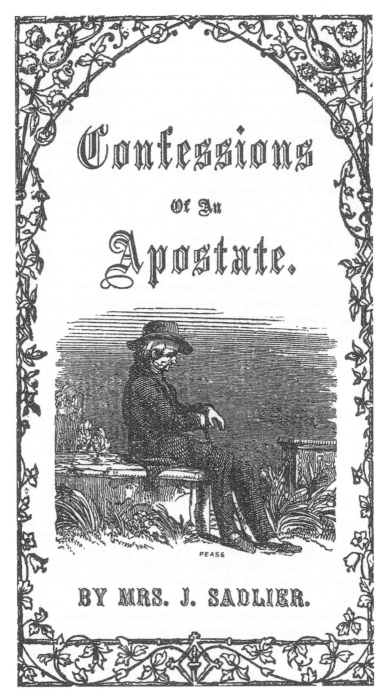

Figure 9.1. In this title page, Sadlier shows Simon O'Hare, now a lonely sad, old man retired to Ireland, regretting his past betrayals of his heritage for the sake of worldly goods.

Sadlier found that readers wanted her to applaud immigrant men who rose to success. When she satirized the new rich in *Old and New*, as when she denied marriage to the heroine of *Alice Riordan*, her readers complained. *Old and New*, like the earlier novel, appeared first as a newspaper serial. Sadlier wrote a new conclusion for the book edition in which she acknowledges her critics: "It has been said . . . that I have dealt too hardly with persons who rise by their own industry from an inferior position in society." In fact, Sadlier was cruel to the new rich in the text of the novel. She describes the Gallaghers as "not, to be sure, overstocked with book-learning" and the husband as a "good-natured, fat, heavy-featured man, remarkably dull in comprehension, so much so, indeed, that it was a matter of astonishment to all his acquaintances how he ever got to the sunny side of this dark world." She also refers to the "*parvenus . . .* the cormorants who have grown fat and lusty on the pennies and shillings of the poor, and are so infatuated by their own purse-proud vanity that they forget the depths from which they have arisen."

In the new conclusion, Sadlier defends herself by pointing to the characters in the book "held up for the reader's respect . . . [who] all raised themselves from an obscure position by honest and persevering exertion. . . . It is not the ascent of our people in the social scale which I have satirized," she wrote, "but the follies and extravagant pretensions of some amongst them when they do succeed in gaining a position."[30]

Sadlier's *Con O'Regan* is the only exception to this model of successful male characters. While it is not the only Sadlier novel in which good Catholics leave a northeastern city, it is the only one in which they leave because they cannot succeed. Sadlier has a unique agenda in this novel. She writes to support the colonization schemes, and she fulfills this agenda by giving a harshly pessimistic, even despairing account of immigrant life in Boston. A bigoted Protestant employer comments that "every respectable house in the city, indeed all New England over, is making it a point to get rid of" the Irish immigrants. The hero of the novel spends his days in "hard, unremitting toil" as a porter and storeman, and tells his sister that "this packing of boxes and barrels and wheeling of trucks . . . is a tiresome thing after all, and a man might be at it for years and years without betterin' his condition."

Sadlier, in this novel, is also the only Irish American novelist of the period to present the dream of America as an outright lie. The hero wonders that "none of these poor unfortunate creatures [in America] ever lets their friends at home know the state they're in," and so those friends keep emigrating. Another Irish immigrant, a former seminarian, explains that when the immigrants find "themselves disappointed" in their "expectation of making a fortune" in this new country, they are "ashamed to own it."[31] Immigrants seeking a good life, in this view, have no choice but to leave Boston for one of the exclusively Irish Catholic western settlements. Even in this novel, the hero eventually becomes quite well off in the settlement.

The authors' depiction of success in the other novels of the time reflects their more typical agenda: to connect faithful Catholic practice with prosperity in the northeastern cities where most immigrants lived—or, to put it negatively, to refute the idea that abandoning Catholicism was the only path to success.

Succeeding in an Anti-Catholic World

Sadlier's conclusion in *Con O'Regan* highlights the conflict in the other novels between the authors' portraits of America as implacably anti-Catholic and their optimistic message about the success of Irish immigrants. Men and women in these novels had to exhibit not only the standard virtues associated with hard work but also the courage to remain faithful Catholics and overcome the prejudice of their Protestant employers. And yet those employers hired and promoted the immigrant characters, so that, in the words of Sadlier in *Willy Burke*, a man could remain a Catholic and also achieve wealth and status.

Some authors simply did not answer the question of how their characters succeeded in the hostile environment. Miles Blake, Tim Flanagan, the new rich in *Old and New*, Mr. Mulroony in *Profit and Loss*, and the older generation of immigrants in both *The Lost Rosary* and *Annie Reilly* are independent businessmen by the time the novels open. The authors give no account, or only the barest account, of their path to success. Quigley's Mr. Mulroony, for example, worked as a "railroad-master for three or four years" before buying his large farm.[32]

In other novels, authors provided some account of their characters' initial employment. In only one, *The Lost Rosary* in 1871, is a major male character hired for his first job by a Catholic, in this case the established Irish immigrant Mr. O'Meara, who hires the young man as a porter/clerk in his store. In Sadlier's *Bessy Conway*, a minor character works in a shoe repair shop owned by a Michael Dooley, but Sadlier never comments on the ethnic or religious background of this employer. The overwhelming pattern is that the immigrants are given their first jobs by non-Catholics. Even in Roddan, who is so explicit about the dangers of mixed societies, the bishop advises the young hero that "Protestants . . . are very numerous, you see, and we are few. Besides, we are poor; and our Catholics depend upon them, in most cases, for a living."[33]

Protestants in the novels in fact readily hire the immigrant characters for the unskilled jobs most of them obtain and also for better jobs that call for some background or education (such as the position obtained by the stockbroker in *Old and New*). In Sadlier's *Confessions of an Apostate*, the captain of the ship that ferried Simon O'Hare to America befriends Simon, then recommends him for a job as "porter in an extensive hardware establishment." Simon gets the job immediately. In *Profit and Loss*, Quigley says that the sons and daughters of the major family in the novel who decide to remain in New York receive "very flattering offers of employment . . . through the influence of some of the many acquaintances which they met immediately after their arrival."[34]

McCorry is as pessimistic as the authors get about their major characters. In *The Lost Rosary*, he says the young male immigrant "saw that their prospects of work were neither so plentiful nor so numerous as he had expected before landing." What this meant, however, is that he took the first job offered, shortly after his arrival, even if it meant leaving the city and his friend.[35] In McCorry's next novel, *Mount Benedict*, the Protestant Mr. Morton is at first reluctant to hire the Irish Catholic immigrant Kate Crolly as companion to his ward Cecilia. But his reluctance quickly fades when Cecilia is impressed with Kate and insists that she be hired.

Even for minor characters, Quigley is the only one of the authors to suggest that Protestants would not hire Catholics. In a brief incident, a Protestant woman on a farm says that her minister always referred to the Bible "when advising us against employing Romanist hired help."[36] On the other hand, all of Quigley's major and minor characters in the novel, including farm laborers, find jobs without difficulty.

The authors never refer to "no Irish need apply" signs, lending further credence to the views of scholars who consider the existence of the signs as an urban myth.[37] Recent research suggests that the Irish may well have suffered discrimination in their search for skilled or white-collar jobs but, as Kevin Kenny has argued, "demand for unskilled male heavy labor and unskilled female domestic labor in the nineteenth century was simply too great for the Irish to have suffered much by way of anti-hiring discrimination" in the lower levels of the job market."[38]

The immigrant characters certainly had to overcome anti-Catholic hostility after they were hired. Protestant employers presented as faithful to their religion criticize the beliefs of John O'Brien, Willy Burke, and Annie Reilly. They also falsely accuse the young men of crimes. John O'Brien and Bessy Conway are required to attend Protestant prayer services, and both are fired for refusing. Simon O'Hare, in Sadlier's *Confessions of an Apostate*, is told to keep his religion quiet. The American-born son Patrick Mulroony, in Quigley's *Profit and Loss*, is encouraged to become a Protestant. Some of the characters succumb, at least temporarily, to the idea that Catholicism is a hindrance to economic success, but they eventually reform. Other characters, like Willy Burke in Sadlier, Paul O'Clery in Quigley, and the major male characters in McCorry and McElgun, never abandon their heritage. And all of these men not only get jobs but also succeed, thanks, in part, to Protestant employers.

On a few occasions, authors simply acknowledge decent Protestants. Roddan's John O'Brien has one such employer during his many years as an apprentice in foster care. The "master" is described as a faithful practicing Baptist who challenges John's beliefs. The master, however, is "unlike most Protestants," who are not only ignorant about religion but also "very foul-mouthed." He stops trying to convert John, does not interfere with his religion, dispenses good advice, and treats him fairly.[39] Roddan's point, however, is to show that such employers are rare; he bases his advice that Catholics avoid mixing with Protestants on the overall pattern of John's life.

For the most part, authors preserve the economic success of their characters and the vision of a hostile environment by ensuring that, while faithful Protestants might hire Catholics, they do not help them advance in their careers.[40] Those who reward Catholics for their good work are

Protestants who eventually convert, or Protestants in name only. Conversions are most common in the novels of the early 1850s, when the authors hope for the eventual triumph of Catholicism. Through the intercession of a priest and a Catholic partner, Sadlier's Willy Burke is hired by a Protestant man, Mr. Weimar, who has fiercely anti-Catholic views. In time, Weimar comes to respect Willy for defending his faith, increases his wages for good work, and eventually converts, attributing his change of heart to the example of his Catholic employee. Paul O'Clery, the young hero of Quigley's first novel, is hired as a tutor by a Mr. Clarke, a "well-bred, full-blooded Yankee," and a member of an Episcopal "literary and religious society." Clarke, too, has anti-Catholic views, but he "could not sanction for an instant any thing like persecution on account of religion." In the end, he, too, converts and brings all of his family and associates along with him.[41]

Catholic women are less likely than men to bring about the conversion of their Protestant employers. Kate Crolly, of McCorry's *Mount Benedict*, accomplishes a rare feat when she brings about the conversion of the young Protestant Cecilia Morton, who had insisted on hiring her, and also of the anti-Catholic father of the family, who had begun life as a Catholic. Women may be less likely than men to inspire conversions because they were not featured in the novels until the 1860s, when the triumphal hope for conversions had passed.

Other employers who treat their Catholic workers fairly and promote them are shown to be faithless Protestants who are critical of their own religion. Mr. Coulter, in Sadlier's *Con O'Regan*, who employs both the title character and his sister, Winny, has anti-Catholic views. Ultimately, though, his commitment to fairness prevails. He tries to promote Con, eventually loaning him the money to move out west. He also finds a job for Winny with his own sisters. Coulter bitterly rejects the Protestant religion. On observing the behavior of his churchgoing wife, he reflects, "if this be the fruit of vital religion, I thank God I have forsworn it long ago. Better . . . the natural promptings of a man's own heart, than the stern, cold, selfish teachings of what is called religion." Coulter's two sisters are also good employers, and their religious views are closer to atheism than Protestantism, showing that their good behavior is motivated not by religion but something like the natural promptings of the heart that motivated their brother.[42]

The authors' third strategy was simply to not identify the religion of the employers who help the immigrant characters advance. This strategy is adopted in novels of the 1870s and suggests some greater willingness to at least imply that good employers might be faithful Protestants. In McElgun's *Annie Reilly*, the hero, James O'Rourke, works in the oil fields and keeps away from the men who participate in the drinking and fighting. He remains a faithful Catholic—the first thing he does on arriving at the site is to locate the nearest chapel—but does not face attacks on his faith or ethnicity. McElgun implies that O'Rourke's boss is Protestant but does not say so explicitly. As James works hard and begins to read the books the priest has given him, his boss, Mr. Lewis, takes note and offers him a job in the office at "a decent salary." McElgun describes Mr. Lewis as an "amiable, just, polite American gentleman, who always made it a rule to reward honesty and industry without regard to creed or nationality," suggesting, without saying, that he is a Protestant. Similarly, the male immigrant in McCorry's *The Lost Rosary* takes a job as a laboring apprentice on a farm. McCorry describes the employer as "an open-hearted, honest American farmer, who . . . appreciated the faithful services" of the young man and eventually helps him to buy a farm of his own. Only the use of the term "American" suggests that he is Protestant. This farmer is influenced by the "good behavior" of the hero and hires two other Irish workers, basing his hiring decisions, not his religious convictions, on the influence of example.[43]

Succeeding in a Catholic Enclave

As the authors adopted various strategies to preserve the idea of a hostile America, all of them except Cannon also showed that their characters could succeed without integrating into its mainstream economy. Successful female and male characters in these novels operate in a separate Catholic economic world. Bessy Conway and Winny O'Regan, as well as the factory workers and apple women who move up to domestic service, are not happy in their work until they are domestic servants with Catholic families. Even Cannon merely suggests that an immigrant's daughter might have worked in the public school system. Successful male characters also operate in a separate economy. They end up as sole owners of their own businesses or they partner with other Catholics. Even the good non-Catholic employers in the novels help the immigrants on their path to an Irish Catholic niche, not into the larger economy. John O'Brien left the Protestant master for a Catholic firm, Willy Burke and the young men in *The Lost Rosary* went into business for themselves, and the O'Regans moved to the Irish Catholic settlement. Only in McElgun's 1873 *Annie Reilly* did the young male lead James O'Rourke become, and remain, a partner of a man not identified as a Catholic. In not specifying the employers' religion, McElgun comes closest to Cannon's willingness decades earlier to show Catholic men integrating into the American economy as journalists and lawyers.

By contrast to the good characters who develop the Catholic enclave, those who abandon the faith seek to enter the larger economy. The young woman in Quigley's *Profit and Loss* who rejects her faith and ethnic heritage becomes a teacher in the public school. In Sadlier's novels, Miles Blake owns his store but has key business dealings with a Protestant, who persuades him to send his son to public school. In Quigley's *Profit and Loss*, the father, who chooses the public school for his son, owns a large farm, but is also running for the office of justice of the peace. Simon O'Hare, in *Confessions of an Apostate*, becomes a partner in a firm established by a Protestant. These characters eventually return to Catholicism once they realize that in giving up their faith and ethnic identity, they have paid a high—and an unnecessary—price for success.

Some male characters abandon their faith and ethnic heritage permanently and, to an even greater degree, have entered the mainstream economy. The most villainous character in Quigley's *Profit and Loss* is a professor in the public school. The American-born Henry Blake, in Sadlier's novel, goes to public school and to Columbia College and becomes a prominent politician.

The authors' preference for male characters who go into business for themselves reflects their preindustrial orientation—essentially, they recreate the economy of Irish villages dominated by small farmers, craftsmen, and merchants. Sadlier writes that the faithful Tim Flanagan and his sons have a thriving firm, and, "what was still more advantageous, their business was altogether managed by themselves." McElgun's Annie Reilly says that it would "break her [mother's] heart to see" her son "working for any one."[44]

The importance the authors attach to being a sole owner also reflects their belief that separation will preserve ethnic and religious identity, a belief shared by leaders of many immigrant groups who came to America after the Irish.[45] Compared to the newer groups, however, the Irish American authors have limited goals; they do not suggest that developing a separate enclave will enhance the immigrants' chances to succeed, develop social capital, or eventually integrate into the mainstream economy. Although they offer two generations of Irish immigrants the ideal of the economic niche, they never use their characters to show readers how to actually establish a business. Their purpose is to link economic separation to group integrity, warning readers that steps they take to improve their economic lives, such as getting a better job outside the Catholic enclave, could have unfortunate consequences for their religious, ethnic, and cultural heritage.[46]

While they do not help readers to develop the Catholic enclave, the authors offer some guidance about the values that should govern behavior within it. The Catholic alternative is a matter of priorities. Heroes and heroines in the novels do not just accept their circumstances; they struggle to succeed, but they never put that goal (or any other goals) ahead of religion and its requirements. For the Irish American authors, this distinguished Catholic from Protestant society, where the desire for material well-being reigned supreme. All of the authors link America's materialism and competitive scrambling to its Protestant origins; Sadlier and Boyce point to social factors as well. For Sadlier's Von Weigels, America's values are a product of the country's

> *newness* . . . the natural effect of the levelling institutions of the country. In new countries . . . where the lines of distinction between . . . classes . . . are not so clearly defined, the people . . . fall into the very natural but very absurd error of supposing that fine dress, fine houses and fine furniture will command . . . distinction.

Moreover, as a nation of immigrants, Americans are essentially a new people as well as a new country. "The great majority of the people" here, Madame Von Weigel says,

> have drifted hither from Old Europe in search of a bare living, denied them at home—being here, they very often succeed in making . . . a fortune . . . and . . . must lead the fashions and astonish others who are not so lucky as themselves. . . . They know of no other way to distinguish themselves.[47]

Similarly, Boyce calls Americans "a new people [who] measure the re-spectability of men and families by the amount of money or property they're possessed of, simply because . . . [they] have no ancestors" or "no houses . . . or pedigrees"; they have nothing else to value, in other words.[48] Since neither Sadlier nor Boyce tell immigrant men in America to be con-tent to remain in their stations, their observations simply highlight the in-sufficiency of striving and possessions as the defining characteristics of a good life.

The Catholic characters in the novels who abandon or neglect the Church adopt the American priorities. The patriarchs in Roddan's *John O'Brien*, Sadlier's *The Blakes and Flanagans*, and Quigley's *Profit and Loss* risk their faith for wealth and status, then jeopardize the faith of their sons by sending them to public schools so they can "rise to . . . a respectable posi-tion." According to Sadlier, Miles Blake, as well as his wife, are "more anx-ious for making money than anything else . . . religion was, with them, only a secondary object. . . . [B]usiness! business! was the grand affair with the Blake family."[49]

The behavior of these characters, whether Protestant or nominally Catholic, is meant to illustrate a basic moral weakness that the authors define as pride, conceit, or vanity. Miles Blake has an air of "self-congratulation" and "wax[es] great in . . . [his] own estimation." Quigley writes that the fa-ther in *Profit and Loss* wants to be a justice of the peace because his "pre-dominant passion" is "vanity. . . . [H]is highest ambition was to be some-body; to hold office; to excel; to have the applause of his fellow-men." The young women in the novels who pursue public education or social life are "self-important" or "proud."[50]

Pride is portrayed as a sin that leads Catholic characters to seek the company and good opinion of Protestants, both to get ahead and to asso-ciate with the wealthy and powerful. Roddan's John O'Brien concludes that "his pride and vanity" were satisfied when he went to Protestant ser-vices, since he thought himself to be "in the company of ladies and gentle-men." Henry Blake enters politics to satisfy his "ambition" for "popu-larity."[51] The moral defect of pride, for some of these authors, could easily be associated with the American values of individualism and liberty.

Good Catholics, unlike Protestants and those who emulate them, subordinate the desire for worldly success to the requirements of their re-ligion. Willy Burke's mother sheds "tears of joy" when the Protestant woman offers to send her son to school. But she changes her mind when she realizes the danger of exposing him this way and declares that she and her son will "never be so foolish as to give up our religion for the sake of the poor perishable things of this wicked world." In *The Blakes and Flanagans*, in which religion is "the sun" of the Flanagans' "solar system," a minor character named Tom Reilly regards "business" as his "chief pleasure." Because Tom is scrupulous in his religious practice, however, the pleasure he takes in business is not portrayed as a problem. Similarly, the "sensible" wife and mother in Quigley's *Profit and Loss* does not object to the wealth and success of her children who remain in New York, or to the eventual wealth of her son after his reformation. She only objects to the risk to their faith posed by her husband's position as justice of the peace and her son's interest in public schools: "What were office, fame, and wealth to her . . . if they may become an impediment in the pursuit of virtue, sanctity, salvation?"[52]

The authors also indicate that material possessions are not the primary ingredient of a good life by devoting relatively little attention to their prosperous characters' worldly goods. The stories in which male characters come to America as poor immigrants focus on their initial experiences in working-class occupations, rather than on the later move to the middle class. Attaining a middle-class occupation (or marriage for most single women) is a reward for leading the exemplary life described in the story. In the novels where the main character has already reached the middle class at the beginning of the tale, the authors stress his previous and continuing good behavior, giving scant attention to the occupation apart from the independence and comfortable living it provided.[53] Roddan and Sadlier say nothing about the possessions of the successful John O'Brien or Willy Burke. Sadlier, McCorry, and McElgun offer no descriptions of the homes or property of the main characters who purchase their own farms. After Quigley's Patrick Mulroony reforms and becomes a wealthy contractor, the author says nothing further about his manner of life.[54]

When the authors mention possessions at all, it is to tell readers that a successful male character has purchased a home in a good neighborhood, without describing much more about either home or neighborhood. In *The Lost Rosary*, McCorry reports that Mr. O'Meara, the older immigrant who has found decent work as a store owner, lives in a "house in a highly respectable locality in New York." Similarly, McElgun's main character, James O'Rourke, who partners with Mr. Lewis in the oil fields and marries Annie Reilly, "purchased a house in a beautiful part of New York City, from which . . . [the family] may be seen driving to the Central Park every Sunday evening." In the same novel, the more established immigrant, Patrick Sweeny, a mechanic who runs his own business, has purchased a house, described variously as "a neat, two-story frame building . . . [that] had a trim little garden in front"; a "cottage"; and a "little white and green dwelling." Over the course of the novel, the faithful Flanagans in Sadlier's novel "removed to a larger house, which they furnished with a view to comfort and convenience, rather than show."[55]

McElgun actually devotes more space to the home of the longshoreman Terence McManus than to the homes of his middle-class characters, to show that working-class people in America, unlike those in England, could lead comfortable lives. McManus brings the newly arrived James O'Rourke to a "neat-looking brick house with a wooden stoop." The two men enter what is clearly an apartment, climbing a "flight of very clean but carpetless stairs to the third story and . . . entered a tidily furnished room of comfortable dimensions." McElgun describes the pictures on the walls, "all very tastefully arranged," including those over "the wooden mantel-piece," and suggests that there are other rooms as well, since Mrs. McManus leaves to prepare a meal.[56]

Sadlier tries to clarify her attitude toward materialism through her portraits of the backsliders, who prize their possessions. While the Flanagans furnish their bigger house with an eye to comfort, the Blakes "had purchased a handsome dwelling . . . and Mrs. Blake was anxious for the opportunity of exhibiting at one and the same time, her new house [and] the richness and elegance of her furniture." The Blakes do not invite any of their Irish friends to the party they give to celebrate their new acquisitions. In *Old and New*, the Gallaghers, who had grown rich from a butcher shop, build a very large house in a "pretentious neighborhood," with "a style of splendor befitting the ambitious pretensions of the family." The Von Weigels, by contrast, reside in an old mansion in a no-longer fashionable neighborhood of New York. They wear plain clothes, surrounded by antique furniture they take for granted and by the books, art, and music that interest them.[57]

The authors also make some effort to apply these general Catholic values to the circumstances of everyday economic life. Most mention, though only in passing, that Catholics give to the Church and to the poor. They also show that Catholics behave morally in their working lives, that is, they do not lie, cheat, or steal. McCorry's established immigrant, Mr. O'Meara, has become a successful store owner through his "integrity in business" as well as his industry and perseverance. (One example of his integrity: as a young man, O'Meara was fired for theft—a crime that, as a good Catholic, he would never have committed. He then refused to lie about the incident in job interviews.)[58]

Another type of conduct that authors use consistently to illustrate Christian morality in economic life is the mutual support family members give one another. The authors may downplay the marriage relationship and traditional nuclear families in their efforts to show the Church as the true home. But they emphasize the obligations of parents to children and, even more, of children to parents. This family support was the primary kind of help the immigrants could rely on—apart from that offered by the Church.

The key family relationships typically involve mothers and children. In novels by Sadlier and Quigley, the Burke and O'Clery parents emigrate for the sake of their offspring. Once in America, they focus mainly on their children's welfare. Sadlier's Con O'Regan, once he is out west with his wife and children, reflects that "he had to work hard at times, and at certain seasons early and late, but what of that when his labor went to improve his own land and to bring in golden crops for the benefit of himself and his family."[59]

The children, in turn, help to support their parents throughout their lives. Single men and women emigrate for the sake of parents left behind. Once in America, well-off married people, single men, and, most especially, single women send money to parents in Ireland. Children raised in America also help their parents. Sadlier's Willy Burke is anxious to go to work, rather than to school, to support his mother. In *Confessions of an Apostate*, the eldest son of the construction worker is, according to his father, "the best son ever poor people had, a boy that wouldn't take a shillin' out of his week's wages 'til he'd bring it home an' put it in his mother's hand."[60]

The authors also highlight helpful relationships among siblings, though to a lesser degree. When Paul O'Clery, the eldest son in Quigley's first novel, earns enough, he buys out the foster care contracts of his younger brothers and sisters. Sadlier's Winny O'Regan helps her brother find employment with Mr. Coulter, then helps him purchase the necessary clothes for the job. When Winny becomes ill, her brother refuses to put her into a charity hospital but pays for her care with the money he had been saving to bring his wife and children to America. And, as mentioned before, Patrick Scanlon, the minor character in Cannon's *Bickerton*, earns enough as a laborer to bring his siblings as well as his wife, children, and parents to America.

Apart from aiding those in their immediate circle, good Catholics—especially in the later novels—help newer arrivals to find employment, but these wider networks never rival the family as a source of support. The established mechanic Patrick Sweeny, the mechanic with his own business, assists Annie Reilly in McElgun's novel to find another job after she leaves her first one. Fellow working-class immigrants direct Manus O'Hanlon, the newly arrived immigrant in Cannon's *Bickerton*, to a job on a labor gang. In McElgun's *Annie Reilly*, an older immigrant Terence McManus helps James O'Rourke find his first job as a longshoreman. Eventually the young men in both novels find these jobs to be unsatisfactory and move on.

While the authors clearly advocate that individuals behave honestly in their economic lives and provide whatever help they can to family members and even to fellow immigrants, they do not consistently distinguish between good and faithless Catholics on these scores. Sadlier acknowledges that Miles Blake, despite his neglect of religious obligations, remains "honest in his dealings" throughout his career. Simon O'Hare, the apostate in her later novel, and the Mulroony father and son in Quigley's *Profit and Loss*, withdraw from mass and the sacraments but do not engage in unethical economic behavior and remain willing to support their mothers. The same can be said about the married women characters who prefer fashion to God. Single women are handled more harshly; if they withdraw from Catholicism they usually behave badly in many areas of life. In *Bessy Conway*, Sally and Mary neglect their work and lie to employers and/or parents. In *The Lost Rosary*, McCorry describes a domestic servant so intent on her social life that she not only abandons religious practice but also causes the death of the child in her care. Yet even Sadlier admits that the Irish domestic servant Bridget, who refuses to go to mass on Sunday or to follow the employer's orders, sends money home to her family in Ireland.

The novelists, in other words, seemed to fear an overweening desire to succeed not because it threatened moral principles but because it threatened ethnic and religious identity.[61] The characters who stop practicing their faith and change their names to be less recognizably Irish often continue to behave in an ethical fashion in their personal and economic lives. This divide between piety and economic conduct suggests again that these authors stressed religious practice more as a mark of group membership than as a basis for good behavior.

Despite this inconsistency, the authors do instruct their readers about the moral rules governing individual behavior and relationships with family and kin. They helped the immigrants to accomplish what John Bodnar in *The Transplanted* sees as a need common to all immigrants: "to provide for their own welfare and that of their . . . household group" by focusing on "that portion of their world in which they actually could exert some power and influence."[62]

By contrast, the authors offered very little guidance specifically to Catholic employers or, more generally, to the Catholic wealthy about what they should do with their power and wealth. Although the novels do not describe an industrial economy but rather a world of farmers, craftsmen, merchants, and servants, much like the one in Ireland, they are describing capitalist structures—Catholic characters own their enterprises and employ workers for wages. In accordance with the message of the novels, these owners should operate on the basis of superior values that will eliminate class conflicts. As Quigley's priest tells the men on the railroads, the Church, which teaches employees to be content with a competency, also teaches "employers . . . [to] treat their men with kindness and justice combined."[63]

As though to implement such expectations, Catholic employers in some novels are shown to hire the immigrants, even if not for their first jobs. In Sadlier's novels, the aristocratic Von Weigels of *Old and New* employ a married couple, a German man and Irish woman, to run their household, and in *Bessy Conway*, Mrs. Delany, a "genuine Irish lady . . . [from] the polished capital of her native land" and "the wife of an eminent physician," hires the heroine for her last job in America.[64] And in McCorry's

The Lost Rosary, the established O'Meara couple hire one of the heroines as a domestic servant after she has left her previous employment. Roddan's John O'Brien obtains his final job with a Catholic law firm with the help of one of the firm's Catholic lawyers; Sadlier's Willy Burke is hired by the Protestant Mr. Weimar, through the intercession of the priest and Weimar's Catholic partner.

Yet the authors make little effort to portray exemplary owner-worker relationships in such Catholic establishments (except, of course, in the matter of religious practice). Most say nothing on the subject, and those who comment are vague. In Roddan's *John O'Brien*, the Catholic lawyer gives John time to study and tutors him, but the author reports nothing about wages, hours, or working conditions. McCorry shows happy dealings between the O'Meara couple and the newer arrival they hire. When the couple take their employee for a drive in a carriage, the domestic servant says that she is not used to such treatment. Mrs. O'Meara responds: "we are in America . . . where mistress and servant, especially a good servant . . . seldom make any particular distinction."[65] Nevertheless, McCorry too ignores such troublesome subjects as wages and working conditions.[66]

Sadlier occasionally shows Irish Catholic employers treating their employees quite harshly. Her Tim Flanagan and his two sons in their leather dressing business "worked into each other's hands; they had nothing to pay out to strangers, except the trifling wages given to the apprentices." In *Bessy Conway*, Sadlier praises the Irish Mrs. Delany for assigning each of her servants a time to go to mass on Sunday. She also notes with admiration that Mrs. Delany had been "obliged to change her cook several times during the first three months." In the same novel, the good Catholic Paul employed in Michael Dooley's shoe store spends his days working in a little room behind the store, "plying the awl from morn till night, and after night, too . . . as he sat hour after hour in that dark little shop." Sadlier's point is not to criticize Dooley for those working conditions but to praise the immigrant for his willingness to work hard to support the old woman he has taken under his wing.[67]

In general, these authors say little about the obligations of wealthier Catholics, apart from very occasional and vague praise of their charity to the poor and contributions to the Church. Roddan is unique when, in his 1850 *John O'Brien*, he suggests that the wealthy might fund Catholic merchants' or apprentices' libraries. No author suggests that established Catholics do anything to help others set up in business, for example. When Sadlier advocates colonization in *Con O'Regan*, she never intimates that wealthy Catholics could fund the scheme; indeed, the lapsed Protestant employer pays for the lead characters to move west. And, certainly, the authors never encourage their readers to rely on, or expect, assistance from better-off Catholics.

In failing to use Catholic standards to persuade the wealthy to alter their behavior, the authors suggest that the religious and economic elites within the immigrant community had the same interests. They also suggest overlapping interests when they advise readers, however understandably, to focus on "the immediate and attainable"—finding a job, working hard, and supporting their extended families—rather than on changing the existing order.[68]

Yet the novels do not present the interests of the Church and the wealthy as identical, and so do not support the idea that the Church and the Catholic middle class in the nineteenth century could simply join forces to promote a hegemonic bourgeois culture, as some scholars have argued.[69] The Catholic authors urge their readers to focus on the areas of life under their control, but they do not go so far as to justify capitalist structures. They also maintain that when religious or moral values conflict with economic ones—as they often do—the moral values should prevail. The authors suggest the divergent interests of religious and economic elites in more immediate ways as well. Priests, not middle-class Catholics, are the community leaders. The novels support the priests in their conflict with trustees over church government and show bishops, not politicians or laymen, leading public campaigns for the schools. The novels also advocate separate economic enclaves to assure group integrity, indicating that religious leaders were quite prepared to limit the ambitions of middle-class and professional men who might wish to enter the economic mainstream. Such divergent interests characterized the relationship of religious leaders not only to the economic elites but also to nationalist leaders, as discussed in chapter 6, and to Catholic politicians, the subject of the next chapter.

Chapter 10

AMERICAN POLITICS

Catholics as Patriotic Outsiders

As they confronted America's political system, the Irish American novelists advanced the same views as their Catholic predecessors, for the most part. They defended rights to Catholic education and opposed the reform movements of the time, particularly abolition. They showed their acceptance of American ideas of church-state separation by taking these clearly political positions without involving any priest characters or advocating any political action, except on issues of religious freedom for Catholics.

The Irish Americans commented on a greater variety of issues than their predecessors, however, including women's rights and temperance in the United States and the national independence movements in Europe. This more extensive commentary reflects the political landscape of the time but also suggests that Catholics, though not the Church or clergy, were becoming more willing to take political positions.

The Irish Americans also emphasized different reasons for their opposition to reform, focusing almost entirely on the movements as manifestations of anti-Catholicism. As they made an exception for the nationalist movement in Ireland, the authors' political positions became another means of reinforcing the group identity of their readers. Although the Irish Americans adopted the prevailing view that African Americans were inferior to other races, they were less supportive of slavery than the earlier Catholic writers—many of whom were native-born American southerners—and they never seemed to doubt, or to assert, their own whiteness.

The Irish American novels also conveyed a cynicism about American politics that was new to Catholic fiction but served to remind readers that priests, not politicians, were the community leaders. At the same time, the novelists asserted even more vigorously than their predecessors that Catholics loved their country and, as a main sign of that love, were willing to fight and die in its wars. Perhaps most important over the long run, the Irish Americans advocated the pluralist position that America could base its unity on adherence to political values and tolerate diversity in cultural and social life. They asserted that pluralist argument globally, as well, maintaining that one political system—even the American one—was not appropriate for all countries.

Supporting Catholic Education and Church-State Separation

Catholic authors, starting with Bryant in 1847, were always willing to use their novels, and their priest characters, to criticize public schools for their sectarianism. Some also proposed remedies for the problem. Bryant (in 1847) and Cannon (in 1855) invoke the right of conscience guaranteed in the Constitution to argue that Catholic and Protestant children in the public schools should be able to read from the Bibles approved by their respective churches. Here, too, the authors were willing to use their priest characters. Bryant is the first of the authors to defend the efforts of Bishop Hughes in New York. He does not comment on the bishop's political activities, such as endorsing a slate of candidates. But he makes the negative case that the bishop did not seek "to have the Bible excluded from the public schools" but only asserted the right of conscience on behalf of Catholic children.[1] Roddan and Sadlier, publishing in Boston in 1850, are more interested in Catholic alternatives for employed young adults than in schools for children. Roddan advocates the Catholic library and educational institutes; Sadlier relies more directly on the Church. The employed Willy Burke in her novel attends an evening school established by the priest and reads books in the priest's library.

With her 1855 *The Blakes and Flanagans*, however, Sadlier comments extensively on the efforts of Bishop Hughes to solve the problem of the public schools. She acknowledges, at least partly, that the bishop led a political struggle; she calls him "the head of the Catholic party." She also expected all Catholics to line up behind him: her good Catholic Tim Flanagan blames Henry Blake's "Protestant heart" for his opposition to the Catholic party. But even Sadlier is extremely vague about the bishop's political activities. His opponents in the novel do not accuse the bishop of meddling in politics, so Sadlier never defends him on that score. She also never specifies the bishop's demands. In the passages from his book that Sadlier cites, the Reverend Bayley says only that "under the advice and active leadership of the Bishop, a systematic attempt was made to call the attention of the community and the public authorities to the subject" of the schools. Sadlier is more eloquent herself about the bishop's activities but equally unwilling to be specific about them. "Fortunately for the young Church of New York," she writes, it was "under the guidance of a prelate ... [who] bent ... his vigorous mind to save the Catholics of the United States, and of New York in particular, from the fearful abyss opened beneath their feet by the *paternal kindness* of the State."[2]

Sadlier is precise only in her conclusion that the bishop did not achieve his goal, whatever it was, which meant that Catholics would have to establish their own school system. Like Bryant earlier, she defends that demand as a matter of freedom, here "freedom of education," claiming that the bishop's opponents, such as Henry Blake, are "opposed to separate schools on principle" and believe that the desire for such schools reflects "a narrow feeling of bigotry, and ... fanaticism."[3] Religious freedom or the right of conscience, which had supported the earlier demand that Catholics be able to read their own Bible in public schools, became the cornerstone of the demand that Catholics should be able to establish their own schools. Although Sadlier is the first of the authors to clearly describe the full-time alternative system and to recommend it to Catholic parents, she never in any way suggests that the bishop or any other Catholic seeks public funding for the separate schools. Like Bryant and Cannon,

Sadlier does not articulate any political demands beyond those that could be couched in terms of religious freedoms guaranteed in the Constitution.

Quigley, in his 1873 *Profit and Loss*, is the next Irish American author to make the schools a central issue. He never hints that political action had been taken in the past to remedy the public system, nor does he mention public funding. His goal is to simply persuade parents to send their children to the full-time Catholic system, and, like Sadlier, he describes the critics of the Catholic position as opposing the very existence of Catholic schools. One preacher, hoping to run for office, says that Catholics wanted "separate schools for their children, a thing that . . . must not be allowed."[4]

Sadlier and Quigley dismiss concerns that Catholic parents would have to make up for the lack of public funding. Sadlier's Miles Blake appears to acknowledge that public schools are free—he comments that he would be "very ungrateful" if he did not send his children to the "Ward School . . . when the State is so good and so kind as to educate our children without meddling with their religion."[5] Yet he does not argue for or against the schools on that ground. In contrast, Mr. Mulroony, in Quigley's 1873 novel, says that parents appreciate the "free schools." Quigley then ridicules the notion of "free," linking it to other objectionable ideas (as when a banner at the public school assembly proclaims "free thoughts, free schools, free religion"). Quigley also suggests that the public schools are not really free. When Mr. Mulroony praises the free schools to his wife, she answers, "that's true, we have plenty of schools, such as they are. But . . . we have to pay dear for them in school-taxes." Quigley neglects to mention that Catholic parents would pay these taxes whether they sent their children to public schools or not. Cannon, by contrast, notes that Catholic parents "were taxed in proportion to their means" for the "schools provided by the State" and hence have an understandable interest in making use of them.[6]

On the question of Catholic school costs, Cannon writes that parishioners pay to support the parish schools, adding further hardship to parents. Sadlier and Quigley, both advocates for Catholic schools, never indicate whether parents pay tuition at St Peter's, the school attended by the Flanagans, or at the Irish Corners school in Quigley's novel. When Sadlier mentions the growth of the Catholic school system by 1855, she lists schools that were by then largely free along with those that charged tuition, without distinguishing between them: The "Brothers of the Chris-

tian Schools and the Jesuit Fathers labor conjointly in the Christian education of youth, doing for boys what the Ladies of the Sacred Heart and the
Sisters of Charity do for girls of all conditions."[7] At the same time, Sadlier
and Quigley feature middle-class families in their novels, for whom tuition
would not be such a hardship.

In their treatment of the schools, the Catholic novels reveal a church
anxious to show that it would not assert its interests in politics except de-
fensively, to protect its religious freedom to go its own way. Contrary to
the arguments of the political scientists Hamburger and Fessenden, discussed in chapter 4, the novels also suggest that this position was not a
new development for the American Church after the defeat of Bishop
Hughes. Before 1847, novelists did not raise the schools issue at all and so
do not provide evidence of a previously more active stance.

The purpose of the novels is not to persuade readers to take political
action in support of Catholic schools; the purpose is to persuade parents
to send their children to those schools, despite the cost. It is possible that
in their praise of separate schools and clerical leadership, the Irish American novels prepared Catholic public opinion for campaigns to gain public
support for the schools, and perhaps for other institutions, at a later date.
But the authors' goals were contradictory since they did little to develop a
base of popular support for clerical or church intervention in politics to
advance a positive rather than defensive agenda for Catholic interests.

The novelists' reluctance to show the Church asserting positive demands in politics is even more pronounced in their discussions of the reform movements of the time, issues that did not so directly involve Catholic interests or lend themselves to claims of religious freedom.

Opposing Reform—Slavery, Abolition,
Women's Rights, and Temperance

From the beginning, Catholic novelists opposed reform movements but
did not define their views as official church positions, or express them
through their priest characters. They also did not suggest that Catholics
take any political action on the issues. At the time, the Church took the position that slavery was a tragic evil that, like war and pestilence, had to be

borne. The American Catholic bishops' councils maintained an official policy of silence on the question of abolition, although commentators at the time interpreted their statements as criticisms of the movement.[8] In the face of such official silence on abolition, the Catholic position was expressed in the personal statements of individual bishops, in the Catholic press—and in Catholic fiction. In the novels, as in these other sources, there was some disagreement about slavery but generally uniform opposition to abolition before the Civil War.

Most of the first generation of Catholic writers were Southerners. They did not directly contradict the Church position that slavery, however inevitable, was an evil, but defended the institution in their novels, most obviously by showing good Catholics as slave owners. In the novels of Pise and Dorsey, the Southern Protestant families who converted to Catholicism owned slaves, as did the Southern Catholic family in Miles's *Loretto*. The slaves were not important characters, and the authors took no pains to describe them. They merely used the characters to show benevolence and charity (on the part of owners) and piety and obedience (on the part of slaves).

Dorsey, more clearly than her colleagues, accepted slavery only as a temporary measure. A good character in her *The Sister of Charity* reflects that he would have his "people, slaves through they be, come with me into the true fold of Christ and *there*, at least, enjoy those equal privileges which, temporarily speaking, are impossible." Yet she describes the "slaves" on the estate of *The Student of Blenheim Forest* as "well clad and happy."[9] Pise uses the slave Moses to illustrate a Catholic life of basic understanding and religious practice, as opposed to the more intellectual Catholicism that appealed to wealthy Protestants. In *Pauline Seward*, the Philadelphia-born Bryant includes a character, Sam, who for forty years had been "the faithful and devoted slave" of a West Indies gentleman. Bryant writes: "In an insurrection of the blacks on the Island of Tobago, Sam had saved his master's life at the imminent risk of his own." As a reward, he was offered his freedom, but "it was long before Sam could be prevailed upon to accept it." Eventually he agreed "to be left as a servant in" the Seward household.[10] There is no suggestion in these early novels that slavery might be unjust, and no mention that slaves were bought and sold or denied a freedom they desired and deserved.

The Irish Americans who dealt with the issue of slavery did not contradict the Church either, though they expressed more ambivalence about the institution than their predecessors. Instead of slave owners, they focused on Irish immigrant characters, referring only occasionally to Southern families and then avoiding the issue of slaves. Quigley, in his first novel, describes a Protestant New Orleans household that employs an "aunt Judy," an African American Catholic woman, who had come to New Orleans at the time of the revolution in her native Santo Domingo "in care of a child belonging to one of the white planters who was murdered." Aunt Judy calls her employers "massa and missus," but Quigley does not explicitly say she is a slave; he refers to her only as a "negro" and says that the household employed "servants of every color and hue." Yet at the end of the novel, he mentions that one of the orphans became a nun and died helping the "negro slaves of New Orleans."[11]

Only Cannon and Boyce communicated a view of slavery, and both spoke of the institution as unjust. In his first novel, *Oran, the Outcast*, published with a secular house in 1833, Cannon's lead character is a free man, the biracial son of a slave and her white owner. A Christ figure throughout the novel, Oran is an outcast because of his race. His father disowns him, and he cannot marry the white woman he loves, although he has saved her life, because of the "barrier that nature—or the prejudices of society—had placed between" them. Cannon voices similar sentiments in his novels published with the Catholic houses. In the 1840s, he ridicules the contemporary view that Catholics were apologists for slavery and Southern interests; Protestants in one of his novels say that priests in Cuba killed black babies in order to eat them and charge that American Catholics wish to control the Southern states to enforce slavery and implement the same practice. In his 1855 short story collection, *Ravellings from the Web of Life*, Cannon again acknowledges the tragic injustices visited upon slaves. In one story, the son of a slave-holding family murders his father and allows a slave to be executed for the crime. The son later repents and devotes the remainder of his life to good works.[12]

Boyce, like Bryant did earlier, includes a story in his novel about a slave who saves a white man's life at the risk of his own. He also mentions a former slave character who escapes to Ireland as a stowaway on a ship. Boyce refers to him only as "Sambo," but tells his readers that slaves—the "unfortunate creatures"—were not typically given surnames. This former slave relishes the fact that he is now "free" and "am good as white man." A conversation about slavery between an Irish woman and the American visitor Ephraim Weeks ends as an indictment of the institution. The Irish woman mentions that she has often heard that the "craturs out there in America warn't so badly off after all," to which Weeks replies, "they're pretty well off for clothes and food . . . but they hain't got their liberty . . . and no American born ought to see a human in slavery and not try to liberate him." The Irish woman then says, "you speak like a Christian. . . . [I]t's a poor sight to see God's craturs bought and sould. . . . [I]t's unnatural."[13]

Yet Cannon and Boyce also maintained, at times, that slaves did not want freedom or that they were no worse off than the immigrants. In some of his stories in *Ravellings*, Cannon includes slave characters who prefer their servitude to freedom, as Bryant had before him. In one story, an African American character named Agamemnon, born a slave, refuses many offers of freedom; he "boasted of his bondage, and looked with pity, if not contempt upon the free" black people in the neighborhood. Cannon also adopted the then-popular view that wage laborers were no better off than slaves, a position also taken by Orestes Brownson. In *Harry Layden*, Cannon writes that the young hero had become "that worst of slaves—a FACTORY BOY!" "Talk ye of the slave of the south? He is a free and happy being compared to the miserable drudge of the Factory; for to him is not denied those common but invaluable blessings—the light of day and the pure free air of heaven."[14] In Boyce, the American Weeks and the Irish woman, who condemns slavery as unnatural and un-Christian, quickly move on to the subject of the immigrants in America. The Irish woman tells Weeks, "still . . . they tell us the poor Irish there isn't trated much better than slaves," forcing Weeks to explain the treatment of the Irish. The implication seems to be that the immigrants must focus on their own plight, which was just as bad, if not worse, than that of slaves.[15]

This tendency to compare the situation of the immigrants to that of slaves occurs in other Irish American novels as well. In Quigley's 1853 *The Cross and the Shamrock*, the priest, in a sermon to the workers, says, "The railroad and day laborer" is forced to "work from dark to dark; he has to take *store pay* for his wages; and he has to obey the . . . arbitrary commands of the . . . most brutal class of men on earth. . . . Is not this slavery?" Quigley also recommends the priesthood as a path to upward mobility for those who do not want to be "the drudges of the earth and the slaves of the world." Sadlier, in *Con O'Regan*, published in 1856 and again in the early 1860s, describes the Irish immigrants in Boston "working like slaves from morning till night."[16]

If there are some differences among the Catholic writers on the subject of slavery, and ambivalence in the attitudes of Cannon and Boyce, the Catholic writers who mentioned abolition were unified in their opposition to the movement. In adopting this stance, the novelists took the same position as the individual bishops who spoke on the question in the years before the Civil War. The bishops raised many considerations, emphasizing that abolition threatened the social order, sought freedom for slaves who were not ready for it, and offered a liberal individualist conception of freedom that would destroy authority and community. Some of the bishops also referred to the anti-Catholicism of the abolitionists and expressed racist views, though their position did not depend wholly on these considerations.[17] The abolitionist movement also threatened the institutional interests of the Church. It would divide the hierarchy and membership on sectional lines, just as it divided other religious denominations in the country. To preserve unity, the Church either kept silent, a tactic adopted by bishops' councils, or voiced outright opposition to abolition, the course followed by some individual bishops.

In defending their opposition to change, the early Catholic novelists emphasized social order. They showed that Catholicism taught masters to be charitable and slaves to be obedient and accepting. When Pise's Father Rowland hears that the slave Moses is a Roman Catholic, he comments that "our religion inspires fidelity." Bryant and Dorsey—writing in the 1840s when the abolitionists were gaining in importance—also emphasize social order above liberty. For Bryant, "the Catholic principle" "preserves alike the crowned head and the majesty of the people; the freeborn and the slave" as opposed to the Protestant idea of "Private Interpretation," which was "weakening the ties of unanimity" in the country, for example, in the "late action of the Methodists, upon the slavery question." Dorsey's priest character tells the father of a slaveholding family that the

> Catholic religion will teach them [slaves] all which can make their inferior position, with its trials, one of merit to themselves here and hereafter. Its holy influences will encourage neither rebellion nor disorders,

neither indolence nor licentiousness, but will prove a salutary check to all those evils which are of common occurrence among them.[18]

American Catholic opposition to abolition, obviously, did not begin with the Irish. In fact, only three of the Irish American authors—Quigley, Sadlier, and to a lesser extent Boyce—voiced opposition; the others were silent. The three Irish Americans also presented a simpler case than the bishops and the first Catholic writers: they opposed abolition primarily because they viewed it as a Protestant anti-Catholic movement. The Catholic press of the time also emphasized this rationale.[19] In one of his author asides, Quigley comments about "the 'Irish,' whom some mad abolitionists would gladly enslave in place of the blacks." In Boyce, the Irish woman who discusses slavery with Weeks says about the New England Protestant employers: "It's a wonder they're not ashamed to purfess so much tinderness for the slaves, and trate the poor Irish so manely as that." Boyce also regarded the abolitionists' concern for slaves as hypocritcal. The American Weeks declares that the "New England ladies" who treat former slaves like princes actually "despise" them.[20]

In portraying abolition as an anti-Catholic and anti-Irish movement, the novels were reflecting reality to some extent; abolition was, in fact, primarily a Protestant movement. Some abolitionist leaders were also prominent anti-Catholics. What is significant about the Irish American novels, however, is that they offered this rationale as the main basis for their opposition to abolition and also ignored any evidence to the contrary. None of the writers mentioned that the Irish political leader Daniel O'Connell opposed slavery and supported abolition or that the abolitionist leader Garrison tried to enlist American Irish Catholics in the cause.[21] None mentioned that some Protestant denominations also opposed abolition. Instead, the writers used the political issue of abolition to mark Catholics off from the rest of American society, once again using "outsiderhood" as a strategy to maintain group cohesion.[22]

The novels' treatment of abolition shows continuity in the Catholic position, in the oppositionist stance as well as in the determination to uphold church-state separation. The Irish Americans of the 1850s and '60s may have been more willing than their Catholic predecessors to name political movements and characterize their leaders—suggesting a shift toward political involvement rather than withdrawal—but this change may reflect only the growing strength of the abolitionist movement. Basically, as the Catholic authors shaped the attitudes of their readers on slavery and abolition, they were careful to keep the Church out of the picture, just as the official church, through the bishops' councils, stayed silent. The authors did not express their opposition through their bishop or priest characters but relied, instead, on author interjections and lay characters. Pise's Father Rowland and Dorsey's priest teach slaves to obey their masters, but they viewed this as advising Catholics, a traditional priestly function, not a political position. In the Irish American novels, no priest comments on slavery even to this extent. The closest any come are the priest in Quigley's first novel, who compares the men working on the railroads to slaves. Again, the authors communicated positions clearly identified as Catholic ones but did nothing to undermine American ideas of separation. On the contrary, they communicated support for the idea that the Church and priests did not belong in politics.

Rather than condemn slavery outright or support the movement to end it, the Catholic novels sent a message that good Catholics treated African Americans well. On this question of individual moral behavior, the novelists invoked their priests. The Irish Americans used this argument as another way to mark off Catholics, who were usually presented as the only characters in the novels who treated African Americans decently. One of Boyce's exemplary Catholics joins the priest in caring for the injured former slave, saying "he's a Christian . . . and perhaps a better Christian, too, than a great many of us." Similarly, in Sadlier's *Bessy Conway*, the Catholic domestic servant, but not the Protestant one, was willing to do some work needed by the old African American male servant, who occupied the lowest position in the servants' hierarchy.[23] Catholic novelists also pointed out that priests and nuns worked faithfully among the African American population. The Irish Americans never mentioned any draft riots or other violent actions by Catholics against African Americans; their orientation in this respect was simply to portray exemplary characters and actions.

Still, the novels communicated the view that African Americans were not equal to whites. Cannon's Oran was the only African American character described as equal in virtue and economic position to his exemplary white colleagues, but he was not equal socially; he was prohibited from marrying the white woman he loved, for example. In the other novels of the period, published by Catholic houses, African American characters were inferior in all respects to white characters, including the Irish. In the early Catholic novels, the African Americans were slaves and so were clearly inferior socially. They were also less educated, as was made clear in their mode of speech. In describing the slave Moses, Pise took pains to portray a dignified character, but in a condescending way. When he is close to death, Moses demonstrates that he knows his religion and can quote scripture, but he speaks in a pronounced accent. The southern Wolburns, on the other hand, have no accent at all. Asked if he adores pictures, Moses answers: "my dear missy, what do de first commandment say: 'thou shalt not make to dyself any graven ting.'" Moses also tells his interlocutors to consult the Bible story of "Gineral Machabee." An onlooker observes that the faith of Moses is "really of an enlightened nature."[24]

Bryant portrayed the former slave Sam—who had heroically rescued his master and was now working as a coachman for the Sewards—as deficient not only in education (as evidenced by his accented speech) but also in judgment. Bryant writes that Sam's "intellect took no note of the conjunctives that connected" words or commands. Sam also "turned his head on one side, and rolling his huge orbs, turned them slowly and incredulously until they were fixed full upon the speaker." In a crisis, Sam grows overexcited, loses control of his horses, and has to be rescued by the white men in the party.[25]

In the Irish American novels after 1850, the authors portrayed African American characters as inferior to an even greater extent than their predecessors. There were no characters during these years with the dignity of Moses. The African Americans were free and might be Catholic, but they did not socialize with or marry Irish Americans, or work with them as equals. Sadlier, in *Bessy Conway*, provides the only instance in which an African American servant is shown working in the same place as Irish domestic servants; she refers to an old man who works in the home of Bessy's employer as "Wash, the colored man" or as the "old darkey." His name indicates his position, which is clearly below that of the Irish immigrant cook and other servants; they order him around and tell him to "shut up" when he displeases them.[26]

The Irish Americans also portrayed African American characters as deficient in speech, character, and behavior. The escaped slave in *Boyce* calls all whites "massa" and says, at one point in the novel, that he is "berry bad . . . berry sick; no tink me live."[27] By contrast, while poor Irish American minor characters might speak with accents, the major characters, whatever their class, speak proper English. In describing physical attributes, the authors also demean African American characters. Cannon describes a porter in *Tighe Lyfford* as "a ferocious-looking and gigantic negro." In *Bessy Conway*, Sadlier refers to a "colored servant in livery. He looked savage" and spoke either "gruffly" or inappropriately "grandly." His employer calls him only "Sambo." Quigley, in 1873, introduces a "colored fortune-teller," a "ferocious-looking darkey enveloped in his greasy habiliments, and surrounded by his half-dozen cur-dogs."[28]

The African Americans were portrayed either as childlike and helpless, or ridiculous. Quigley's African American "servant" aunt Judy displays "childish and helpless simplicity," while the Irish girl who befriends her responds with "kind and good-natured condescension."[29] Sadlier's old Wash "blubbered like a great baby" when the mistress was leaving the country, and in *Old and New*, "Hardman E. W. R. White, a colored gentleman, lately escaped from slavery," lectured "in the Tabernacle . . . to raise funds *to educate himself.*" When an Irish visitor asked, "Now on what do you suppose will this alphabetically-great colored individual hold forth for public enlightenment?" he is told the subject will be "abolitionism, of course—and a capital audience he'll have, too—I can tell you that!"[30]

These crude portrayals have implications for the debate among scholars about the Irish immigrants' attitudes toward race and claims of whiteness.[31] The novels present the Irish as clearly superior to African Americans, in general appearance, speech, character, and occupation. Since the novels never show Irish immigrants struggling to find low-level jobs, their negative attitude toward African Americans suggests they were more concerned about status or caste than about employment. While the authors never indicate that Irish characters fear job competition, they suggest a great fear of association with a race seen as inferior in American society. The novels do not show African American women in domestic service or African American men on the canals, because their presence, in the authors' view, would signify that the job was at the bottom rung of the status hierarchy. As Bruce Nelson has argued in his recent study of Irish nationalism, the immigrants sought to distinguish themselves from a "despised and powerless race," to avoid being condemned to "the margins of the society they had chosen as their home."[32]

At the same time, the novelists' provide no evidence of the immigrants' struggle to attain "whiteness." The authors do not refer to the immigrants as members of the white race or as white. Nor do they emphasize such physical attributes as pale skin or hair. Cannon describes the "complexion" of the immigrant's daughter in *Bickerton* as "a healthful brown," for example.[33] When they speak of the stereotypes prevailing in Protestant opinion, they emphasize the attacks on the immigrants' faith and ethnicity, not the efforts to align them with African Americans. Only Quigley refers to the Thomas Nast portraits that appeared in *Harper's Weekly*, calling them "Harper's *Nasty* Pictorials" and emphasizing the attack on Irish Catholics for their moral character: the cartoon is a "hideous picture of a party of drunken Irish Catholics, murdering a family of innocent American Methodist Protestants.[34] The authors seem simply to assume that the Irish are white and make no effort to underscore this point. They also have no interest in proclaiming their unity with American Anglo-Saxons on racial or any other grounds.[35] If, as scholars have argued, "whiteness" is about cultural characteristics associated with respectability rather than skin color, then certainly the Irish struggled for whiteness, but then the term seems to have lost all meaning. The novels show that the Irish fought to be considered respectable and equal, especially to the dominant Anglo-Saxons, but did not define that equality in racial terms.

In fact, when they spoke of the immigrants' race, the authors adopted a typically imprecise nineteenth-century view of the subject. They refer to "the Irish race in America" as opposed to the "American French, or German, or Spanish, Swedes, Danes or Norwegians . . . those other races."[36] The novelists did not mind being "racialized" as Irish or Celtic, with inherited qualities; they minded any implication that their race was an inferior one. In Cannon's *Tighe Lyfford*, the Catholic speaker objects to the idea that America owes all of her prosperity "to the Anglo-Saxon energy diffused among us through Puritan blood." "Some little credit," he says, "is certainly due to the other races of which we are composed."[37]

The Irish Americans advanced their positions on slavery and abolition in novels written before and during the Civil War but did not take sides on the war itself. Cannon is more explicit than the others: in 1859, he writes that "the Public Opinion of the North and the South . . . having very little in common, . . . it follows . . . that some of these opinions must be wrong."[38] In refusing to take sides, the novels followed the lead of the bishops' councils, which also remained neutral, since northern bishops, like Hughes, supported the Union, while southern bishops supported the Confederacy.

Like the bishops themselves, though, some of the writers took positions as individuals. Pise was known to be pro-Union, and Dorsey's son was killed fighting with the Union army. The owners of the publishing companies in New York and Massachusetts, with the exception of the Sadliers, were active Union supporters.[39] The Irish population fought mainly for the Union, but some fought on the Confederate side as well. After the war, Quigley's editor, Patrick Donahoe, like Bryant in the 1840s, traced the conflict to religious divisions in America, as though a wholly Catholic society could have found a way to resolve problems like slavery. In his 1853 novel, Quigley predicts beneficial results from the inevitable decline of Protestantism: "there can never be a real union among the States till the minds of the people, north and south, are united in faith and sentiment," he writes. In a footnote to a postwar edition of the novel, the editor comments: "the late war and its horrors, undoubtedly brought about by sectarian fanaticism prove that the predictions of the author of this book were true."[40]

The novelists' positions on slavery and abolition served many purposes. They communicated the typical nineteenth-century Catholic opposition to reform, with arguments that reinforced the conception of Irish Catholics as an isolated, beleaguered group. They also asserted that Irish immigrants were superior in every way to African Americans, although they too were racially as well as religiously distinct from the dominant Anglo-Saxons. The novels also communicated support for American ideas of church-state separation and did nothing to justify clerical involvement in electoral politics or policy-making.

Slavery and abolition were not the only reform issues that surfaced in the novels. The Irish Americans advanced positions on the movements for women's rights and temperance and also on the European movements for independence and representation. In taking these positions, they depart from their predecessors, who tended to ignore such issues. The Irish

Americans remained careful to support the idea that the Church stood apart from politics, articulating their views without reference to church interests through lay characters and author interjections, not through priests. They also did not translate their Catholic political opinions into endorsements of any political action.

Quigley, Sadlier, and McCorry voice the opposition to the women's rights movement, mostly in novels of the 1860s and '70s, though Quigley expresses his opposition in 1853 as well. The three authors characterize the women's movement as a single set of proposals, not distinguishing the call for voting or property rights from other demands. Typically, they justify their opposition primarily by portraying the leaders and adherents of the women's movement as Protestant and anti-Catholic.

Quigley lists "Bloomer women" as well as "spiritual rappers" as evidence of the "diseased public mind" caused by "sectarianism."[41] Sadlier calls two Protestant women, one a Reverend and the other named after Mary Wollstonecraft, a "pair of feminines" "of the Bloomer school." The two women, who visit Madame Von Weigel seeking signatures for a petition supporting women's rights, dismiss the opinions of St. Paul. Like Quigley, Sadlier links the women's movement with other progressive movements of the day, including "Physiology and Animal Magnetism and Bi-ology, . . . Spiritualism and Negro Slavery."[42] Protestant women in McCorry's *The Lost Rosary* regard their minister, Mr. Sookes, as weak because he "did not believe in his own advocacy of women's rights." The women are also shown to be prejudiced against Irish Catholics. They urge the minister to attend to the "benighted things from Ireland . . . poor, ignorant creatures, sent . . . by the hand of Providence, who, in order to reach the hardened hearts of idolators, punishes and afflicts them for His wise ends." One of the women calls a policeman with an Irish accent an "impudent Irish boor"; another calls him a "vile Irish wretch."[43]

On this issue, more than on abolition, the novelists explain the reform movement, which they view as advocating the right to assert one's own interests, as a logical development of Protestant individualism. All three of the authors object to the women's advocates speaking in public or, as McCorry puts it, "brawling and screaming on public platforms." Sadlier's two advocates are petitioning for their "trampled rights as women," specifically for the right to speak "in the councils of the nation." Sadlier links the claiming of rights in the political sphere to self-assertion in private life. The two advocates "seated themselves with the air of persons who felt they had a *right* to be seated, stand who would."[44]

For all three authors, the very concept of women's rights violates norms of family life and gender. For McCorry, the women's movement places a "knife . . . at the throat of the present marriage system." Sadlier focuses on the threat to authority. Madame Von Weigel tells the advocates that she belongs to a church that agrees with St. Paul that "women should *obey* their husbands and . . . keep silent in public assemblies." This reflects "a merciful dispensation . . . and a wise provision of the Divine Ruler for the wants of the human family."[45] Sadlier's treatment of women in her novels is more favorable regarding their independence and equality than this statement would suggest. But for her, as for her male colleagues, women's equality ends at the door into public life.

All three authors also connect women's rights to sexual liberation or deviance. Quigley's women's rights characters advocate and practice "free-love" and divorce. McCorry ties women's rights to sexual license more generally, saying that "Women's Rights . . . are devil's rights, calculated to destroy virtue; to prostitute all that we love and admire . . . and plunge the good and true into the . . . maelstrom of vice." Sadlier suggests that the advocates so violate norms of gender that they are not really women at all. She describes them as "attired in a fashion half masculine, half feminine but rather inclining to the former," with "rakish-looking hats . . . Turkish trowsers . . . stout buskins . . . [and] buckskin gloves, or rather gauntlets." One of the women speaks "in loud emphatic tones—meant probably for masculine."[46]

As with abolition, the writers do not find it necessary to justify their taking a position on the issue, but they also do not connect their opposition to the interests of the Church. They never suggest that women's participation in public life might disrupt the alliance between priests and women that helps to maintain Catholicism in the home and community. They also do not cite statements of American bishops or priests about the women's rights movement, instead communicating their opposition to the movement through author interjections.[47]

The Irish American novelists were also quite willing to assert their views on European affairs, again without involving their priest characters.

The earlier Catholic writers extolled their religion for its contribution to peace and order but did not allude to contemporary European revolutions. The Irish Americans, by contrast, portrayed the European reformers— except for the Irish nationalists—as part of the anti-Catholicism of the time, tying the Europeans to the American reform movements and even to American political associations generally. Their emphasis was on the unity of their opponents and the need for Catholic unity in response.

The authors objected to the European reformers because they directed their political activities against the Church, pope, and clergy. Roddan, in 1850, terms the French revolution "wicked" without further elaboration, points out that "General Bonaparte treated the holy father very badly," and refers to "the late godless movements in Europe." Through his account of European movements, Cannon highlights the hypocrisy of American anti-Catholics who oppose some, but certainly not all, foreign influences. He recounts a demonstration through a Catholic neighborhood "by which foreignism—not, of course, Kossuth-foreignism, or red-republican-French-foreignism, or radical-English-foreignism, or infidel-German-foreignism,—but popish-foreignism, was to be frightened out of the land." Boyce applauds his Irish revolutionary Randall Barry because he was "without a trace of the socialist or the red republican." Quigley refers to the "satanic acts" of the Paris Commune, men who "immortalized themselves for what they did to priests and churchmen in our own day."[48]

By connecting European reform to the movements in the United States, the Irish American authors reinforced a sense of the hostile, anti-Catholic external world that made Catholic unity and defensiveness all the more crucial. Their determination to define Catholic boundaries continued even on issues, such as temperance, where many of them acknowledged the problems and shared the concerns of other American organizations.

Except for Cannon, the early Catholic authors who included Irish characters in their stories did not raise immigrants' drinking as an issue. Neither did most of the Irish Americans in the 1850s. The Protestant characters who attack the immigrants on grounds of ethnicity without reference to religion usually allege that the Irish are dirty, lazy, and ignorant, focusing, in other words, on qualities associated with poverty. In Sadlier's novel, when Mrs. Burke tells the Protestant employer that she cannot send her son to the public school, the woman replies: "It is true, I had often heard that you Irish are too lazy and indolent to apply yourselves to learn anything." In Roddan, John O'Brien hears from his schoolmates that those who attend the "Paddy church" are "low, dirty, and vulgar" fellows who "couldn't speak plain English."[49]

Cannon, the American-born son of immigrants, is willing to consider the tendency to associate the Irish with drinking. He traces some of that reputation to bigotry: The local farmers in his 1855 *Bickerton* refuse to help an immigrant dying in the street because they assume he is "some Irishman . . . who's taken too much of the 'cratur,' and lied down for a snooze." But there are times when Cannon acknowledges the problem. In his novels of the 1840s, he says that some people, although certainly not all, are poor because of "intemperance." Jack Toland Sr., the immigrant father in *Scenes and Characters*, takes to drink after the death of his wife. Cannon is most direct in *Bickerton*, where the Irish men working on the canals are "almost brutified by the constant use of alcoholic poisons," and "left a stain upon the Irish name . . . which will not soon, if ever, be effaced." In the town also, the immigrants give in to the "evil of intemperance," and their conduct has "only too often given just grounds for reproach from their more circumspect neighbours."[50]

In the succeeding decades, the novels continue to express resentment at attacks on the Irish because of their poverty or class position. Sadlier's Con O'Regan says that all the immigrants ever heard was "'stupid Irish' and 'ignorant Paddies.'" For Boyce, the American Ephraim Weeks "like many of his countrymen . . . fancied the Irish he saw about him never could have an idea in their heads above the pick or the spade; a ragged coat and an Irish *brogue*, being in his mind synonymous with consummate ignorance and absolute barbarism."[51]

But in these years, the authors also began to deal with attacks on the Irish for drinking. Boyce and Quigley emphasize the hostile stereotypes. In the latter's *Profit and Loss*, as mentioned before, the news media turns a minor incident in which a laborer hits his employer into a story about a "party of drunken Irish Catholics" who murder an innocent Methodist.[52] Sadlier, like Cannon, simply acknowledges the problem: in *Bessy Conway*, the heroine writes to her parents that "there's a power of money made here, but there's many a one makes it that would be as well without it for there's a good many of them turns to drink." McElgun, in the 1870s, follows suit. His immigrant hero gazes at a "rum-shop" and reflects "what a woeful blight to his countrymen in America love of such places proved." Sadlier also sees drinking as a cause of domestic abuse. Male characters who drink excessively "beat" their wives or "gave . . . [them] a kick."[53]

The authors give varying explanations for the problem. Cannon attributes the behavior of the canal laborers to deplorable living and working conditions, namely, the "iniquitous laws" of England "under which they were born," the absence "of a priesthood who had exercised over them a salutary authority," the alcohol "supplied . . . without stint at the store of the contractor," and the many saloons in the poor Irish neighborhoods, "where every other cellar was turned into a dram shop."[54]

Sadlier's explanations depend on her agenda. In *Bessy Conway* she blames the immigrants themselves. Her heroine writes to her parents that "there's hundreds and hundreds" of Irish people in America "that might do better than they do, if it wasn't for the liquor." In this novel, Sadlier also blames the immigrants for the prevalence of saloons. A good character tells the future saloon owner, Ned Finigan, that "the curse of sin" blighted the business of saloon-keeping, which was "the cause" of "drunkenness," and of men taking money from cold, starving, "heart-broken" wives and children. But in *Con O'Regan*, where her goal is to encourage immigrants to move west, Sadlier blames life in Boston, "where there's ten or twelve Irish families in one house"; the drinking "comes from there being so many of them cramped up together."[55] McElgun in the 1870s traces the drinking to the harsh conditions in the oil fields, where "men . . . from every part of America and Europe . . . cared for nothing but drinking, carousing, and fighting." But on the whole, he blames the immigrants. The hero of his novel says that older men were still doing "hard labor" in the oil field because in their youth they had not saved money but spent it on whiskey; "the greater part of them have themselves only to blame for their misery."[56]

Despite their concern, the authors did not go so far as to call for political action to remedy conditions or for any alliance with the existing American temperance movement. Again, as with abolition and women's rights, the novelists correctly saw that the temperance movement was led by Protestants, and again equated Protestant with anti-Irish and anti-Catholic. Quigley names the secret oath-bound "Sons of Temperance"— an organization founded by the Freemasons that had been condemned by the Church—as an example of "fanaticism."[57] The other authors do not name a temperance organization. As in their account of the abolitionists, the authors never show temperance advocates reaching out to Catholics or Catholic temperance leaders reaching out to Protestants. If a few mention the work of the Irish priest Father Theobold Mathew, who journeyed through America from 1849 to 1851 advocating temperance, they refer only to his work among Catholics, even though he was invited to America by a mainly Protestant temperance association and tried to enlist Protestants as well as Catholics.

Rejecting the idea of any alliance with the temperance movement, the novelists urge readers to tackle the problem on their own by practicing sobriety—but not necessarily total abstinence—in accord with Church teachings. Those who needed help could rely on the Church and its priests. Once drinking was defined as a moral issue that individuals could handle within the community, the authors involved their priest characters. Quigley's priest gives a sermon to the men on the railroad gang, advising them to "guard against drunkenness." Cannon describes the role of a new pastor who inculcates in his parishioners "something of the decorum more becoming a Christian people." He goes from "house to house, and to every family in each house" encouraging them to take "the temperance pledge," and appealing not only to their "religious feelings" but also to "what was even more powerful in most, their national pride."[58]

This orientation—that readers rely on themselves, and the Church, to solve their problems—conditioned the Irish American authors' attitudes not only to reform and charitable organizations but also to the government itself. Again, the novels conveyed a deep suspicion of American institutions, including its electoral and policy-making politics.

The Political System: Low Expectations, Cynicism, and Patriotism

The Irish Americans, while focused on upward mobility, did not entirely ignore the immigrants' poverty.[59] They describe general conditions, show their characters enduring poverty in their first years in America, and allow minor figures to remain or become poor. In these accounts, some of the authors also assign responsibility for the harsh conditions in which immigrants lived and worked. Cannon blames the contractor on the canal site, who supplies "alcoholic poisons" to the laborers at his own store and "cared not" how the men "spent their earnings, provided they were spent to his profit."[60] On very rare occasions, authors single out government for its failure to regulate economic enterprises. Quigley blames "Uncle Sam" for not exercising control over the "unjust and cruel" contractors. "The whole fault is yours, 'Uncle,' and lies at the doors of people who, having the power to protect the laborer by law, neglect to exercise that power." McElgun comments that it is a "standing shame for the city" to allow so many unscrupulous people to operate the licensed boarding houses.[61]

Some authors also trace continuing poverty simply to illness, accidents, or other circumstances beyond the immigrants' control, but if they blame the immigrants themselves, they tend to focus on drink. Sadlier's successful hero in *Con O'Regan* does not drink, while another character, who works on the docks and earns "plenty of money," spends it all on liquor. McElgun's hero calls an Irish laborer in the oil fields a "drunkard" and chastises him for squandering his money. By contrast, the successful immigrant in the novel is a "sober, industrious mechanic" who has been "strictly temperate from the day he came to New York, he spent none of his money in the grog-shop."[62]

Apart from the isolated comments of Quigley and Cannon, authors never suggest that political action could be a remedy for these harsh conditions. They also consistently warn readers that public, or Protestant, charities are designed mainly to lure Catholics from their faith. The remedy for poverty, as for drinking, is personal effort aided by the Church and priests. Even Sadlier's colonization scheme is funded by the individuals involved, aided by benefactors they recruit. Quigley, who criticizes Uncle Sam for its neglect, never suggests that the immigrants take action, and traces the improvement in their lives to the priest, who speaks for the "cruelly-oppressed" workers and also encourages the men to reduce their drinking and fighting. Sadlier is the only author to mention the efforts of Catholic charities as well as of individual priests. In a footnote to Bessy Conway's letter to her parents, in which she describes the poverty she has seen in New York City, Sadlier points out that "now," as opposed to the time of which her heroine wrote, the "deserving poor have found active and devoted friends in the Society of St. Vincent de Paul."[63]

The Irish American novelists not only dismissed the government as a source of help to the immigrants, they also communicated suspicion of the system and of politicians, both Protestant and Catholic. In many novels, politicians are portrayed as hypocrites who seek the people's votes for their own ends. Despite Cannon's resentment of nativist efforts to deny Catholics the full rights of citizenship, he calls the rival parties "the Tweedledums and the Tweedledees" and says that around election time, the parties "vied with each other in showering compliments on those who were at other times mere 'Bogtrotters' or 'Troglydytes.'" In Sadlier, Henry Blake, the Democratic Party and Tammany leader, explains to his wife that his "*Irish blood*" has served him well "thanks to the 'gullibility' of our worthy Irish citizens. They are always ready to swallow the bait if it be only covered with liberality or nationality or what shall I call it—religionality." Quigley, the only author to acknowledge the growing political power of Catholics in 1853 (even if he does not incorporate that acknowledgment into his message), makes the more typical assertions in his *Profit and Loss* twenty years later. Politicians, he says, only attend to their constituents when it suits them, visiting the saloons "a few days before election." A good character in the novel asks, "What enables one party of politicians to triumph over another party? The numbers and the boldness of the lies they tell."[64] None of these Irish American authors ever introduces a Catholic politician who promotes Irish or Catholic interests. No good political leader—of any religion—ever appears in the novels, in fact. Any Catholic characters who seek political office—like Henry Blake or the Mulroony father and son—end up abandoning their faith temporarily or permanently.

This cynicism about American politics was new in Catholic fiction. The previous generation of writers, if they spoke of American politics at all, praised its operations, portraying the native-born and converted Catholic heroes of their novels as the leading men of their communities from families who had played that role for generations. The converts in Dorsey are from "one of the oldest and proudest families of Carolina," and the patriarch of the Catholic family in Miles *Loretto* is the "principal man in all the neighborhood."[65] The Irish American authors' accounts of American politics and politicians, in contrast, encourage readers to define themselves exclusively as Catholics under the leadership of the priests and not as Democrats (or Irish nationalists) led by any politicians, Catholic or otherwise.

While they voiced their criticism and suspicion of American culture, society, and politics, the Irish American authors also declared—with varying degrees of frequency, consistency, and ardor—that Irish Catholics "loved" and were loyal to this country. They were more likely than their predecessors to proclaim Catholic patriotism because the early authors could make their point through prominent male characters whose families had long contributed to the country's public life.

In the Irish American novels, the immigrants maintain their loyalty despite being treated unjustly. Boyce most poignantly asks the immigrants to remember "the stalwart limbs you gave your adopted country . . . now wasted away in her service . . . the blood you shed in her battles, the prayers you offered for her prosperity, . . . and . . . the only return she makes . . . is to hate and spurn you."[66]

The immigrant characters love America because they have been able to make a life here. Cannon says that the American "government . . . has, as it eminently deserves to have, a right to my allegiance, and the allegiance of every one whose person and property it protects, whether he be native here, or . . . has by adoption made this land his own." America also afforded religious freedom, which had—despite all the difficulties—allowed the immigrants to practice their faith and build their institutions. Quigley comments that "the Irish Catholic is the best lover of this country . . . for his sufferings in the cause of liberty and of conscience have been such as to give him the strongest title deed to the liberties and privileges . . . of this favored land." The Irish Americans were quite willing to use their priest characters to assert this love of country. Cannon cites the bishops who say in their pastoral letter that "as citizens of this great and flourishing republic, we should be grateful to God for the blessings which its noble institutions scatter among all its citizens alike," namely, "the glorious boon of equal rights and equal protection."[67]

The immigrants also contribute to their new country. The Irish Americans apply to themselves the argument that the earlier writers applied to the slaves: thanks to Catholicism and its priests, the immigrants obey lawful authority. The priest in Quigley's *The Cross and the Shamrock* persuades the men on the railroads to peaceful rather than violent action. In McCorry's novel, the bishop and priest prevent the Irish Catholics from confronting the mob attacking the convent and from seeking revenge afterward. Sadlier and Quigley indicate that the Church teaches Catholics to obey their employers.

The immigrants work hard and, in that regard, contribute to the country's prosperity. They may not be the leading men of their districts, but, as Quigley says, with their "busy hands and stalwart arms" the Irish Catholics farm land, build houses, man ships, work factories, and dig railroads and canals. Cannon maintains that America owes its prosperity not only to Anglo-Saxons but also to the "other races of which we are composed," who had displayed "unflagging industry."[68]

The Irish Americans were less likely than their predecessors to invoke the Catholics who had contributed to America over its history. They were concerned with the present-day immigrants and barely touched on the fact that many Catholics were native-born Americans because that could suggest some problem with foreigners. Cannon, the holdover from the previous era, was the exception. In *Bickerton*, the Protestant Fred Hubbard responds to nativist demands for an "America for the Americans" against the "foreign religion" of Catholicism by pointing out that "all Catholics are not foreigners. Indeed, some of our oldest and best American families— American in feeling a well as by birth—are Catholics."[69]

Most of the Irish Americans also did not include political participation in their concept of patriotism or love of country. As discussed above, they object to nativist and Know-Nothing movements as examples of anti-Catholicism but do not describe their platforms or their proposals to limit the political rights of the immigrants. The authors do not advise against voting, they simply do not mention it. They do not show good Catholic characters being active citizens; indeed, as discussed, they disparage characters who seek political office. In fact, there was no major good Catholic character in any of the novels who is shown to be a public-spirited citizen in the sense of participating in American social or public life.[70] This absence of Catholic public figures in their work may be the authors' response to Protestant fears of Catholic political intentions, but, on the other hand, it also distinguished the Irish Americans from their Catholic predecessors and reinforced the idea that the Church, not the American social and political order, was the immigrants' home.

On the question of citizenship, as on that of a Catholic contribution to American history, Cannon was the exception. Again, he conveys a sensibility that differs from the immigrant authors; he writes from an American, rather than Irish, experience and shares attitudes with his fellow Americans, including both writers and readers. He saw anti-Catholicism and nativism primarily as movements to limit the political—and hence, the social and cultural assimilation—of Irish Catholics. His major purpose is to assert immigrants' claim to full citizenship. In *Bickerton*, the elder Mr. Hubbard objects to political parties "endeavoring to enlist their [the immigrants'] aid at every election, by appealing to them *as* foreigners or Romanists." He calls this a "distinction that should no longer be remembered" because once the immigrants become citizens, they are simply Americans.[71] The son, Fred Hubbard, sees the role of citizen as a source of unity amid religious and other differences because citizens are bound to their government "by the ties of sympathy and interest" and are prepared to "come forward . . . to give . . . government a ready and cheerful support."[72]

Like their predecessors, all of the Irish American authors also highlight military service as evidence of patriotism. In the novels of the first generation of Catholic writers, Colonel Wolburn in Pise fights in the revolutionary war. In *Father Felix*, Cannon points out that "in our revolutionary struggle, the few Catholics among us were neither the least active nor the least efficient of the friends of American Independence."[73] Among the later Irish Americans, Quigley reminds his readers that "it was not all native blood that was spilled in the establishment of the republic," and Boyce notes the blood the immigrants have shed in America's battles.[74] The Irish Americans also emphasize the immigrants' current willingness to fight for the country. In *Bickerton*, Cannon quotes the bishops who advise Catholics: "if you should be called on to rally around its [the country's] flag, you should be always ready to obey cheerfully the call, and, if need be, to pour out your blood in its defense." Echoing the bishops' language, Sadlier's good Catholic American-born sons of the immigrants are "fully prepared to stand by this great Republic . . . even to shedding the last drop of . . . [their] blood, were that necessary." One of the young men is willing to shed his blood as a soldier for either Ireland or America.[75] However, the novels of the 1860s and '70s do not specifically mention those who fought in the Civil War. Except for Cannon, the Irish Americans differ from their predecessors not in emphasizing military service but in making that service the main example of public spirit in a community that for the most part, otherwise kept to itself.

The novels are evidence that as the Church refrained from taking official positions, it found other ways to advance political views that met its

interests. The Catholic point of view was expressed not only in the statements of individual bishops but also in the Catholic press—which included papers that were the official organs of a diocese—and in novels
identified and advertised as Catholic books, published by Catholic firms.
The political opinions advanced the institutional interests of the Church
and the group identity and cohesion of the Irish Catholic community. The
novelists wrote as though they were the only group in America to seek a
separate school system or to oppose the reform movements, so that the
immigrants' political opinions, like the other aspects of their lives, marked
them as distinct from the rest of the anti-Catholic American society. Since
most of these political opinions were also opposed to contemporary movements, Irish Catholic identity was based to a significant extent on suspicion and disputes with the larger society. The novels also suggest that the
eventual emergence of Irish Catholic politicians or an Irish Catholic voting bloc would not do anything to change this oppositional stance.

But Catholic unity was not just a matter of shared views; the people
were part of an institution with an organized leadership structure. In communicating such overwhelmingly favorable attitudes toward priests and
such suspicion of politicians, the novelists sought to ensure that the clergy
would not have rivals for the leadership role. Only the clergy spoke and
acted in the best interests of Catholics; only they would define Catholic issues.

American Pluralism—The Merits of Diversity

The Irish American authors advocated separation but also maintained,
both directly and by illustration, that a group's determination to preserve
its own culture and institutions did not jeopardize America's political unity.
They made the case for pluralism—that wide diversity in religion, and in
the cultural and social life that supported it, was compatible with the country's unity so long as citizens shared a commitment to political values and
institutions. Even Sadlier, who disliked America and sent so many of her
lead characters back to Ireland or to a western settlement, had no doubt
that the Catholics who remained would be good Americans. The good
Catholic Edward Flanagan was, he claimed, "Irish in heart—Catholic, I
hope, in faith and practice, and yet I am fully prepared to stand by this

great Republic, the land of my birth. . . . I am both Irish and American." In Sadlier's *Old and New*, another good Catholic son, who has just graduated from West Point, declares that he has "two countries: Ireland . . . [and] America . . . [and] both are equally dear to my heart."[76]

The authors definitely rejected the advice of Orestes Brownson, who criticized the Irish American novelists for their tendency to "seek . . . strength in a foreign nationality," urging them to adapt by "assimilating themselves to the Anglo-Americans and becoming animated by their spirit."[77] Instead, Catholics in these novels would create an ideal community, with a distinct culture and set of institutions, that would not threaten and in some ways would support the larger American society.

With their ties to another country, and with their membership in a universal church, all of the Catholic authors also retained some perspective about American political values and institutions; their patriotism did not reach the level of a religious Americanism. The political system suited this country but was not necessarily ideal in all circumstances. Bryant and Cannon maintained that because it confined itself to spiritual matters, the Church could live with any form of government. A Catholic speaker in Cannon's last novel refuses to say "whether the government under which we live . . . be as well adapted to the wants of every other people as it is to ours, as the Public Opinion of America would have us think."[78]

Some of the authors were sarcastic about the Americans' propensity to regard themselves as superior to every other people. Boyce's Ephraim Weeks believes it is "the duty of every American to enlighten mankind . . . to redeem the world from ignorance . . . and we must be known to be imitated." Throughout the novel, of course, Weeks is humiliated by the Irish characters he encounters. Boyce also satirizes America's tendency to assert its superiority as a nation. For Weeks, America, a "powerful" nation, has "flung our right arm across the Gulf, and laid hold of Mexico by the hair of the head . . . and . . . [is now] ready to extend our left over your British American possessions, at any day or hour we please"; "our destiny is universal empire."[79]

With their determination to maintain their faith and culture, and build institutions to embody them, the Irish Americans made important contributions to American political thought and practice. Their experience provided a model for other immigrant groups and continues to stimulate reflection on both the merits of diversity and the sources of national unity.

CONCLUSION

My own family's experience in America testifies to the endurance and adaptability of the mid-nineteenth-century Irish Catholicism discussed in these chapters—and also to the serious challenges it faces for the future. My parents came to New York City from Ireland in the 1930s, when the Catholic Church was entering what has been termed its period of "triumph."[1] They lived for the most part in an Irish Catholic world, socializing mainly with extended family, living in a neighborhood filled with Irish immigrants, and working for organizations, including the New York City Fire Department, that had a long association with Irish Catholics. They were typical practicing Catholics, attending mass and the sacraments regularly and participating in their share of the religious activities—novenas, missions, devotions—that began to flourish in the late nineteenth century. Looking back, it seems to me that the pastors and priests of the parish were mostly of Irish origin, as were most of the women who ran the parish religious associations. Apart from family and work, the local parish was the most important institution in these people's lives. Faced with family conflicts, unemployment, and bereavements of all sorts, they turned to the priests for advice and help.

Growing up in the 1950s, I attended the local parish school and continued on to an excellent Catholic high school outside the neighborhood.

While most of my fellow students—and most of the nuns and priests who taught us—were of Irish ancestry, many were not, testifying to the ability of the Church to incorporate many immigrant groups over the decades. My world was Catholic rather than simply Irish. Yet key aspects of the Irish Catholicism described in the mid-nineteenth-century novels remained. We were encouraged to prefer Catholic society and institutions to non-Catholic ones. We certainly attended only Catholic religious services but also belonged to Catholic educational, social, and recreational associations. While we no longer feared deliberate plots to convert Catholics, we had a general sense that the non-Catholic world was prejudiced against us and, even more, propagated doctrines and morality that would somehow endanger our faith. We studied apologetics, learning how to defend Catholicism, and if we did not attack or ridicule Protestants, we considered them heretics and did not seriously examine their views. We learned the same basic sexual morality as preached in the novels—the culture wars that brought issues like abortion and homosexuality to the fore were still to come—and, above all, we learned that morality meant considering the interests of others, especially the poor and vulnerable, as well as ourselves. Like the mid-nineteenth-century novelists, we did not consider these moral principles with reference to larger political issues like racism or capitalism but confined our political discussions to a general endorsement of the American system. About five percent of my high school classmates entered the convent; most went to college, and to a Catholic college, mostly as a matter of preference, although the high school also refused to write recommendations to non-Catholic private colleges and universities.

In other words, in a northeastern city a century after the fiction described in this book, the Church still provided a supportive safe community—staffed with priests and nuns, filled with ritual, advocating moral principles to govern interpersonal life—for a people encouraged to be fearful and suspicious of the external world.

The expectation that this Catholic world would continue into another generation was confirmed as all of my family members and good friends from school married Catholic men, of varied ethnic backgrounds. But the lives of the next generation were different, for many reasons, including the election of John Kennedy—which was taken as a sign of arrival and acceptance, especially by Irish Catholics—and the ecumenical teachings of the Vatican Council. The men and women born in the twenty-five years after these developments — my nephew and nieces — grew up in middle-class and even upper-middle-class families, attended public as well as Catholic schools, and moved easily outside Catholic circles in their choice of friends, spouses, and employment, all the while regarding themselves as fully American. They do not need a safe haven from a world they perceive as dangerous to them, as Catholics or as descendants of immigrants. They do not see priests as uniquely qualified leaders, and the women do not need the Church to provide unique opportunities for social or professional fulfillment. They are members of a generation the Church is finding it difficult to reach, according to both national research and local bishops. Yet these men and women still need community; responsible leaders they can admire and trust; and moral principles consistent with their ideas of human dignity to guide their conduct as individuals, professionals, and citizens. Perhaps above all, they need to believe that their lives have meaning. Is there a type of Catholicism that can speak to them as successfully as the Catholicism of the mid-nineteenth century spoke to the Irish immigrants? And can Catholics use modern media to reach their hearts and minds, as successfully as the mid-nineteenth-century novelists used stories to reach their immigrant audience?

NOTES

Introduction

1. For a discussion of the role of popular literature in sustaining Catholic identity and institutions, see Massa, "'As If in Prayer': A Response to 'Catholicism as American Popular Culture,'" 2:112–18. Also see R. M. Smith, *Stories of Peoplehood*, for a general account of stories and group identity.

2. For data on the Catholic and Irish immigrant populations in the middle decades of the nineteenth century, see McCaffrey, "Irish Americans," 203–10; Taves, *The Household of Faith*, 7; Miller, *Emigrants and Exiles*, 291, 569. For data on church infrastructure, see *The Metropolitan Catholic Almanac and Laity's Directory*, 1841, 68; *The Metropolitan Catholic Almanac and Laity's Directory*, 1860, 264–66; *Sadlier's Catholic Directory, Almanac, and Ordo*, 1875, 22.

3. Brownson, "Review of *Thornberry Abbey: A Tale of the Times*," 131. For Brownson's recognition of the importance of the novels in reaching the "mind and heart" of uprooted immigrants, see also his "Catholicity and Literature," 460. Scholars vary in their estimates of how many of the estimated 2.5 million Irish Catholics who immigrated to the United States between 1840 and 1870 were literate in English. There is general agreement, however, that sizeable proportions could read the language. Fanning, *The Exiles of Erin*, 92; Taves, *The Household of Faith*, 9; Miller, "For Love and Liberty," 53.

4. Charles Fanning, in *The Exiles of Erin* and *The Irish Voice in America*, is the most important scholar of Irish American literature. He is interested in the

278

tradition of American Irish, rather than American Catholic, fiction and so considers the novelists in the context of the Irish immigrant writers, primarily Protestant, who preceded them. When the novelists are viewed in the tradition of Catholic literature, some distinct issues are raised about the authors' purposes in writing fiction; their definitions of the moral life; their attitudes toward economic success; and their views of the Church, clergy, and church-state relations, among others. Thorp, *Catholic Novelists in Defense of Their Faith, 1829–1865*, is a valuable historical account of Catholic writers and novels. Catholic fiction of later periods is analyzed in Messbarger, *Fiction with a Parochial Purpose*, and in Sparr, *To Promote, Defend, and Redeem*.

5. The seven novelists were advertised, serialized, and reviewed more frequently than any others in the Catholic publications of the time. They are also the authors mentioned most frequently in current books and articles on mid-nineteenth-century Irish American literature. They are also identified as the representative Irish American voices of the time by Charles Fanning in both of his books.

6. Between 1850 and 1875, novels by the Irish Americans appeared, for example, in Louisville in the *Catholic Advocate*; Minnesota in the *Northwestern Chronicle*; New Orleans in the *Morning Star*; New York in the *Irish News*, the *Emerald*, and the *Irish World*; and in St. Louis in the *Leader*. Fanning, *The Exiles of Erin*, 92–95.

7. Amusements Section, *New York Times*, December 9, 1861; October 29, 1852; and May 29, 1866.

8. See, for example, announcements of a Cannon lecture on the Irish in America in the *New York Times*, February 12, 1852, and of a Boyce lecture on Mary Stuart in the *New York Times*, December 17, 1852.

9. *New York Times*, December 17, 1852.

10. From *The Boston Pilot*, October 23, 1847, as quoted in Frawley, *Patrick Donahue*, 32. J. E. Ryan in *Faithful Passages* describes the publishers' "direct ties to the institutional church" (115). In 1858, Donahoe changed the newspaper's name to *The Pilot*.

11. For an analysis of the publishers, their enterprises, and their successes, see Sullivan, "Community in Print." For more detail on the evidence of success, see chapter 2 below. Also see Messbarger, *Fiction with a Parochial Purpose*, 50–60, and Fanning, *The Irish Voice*, 77.

12. Carroll, *American Catholics in the Protestant Imagination*, 30–35. Similarly, Light comments in *Rome and the New Republic* on the "lack of religious fervor among immigrants to Philadelphia" in the middle decades of the nineteenth century and the determination of the bishops to do something about it (294).

Also see Dolan, *The Irish Americans*, 108–11, and *The Immigrant Church*, 56; Meagher, *The Columbia Guide to Irish American History*, 89; and Miller, *Emigrants and Exiles*, 331–32.

13. Miller, *Emigrants and Exiles*, 331.

14. As quoted in M'Clintock and Strong, *Cyclopaedia of Biblical, Theological, and Ecclesiastical Literature* 9:83, 84. The citation from Bishop Spalding is from his biography of his uncle Martin J. Spalding, the Archbishop of Baltimore.

15. For analyses of the cultural work of fiction, see Glover and Mc-Cracken, "Introduction," *The Cambridge Companion to Popular Fiction*; Cappell, *American Talmud*; Bontatibus, *The Seduction Novel of the Early Nation*; Davidson, "Preface: No More Separate Spheres!"; Dobson, "Reclaiming Sentimental Literature"; and Tompkins, *Sensational Designs*.

16. Meagher, *The Columbia Guide to Irish American History*, 89, 90.

17. Carroll, *American Catholics in the Protestant Imagination*, 29.

18. Dolan, *The Irish Americans*, 106.

Chapter 1. The Origins of American Catholic Fiction

1. Pise, *Father Rowland: A North American Tale*; *The Indian Cottage: A Unitarian Story*; and *Zenosius; Or, The Pilgrim-Convert*. In further text and citations, these novels, and all of the novels discussed in this chapter, are referred to by their lead titles, omitting subtitles.

2. Pise, *Father Rowland*, 3. Information on editions for Pise and for the other authors discussed in the chapter is from the library collections at www.worldcat.org.

3. Ibid., 195.

4. Indicating that such predominantly doctrinal novels were not the exclusive domain of Catholics, Pise based his work on a novel by Orestes Brownson published five years earlier by Little, Brown, in which the title character, Charles Elwood, engages in conversations and travel to examine the important philosophical and reform movements of the time, ending with an admiration for Catholicism but still hoping for a new Christian synthesis. The conversations and travels of Zenosius, of course, culminate in Rome and the pope, that "beacon of truth" (195).

5. *New York Times*, December 27, 1896.

6. Dorsey, *The Sister of Charity*, 2 vols.; and *The Student of Blenheim Forest*. One of Dorsey's novels was also published in Dublin and London, and Murphy issued the other in several revised editions. For an account of the number

of Dorsey works and their editions, see Thorp, *Catholic Novelists in Defense of Their Faith, 1829–1865*, 87, 89.

7. Bryant, *Pauline Seward: A Tale of Real Life*, 2 vols.

8. Bryant, *Pauline Seward*, 1:3.

9. Dorsey, *The Sister of Charity*, 1:6.

10. Pise, *Father Rowland*, 26, 27.

11. Dorsey, *The Sister of Charity*, 2:73.

12. Pise, *Zenosius*, 41, 106; Bryant, *Pauline Seward*, 1:98, 100–101.

13. Bryant, *Pauline Seward*, 1:249. Sometimes the authors include explanations of doctrines that did not figure so prominently in Protestant attacks. *Zenosius* includes a summary of what every Catholic must believe on the Trinity, for instance (50–51, 71). And Dorsey's heroine readily accepts the doctrine of the Real Presence once it is explained to her (*The Sister of Charity*, 2:29).

14. Dorsey, *The Oriental Pearl; Or, The Catholic Emigrants*.

15. Miles, *Loretto; Or, The Choice*; and *The Governess; Or, The Effects of Good Example: An Original Tale*. Both novels were first published serially in the late 1840s.

16. Miles, *The Governess*, 251.

17. Miles, *Loretto*, 130.

18. Miles, *The Governess*, 138–39.

19. Dorsey, *The Oriental Pearl*, 42; Miles, *The Governess*, 49.

20. Dorsey, *The Oriental Pearl*, preface; Miles, *The Governess*, preface.

21. Dorsey, *The Sister of Charity*, 2:167.

22. Bryant, *Pauline Seward*, 1:5.

23. Bryant, *Pauline Seward*, 1:15; Dorsey *The Student of Blenheim Forest*, 9.

24. Miles, *Loretto*, 10, 106.

25. Miles, *The Governess*, 14, 13.

26. Dorsey, *The Oriental Pearl*, 38, 108. See also J. E. Ryan's discussion of Dorsey in *Faithful Passages*, 104–5.

27. Pise, *Father Rowland*, 189, 142–47.

28. Miles, *Loretto*, 145, 146, 152–53.

29. Miles, *The Governess*, 14.

30. Bolger, *The Irish Character in American Fiction, 1830–1860*, 154–56.

31. See Dowd, *The Construction of Irish Identity in American Literature*, 2–3.

32. Bryant, *Pauline Seward*, 1:205.

33. Miles, *Loretto*, 281, 279.

34. Miles, *The Governess*, 48–49.

35. Dorsey, *The Student of Blenheim Forest*, 220.

36. Ibid., 230, 228, 227.

37. Ibid., 231, 232, 222.

38. Ibid., 232–33, 229–30, 231, 339.

39. Pise, *Father Rowland*, 26, 97, 40.

40. Pise, *Zenosius*, 79, 208, 6. Pise is particularly outraged at the "incredible presumption" of a recent Presbyterian Convention, which said that Catholics were not even Christians (6). Even in this, his harshest work, Pise ends on an optimistic note. As Zenosius reaches the end of his European journey, the pope tells him to return to his "native land, and be an example and an encouragement to thy well-disposed, and thy truth-seeking countrymen" (278). Pise also clarifies at a few points that such well-disposed Protestants did exist: "When, in a paroxysm of controversy, Editors and Preachers . . . rave, at random, against a church and its doctrines, of which they know nothing . . . they excite the contempt of all liberal men, of every denomination" (79–80).

41. Bryant, *Pauline Seward*, 1:139, 13, 173.

42. Ibid., 199–202.

43. Dorsey, *The Sister of Charity*, 1:20, 60.

44. Dorsey, *The Student of Blenheim Forest*, 13, 4.

45. Dorsey, *The Sister of Charity*, 1:168, 117.

46. Dorsey, *The Oriental Pearl*, 13, 37.

47. Miles, *The Governess*, 11.

48. Ibid., 73, 105. On other occasions, anti-Catholic attitudes in Miles reflect only unthinking inherited opinions, which indicate the characters' general indifference to religion. The Protestant heroine of *Loretto*, whose father gave her a "Protestant Episcopalian education" initially, "knew little" of Catholicism "save from stereotype calumny, and from her own juvenile observations in France, Spain and Italy" (37). Miles does not specify her opinions. In *The Governess*, Miles includes a few typical attacks. Protestants say that Catholicism is "idolatry" (10), "antiquated mummery" (12), and "Popish superstition" (81).

49. Miles, *The Governess*, 25, 92. In Pise also, Zenosius endures verbal attacks but not material injury.

50. Bryant, *Pauline Seward*, 1:237.

51. Cannon, *Oran, the Outcast; Or, A Season in New York*, 2 vols., 2:141, 174.

52. Cannon, *Harry Layden: A Tale; Mora Carmody; Or, Woman's Influence: A Tale*; and *Father Felix: A Tale*.

53. Cannon, *Harry Layden*, 35.

54. Brownson, "Review of *Mora Carmody*," 134.

55. Cannon, *Father Felix*, preface. Information on printings and translations is from Meehan, "Catholic Literary New York, 1800–1840," 413, as well as from library catalogues.

56. Cannon, *Scenes and Characters from the Comedy of Life*. The novel is referred to throughout the text as *Scenes and Characters*.

57. Cannon, "The Beal Fire," 102.

58. Cannon, *Harry Layden*, 29; *Mora Carmody*, 28.

59. Cannon, *Father Felix*, 160–61, 54–55, 50.

60. Cannon, *Mora Carmody*, 55.

61. Cannon, *Harry Layden*, 22.

62. Cannon, *Mora Carmody*, preface.

63. Cannon, *Oran, the Outcast*, 1:99.

64. Ibid., 1:104, 105.

65. Ibid., 1:37, 36.

66. Cannon, *Harry Layden*, 95, 81.

67. Ibid., 13, 15, 98.

68. Cannon, *Father Felix*, 75, 72, 74, 77.

69. Cannon, *Scenes and Characters*, 61, 31, 77–80.

70. Cannon, *Harry Layden*, 95.

71. Cannon, *Mora Carmody*, 36–43, at 36, 39; 55–56.

72. Cannon, *Father Felix*, 62.

73. Cannon, *Scenes and Characters*, 61, 98.

74. Cannon, *Oran, the Outcast*, 1: dedication page, and 1:19.

75. Cannon, *Harry Layden*, 95; *Scenes and Characters*, 34.

76. Cannon, *Harry Layden*, 118.

77. Cannon, *Scenes and Characters*, 206–13.

78. Cannon, *Harry Layden*, iii–iv, 35; *Mora Carmody*, preface.

79. Cannon, *Mora Carmody*, postscript, 140; *Father Felix*, 69, 85, 165.

Chapter 2. The Irish Americans

1. Although the Irish dominated American Catholic fiction from 1850 through the 1870s, writers of other backgrounds, including native-born Catholics as well as converts, continued to publish Catholic fiction. Anna Dorsey remained prolific, and other authors included Jedediah Vincent Huntington, Thomas Low Nichols, and many women—Cora Berkley, Mary L. Meany, Mary Miller Meline, Fannie Warner, Mary Jane Hoffman, and Julia Amanda Wood. For brief discussions of these writers, see Thorp, *Catholic Novelists in Defense of Their Faith, 1829–1865*, and Messbarger, *Fiction with a Parochial Purpose*.

2. Quigley, *The Cross and the Shamrock; Or, How to Defend the Faith: An Irish-American Catholic Tale of Real Life*; Sadlier, *Con O'Regan; Or, Emigrant Life in the*

New World, Boyce (writing as Paul Peppergrass), *Mary Lee; Or, The Yankee in Ireland*. In further text and citations, these novels, and all of the novels discussed in the chapter, are referred to by their lead titles, omitting subtitles. Sadlier the novelist is listed by her last name only; initials of their first names are included on the few occasions when other members of the Sadlier family appear in the notes.

3. Roddan, *John O'Brien; Or, The Orphan of Boston: A Tale of Real Life*; Sadlier, *Willy Burke; Or, The Irish Orphan in America*.

4. McCorry (writing his fiction as Con O'Leary), *The Lost Rosary; Or, Our Irish Girls, Their Trials, Temptations, and Triumphs*. The other two novels focused on single women are Sadlier, *Bessy Conway; Or, The Irish Girl in America*, and John McElgun, *Annie Reilly; Or, The Fortunes of an Irish Girl in New York: A Tale Founded on Fact*.

5. Roddan, *John O'Brien*, v, vi.

6. Sadlier, *Willy Burke*, 3; *Bessy Conway*, iv, iii.

7. Sadlier, *The Blakes and Flanagans: A Tale Illustrative of Irish Life in the United States*, vi. In her 1862 *Old and New; Or, Taste Versus Fashion*, Sadlier departs from her usual practice of using titles to identify her audience. But in a conclusion written to accompany the book—which previously had appeared serially in a Catholic newspaper—she clarifies that she is directing the novel to "our would-be somebody American-Irish Catholics," that is, newly middle-class immigrant women and their daughters, who are "ashamed of their Irish ancestry, or join in holding up their fatherland to the ridicule and contempt of others" (485, 486).

8. Quigley, *Profit and Loss: A Story of the Life of the Genteel Irish-American, Illustrative of Godless Education*.

9. Brownson, "Review of *Tigh* [*sic*] *Lyfford*," 410.

10. Information on editions, printings, and translations is from the library catalogues at www.worldcat.org. Information on the sales of Sadlier's novels is also available from A. T. Sadlier, "Mrs. Sadlier's Early Life, Her Books and Friends," 331. Information on Cannon's work is in Meehan, "Catholic Literary New York, 1800–1840."

11. For an argument that the Church recognized that immigrants needed advice on how to behave, not dogma, see T. L. Smith, "Religion and Ethnicity in America."

12. Roddan, *John O'Brien*, vi.

13. Quigley, *The Cross and the Shamrock*, 6, 8, 7–8.

14. Sadlier, *Willy Burke*, 3.

15. Quigley, *The Cross and the Shamrock*, 8.

16. McElgun, *Annie Reilly*, 206. See also Sadlier, *Elinor Preston: Or, Scenes at Home and Abroad*, 210–11. This novel is written as a memoir of a middle-class Irish woman who emigrates to Canada. Elinor meets some Irish immigrants

when she stops in New York City on her way to Montreal. She finds they have adopted American culture and become cold, selfish, and materialistic.

17. Sadlier, *Bessy Conway*, iii.

18. McCorry, *The Lost Rosary*, 64.

19. McCorry (writing as Con O'Leary), *Mount Benedict: Or, The Violated Tomb: A Tale of the Charlestown Convent*, preface, v.

20. McCorry, *Mount Benedict*, 234, 233. The most McCorry will allow is that "Already we observe indications of a better spirit appearing. . . . [T]his change . . . was long needed, but come it has at last, and we welcome it as the sweet harbinger of a peaceful future wherein men will disdain to outrage civilization" (234–35).

21. Boyce, *Mary Lee*, 3, 6.

22. Ibid., 15, 16, 18.

23. An Irish woman in the novel receives a letter from a niece working as a domestic servant in America who complains bitterly that the Protestant mistress insults her faith and ethnicity (234). Boyce also says that in America there is "a universal scramble, in which every body snatched at what came handiest" and everybody is motivated by "one idea—one object—one aspiration—money" (125).

24. Cannon, *Bickerton; Or, The Immigrant's Daughter: A Tale*.

25. Cannon, *Tighe Lyfford: A Novel*. James Miller, the publisher of the work, advertises himself at the end of the novel as a bookseller, publisher, bookbinder, and importer in New York City, located on Broadway, not Barclay Street. The advertisement does not indicate that he is a Catholic publisher, which suggests that he is not, since the other firms always advertise themselves as such. Miller's list, moreover, includes a wide variety of books, such as a guide to NYC; a play by a Captain Berryman; nineteen volumes of Dickens, and children's books. The only religious works on the list are not Catholic; they are *The Duties of Human Life, tr from a Sanscrit manuscript*, and *Mento-Theology: Being Parables for the Clergy but Intelligence for the People* (271–75). Cannon also published two collections of short stories with the Sadlier firm in the 1850s.

26. Cannon, *Bickerton*, 3.

27. Cannon, *Tighe Lyfford*, preface, 3.

28. Sadlier's *Elinor Preston* is also an exception, but it is about an immigrant to Canada not the United States. The novel was published in 1861 but probably written earlier. It brings the heroine to Canada and describes her life there in the 1850s, a period roughly contemporaneous with publication.

29. The novels are Quigley's 1853 *The Cross and the Shamrock*, Sadlier's 1861 *Bessy Conway*, and McCorry's 1871 *Mount Benedict*. In novels published in the 1850s, the immigrants in Sadlier's *Willy Burke* and Cannon's *Bickerton* also come in the 1830s. The authors are usually not very explicit about the dates of their characters' emigration; the reader has to figure it out from rather vague references.

30. The lead character in Sadlier's *Confessions of an Apostate; Or, Leaves from a Troubled Life* comes between 1810 and 1815. The leads in her *The Blakes and Flanagans* and *Old and New* come in the 1820s.

31. The male leads in McCorry's 1870 *The Lost Rosary* come in the early 1840s, as do the leads in Sadlier's 1864 *Con O'Regan*. Quigley, in *Profit and Loss*, and McElgun, in *Annie Reilly* (both published in 1873), focus on immigrants arriving in the 1850s.

32. Sadlier, *Willy Burke*, 8.

33. Sadlier, *Confessions of an Apostate*, 56. Similarly, Sadlier's Elinor Preston cannot describe her vacation in Killarney without highlighting "the ruined abbeys" (142) and the ancient monks who contributed to "the chronicles of the nation," both "shedding a halo of supernatural glory even now over the natural beauties of that romantic region" (*Elinor Preston*, 146).

34. Quigley, *The Cross and the Shamrock*, 46; *Profit and Loss*, 8.

35. McElgun, *Annie Reilly*, 198.

36. Sadlier, *The Blakes and Flanagans*, 20.

37. Sadlier, *Confessions of an Apostate*, 43.

38. Quigley, *The Cross and the Shamrock*, 46.

39. Boyce, *Mary Lee*, 188, 162–63.

40. Cannon, *Bickerton*, 8, 7.

41. Sadlier, *Willy Burke*, 5; Quigley, *The Cross and the Shamrock*, 55; Quigley, *Profit and Loss*, 9.

42. Sadlier, *Old and New*, 147, 194.

43. In all but three novels published after 1860, the main characters are single people. The three exceptions are Quigley's *Profit and Loss*, and Sadlier's *Old and New*, in which families emigrate, and Sadlier's *Con O'Regan*, who comes without his wife and children.

44. McCorry, *Mount Benedict*, 31.

45. Sadlier, *Confessions of an Apostate*, 20.

46. Sadlier, *Willy Burke*, 7–8.

47. Quigley, *The Cross and the Shamrock*, 53.

48. Quigley, *Profit and Loss*, 24.

49. McElgun, *Annie Reilly*, v, 40–41, 30.

50. Sadlier, *Willy Burke*, 7.

51. Sadlier, *Bessy Conway*, 7, 258; *Confessions of an Apostate*, 31, 34, see also 29–30.

52. McElgun, *Annie Reilly*, 11.

53. McCorry, *The Lost Rosary*, 53, v.

54. McElgun, *Annie Reilly*, 39, 71, 10, 25, 11.

55. McCorry, *The Lost Rosary*, 36–37.

56. Quigley, *The Cross and the Shamrock*, 26, 73.

57. Quigley, *Profit and Loss*, 22, 25.

58. Cannon, *Bickerton*, 5, 9.

59. Ibid., 18.

60. Sadlier, *Old and New*, 91.

61. Quigley, *The Cross and the Shamrock*, 114–15; Cannon, *Tighe Lyfford*, 115, and *Bickerton*, 44; Sadlier, *Con O'Regan*, 48–49.

62. Cannon, *Bickerton*, 150; Sadlier, *Con O'Regan*, 128.

63. Sadlier, *Con O'Regan*, 280.

64. One exception: McCorry's *Mount Benedict*, where Kate Crolly and her brother Patrick are separated for some unexplained reason, and Kate has to find work as a companion. Patrick seems to be able to devote all of his efforts to locating her, apparently not needing to find employment.

65. McElgun, *Annie Reilly*, 148–50, at 148, 160.

66. Quigley, *The Cross and the Shamrock*, 53; and *Profit and Loss*, 8–9.

67. McCorry, *The Lost Rosary*, 168; Cannon, *Bickerton*, 31.

68. Quigley, *The Cross and the Shamrock*, 8.

69. Boyce, *Mary Lee*, 154, 124, 105.

70. Sadlier, *Alice Riordan, The Blind Man's Daughter: A Tale for the Young*, 2.

71. Boyce, *Mary Lee*, 106.

72. McElgun, *Annie Reilly*, 118.

73. Quigley, *The Cross and the Shamrock*, 54.

74. Sadlier, *Elinor Preston*, 76.

75. Ibid., 22.

76. Ibid., 159–60. Elinor does not like to depend on friends, for despite "their kindness, I cannot divest myself of the feeling of dependence; and . . . the bread of dependence is bitter!" (157). Elinor is also attracted to the "adventure": "There was somewhere far down in my heart or mind . . . a desire to see the world abroad" (156).

77. Ibid., 191.

78. Sadlier, *Bessy Conway*, 258, 259, 261, 271.

79. McCorry, *The Lost Rosary*, 44, 97.

80. Ibid., 111.

81. Ibid., 97, 108.

82. Ibid., 97, 54–55.

83. Ibid., 53.

84. Ibid., 54.

85. Sadlier, *Willy Burke*, 6, 7–8.

86. Sadlier, *Bessy Conway*, 7; McElgun, *Annie Reilly*, 81.

87. McCorry, *The Lost Rosary*, 48, 51–52.

88. Sadlier, *Confessions of an Apostate*, 31, 33. Similarly, the "dream" of Bessy Conway's "young heart" for many years has been "to 'see the world'" (7). But Bessy also knows that she can earn money in America to send back to her home: her "delicious dream" is that "If I ever have money enough to go home with, there's many a thing I can do!"(205).

89. Sadlier, *Con O'Regan*, 10; McElgun, *Annie Reilly*, 78, 190.

90. Even those who come to America for more selfish reasons help those they left behind. The young man in *Annie Reilly* flees Ireland after he is falsely accused of raiding a barracks. Once in America though he "continued to work along shore for several months, saving up all the money he could, and sending it to his father" (148).

91. Sadlier, *Confessions of an Apostate*, 33, 34; McElgun, *Annie Reilly*, 11.

92. McCorry, *The Lost Rosary*, 42, 47, 57.

93. Quigley, *The Cross and the Shamrock*, 26.

94. See *Willy Burke*, *Bessy Conway*, *The Lost Rosary*, and *Annie Reilly*.

95. Hasia Diner, *Erin's Daughters in America: Irish Immigrant Women in the Nineteenth Century*, chaps. 1, 2, 4, 6, esp. 7–8, 34, 70, 127; Janet A. Nolan, *Ourselves Alone: Women's Emigration from Ireland, 1885–1920*, introduction and chapters 2 and 3, esp. pp. 3, 36–37, 47–53.

96. McElgun, *Annie Reilly*, 79.

Chapter 3. American Anti-Catholicism

1. For a recent argument making this case, see Doyle, "The Remaking of Irish-America, 1845–1880." Similarly, Light in *Rome and the New Republic* cites Bishop Hughes acknowledging that Nativism had never posed a real danger but had proven useful because it unified Catholics and destroyed "that spurious liberality . . . which had prevailed to a great extent" (318–19).

2. For classic accounts of the history of American anti-Catholicism, see Hueston, *The Catholic Press and Nativism, 1840–1860*; McAvoy, *The Formation of the American Catholic Minority, 1820–1869*; and Billington, *The Protestant Crusade, 1800–1860*. For more recent accounts, see Meagher, *The Columbia Guide to Irish American History*, esp. 91, and Jensen, "'No Irish Need Apply,'" 419. For an analysis of anti-Catholic popular literature, including the nativist or Know-Nothing fiction of the 1850s, see Griffin, *Anti-Catholicism and Nineteenth-Century Fiction*.

3. Roddan, *John O'Brien*, 59, 60.

4. Sadlier, *The Blakes and Flanagans*, 10.

5. Sadlier, *Old and New*, 116–30, at 121, 124, 126, 128.

6. McCorry, *Mount Benedict*, v–vi.

7. Quigley, *Profit and Loss*, 105, 391. For Quigley's general accounts, see also 102–4, 392–93.

8. Boyce, *Mary Lee*, 16.

9. Quigley, *Profit and Loss*, 234.

10. Roddan, *John O'Brien*, 202, 185; Boyce, *Mary Lee*, 278.

11. Roddan, *John O'Brien*, 240, 244, 242.

12. Boyce, *Mary Lee*, 203, 204, 269.

13. Sadlier, *Con O'Regan*, 191, 194. In her *Confessions of an Apostate* also, Sadlier suggests that "liberal" Protestants try to be fair to Catholics. When he is confronted with a particularly egregious charge, the now Protestant lead character reflects: "had I been a real, sincere Protestant, with my disposition, I might have been liberal enough to defend Catholics against charges which I knew to be false or exaggerated, if only for love of fair play" (186). These are not the Protestants, however, who see to it that the young man has to hide and neglect his faith in order to be successful.

14. Boyce, *Mary Lee*, 234.

15. Quigley, *Profit and Loss*, 424.

16. The changed orientation reflected the times in which the novels were published but not the times in which the stories ostensibly take place. The lead characters of the post-1860 novels in which anti-Catholicism is peripheral are in America from the 1830s to the 1850s, the same years as the characters in the novels that make anti-Catholicism the central theme.

17. Sadlier, *Bessy Conway*, 135, 187, 121, 226.

18. McCorry, *The Lost Rosary*, 76, 130, 128.

19. McElgun, *Annie Reilly*, 179, 183.

20. Sadlier, *Old and New*, 485, 486. In Sadlier's *Elinor Preston*, an immigrant in New York City explains, "Society here is, for the most part, a meretricious glitter. . . . [P]eople are straining might and main to outshine their neighbors. . . . Money we make here, but happiness and social enjoyment are myths" (211).

21. Boyce, *Mary Lee*, 54, 55, 106.

22. Sadlier, *Bessy Conway*, 163.

23. Quigley, *Profit and Loss*, 321, 322.

24. Sadlier, *Old and New*, 229.

25. McElgun, *Annie Reilly*, 203–12, 221–35; at 203, 222, 227–28, 225–26.

26. Sadlier, *Bessy Conway*, 88–89, 148, 149, 205–8 at 207. In his article "Irish Domestic Servants," Urban provides one illustration (from Quigley's first

novel) of an incident in which an Irish Catholic girl is approached sexually in an insinuating way by a Protestant minister. He is illustrating the Irish American writers' determination to refute stereotypes of Irish domestic servants as aggressive and incompetent by portraying them as heroines enduring frequent harassment. The "sexual" incident from Quigley is unique in the novels; far more typical are Urban's other examples of harassment based on the servant's faith and ethnicity, always the chief concern of the Irish American writers. "Irish Domestic Servants, 'Biddy' and Rebellion in the American Home, 1850–1900."

27. McElgun, *Annie Reilly*, vii–viii, 167–71, 181. The anti-Catholic episodes in McCorry's *The Lost Rosary* involve only minor characters, especially the poor Baptist minister whose female parishioners refer to the "benighted things from Ireland" (116). This novel's account of a more serious anti-Catholicism concerns immigrant characters from the previous generation. Mr. O'Meara, a now successful store owner, reports that he had once been falsely accused of theft, called an "Irish brat of a papist," and summarily fired. He then had a very difficult time before finding his next decent employment (166).

28. Roddan, *John O'Brien*, 163.

29. Sadlier, *Confessions of an Apostate*, 47.

30. Quigley, *Profit and Loss*, 243.

31. Roddan, *John O'Brien*, 163.

32. Sadlier, *The Blakes and Flanagans*, 15, 377–78.

33. Sadlier, *Bessy Conway*, 134.

34. Quigley, *The Cross and the Shamrock*, 78–79.

35. Ibid., 79, 15, 6, 4.

36. Quigley, *Profit and Loss*, 33, 34, 38.

37. For a discussion of the importance of group boundaries and the relative unimportance of the "stuff" enclosed within them, see Meagher, *The Columbia Guide to Irish American History*, 9–11. Irish American fiction suggests that the enclosed "stuff" might be crucially important at some periods for those seeking to create and reinforce boundaries.

38. Sadlier, *Willy Burke*, 80.

39. Sadlier, *The Blakes and Flanagans*, 302; Quigley, *The Cross and the Shamrock*, 82.

40. Roddan, *John O'Brien*, 164.

41. Sadlier, *Willy Burke*, 175.

42. Roddan, *John O'Brien*, 108–9; Quigley, *The Cross and the Shamrock*, 83–85.

43. Sadlier, *The Blakes and Flanagans*, 304, 301.

44. Taves, *The Household of Faith*.

45. Sadlier, *The Blakes and Flanagans*, 304.

46. Ibid., 365, 386.

47. Sadlier, *Willy Burke*, 48.

48. Dolan, *The Irish Americans*, 58. Carroll, in *American Catholics in the Protestant Imagination*, has recently argued that the "affinity" between the discipline required in religious practice and in domestic service explains why Irish women and, through them, Irish men adopted this "mass and the sacraments" type of Catholicism. This may well be true, but the novels suggest that the practices also served for men and women as visible badges of membership in a community resisting the surrounding social world.

49. Roddan, *John O'Brien*, 172.

50. Sadlier, *The Blakes and Flanagans*, 336.

51. Roddan, *John O'Brien*, 63.

52. Sadlier, *The Blakes and Flanagans*, 192.

53. Sadlier, *Willy Burke*, 39.

54. Sadlier, *The Blakes and Flanagans*, 337.

55. Boyce, *Mary Lee*, 16.

56. Roddan, *John O'Brien*, 175; Quigley, *The Cross and the Shamrock*, 150–51.

57. Sadlier includes no attacks on practice in either *Elinor Preston* or *Old and New* and none on priests in *Bessy Conway*. The brief exchanges cited are at *Bessy Conway*, 88–89, and *Annie Reilly*, 168–71. By contrast, Protestant characters in Quigley's *Profit and Loss* say that Catholics "follow odd superstitions like fasting, confession, and praying to the dead; are not allowed to read the bible; and blindly follow their priests" (69, 183–84, 241, 244, 456).

58. Roddan, *John O'Brien*, 18; Sadlier, *Willy Burke*, 38.

59. Roddan, *John O'Brien*, 112, 90; Quigley, *The Cross and the Shamrock*, 178.

60. McCorry, *The Lost Rosary*, 116; Quigley, *Profit and Loss*, 45; Sadlier, *Con O'Regan*, 35. In Sadlier's *Old and New*, the women from the ward mission who visit Madame Von Weigel say that Irish immigrant parents are "addicted . . . to . . . blasphemy," and "besotted" by the "degrading superstitions of Popery" (118). Backsliding Catholics repeat the same charges. In Quigley's novel, the young lead character tells his mother that the teachings she brought from "the old country" are "old and antiquated" (180).

61. Sadlier, *Confessions of an Apostate*, 185, 50.

62. Bryant, *Pauline Seward*, 1:181–86, at 185.

63. Roddan, *John O'Brien*, 43, 47, 45, 48.

64. Sadlier, *Willy Burke*, 38, 40, 41.

65. Quigley, The *Cross and the Shamrock*, 79–80.

66. Roddan, *John O'Brien*, 47. Sadlier in 1850 is not clear even about a full-time Catholic alternative in the future. When Willy Burke receives a legacy at the end of the novel, he says he will leave some portion of it to the Church; the

priest replies that the bishop will be grateful since he has been "harassed lately for want of funds to carry on some buildings"; there are "no less than three of them going forward." Sadlier never identifies the buildings (260).

67. Quigley, *The Cross and the Shamrock*, 80.

68. Sadlier, *The Blakes and Flanagans*, 251, 250.

69. Ibid., 251, 250–51.

70. Ibid., 250.

71. Ibid., 36, 14, 19, 87.

72. Ibid., 20, 14, 26, 30.

73. Quigley, *Profit and Loss*, 34, 82, 61–62.

74. Sadlier, *The Blakes and Flanagans*, 87–88, 29.

75. Quigley, *Profit and Loss*, 380, 54, 379.

76. Sadlier, *The Blakes and Flanagans*, 388–89, 379, 378.

77. Quigley, *Profit and Loss*, 403–13, at 411, 410, 359, 380, 458.

78. In her 1864 *Con O'Regan*, Sadlier continues these arguments against the public schools of Boston. A good Irish Catholic immigrant, Andy Dwyer, a former seminarian, says that in public schools, children are "sure to learn more of evil than of good." He calls them "infidel schools—heathen schools" and goes so far as to say they can be called "the Devil's Schools, as far as Catholics are concerned" (214, 215).

79. Cannon's second novel of the decade, *Tighe Lyfford*, was published in 1859 by James Miller and does not focus on anti-Catholicism.

80. Cannon, *Bickerton*, 3, 85, 155.

81. Ibid., 110.

82. Ibid., 109–10.

83. Ibid., 76–77.

84. Ibid., 110.

Chapter 4. Catholics and Religious Liberty

1. McGreevy, "Introduction: The American Catholic Century," 2. For another discussion of support for religious liberty and church-state separation among Catholic laity and some clergy—but not theologians before the 1950s and 1960s—see Ellis, *The Catholic Priest in the United States: Historical Investigations*, esp. 36–37.

2. Pise, *Father Rowland*, 180. In his more uncompromising *Zenosius*, the only reference Pise makes to "persecution" or force concerns pagans against early Christians and current Protestant nations such as England, which not only oppose "the truth" but also "persecute it" (130). Dorsey, *The Sister of Charity*, 1:169.

3. Bryant, *Pauline Seward*, 1:266; Dorsey, *The Student of Blenheim Forest*, 213, 214. See also Pise, *Zenosius*, 185, 8.

4. Dorsey, *The Oriental Pearl*, 13; Miles, *The Governess*, 137, 139–40.

5. Pise, *Father Rowland*, 156; Bryant, *Pauline Seward*, 1:133. In Dorsey's *The Student of Blenheim Forest*, the newly faithful Catholic mother challenges the Protestant father and asks "by what right" he punishes his son "because he sees fit and finds it necessary to his salvation to change his creed?" (111).

6. Pise, *Father Rowland*, 12; *Zenosius*, 273, 43.

7. Miles, *Loretto*, 245, 281.

8. Pise, *Zenosius*, 210–11.

9. Dorsey, *The Sister of Charity*, 1:165–71, at 166, 169. Miles makes this argument also. One of his good characters says that Italy is superior to England or Germany "in every virtue and in every art" (*The Governess*, 137).

10. Bryant, *Pauline Seward*, 1:264, 266–67. This use of religious divisions as explanation for the political conflict was common in Catholic circles, especially in Europe. Mark A. Noll, *The Civil War as a Theological Crisis*.

11. Pise, *Father Rowland*, 47, 141.

12. Bryant, *Pauline Seward*, 1:140, 272, 306.

13. Pise, *Zenosius*, 18; Bryant, *Pauline Seward*, 1:135, 217, 220; Miles, *Loretto*, 218, 279, 271.

14. Bryant *Pauline Seward*, 1:169; Miles, *Loretto*, 271.

15. Pise, *Father Rowland*, 104; Dorsey, *The Student of Blenheim Forest*, 128.

16. Pise, *Zenosius*, 20; Bryant, *Pauline Seward*, 1:279; Miles, *The Governess*, 244. Most of the novelists do not include many specific references to the priests' holiness beyond their accounts of his actions and motivations. Cannon is satisfied to refer once to Father Felix's piety (67). He also dedicates the novel to the Bishop of Chicago, "in whom the zeal of The Christian Minister is equalled only by the Kindness of the Man." The exceptions are Miles on occasion and Dorsey quite often. In her *The Sister of Charity*, she refers to the priest's "holy expression" and to his "countenance which always wore the meek look of a saint" (2:20).

17. Pise, *Father Rowland*, 81.

18. Quigley is the sole exception. In his 1873 *Profit and Loss*, Protestant characters refer, without further specification, to "the spirit of popery so dangerous to 'our liberties'" (105) and assert that the Catholic Church is "aiming at political power" (145), or wants to "rule our country" and "subvert our government" (106).

19. Roddan, *John O'Brien*, 48, 113, 48–49; Sadlier, *Willy Burke*, 40.

20. Roddan, *John O'Brien*, 190; Quigley, *The Cross and the Shamrock*, 116.

21. A rare example comes in Quigley's *Profit and Loss* when the family of a Protestant man who wants to convert to Catholicism makes it difficult for

Father John to see him. The priest asks the man's wife if she believes in "freedom of conscience" and then "administered a well-deserved rebuke" to the family "for their bigotry" (207, 208).

22. Quigley, *The Cross and the Shamrock*, 117, 118.

23. Quigley, *Profit and Loss*, 226. At another point Quigley writes that the "clerical spouters" at the assembly "delivered themselves of the usual rant in praise of religious liberty, the Bible, free schools, and free thoughts" (230).

24. Sadlier, *The Blakes and Flanagans*, 337–38; *Bessy Conway*, 207.

25. Sadlier, *Willy Burke*, 4.

26. Quigley, *The Cross and the Shamrock*, 162.

27. Quigley, *Profit and Loss*, 233.

28. Boyce, *Mary Lee*, 224; Sadlier, *Old and New*, 187.

29. Sadlier, *Confessions of an Apostate*, 22, and *Con O'Regan*, iv.

30. Sadlier, *The Blakes and Flanagans*, 377.

31. Quigley, *The Cross and the Shamrock*, 14, 101, 149, 264.

32. The priest Father Rivas in *Tighe Lyfford*, Cannon's final novel, written for a secular publisher, is old and dies at the end of story. It would seem that Cannon reverts to the strategy of old priests when he addresses a general audience.

33. Sadlier, *Willy Burke*, 62–63, 289. Quigley's old priest O'Shane weeps "heavy tears" for the plight of the widow and her children in *The Cross and the Shamrock*, but the more robust Father Ugo in the same novel does not weep (20).

34. McCorry, *Mount Benedict*, 232; Sadlier, *Bessy Conway*, 61; Quigley, *Profit and Loss*, 399. The fictional priest assisting Bishop Fenwick in *Mount Benedict* does not cry at the conversion of the Protestant ward or during the mob attack, but when he is told of a nun's efforts to save the tabernacle he "could not avoid shedding tears of pity and admiration" (225).

35. Quigley, *Profit and Loss*, 227, 228.

36. Sadlier, *The Blakes and Flanagans*, 251, 252.

37. Cannon, *Mora Carmody*, 23; *Father Felix*, 35. In *Scenes and Characters*, Protestants say that the Catholic Church threatens "the institutions of our country," and that "While popery, like the yellow fever, was confined to the seaboard, it was well enough to say 'Let it alone,' but now, that it has sent its contagion into our small towns and villages . . . it behooves every lover of his country to be up and doing, to purify the atmosphere of its noxious vapors" (97).

38. Cannon, *Bickerton*, 83.

39. Cannon, *Mora Carmody*, 26; *Father Felix*, 38.

40. Cannon, *Father Felix*, 66–67.

41. Ibid., 67.

42. Cannon, *Father Felix*, 54–58; *Bickerton*, 106.

43. Cannon, *Bickerton*, 106, 108. In *Scenes and Characters*, Cannon refers to the "rust" that the priest character, Father Quigley, "had brought with him from home," a home he shares with his immigrant congregation (31). Other of Cannon's priests are more typical. Father Felix is American and a convert; his parents were "hereditary Protestants. One the descendent of a Huguenot family; and the other of Puritan blood" (156). In his first doctrinal novels, *Harry Layden* and *Mora Carmody*, Cannon says nothing about the backgrounds of the priest characters.

44. Cannon, *Harry Layden*, 118.

45. Cannon, *Mora Carmody*, 57, 58–59, 60; *Father Felix*, 41.

46. Cannon, *Bickerton*, 98–103, at 98, 102.

47. Ibid., 129–39, at 129, 129–30, 139.

48. Ibid., 129, 130, 134.

49. Ibid., 97, 103, 102, 101.

50. Ibid., 133. Hubbard also says that for the Protestant, "the right of private judgment in matters of conscience" takes precedence while the Catholic "believes that, in spiritual affairs, the decisions of the Church ought to overrule the individual judgment" (133).

51. Ibid., 133.

52. Ibid., 132, 75–76.

53. Ibid., 136, 132.

54. Ibid., 137, 139.

55. Ibid., 136, 138–39.

56. Cannon, *Tighe Lyfford*, 130–44, at 136, 137, 138, 139.

57. Cannon, *Bickerton*, 191.

58. Hamburger, *Separation of Church and State*, esp. 240–43. See also Hamburger's article "Against Separation," and Fessenden, "The Nineteenth-Century Bible Wars and the Separation of Church and State."

59. Hamburger, for example, offers as evidence only Archbishop Hughes's statements that he supports separation, has not voted in elections, and has intervened in politics only once to defend the rights of Catholics to equal treatment in regard to public funding for schools and to reveal fraud on this issue in an election campaign. But this is evidence only for Bishop Hughes, not for all the American Catholic clergy. Moreover, even for Hughes it is not evidence of any complete withdrawal. After making the statement that Hamburger cites, for example, Hughes continues to take public positions on issues of American politics, including abolition, the Civil War, and women's rights. And years after making the statement, Hughes travels to Europe for President Lincoln to gain

support for the Union cause from Catholic countries. Indicating his narrow interpretation of separation, Hughes accepts the task but not an official position. Moreover on the issue of intervening in electoral politics, Hughes says that if a similar situation over the schools arose in the future he would behave in the same way. See McGreevy, *Catholicism and American Freedom*, and Shaw, *Dagger John: The Unquiet Life and Times of Archbishop John Hughes of New York*. For Hughes's position, see especially his letter to the *Freeman's Journal*, April 17, 1855. See also Lannie, *Public Money and Parochial Education*, and McAvoy, "The Formation of the Catholic Minority in the United States, 1820–1860."

Chapter 5. The Anti-Protestant Novel

1. For accounts of the anti-Catholic popular literature, see Griffin, *Anti-Catholicism and Nineteenth-Century Fiction*, and Franchot, *Roads to Rome*.

2. Pise, *Father Rowland*, 81–82.

3. Bryant, *Pauline Seward*, 1:198, 194, 191.

4. Pise, *Father Rowland*, 86. Similarly, a friend of Bryant's Pauline Seward, observing her conversation with Dr. Bogus about apostolic succession in the Anglican Church, sees that Pauline is able to "skillfully wield the Reverend Doctor's own weapons, and completely corner him on the queen's commissions, and church authority" (Bryant, *Pauline Seward*, 1:122).

5. Miles, *The Governess*, 140–41, 142.

6. Pise, *Father Rowland*, 102, 83.

7. Miles, *The Governess*, 206.

8. Pise, *Father Rowland*, 83.

9. Dorsey, *The Sister of Charity*, 1:77.

10. Miles, *The Governess*, 10, 88–91, 136–42.

11. Pise, *Father Rowland*, 81.

12. Dorsey, *The Student of Blenheim Forest*, 110. Similarly, Pauline Seward expects Dr. Bogus to be a "cold and dogmatical theologian" but instead finds him to have an "easy and graceful carriage; and in conversation energetic and beyond expression winning" (Bryant, *Pauline Seward*, 1:111).

13. Miles, *The Governess*, 142.

14. Pise, *Zenosius*, preface, 5; 208.

15. Bryant, *Pauline Seward*, 1:237.

16. Pise, *Zenosius*, 8, 279, 6, 35, 20, 54.

17. Ibid., 6.

18. In *Oran, the Outcast*, Cannon presents at least a mixed portrait even of a Protestant minister. He describes the minister's sermon on death and the im-

mortality of the body as ridiculous, but he still calls the man pious, cheerful, and liberal (2:90). At another point, he says the minister delivered "an excellent sermon" (2:75). In this, his first novel, Cannon reserves his satire for the pretentious wealthy.

19. Cannon, *Father Felix*, 21, 167.

20. Ibid., 156, 40, 171–72.

21. Cannon, *Harry Layden*, 46. In *Father Felix*, the hero comes upon a Millerite encampment, a tent "crowded with human beings of both sexes, of all ages and conditions, and of every shade of complexion," where a preacher is "shouting" a "harangue" (178, 180).

22. Cannon, *Scenes and Characters*, 79. In only a few places in the novel, Cannon adopts the more traditional account of anti-Catholicism. He reports, for example, that a minister accused Catholics of paying priests for the forgiveness of sins. Even then he adds a footnote telling his readers that this "stale and ridiculous charge is still repeated by the sectaries" (62).

23. Ibid., 47, 48, 215, 64–65, 114.

24. Ibid., 64, 57–58.

25. "Review of Cannon's *Scenes and Characters from the Comedy of Life*," 258.

26. Cannon, *Scenes and Characters*, 206, 68, 210, 211, 212–13, 216.

27. Roddan, *John O'Brien*, 200, 201. In Cannon's 1855 *Bickerton*, the part-time preacher Scroggs organizes nativist meetings in the basement of his church and "ministers . . . of three or four other churches" participate. As a result, a mob attacks the priest and the Irish Catholic neighborhood. *Bickerton*, 74; see also 157–59, 181.

28. Quigley, *The Cross and the Shamrock*, 117.

29. Ibid., 146, 155–60.

30. Roddan, *John O'Brien*, 59, 60; Quigley, *The Cross and the Shamrock*, 35, 63–64; Cannon, *Bickerton*, 180–82.

31. Roddan, *John O'Brien*, 191.

32. Cannon, *Bickerton*, 51–52, 64.

33. Quigley, *The Cross and the Shamrock*, 184.

34. Sadlier, *Willy Burke*, 185, and *Confessions of an Apostate*, 205; Quigley, *The Cross and the Shamrock*, 194.

35. Roddan, *John O'Brien*, 257; Sadlier, *Willy Burke*, 299.

36. Quigley, *The Cross and the Shamrock*, 37, 193–94. Quigley ascribes the same motives to Protestant journals "such as the Harper's publications and the religious organs," which abuse Catholics so "shamefully." He calls them "journals of a mercenary character" (*Profit and Loss*, 49). When Cannon's Rev. Scroggs finds that his first denomination, Universalism, "is by no means a paying one, for somehow people are generally better pleased to hear that their friends and

neighbors are in danger of hell-fire, than to be assured of their own salvation," he begins to preach as "'Fire and Brimstone' Scroggs" and is then "'called,' from a comparatively poor congregation . . . to . . . a parsonage fit for a prince's dwelling, and a salary of five thousand a year" (*Bickerton*, 53–54).

37. Cannon, *Bickerton*, 55.

38. Quigley, *The Cross and the Shamrock*, 36.

39. Roddan, *John O'Brien*, 200, 255; Quigley, *The Cross and the Shamrock*, 261.

40. Quigley, *The Cross and the Shamrock*, 116–17.

41. Cannon, *Bickerton*, 130.

42. In Quigley's *Profit and Loss*, when the wife of a dying Protestant is afraid to grant her husband's request to see a priest because it "is such a disgrace . . . to join the Catholics. . . . [T]he ministers will all be so hard on us," the priest asks if she "believed in freedom of conscience" (207). McCorry notes that the attack on the Charlestown convent violated the American Constitution (*Mount Benedict*, 233). In Sadlier's *Confessions of an Apostate*, Deacon Samuels says that "Popery is a monstrous thing." The lead character Simon—by now a Protestant—remarks to his wife that "Protestants are much given to talking of Popish intolerance. . . . What a pity they don't see their own faults" (176, 177).

43. Boyce, *Mary Lee*, 262–63. Even McCorry, who blames Rev. Alvah Morton Jr. for the attack on the Charlestown convent, manages to undermine the minister's authority in the end. Although the thugs who perpetrated the attack "were simply puppets in the hands of . . . Morton . . . and other evangelicals of a like type," the minister cannot control the public. In the end, "the stream of locked-up bigotry was let loose, and the people became literally frenzied" (*Mount Benedict*, 194, 193).

44. Sadlier, *Con O'Regan*, 191.

45. Sadlier, *Confessions of an Apostate*, 205–10, at 205, 207, 208, 210.

46. McElgun, *Annie Reilly*, 174, 172, 176–77.

47. Quigley, *Profit and Loss*, 86, 301, 302.

48. Cannon, *Bickerton*, 53.

49. Sadlier, *Bessy Conway*, 207. In Quigley's *Profit and Loss*, the principal consenting to marry the minister says: "I shall be true to you, as far as your and my interests will permit" (91).

50. Quigley, *The Cross and the Shamrock*, 89, 91.

51. McCorry, *The Lost Rosary*, 83, 204.

52. Sadlier, *Willy Burke*, 300.

53. Quigley, *The Cross and the Shamrock*, 105.

54. Ibid., 140.

55. Roddan, *John O'Brien*, 256–57.

56. Cannon, *Bickerton*, 65, 66.

57. Sadlier, *Elinor Preston*, 271–72.

58. Quigley, *Profit and Loss*, 189–92, at 189.

59. McCorry, *Mount Benedict*, 194, 191.

60. McCorry, *The Lost Rosary*, 118, 84, 123, 117. In Boyce's *Mary Lee*, the colporteur is named Sweetsoul and described as "snivelling" (275).

61. Quigley, *Profit and Loss*, 85. See also 50–52, 141–43, 304–7.

62. Sadlier, *Old and New*, 125, 126, 127.

63. Roddan, *John O'Brien*, 168, 252–53.

64. Cannon, *Bickerton*, 42.

65. Quigley, *The Cross and the Shamrock*, 233, 174, 156–57, 193, 194.

66. Other denominations were not off the hook, however. In Sadlier's *The Blakes and Flanagans*, an Irish immigrant remarks that the "conscience" of many Protestants tells "them from day to day what the old Quaker said to his son, by way of a parting advice: 'Make money, Obadiah—honestly, if thee can—but be sure thee make it'" (338). Quigley cites "Benjamin Lifford the Quaker" who speaks of the "inflooence of the speerit" and his desire to "sarve thee" (*The Cross and the Shamrock*, 155).

67. Boyce, *Mary Lee*, 96, 205. Boyce exempts the Irish Anglican from his criticism. This man is not anti-Catholic, supports the revolutionary, befriends the priest, and despises both the hypocritical Presbyterian and the canting Methodist. He does not convert to Catholicism because he has some reservations about confession.

68. Sadlier, *Confessions of an Apostate*, 151–52. In the same novel, Sadlier says that a young handsome minister has "little of the Puritan about him," although he is forced to repress his "happy vein of humor . . . within the very narrowest bounds, in virtue of his standing amongst 'the chosen'" (141). McElgun makes the same criticism. Dr. Brassman, the minister in *Annie Reilly*, gives an incoherent sermon that seems to favor the implementation of the "old law" or the death penalty, even for minor crimes, indicating the harshness of his theology (175–76).

69. Roddan, *John O'Brien*, 185; Boyce, *Mary Lee*, 263, 61; Quigley, *Profit and Loss*, 82.

70. Roddan, *John O'Brien*, 254, 255. As examples of fanatics, Roddan refers to Matthias (the upstate New York carpenter who founded a kingdom); Mormons; and William Miller (a forerunner of Adventists), who expected the world to end imminently (255).

71. Quigley, *The Cross and the Shamrock*, 238.

72. Cannon, *Bickerton*, 188. Among the newer denominations, Unitarians come into their share of criticism. Roddan—explaining that Protestants can only appeal to man not to God—concludes that "the Unitarian makes his

appeal to the man, rational and animal, and tries to make him do well because it is gentlemanly to do so" (185). Quigley also emphasizes the rationalism of the denomination. "His honor Squire Wilson the Universalist" considers a Protestant "rather simple to allow . . . the priest to come into his house" (*The Cross and the Shamrock*, 155).

73. Quigley, *The Cross and the Shamrock*, 158; *Profit and Loss*, 435.

74. Sadlier, *Bessy Conway*, 206–7. In Sadlier's *Con O'Regan*, Rev. Shillingworth preaches "after no man's fashion but out of the fullness of his own soul, which was, as he said, an overflowing cistern of sweet water for the children of God's covenant" (191).

75. Quigley, *Profit and Loss*, 41, 81. See also Sadlier, *Elinor Preston*, 271.

76. Cannon, *Bickerton*, 40–41.

77. Quigley, *The Cross and the Shamrock*, 238.

78. Quigley, *Profit and Loss*, 82.

79. Roddan, *John O'Brien*, 202.

80. Quigley, *Profit and Loss*, 141, 142. See also *The Cross and the Shamrock*, 160.

81. Sadlier, *Confessions of an Apostate*, 107, 221; McCorry, *Mount Benedict*, 233, 53.

82. Sadlier, *Confessions of an Apostate*, 109; McCorry, *Mount Benedict*, 194; Quigley, *Profit and Loss*, 435.

83. Sadlier, *The Blakes and Flanagans*, 378.

84. McCorry, *The Lost Rosary*, 119; *Mount Benedict*, 94; Quigley, *Profit and Loss*, 206.

85. Roddan, *John O'Brien*, 185; Sadlier, *Con O'Regan*, 190; McCorry, *The Lost Rosary*, 119.

86. Roddan, *John O'Brien*, 202, 191.

87. Quigley, *The Cross and the Shamrock*, 152; Sadlier, *The Blakes and Flanagans*, 306.

88. Quigley, *The Cross and the Shamrock*, 7–8; *Profit and Loss*, 244.

89. Sadlier, *Con O'Regan*, 194. In *Confessions of an Apostate*, Sadlier's lead character, now a disillusioned Protestant, regards their baptisms as illegitimate. He reports that his children are being baptized by a Protestant minister, but since "births and baptisms were, of course, wholly unconnected with us, it was not till the child was able to use both limbs and tongue in their legitimate functions that the ceremony was gone through, such as it was" (186–87).

90. McCorry, *Mount Benedict*, 94.

91. Quigley, *The Cross and the Shamrock*, 233; Sadlier, *The Blakes and Flanagans*, 378, 291; Cannon, *Bickerton*, 41.

92. Sadlier, *Willy Burke*, 218, 219; *The Blakes and Flanagans*, 206.

93. Quigley, *The Cross and the Shamrock*, 238, 239; *Profit and Loss*, 244.

94. Quigley, *Profit and Loss*, 36–37, 38.

95. Roddan, *John O'Brien*, 63; Sadlier, *The Blakes and Flanagans*, 194.

96. Quigley, *Profit and Loss*, 456, 434, 457.

97. Sadlier, *Old and New*, 305, 304–5.

98. Sadlier, *Confessions of an Apostate*, 62, 61, 74.

99. Sadlier, *Willy Burke*, 72–73, 151.

100. Sadlier, *Con O'Regan*, 305, 24, 236, 367.

101. Quigley, *Profit and Loss*, 34, 32, 408, 410.

102. Sadlier, *Old and New*, 18, 382.

103. Sadlier, *Bessy Conway*, 72.

104. Quigley, *The Cross and the Shamrock*, 239.

105. Quigley, *Profit and Loss*, 187; Sadlier, *Old and New*, 128, 129; McCorry, *The Lost Rosary*, 119, 5.

106. McCorry, *The Lost Rosary*, 144, 81.

107. Boyce, *Mary Lee*, 207, 220–21, 207.

108. Cannon, *Bickerton*, 102, 77.

109. Ibid., 9, 60, 61, 65, 54.

110. Cannon, *Tighe Lyfford*, 130–44, at 136, 137, 138, 139.

111. Noll, *The Civil War as a Theological Crisis*, 127.

Chapter 6. The Church as Family

1. Reynolds, *Faith in Fiction*, especially chapter 8.

2. Pise, *Father Rowland*, 140.

3. Miles, *Loretto*, 217, 224, 235–38, 251–52.

4. Miles, *The Governess*, 13, 108.

5. Dorsey, *The Oriental Pearl*, 28, 29.

6. Ibid., 102, 60.

7. Pise, *Father Rowland*, 156, 14.

8. Cannon, *Mora Carmody*, 44, 45.

9. Pise, *Father Rowland*, 30.

10. Pise, *Zenosius*, 43; Miles, *Loretto*, 281. See also discussion of liberty of conscience in chapter 4.

11. Pise, *Zenosius*, 47, 272, 273.

12. Miles, *The Governess*, 107; *Loretto*, 279.

13. Cannon, "The Beal Fire," 102, 115.

14. Cannon, *Scenes and Characters*, 31, 32. Describing the senior Tolands, a character in the novel says that about twenty years before, an "Irish family . . . poor and illiterate" had come to America (61).

15. Sadlier, *Willy Burke*, 3, 41; *The Blakes and Flanagans*, 31; *Con O'Regan*, 342; *Confessions of an Apostate*, 19; Quigley, *The Cross and the Shamrock*, 53, 82; McElgun, *Annie Reilly*, 181.

16. Quigley, *The Cross and the Shamrock*, 59; Cannon, *Bickerton*, 116.

17. Quigley, *The Cross and the Shamrock*, 7; McCorry, *The Lost Rosary*, 63, 64.

18. Sadlier, *Old and New*, 97–98; McCorry, *Mount Benedict*, 226.

19. Sadlier, *The Blakes and Flanagans*, 31, and *Old and New*, 186–87.

20. Quigley, *The Cross and the Shamrock*, 137.

21. Comment from Harriet Spofford in 1881, quoted in Lynch-Brennan, "Ubiquitous Bridget," 337.

22. Sadlier, *Con O'Regan*, 7. Similarly, in McElgun's *Annie Reilly*, the young immigrant's employer treats her with "lofty scorn" and gives her only a miserable room with ceilings too low to stand up in (159, 160).

23. McElgun, *Annie Reilly*, 149–56.

24. Sadlier, *The Blakes and Flanagans*, 11.

25. Quigley, *Profit and Loss*, 33, 27.

26. Sadlier, *The Blakes and Flanagans*, 20.

27. Roddan, *John O'Brien*, 65, 261–62, 51.

28. McCorry, *The Lost Rosary*, 73, 182. McElgun's hero in *Annie Reilly* works in the oil fields, which employ men "from every part of America and Europe." He finds his fellow workers "for the most part a very reckless set of fellows, who cared for nothing but drinking, carousing, and fighting." James "keeps apart from them as much as possible . . . in the evenings sitting alone by himself, thinking of home" (179).

29. Sadlier, *Bessy Conway*, 214, 134. In *The Blakes and Flanagans*, Sadlier sums up the Flanagans' social life by describing "a family party" to which all their Irish family, friends, and neighbors are invited. The first dance is an "Irish jig" and the author describes "the fun" and "joy" of all the guests, a rare mention of Irish music and dancing in these novels (160–76, at 160, 165, 166, 167).

30. Sadlier, *Con O'Regan*, 364, 373.

31. McCorry, *Mount Benedict*, 32, 84.

32. On rare occasions, an author is willing to countenance marriage in America between Catholics and unconverted Protestants for very minor characters. In Quigley's *The Cross and the Shamrock*, a character given only the name of Knicks describes his family: his mother was a Catholic convert from England who always had the best of any arguments with her Protestant husband and his ministers. Knicks also says that he "never met a Christian but my mother," and "If I were to embrace any religion, it would be the Roman Catholic religion; for it is the only *honest religion* there is." In the end, Knicks's "father turned with

mother, and had the Irish priest O'Shane to attent him afore he died. Mother got us all baptized too." This character never appears in the story again (34, 35).

33. Sadlier, *Old and New*, 109, 209, 89, 96–97.

34. Quigley, *Profit and Loss*, 406; McElgun, *Annie Reilly*, 124.

35. An editor of the Sadlier family-owned newspaper, the *New York Tablet*, claimed in a letter to the *New York Times* that he had been fired by the three Sadlier partners (Dennis, James, and Mary Anne Sadlier) after writing an article denouncing the Southern secession. The editor charges that although the Sadliers claim to preserve a "Baltimorean neutrality," in fact they objected to his position. According to the editor, Dennis is the only one of the partners to be an American citizen, while the other two are "outspoken sympathizers with the rebellion, one violently so." That one has "a hatred of this country, its institutions (except slavery) and its people" (*New York Times*, September 22, 1861).

36. Sadlier, *Willy Burke*, 312. Sadlier does not give the man a name or specify his ethnic background.

37. Sadlier, *Old and New*, 480, 461.

38. McCorry, *The Lost Rosary*, 64, 65, and *Mount Benedict*, 172–73.

39. Sadlier, *Old and New*, 101, 178, 224.

40. To further show the contrast between Sadlier's views of the old and new worlds, even the educated Elinor Preston, en route to Canada, rejects a proposal from an admirable English Protestant man named William Wortley because, as Elinor explains to the young man's father, "William is a staunch Protestant and I am, I thank God for it! as staunch a Papist. . . . [T]here is a yawning gulf between us. . . . In all probability I shall never marry, but if I do, the man of my choice must be a Catholic" (201–2).

41. Boyce, *Mary Lee*, 138–39. When Barry worries that Mary Lee "could never be happy with the heretic and revolutionist I am," the old Irish woman replies that if Mary marries him "she'd make a Catholic iv ye in three weeks. . . . [S]he'd make her religion look so good an holy in yer eyes, jist by her ivery day ways, that ye cudn't help lovin it yerself" (139).

42. Neither McCorry nor McElgun communicates a consistent vision of the Church.

43. Roddan, *John O'Brien*, 213, 150, 152, 242.

44. Ibid., 242, 199.

45. Quigley, *The Cross and the Shamrock*, 85; Sadlier, *Willy Burke*, 41. Quigley's character also says that "the church is my mother; and when she prohibits an indifferent thing, I, as a good child, am bound to obey her" (85). In another Sadlier novel, Edward Flanagan asserts that Catholics "believe and practice, but

never presume to discuss the wise teachings of the Church" (*The Blakes and Flanagans*, 304).

46. Sadlier, *The Blakes and Flanagans*, 88.

47. Quigley, *The Cross and the Shamrock*, 44.

48. Sadlier, *The Blakes and Flanagans*, 381, 390; *Confessions of an Apostate*, 204, 233–48. Sadlier does the same thing in *Willy Burke*. After showing her characters asserting their obedience to the Church and describing the dire consequences for Peter Burke when he rejects that authority, Sadlier concludes that her purpose has been to place before her reader "Religion . . . as she really is — mild, and cheerful, and softening in her influence" (314).

49. Boyce, *Mary Lee*, 117, 326.

50. Ibid., 326, 324, 325.

51. Ibid., 323, 167, 164, 175, 117.

52. Ibid., 162, 167, 323, 165.

53. Ibid., 323, 326, 387.

54. Brownson, "Review of *The Yankee in Ireland*," 89, 91, 93.

55. Boyce, *Mary Lee*, 124–25. Quigley at times also suggests that the older aristocratic societies of Ireland and Europe are superior to America. Father Ugo, the priest in *The Cross and the Shamrock*, is "highly educated, and accustomed in Europe, where he was chaplain to Lord C___d, to the most aristocratic society. . . . [H]e entertained no small contempt for the mushroom aristocratic imitations that he witnessed in America" (149). Sadlier defends her idea of an aristocratic order in *Old and New*, 91, and *Bessy Conway*, 162.

56. Cannon, *Bickerton*, 141, 144, 143.

57. Sadlier, *Elinor Preston*, 62, 63, 47.

58. Brownson, "Review of C. J. Cannon's Works," 504, 527, 525.

59. Sadlier, *Bessy Conway*, 123–31, at 123.

60. Cannon, *Bickerton*, 108–11; Sadlier, *The Blakes and Flanagans*, 125. See discussion in chapter 7.

61. Sadlier, *The Blakes and Flanagans*, 87, 89, 390, 373.

62. Ibid., 391, 87, 37.

63. Ibid., 19–20. Quigley, *Profit and Loss*, 35.

64. Sadlier, *The Blakes and Flanagans*, 390, 254.

65. Ibid., 206, 290, 288.

66. Sadlier, *Old and New*, 483–84.

67. McCorry, *Mount Benedict*, 195, 211, 197.

68. Sadlier, *Bessy Conway*, iv, 296.

69. Sadlier, *Con O'Regan*, iii, iv, 159–60, 342.

70. Ibid., iii–iv.

71. Sadlier, *Elinor Preston*, 58.

72. Sadlier, *Old and New*, 321, 323, 325.

73. Sadlier, *The Blakes and Flanagans*, 244, 247–48.

74. McElgun, *Annie Reilly*, 71.

75. For discussions of the tensions and conflicts, see Joyce, *Editors and Ethnicity*, and T. N. Brown, *Irish-American Nationalism, 1870–1890*. Jenkins and Rafferty discuss the ambivalence of the American clergy (which included some voices in favor of physical force nationalism) and also of the hierarchy, which refused to publicly condemn the Fenians by name mainly because they feared alienating their Irish constituents. Jenkins, *Irish Nationalism and the British State*, and Rafferty, "Fenianism in North America in the 1860s."

76. Cannon, "The Beal Fire," 102, 103, 115.

77. McCorry, *The Lost Rosary*, 97.

78. Cannon, *Harry Layden*, 95; "The Devil's Chimney," 276.

79. Quigley, *Profit and Loss*, 7–8.

80. Cannon, *Bickerton*, 5–6.

81. Boyce, *Mary Lee*, 140, 130, 212, 220.

82. Ibid., 140, 140–41.

83. Ibid., 299, 374–88.

84. Ibid., 162.

85. Meagher, *The Columbia Guide to Irish American History*, 6.

Chapter 7. The Maternal Priest

1. Tocqueville, *Journey in Ireland*, 48, 126.

2. Pise, *Zenosius*, 62.

3. Bryant, *Pauline Seward*, 1:97, 317.

4. Pise, *Father Rowland*, 23; Dorsey, *The Sister of Charity*, 1:172.

5. Pise, *Zenosius*, 103–27, at 104.

6. Cannon, *Father Felix*, 159.

7. Cannon, *Harry Layden*, 6, 99; *Father Felix*, 44–48, 55–57, 208–15.

8. Dorsey, *The Oriental Pearl*, 80, 109–110, 50.

9. Miles, *Loretto*, 65; *The Governess*, 46, 89–90.

10. Cannon, *Scenes and Characters*, 31.

11. Pise, *Father Rowland*, 23; Dorsey, *The Student of Blenheim Forest*, 128, 129; Miles, *The Governess*, preface. In Dorsey's *The Sister of Charity*, the priest also speaks six languages in addition to English, and is a person of "deep learning," well able to engage in "intellectual conversation" (1:161, 159, 173).

12. Dorsey, *The Sister of Charity*, 1:161–62; Pise, *Father Rowland*, 23.

13. Dorsey, *The Oriental Pearl*, 79, 108.

14. Cannon, *Mora Carmody*, 106; *Father Felix*, 67; *Scenes and Characters*, 30–31.

15. Cannon, *Harry Layden*, 99; *Scenes and Characters*, 30.

16. Dorsey, *The Oriental Pearl*, 60, 58. As soon as she implies this criticism of the priest for excessive severity and lack of understanding, however, Dorsey withdraws it. The young man acknowledges that the fault was his own and reflects that perhaps the priest's harshness and "severity" "were salutary" (81–82, 72).

17. Miles, *Loretto*, 266.

18. Ibid., 65, 73, 267, 268. Similarly, in Miles's other novel, when the governess resolves to seek the advice of her confessor about remaining in her employment with the Protestant family, she decides that if the priest tells her to leave the job, she will do so (*The Governess*, 89–90).

19. Miles, *The Governess*, 90.

20. McElgun, *Annie Reilly*, 119.

21. Sadlier, *Willy Burke*, 35; McCorry, *The Lost Rosary*, 99, 101; McElgun, *Annie Reilly*, 68, 72, 73.

22. Quigley, *The Cross and the Shamrock*, 26.

23. Sadlier, *Willy Burke*, 10–14. Boyce's priest lives in Ireland where the action of the novel takes place. I consider him in the section on the priest in America because Boyce does not portray an Irish and then an American priest; his Irish priest is his sole illustration.

24. Sadlier, *The Blakes and Flanagans*, 122. In some cases, the reader can assume a priest is Irish even if the author does not specify his background. Quigley's second priest in *The Cross and the Shamrock*, Father Ugo, who defends the laboring men, is described only as European, but it seems likely that this name is a variant of the author's own first name, Hugh, and so European can be interpreted as Irish. Quigley follows this pattern in describing the priest who accompanies the immigrants in their passage to America, calling him "Rev. H. O'Q—" (55).

25. Quigley, *Profit and Loss*, 199, 201.

26. Cannon, *Bickerton*, 107; *Tighe Lyfford*, 223.

27. Roddan, *John O'Brien*, 107; Sadlier, *Willy Burke*, 39.

28. Sadlier, *Willy Burke*, 111, 103, 112.

29. Quigley, *The Cross and the Shamrock*, 24, 43, 45.

30. Cannon, *Bickerton*, 119, 119–20.

31. McElgun, *Annie Reilly*, 197. McElgun does not take a position on church authority, but he subscribes to the nurturing view of the priest.

32. The heroines of *The Lost Rosary* and *Annie Reilly* are helped by married friends; Bessy Conway is advised by one of the author's priest substitute characters, a deformed, dwarf-like, unmarried man devoted to the Church.

33. Quigley, *The Cross and the Shamrock*, 15; Cannon, *Bickerton*, 110.

34. Quigley, *The Cross and the Shamrock*, 15; Cannon, *Bickerton*, 23; McCorry, *Mount Benedict*, 212.

35. Boyce, *Mary Lee*, 320, 319; Quigley, *The Cross and the Shamrock*, 46, 97.

36. Cannon, *Bickerton*, 143; Quigley, *The Cross and the Shamrock*, 118.

37. Sadlier, *Bessy Conway*, 56, 57.

38. Quigley, *The Cross and the Shamrock*, 116; McCorry, *Mount Benedict*, 209, 232; Sadlier, *Con O'Regan*, 288, 390, 391.

39. Roddan, *John O'Brien*, 107. McCorry, twenty years later, comments that "the valuable collection of books belonging to Bishop Fenwick, which contained many rare and valuable works on science, philosophy, and theology were scattered before this uneducated" crowd and burned (*Mount Benedict*, 213).

40. Sadlier, *Confessions of an Apostate*, 91, 67, 68; *Con O'Regan*, iv.

41. Quigley, *The Cross and the Shamrock*, 149, 226, 227, 150.

42. The only reference to manners is Sadlier's description of the Jesuit superior at Clongowes, who receives the visitors "with the simple, unaffected urbanity which ever distinguishes the truly religious" (*Elinor Preston*, 49). When the authors refer to the American priests as "gentlemanly," they do not mean manners. Sadlier is concerned with pious and studious qualities as she describes Father Daly on board ship in *Bessy Conway* as "gentlemanly" (56). Cannon is concerned with moral qualities when a Catholic character refers to the priest of *Bickerton* as a "Christian and a *gentleman*" (124).

43. Quigley, *The Cross and the Shamrock*, 149.

44. Cannon, *Bickerton*, 172; McCorry, *Mount Benedict*, 210, 234.

45. Roddan, *John O'Brien*, 64.

46. Sadlier, *Willy Burke*, 61; *Confessions of an Apostate*, 98; Quigley, *The Cross and the Shamrock*, 123, 124.

47. Boyce, *Mary Lee*, 116–17; Sadlier, *The Blakes and Flanagans*, 73, 249; Quigley, *Profit and Loss*, 201, 270.

48. Boyce, *Mary Lee*, 38, 298, 188, 116.

49. Ibid., 161, 118, 116.

50. Ibid., 162, 163, 330.

51. Ibid., 299, 302, 363–64.

52. Ibid., 163, 166, 185, 387.

53. Sadlier, *The Blakes and Flanagans*, 377, 73; Quigley, *Profit and Loss*, 252.

54. Sadlier, *The Blakes and Flanagans*, 73, 87, 89, 289–90.

55. Quigley, *Profit and Loss*, 210, 223, 268, 269, 373.

56. Ibid., 35, 405.

57. Sadlier, *The Blakes and Flanagans*, 118, 121, 117.

58. Cannon, *Bickerton*, 27.

59. Ibid., 108–11, at 108–9; Sadlier, *The Blakes and Flanagans*, 125.

60. Cannon, *Bickerton*, 173, 174. McCorry makes a similar point in *The Lost Rosary*, commenting that the Church permitted the once pagan custom of May celebrations, "thus proving her wisdom in changing, and in many instances sanctifying, instead of destroying popular customs" (13).

61. Cannon, *Bickerton*, 110; Sadlier, *The Blakes and Flanagans*, 87.

62. Boyce, *Mary Lee*, 389–90, 138–39.

63. Cannon, *Bickerton*, 190.

64. Sadlier, *The Blakes and Flanagans*, 206, 290.

65. Quigley, *Profit and Loss*, 35, 405; Sadlier, *The Blakes and Flanagans*, 125.

66. Quigley, *Profit and Loss*, 223.

67. Sadlier, *The Blakes and Flanagans*, 37, 184, 212; Quigley, *Profit and Loss*, 411.

68. Quigley, *Profit and Loss*, 412.

69. Ibid., 406, 294.

70. Sadlier, *Con O'Regan*, 216–17.

71. Sadlier, *The Blakes and Flanagans*, 122, 377; Quigley, *Profit and Loss*, 269.

72. Roddan, *John O'Brien*, 98; Sadlier, *Willy Burke*, 134.

73. Sadlier, *The Blakes and Flanagans*, 337, 104, 386, 253–54, 288, 291–92. In Quigley's novel, an Irish immigrant laborer, who calls the priest a "treasure" for having saved his mother's life, makes the strongest claims for the priest's authority. He explains to a Protestant that "our priests have *power*. . . . Their influence is with God," and then quotes scripture to support the claim that "Christ had all power from the Eternal Father, and that same power is confided to the priests of our Church" (*Profit and Loss*, 400, 252).

74. Sadlier, *Bessy Conway*, 312, 132; *Confessions of an Apostate*, 99; *The Blakes and Flanagans*, 31, 72, 78. For a discussion of Sadlier's use of physical punishment to enforce authority relations, see Howes, "Discipline, Sentiment, and the Irish-American Public."

75. Sadlier, *Bessy Conway*, 188, 189.

76. Sadlier, *Confessions of an Apostate*, 216, 188, 189, 216, 215, 225–28, at 226, 227.

77. Quigley, *Profit and Loss*, 357, 370.

78. The other novel in which most of the lead characters leave America is Quigley's *The Cross and the Shamrock*. Quigley is not making a statement about America, however. One of the orphans becomes a nun and remains here; the

eldest becomes a priest and missionary; and another buys the family farm in Ireland. In Quigley's later book, the lead becomes a successful businessman in America.

79. Sadlier's *Elinor Preston* is different in one respect. The heroine has a relationship with a French Canadian priest, who hires her as a teacher for his school. But Elinor still never finds a home in French Canada to replace the one she left in Ireland. Her attitude to the priest symbolizes this lack of community. He is "worthy" and "good" but no match for the Irish Jesuits. Elinor seems the superior figure; she helps the priest by agreeing to be the teacher in his small school; she speaks French to him because he does not speak English; and she teaches Irish history to him. The priest is not used to such accomplished company; his only other companion is his sister, who is not interested in serious subjects. Elinor is not even confident that the priest will appreciate the value of her memoirs; she leaves the manuscript with him but only in the hope that "some wanderer from my own loved land" might find it. Elinor finds her "Father, Brother, Friend" not in a priest but in "the churches," in "God's holy house," and, ultimately, she looks forward to her "home in the everlasting mansions" (256, 258, 21, 293, 233).

80. Sadlier, *Confessions of an Apostate*, 17; *Bessy Conway*, 295, 303.

81. Sadlier, *Con O'Regan*, 81, 159–60, 401.

Chapter 8. A Woman's Place

1. Later in the nineteenth century, African American novelists would advance still another construction of the American woman reflecting unique racial, social, and economic circumstances. The scholarship on African Americans includes Romero, *Home Fronts*; Tate, *Domestic Allegories of Political Desire*; and Carby, *Reconstructing Womanhood*.

2. For discussions of the domestic ideal and the role of religion in shaping constructions of women, see DeVries, "Rediscovering Christianity after the Postmodern Turn"; Bednarowski, "Women, Spirituality, and History"; Hall, "Beyond Self-Interest"; Kelley, "Beyond the Boundaries"; Fessenden, "The Convent, the Brothel, and the Protestant Women's Sphere"; and Keddie, "The New Religious Politics and Women Worldwide."

3. See, for example, Wald, "Immigration and Assimilation in Nineteenth-Century US Women's Writing," and Griffin, "Women, Anti-Catholicism, and Narrative in Nineteenth-Century America." Also see McDannell, *The Christian Home in Victorian America, 1840–1900*.

4. Other scholars who argue that women writers should be considered along with their male contemporaries include Burstein, *Narrating Women's History in Britain, 1770–1902*; Kete, *Sentimental Collaborations*; and Ellison, *Cato's Tears and the Making of Anglo American Emotion*. For a discussion of the concepts of "system writers" and "system discourse"—the premise that a set of writers share so many assumptions that they can be understood only as a group—see Kucukalioglu, "The Representation of Women as Gendered National Subjects in Ottoman-Turkish Novels (1908–1923)," 4.

5. Kelley, "Beyond the Boundaries," summarizes the literature on the Protestant cult of domesticity and the challenges to it. Also see Scott, "Feminism's History." For the cultural work the domestic literature performed in advancing interests of middle-class Protestant Americans, see Bontatibus, *The Seduction Novel of the Early Nation*; Davidson, "Preface: No More Separate Spheres!"; Dobson, "Reclaiming Sentimental Literature"; and Tompkins, *Sensational Designs*.

6. Brownson, "Religious Novels," 146.

7. Dorsey, *The Student of Blenheim Forest*, 43.

8. Miles, *The Governess*, 15.

9. Cannon, *Father Felix*, 193.

10. Dorsey, *The Oriental Pearl*, 108, 137; Miles, *The Governess*, 13.

11. Miles, *The Governess*, 17, 24.

12. Ibid., 14.

13. McCaffrey, "Irish Americans," 204–5; Miller, *Emigrants and Exiles*, 352, 581, 582; Diner, *Erin's Daughters in America*, 31–33; Nolan, *Ourselves Alone*, 47–53.

14. Only Bertha Von Weigel in Sadlier's *Old and New* leaves her Irish castle to join her mother in America.

15. Sadlier, *Bessy Conway*, 294; McCorry, *The Lost Rosary*, 129.

16. Sadlier, *Bessy Conway*, 295.

17. Sadlier, *The Blakes and Flanagans*, 215–16; McCorry, *The Lost Rosary*, 83. For examples of apple women, see *Mount Benedict*, 229–30. Domestic servants are usually maids or cooks. One of the heroines of McCorry's *The Lost Rosary* is hired for child care, and Sadlier's Winny O'Regan eventually becomes a seamstress.

18. Sadlier's Elinor Preston in Canada is employed first as a companion and then as a teacher. In this last employment, she is unique; no Irish immigrant in America works as a teacher.

19. McCorry, *The Lost Rosary*, 147.

20. And Sadlier complains about the idle daughters of the new rich in *Old and New* because they think themselves too good to do their own housework, not because they do not take jobs (13–14).

21. Sadlier, *Willy Burke*, 208; Cannon, *Bickerton*, 144.

22. Sadlier, *Alice Riordan*, 270.

23. For a discussion of Sadlier's use of the conventions of romance for other purposes, see Lacombe, "Frying-Pans and Deadlier Weapons: The Immigrant Novels of Mary Anne Sadlier."

24. Sadlier, *Alice Riordan*, 265, and preface. As Sadlier reports, the work first appeared in the *Boston Pilot* in 1850 and as a book published by Patrick Donahoe in 1851. It was issued in another edition in 1854 with a preface in which Sadlier explains the changes she has made. Also see Lacombe, "Frying-Pans and Deadlier Weapons: The Immigrant Novels of Mary Anne Sadlier."

25. Sadlier, *Con O'Regan*, 383, 386, 393, 398, 399.

26. In *Mount Benedict*, McCorry devotes an entire chapter to the baptism of the formerly Protestant heroine Cecilia, saying that the young woman was "at the summit of earthly happiness" (162). McCorry devotes much less space to the courtship of Cecilia and Patrick Crolly, the man who had rescued her from the mob (212, 230, 236). McElgun is unique among these authors because he indicates that his heroine is happier after the reunion with her fiancé than she had been before. In the past, he writes, Annie was "not very unhappy, but the painful sense of something wanting, which distressed her so often during those years, was now banished. Now her heart was full, overflowing with joy" (242).

27. Brownson, "Review of *The Yankee in Ireland*," 87.

28. Sadlier, *Old and New*, 459, 452–53.

29. Intact nuclear families in America appear as minor characters in Roddan's *John O'Brien*, Sadlier's *Con O'Regan* and *Confessions of an Apostate*, McCorry's *The Lost Rosary*, and McElgun's *Annie Reilly*. Also the single women who are married in the closing pages of novels will be part of such families in the future.

30. Sadlier, *Willy Burke*, 111; McCorry, *The Lost Rosary*, 56. For the apple women, see Boyce, *Mary Lee*, 133, 281; and Sadlier, *The Blakes and Flanagans*, 84.

31. Sadlier, *Con O'Regan*, 284. A few poor wives do not work, even if their families are desperate. In Sadlier's *Confessions of an Apostate*, for instance, the wife in a poor family does not work even after her husband loses his job due to an injury and her eldest son dies. But even she plans to take in boarders once there is room for them (51, 85–90).

32. Quigley's Mrs. O'Clery, in *The Cross and the Shamrock*, is unusual in her willingness to depend on others for financial support. Newly destitute, she travels to upstate New York with her children "hoping to make out certain acquaintances of her husband, whom she heard were settled" there (58).

33. Sadlier, *Old and New*, 33.

34. McCorry, *The Lost Rosary*, 150.

35. See especially McDannell, "Catholic Domesticity, 1860–1960." See also note 54 below.

36. McCorry, *Mount Benedict*, 229.

37. Quigley sends minor characters in this direction. Two of the orphaned daughters in *The Cross and the Shamrock* enter the convent, as does one of the daughters in *Profit and Loss*.

38. Sadlier, *The Blakes and Flanagans*, 107–8; McCorry, *Mount Benedict*, 113, 112.

39. See, for example, Meagher, *The Columbia Guide to Irish American History*, 178.

40. Sadlier, *Bessy Conway*, 119–20.

41. Cannon, *Bickerton*, 29; Sadlier, *Willy Burke*, 309–10, 245–46.

42. Sadlier, *The Blakes and Flanagans*, 108. See also McCorry, *Mount Benedict*, 207–8. The conflicts for nuns between forgetfulness of self and professional accomplishment are discussed in Cohen, "Miss Read and the Superiors," and also in the work of Margaret Susan Thompson.

43. Boyce, *Mary Lee*, 376; McCorry, *The Lost Rosary*, 150, 87. In *Mount Benedict* Biddy the apple woman is also somewhat "warlike." She maintains: "I'm fit to purtect myself," and when thugs approach as she and Patrick are rescuing Cecilia, she tells Patrick, "I can do for one o' them an' you can do for the other" (78, 72, 76).

44. McCorry, *Mount Benedict*, 42, 196. In Boyce's novel, Else Curley expresses what most would regard as a normal reaction to injury even if it might violate the injunctions to forgiveness dutifully expressed by Mary Lee. In response to pleas to consider the salvation of her soul, Else says that she had "fursaked God an' salvation thirty odd years ago." And again later she says, "I knew no God these thirty years. . . . I have no soul, I lost it thirty years ago" (130, 285).

45. McCorry, *Mount Benedict*, 16. See also Boyce, *Mary Lee*, 139.

46. McCorry, *Mount Benedict*, 228, 78, and *The Lost Rosary*, 72, 150. See also Boyce, *Mary Lee*, 383, 381.

47. McCorry, *The Lost Rosary*, 113, 52, 79.

48. Roddan, *John O'Brien*, 206; Sadlier, *Con O'Regan*, 50. For another discussion of Irish servants in nineteenth-century fiction, which emphasizes the motivation of service more than the determination to be economically independent, see M. Murphy, "The Irish Servant Girl in Literature," and "Bridget and Biddy."

49. Sadlier, *Old and New*, 131.

50. The novels include only one exception to this overall pattern of good wives regretting the loss of community. In the Byrne family, minor characters in Sadlier's *Confessions of an Apostate*, the wife initiates the emigration. The husband of the family tells Simon, the lead character: "My woman has got the notion in

her head, an' I'm not much again it myself either, for we have a family growin' up, you see, an there's no prospect here for them but hard work an' little for it" (33).

51. Sadlier, *Willy Burke*, 7–8; Cannon, *Bickerton*, 7; Quigley, *Profit and Loss*, 21; McCorry, *The Lost Rosary*, 57. See discussion in chapter 2.

52. Sadlier, *Con O'Regan*, 51; *Bessy Conway*, 79–80, 205.

53. Sadlier, *Confessions of an Apostate*, 78, 22.

54. Colleen McDannell has done the best work on Catholic and Protestant attitudes to home and church in the nineteenth century. See especially *The Christian Home in Victorian America, 1840–1900*, and "Catholic Domesticity, 1860–1960." She maintains that the novelists of the mid-century period, Sadlier and McCorry in particular, began to develop a domestic ideology that took root later in the century as the Irish became more middle class. While she analyzes the differences between Catholics and Protestants, especially concerning the role of the institutional church, McDannell emphasizes the similarities in their view of the home and the role of the woman within it. Essentially, she argues, both religious groups developed a domestic ideology. This view, I think, underestimates the degree to which the mid-century novels legitimated the lives of working-class women. It also underestimates the relationship of women to the Church and priests and therefore the woman's role in her community rather than her home. Other authors who stress that Catholics followed Protestants in developing a domestic ideology include Mannard, "Maternity . . . of the Spirit," and Kennelly in her foreword to *American Catholic Women*.

55. Sadlier, *Confessions of an Apostate*, 22, 23. In the same way, McCorry in *The Lost Rosary* explains that his heroine, who has two parents until she is in her late teens, remains faithful to her heritage because of the lessons she has been taught "by her mother and by her teachers at the Old Chapel School" (44). See also McElgun, *Annie Reilly*, 10.

56. Quigley, *Profit and Loss*, 403, 413.

57. Ibid., 114–15, 370.

58. Brownson, "Review of *The Blakes and Flanagans*," 31.

59. Sadlier, *Willy Burke*, 139–40; McCorry, *The Lost Rosary*, 127, 73.

60. Sadlier, *Old and New*, 129. In *Mount Benedict*, McCorry criticizes the Protestant Mr. Morton, saying that "the Slave of the Lamp was never more subservient to another's will than was Alvah Morton to his wife." As he begins to reform, Morton says that he will "reinstate myself in my proper position as head of this house!" (169, 171).

61. Sadlier, *The Blakes and Flanagans*, 15. In such cases of agreement, the woman can, at most, influence her husband in the direction of greater faithfulness. When Edward Flanagan, the son of the family, and his wife Margaret receive an invitation to a dinner party at the home of the backsliding Henry Blake,

"Margaret was, for once, obstinate, or rather firm" that she would not attend but that Edward should go to avoid a family quarrel. Margaret's wishes prevail (300).

62. Ibid., 96–97, 87, 290, 373.

63. Ibid., 17, 20–21.

64. Quigley, *Profit and Loss*, 55–56.

65. Sadlier, *The Blakes and Flanagans*, 390; Quigley, *Profit and Loss*, 412–13. See also Roddan, *John O'Brien*, 47.

66. Quigley, *Profit and Loss*, 37.

67. Sadlier, *Willy Burke*, 245–46; McCorry, *The Lost Rosary*, 88; Cannon, *Bickerton*, 178; Sadlier, *Bessy Conway*, 120.

68. Quigley, *Profit and Loss*, 456.

69. Roddan, *John O'Brien*, 3; Sadlier, *The Blakes and Flanagans*, 13, 12, 10, 114, 113.

70. Quigley, *Profit and Loss*, 269, 36.

71. Roddan, *John O'Brien*, 65.

72. Boyce, *Mary Lee*, 171; Sadlier, *Willy Burke*, 63; McCorry, *Mount Benedict*, 166; Quigley, *Profit and Loss*, 113. See also Sadlier, *The Blakes and Flanagans*, 84.

73. Quigley, *Profit and Loss*, 361, 409–10; McElgun, *Annie Reilly*, 68–73; McCorry, *The Lost Rosary*, 97–101.

74. Nuns opposed bishops to safeguard the mission of their orders, and laywomen challenged priests to protect the integrity of their families and communities. For accounts of nuns opposing clergy, see, Thompson, "Women, Feminism, and the New Religious History." Delay in "Confidantes or Competitors?" examines laywomen's challenges to priests. Also see Katzenstein, *Faithful and Fearless*.

75. Gudorf analyzes the feminization of Catholicism by its opponents, beginning in the late Renaissance, in "Renewal or Repatriarchalization?"

76. Brownson, "Review of *The Yankee In Ireland*," "Religious Novels," and "Catholicity and Literature." See also Brownson, "Literature, Love, and Marriage," and "Women's Novels."

77. Gudorf notes that the priests' nurturing role challenged contemporary definitions of gender. Jenny Franchot makes the same point in *Roads to Rome*. For feminization in the Protestant context, see Douglas, *The Feminization of American Culture*.

78. In Ireland, by contrast, the English governors had, by the mid-nineteenth century, turned over the social and especially the educational institutions of the country to the Church and provided state funds for them. Lee, "Women and the Church since the Famine." See Inglis, *Moral Monopoly*.

79. See, for example, Armstrong, "What Feminism Did to Novel Studies"; Wald, "Immigration and Assimilation in Nineteenth-Century US Women's Writing"; Miller, "For Love and Liberty"; and Stansell, *City of Women*.

Chapter 9. Catholics and Economic Success

1. McElgun, *Annie Reilly*, 157, 203. Also see McCorry, *The Lost Rosary*, 75.

2. Sadlier, *The Blakes and Flanagans*, 10; McElgun, *Annie Reilly*, 242; Sadlier, *Confessions of an Apostate*, 81. See also McCorry, *The Lost Rosary*, 166.

3. McElgun, *Annie Reilly*, 167, 199.

4. Sadlier, *Bessy Conway*, 160; McElgun, *Annie Reilly*, 183.

5. Sadlier, *Old and New*, 12, and *Elinor Preston*, 156; Cannon, *Tighe Lyfford*, 16.

6. Sadlier, *Willy Burke*, 143; McElgun, *Annie Reilly*, 197; Sadlier, *Confessions of an Apostate*, 54. See also Roddan, *John O'Brien*, 124–25, and Quigley, *The Cross and the Shamrock*, 136.

7. McElgun, *Annie Reilly*, 83; Sadlier, *Bessy Conway*, 64, 151, 163; McCorry, *The Lost Rosary*, 170.

8. Boyce, *Mary Lee*, 235.

9. Lynch-Brennan, "Ubiquitous Bridget," 336. Scholars involved in the debates about "whiteness" and gender also show that Irish American domestic servants were caricatured as aggressive and insubordinate, requiring careful teaching and monitoring from their Protestant mistresses. See Schultz, "The Black Mammy and the Irish Bridget"; Enobong and Wooten, "Suitable for Service"; Urban, "Irish Domestic Servants"; and Moloney, "Who's Irish?"

10. Boyce, *Mary Lee*, 235.

11. Quigley, *The Cross and the Shamrock*, 125; *Profit and Loss*, 258.

12. Sadlier, *Con O'Regan*, 57; *Bessy Conway*, 201.

13. McCorry, *The Lost Rosary*, 88. McElgun's Annie Reilly bears "patiently with every hardship and insult, but always bravely and intelligently defending her race and creed." She finally quits her job because the employers criticize her work and fight strenuously with one another (*Annie Reilly*, 186, 160–61).

14. McCorry, *The Lost Rosary*, 129.

15. Sadlier, *Bessy Conway*, 205; *Con O'Regan*, 10, 190.

16. Sadlier, *Bessy Conway*, 3–4; *Willy Burke*, 3.

17. McCorry, *The Lost Rosary*, 73–74.

18. Roddan, *John O'Brien*, 247; Cannon, *Bickerton*, 144, and *Tighe Lyfford*, 12–13.

19. Sadlier, *Old and New*, 147, 194.

20. Cannon, *Bickerton*, 175; McElgun, *Annie Reilly*, 117–18, 119.

21. McCorry, *The Lost Rosary*, 79–80, 168.

22. Sadlier, *The Blakes and Flanagans*, 114, 15, and *Bessy Conway*, 65. Sadlier also describes a character in *Con O'Regan* as a "careless, improvident, good-natured fellow" (266), and she calls Elinor Preston's father—who dies in debt leaving his family penniless—"one of those good, easy men" (22).

23. Sadlier, *The Blakes and Flanagans*, 10, 135.

24. McCorry, *The Lost Rosary*; Sadlier, *Con O'Regan*; and Quigley, *Profit and Loss*. McCorry advises anyone coming to America with knowledge of farming to stay with that work. It may not have immediate attractions, he writes, "but a few years will make the steadfast worker a landed proprietor," where "the sun of independence dawns . . . and hails him as a Man!" (*The Lost Rosary*, 82).

25. McElgun, *Annie Reilly*, 239, 242.

26. Quigley, *The Cross and the Shamrock*, 263. Even minor characters in the novels seldom become priests. Those who do are typically the sons of one of the important families, such as Sadlier's Flanagans, and are briefly extolled as exemplary characters who are away studying (135). They may also be introduced in a novel's final pages as the author reports that the major characters have married and raised a son who becomes a priest. McCorry, *The Lost Rosary*, 220.

27. Boyce, *Mary Lee*, 124; McCorry, *The Lost Rosary*, 113–14; Quigley, *The Cross and the Shamrock*, 124.

28. Sadlier, *The Blakes and Flanagans*, 117, 372. On the subject of education, also, Sadlier is not willing to stay with mercantile as opposed to classical education. When Miles Blake defends the public schools as producing "an enlightened American" fit for a profession, a Catholic character responds: "Do you meant to insinuate, sir, that Irish teachers are not as fully competent to form the mind and cultivate the intellect as Americans, or any others?" (163).

29. Sadlier, *Confessions of an Apostate*, 197.

30. Sadlier, *Old and New*, 478, 31, 75–76, 478–79.

31. Sadlier, *Con O'Regan*, 44, 45, 277, 102.

32. Quigley, *Profit and Loss*, 26.

33. Roddan, *John O'Brien*, 109.

34. Sadlier, *Confessions of an Apostate*, 38; Quigley, *Profit and Loss*, 26.

35. McCorry, *The Lost Rosary*, 79.

36. Quigley, *The Cross and the Shamrock*, 203.

37. Jensen, "'No Irish Need Apply,'" esp. 418–19.

38. Kenny, "Race, Violence, and Anti-Irish Sentiment in the Nineteenth Century," 372. For data showing demand for unskilled labor and likely discrimination for skilled and white-collar jobs, see Ferrie, *Yankeys Now*, especially chapters 3, 5, and 8. Guides written for potential Irish immigrants also suggest that finding low-level employment in America was not a problem. John Francis Maguire, no lover of American cities, advises Irish women in 1868 that they can find jobs in any season of the year. He inserts one qualification for men: if they are seeking outside work, they should come in the spring. *The Irish in America*, 208.

39. Roddan, *John O'Brien*, 188–246, at 188.

40. The good Protestant Hubbards in Cannon's *Bickerton* are not employers. Sadlier's Elinor Preston in French Canada has a faithful and good Protestant employer. Sadlier grows harsher on all subjects when she treats working-class immigrants in America, but Elinor, too, does not find any level of contentment until she is employed in the Catholic school (*Elinor Preston*, 254–57).

41. Quigley, *The Cross and the Shamrock*, 164, 168.

42. Sadlier, *Con O'Regan*, 146, 191, 194.

43. McElgun, *Annie Reilly*, 201, 199; McCorry, *The Lost Rosary*, 202, 212.

44. Sadlier, *The Blakes and Flanagans*, 135; McElgun, *Annie Reilly*, 190.

45. For discussions of theories of assimilation and enclaves, as well as differences between older and newer immigrant groups, see the issue of *Daedalus* 142, no. 3 (Summer 2013); Alba and Nee, *Remaking the American Mainstream*; Suarez-Orozco, "Everything You Ever Wanted to Know about Assimilation but Were Afraid to Ask"; Jacoby, *Reinventing the Melting Pot*; and Bodnar, *The Transplanted*.

46. See Alba and Nee, *Remaking the American Mainstream* (125), for a discussion of how individuals take steps to improve their lives without understanding the consequences for their identity and assimilation.

47. Sadlier, *Old and New*, 91–92.

48. Boyce, *Mary Lee*, 212, 61. This preference for Europe expressed by Sadlier and Boyce is not typical of the authors. Cannon, as usual, prefers America and says that this country "if she be but true to herself, must yet be the regenerator of Europe" (*Bickerton*, preface, 3).

49. Quigley, *Profit and Loss*, 53; Sadlier, *The Blakes and Flanagans*, 11–12. The lead character in Sadlier's *Confessions of an Apostate* wants "wealth and consideration amongst men" (212) and also the love of a Protestant woman. The resisting brother, Peter, in her *Willy Burke*, disregards the advice of his mother, brother, and priest to take the job with a Protestant couple who promise to send him to school and pay him a very good wage.

50. Sadlier, *The Blakes and Flanagans*, 104, 125; Quigley, *Profit and Loss*, 55–56, 404, 408; Sadlier, *Bessy Conway*, 135.

51. Roddan, *John O'Brien*, 126; Sadlier, *The Blakes and Flanagans*, 243.

52. Sadlier, *Willy Burke*, 35, 45–46; *The Blakes and Flanagans*, 121; Quigley, *Profit and Loss*, 34, 56.

53. Roddan says that John O'Brien earns enough to support a family before he gets married (261–62); McElgun describes the established immigrant Patrick Sweeny and his family, who helped the immigrant Annie Reilly, as living "comfortably" (140), and his hero James O'Rourke is on the road to wealth by the end of the novel.

54. Sadlier also says nothing about the home or the shop of Mrs. Williams, who owns the millinery business and uses her money to raise the Burke daughters (112, 189–90).

55. McCorry, *The Lost Rosary*, 166; McElgun, *Annie Reilly*, 244, 140, 245; Sadlier, *The Blakes and Flanagans*, 136. Tom Reilly, the minor character in the last novel, who takes care of his mother, lives in a "quiet, happy home"—"a nicely-furnished house, small indeed, but tasteful and comfortable" (387, 388).

56. McElgun, *Annie Reilly*, 119.

57. Sadlier, *The Blakes and Flanagans*, 131, 132; *Old and New*, 9, 11, 73–75.

58. McCorry, *The Lost Rosary*, 166, 166–68.

59. Sadlier, *Con O'Regan*, 401.

60. Sadlier, *Confessions of an Apostate*, 88.

61. For an analysis of Sadlier's *Willy Burke* and Quigley's *The Cross and the Shamrock*, which makes a similar point about the authors' concern for identity rather than moral scruples (and also highlights the lead characters' separation from the mainstream economy), see Dunne, *Antebellum Irish Immigration and Emerging Ideologies of 'America'*, esp. chapter 4.

62. Bodnar, *The Transplanted*, xvi, 209. See also 208.

63. Quigley, *The Cross and the Shamrock*, 124. Similarly, a good Catholic in Miles's *Loretto* claims that "If Christian charity were more in vogue, socialism which only lives in its absence, would be out of fashion" (146–47).

64. Sadlier, *Bessy Conway*, 211, 208. In the same novel, the good Catholic Paul gets his first job at the "small shoe store" of a Michael Dooley (62).

65. McCorry, *The Lost Rosary*, 190, 193.

66. The authors basically never criticize Irish Catholic employers. McElgun raises the issue of Catholic employers exploiting co-religionists in Ireland, where a Catholic landlord mistreats his tenants (*Annie Reilly*, v). The landlord in question, however, pretends that he is English, emphasizes his Norman ancestry, and eventually changes his religion. See also chapter 2 above.

67. Sadlier, *The Blakes and Flanagans*, 135; *Bessy Conway*, 208, 63. Sadlier's increasing harshness as she comes to write about immigrants in America can be seen by comparing her portrait of Mrs. Delany in New York with the Mrs. Brady in Canada, who employs a newly arrived immigrant as a domestic servant in *Elinor Preston*. Sadlier praises Mrs. Brady for hiring the immigrant: she is a "widow lady with a large family of grown-up sons and daughters, having plenty of means, and the heart to divide them in a measure with those who had none" (212). Sadlier never directly praises a Catholic woman in America for hiring a fellow Catholic.

68. Bodnar, *The Transplanted*, 211.

69. For an argument about the role of the middle class in forging Irish American identity, see Miller, "Class, Culture, and Immigrant Group Identity in the United States." For evidence regarding competing elites within immigrant groups, see Light, *Rome and the New Republic*, 291; Bodnar, *The Transplanted*, chapter 4; and Alba and Nee, *Remaking the American Mainstream*, esp. chapters 2 and 4.

Chapter 10. American Politics

1. A Protestant character in the novel accusing Catholics of seeking to ban the Bible from the schools asks: "has not the bishop of N_Y_ been lately using all his influence with the people and legislature of that state to corrupt them to sanction the nefarious design?" Pauline Seward denies the charge and reads a letter in which the bishop says that Catholics "merely desired for their children the liberty of using the Catholic version" of the Bible, a liberty guaranteed in the Constitution (Bryant, *Pauline Seward*, 1:184–86, at 184).

2. Sadlier, *The Blakes and Flanagans*, 249–57, at 252, 253, 250, 249–50.

3. Ibid., 379, 251, 252.

4. Quigley, *Profit and Loss*, 95.

5. Sadlier, *The Blakes and Flanagans*, 20. See also *Willy Burke*, 30.

6. Quigley, *Profit and Loss*, 31, 226, 31–32; Cannon, *Bickerton*, 110.

7. Sadlier, *The Blakes and Flanagans*, 378.

8. For accounts of the Catholic Church position on slavery and abolition, see Nelson, *Irish Nationalists and the Making of the Irish Race*; Noll, *The Civil War as a Theological Crisis*; Quinn, "Three Cheers for the Abolitionist Pope"; McGreevy, "Catholicism in America" and *Catholicism and American Freedom*; and Rice, *American Catholic Opinion in the Slavery Controversy*. In the years before the Civil War, the bishops' councils issued statements about obedience to law that were interpreted then and now as opposed to the abolitionists. See Rice. Individual bishops, moreover, including England, Kenrick, and Hughes, made clear public statements against abolition—at least for the foreseeable future—whether it was sought by peaceful or violent means. While the positions of the bishops were uniform before the war, disagreements emerged during the conflict.

9. Dorsey, *The Sister of Charity*, 2:52 (also 2:67–68); *The Student of Blenheim Forest*, 41.

10. Pise, *Father Rowland*, 7, 142–47; Bryant, *Pauline Seward*, 1:162.

11. Quigley, *The Cross and the Shamrock*, 246, 247, 242, 264.

12. Cannon, *Oran, the Outcast*, 2:169; "The Two Spirits: A Legend." Cannon does not mention slaves or African Americans in *Bickerton*.

13. Boyce, *Mary Lee*, 335, 237, 336, 233–34.

14. Cannon, "The Devil's Chimney," 288; *Harry Layden*, 22. For Brownson, see "The Laboring Classes."

15. Boyce, *Mary Lee*, 234.

16. Quigley, *The Cross and the Shamrock*, 114, 263; Sadlier, *Con O'Regan*, 45.

17. See Rice and others cited in note 8 above.

18. Pise, *Father Rowland*, 50; Bryant, *Pauline Seward*, 1:266, 265; Dorsey, *The Sister of Charity*, 2:49–50.

19. See authors cited in note 8 above and note 21 below; see also Hueston, *The Catholic Press and Nativism, 1840–1860*.

20. Quigley, *The Cross and the Shamrock*, 250; Boyce, *Mary Lee*, 234, 233.

21. For accounts of the relationship between O'Connell and abolitionist leaders, see Kinealy, *Daniel O'Connell and the Antislavery Movement*, and A. F. Murphy, *American Slavery, Irish Freedom*.

22. Moore, *Religious Outsiders and the Making of Americans*.

23. Boyce, *Mary Lee*, 119; Sadlier, *Bessy Conway*, 197.

24. Pise, *Father Rowland*, 143, 144, 147.

25. Bryant, *Pauline Seward*, 1:163, 165–66.

26. Sadlier, *Bessy Conway*, 71, 197, 89.

27. Boyce, *Mary Lee*, 176.

28. Cannon, *Tighe Lyfford*, 111; Sadlier, *Bessy Conway*, 176, 177; Quigley, *Profit and Loss*, 304. In this, as in his other novel, Quigley insults many groups: he asks, "why should we censure the ignorant black man, the brown gypsy, the red Indian, or the cream-colored Asiatic, for the practice of those arts of imposition . . . when we pardon the like tricks . . . by members of our own advanced, enlightened, and godly Anglo-Saxon race of people?" (312).

29. Quigley, *The Cross and the Shamrock*, 246–49, at 249.

30. Sadlier, *Bessy Conway*, 139; *Old and New*, 212.

31. For arguments that the Irish defined their struggle in racial terms, see Roediger, *The Wages of Whiteness*, and *Working toward Whiteness*; and Ignatiev, *How the Irish Became White*. For the limitations of this argument, see Kenny, "Race, Violence, and Anti-Irish Sentiment in the Nineteenth Century," and Meagher, *The Columbia Guide to Irish American History*. For other very good discussions of the attitudes toward race expressed in Irish American novels, particularly Boyce's *Mary Lee*, which concerns group relations in Ireland, see Pearl, "White, with a Class-Based Blight," and Eagan, "'White,' If 'Not Quite.'"

32. Nelson, *Irish Nationalists and the Making of the Irish Race*, 67. Nelson argues that labor competition is the least satisfactory explanation of Irish American attitudes toward African Americans, free or slave. Over time, the Irish were

victors in the labor market and, relative to African Americans, they were victors early on (70).

33. Cannon, *Bickerton*, 55.

34. Quigley, *Profit and Loss*, 263–64.

35. Guglielmo, in *White on Arrival*, argues that Italian immigrants also considered themselves white on arrival. Some of the scholars interested in the racialization of nineteenth-century domestic servants (cited in chapter 8) also challenge the idea that Irish women had to struggle to be considered white, showing that even Protestants interested in associating domestic service occupations with nonwhite groups had to regard Irish women as white, in the end. See Schultz, "The Black Mammy and the Irish Bridget"; Urban, "Irish Domestic Servants"; and Enoberg and Wooten, "Suitable for Service."

36. Sadlier, *Old and New*, 484, 486.

37. Cannon, *Tighe Lyfford*, 135–36.

38. Ibid., 132–33.

39. For Pise, see Thorp, *Catholic Novelists in Defense of Their Faith, 1829–1865*, 28–29. Patrick Donahoe organized Irish Regiments in the Union Army (*New York Times*, March 18, 1862). Patrick O'Shea sent letters advocating the Union cause to the *Pilot* in Boston and the *Nation* in Dublin, signing them "an American Citizen" (see "Obituary Patrick O'Shea," 874; Connors, "Patrick O'Shea," 2:347; and "Catholic Publisher Dies"). James Kirker, who succeeded Dunigan, was a major in the 69th regiment, a friend of General Corcoran and, until his death, an active sponsor of charities for the families of soldiers. The Sadliers alone among the Northerners seem to have had an ambiguous position on the war. As discussed in note 35 of chapter 6, a former editor of their paper charged that the Sadlier partners claimed to preserve a "Baltimorean neutrality" but in fact favored the South. James and Mary Anne especially were "outspoken sympathizers with the rebellion, one violently so." One of them had "a hatred of this country, its institutions (except slavery) and its people" (*New York Times*, September 22, 1861).

40. Quigley, *The Cross and the Shamrock*, 162–63. This use of religious divisions to explain the political conflict was common in Catholic circles, especially in Europe. Noll, *The Civil War as a Theological Crisis*.

41. Quigley, *The Cross and the Shamrock*, 7, 6.

42. Sadlier, *Old and New*, 126, 129.

43. McCorry, *The Lost Rosary*, 116, 126.

44. Ibid., 219; Sadlier, *Old and New*, 127, 126.

45. McCorry, *The Lost Rosary*, 5; Sadlier, *Old and New*, 129, 130.

46. Quigley, *Profit and Loss*, 244, 226, 304; McCorry, *The Lost Rosary*, 5; Sadlier, *Old and New*, 125–26, 127.

47. The closest they come is when Quigley's priest wonders why the banners at the assembly do not include "free-love" along with the listed "free schools" and "free religion" (*Profit and Loss*, 226).

48. Roddan, *John O'Brien*, 13–14, 243; Cannon, *Bickerton*, 164; Boyce, *Mary Lee*, 140; Quigley, *Profit and Loss*, 391. Sadlier's Henry Blake corresponds with Mazzini, challenges the temporal authority of the pope, and calls Pius IX "a religious tyrant" and "the despot of Rome" (*The Blakes and Flanagans*, 387).

49. Sadlier, *Willy Burke*, 43; Roddan, *John O'Brien*, 58.

50. Cannon, *Scenes and Characters*, 20; *Bickerton*, 37, 27, 28, 172, 171.

51. Sadlier, *Con O'Regan*, 45; Boyce, *Mary Lee*, 154.

52. Quigley, *Profit and Loss*, 263–64. Boyce uses drinking as a way for the Irish hosts to show up the American visitor, Weeks, who is ostensibly a teetotaler. The Irish aristocratic Anglican character comments that abstention from drinking might be appropriate for the poor, but a gentleman should be able to hold his liquor (*Mary Lee*, 255).

53. Sadlier, *Bessy Conway*, 133, 225, 217; McElgun, *Annie Reilly*, 185.

54. Cannon, *Bickerton*, 27, 172.

55. Sadlier, *Bessy Conway*, 67; *Con O'Regan*, 92. In the latter novel, Sadlier also defends the Irish from exaggerated charges. They drink and fight but are not "addicted to the dark, secret, unmentionable crimes, which are of daily occurrence amongst other sections of the community" (57, 56).

56. McElgun, *Annie Reilly*, 179, 183.

57. Quigley, *The Cross and the Shamrock*, 161.

58. Ibid., 123; Cannon, *Bickerton*, 171, 172.

59. This subject is also taken up in chapters 2 and 9.

60. Cannon, *Bickerton*, 27.

61. Quigley, *The Cross and the Shamrock*, 115; McElgun, *Annie Reilly*, 134–35, at 135.

62. Sadlier, *Con O'Regan*, 19; McElgun, *Annie Reilly*, 182, 140, 146.

63. Quigley, *The Cross and the Shamrock*, 116; Sadlier, *Bessy Conway*, 134.

64. Cannon, *Bickerton*, 81; Sadlier, *The Blakes and Flanagans*, 365; Quigley, *Profit and Loss*, 66, 394.

65. Dorsey, *The Sister of Charity*, 2:167; Miles, *Loretto*, 10.

66. Boyce, *Mary Lee*, 223–24.

67. Cannon, *Tighe Lyfford*, 134; Quigley, *The Cross and the Shamrock*, 74; Cannon, *Bickerton*, 98.

68. Quigley, *The Cross and the Shamrock*, 74–76, at 74; Cannon, *Tighe Lyfford*, 135–36. Sadlier in *The Blakes and Flanagans* extolls the Catholic school because "many a valued citizen did it bring up for the State." She is referring to the eco-

nomic rather than the political contributions of the graduates since she continues that "not a few of the boys . . . have since attained a good position in society by their industry and conduct, not to speak of the sound business education" they received (15).

69. Cannon, *Bickerton*, 95, 96, 97. In the 1840s Cannon cites the contributions of John Carroll and John Barry and also the Catholic soldiers from France and Poland who fought in the revolutionary war (*Mora Carmody*, 25). The lead characters in *Father Felix* are "hereditary Catholics, whose ancestor came to this country with . . . Lord Baltimore" (41).

70. Sadlier on a rare occasion suggests that good Catholics might play a role in American public life. In *Old and New*, she describes the father and son of a good and successful Catholic family as "public-spirited, and ever willing to go into any movement having the good of the people in view" (455–56). She mentions no such movement, however.

71. Cannon, *Bickerton*, 75.

72. Ibid., 132, 135. This subject is also discussed in chapter 4.

73. Pise, *Father Rowland*, 6; Cannon, *Father Felix*, 38.

74. Quigley, *The Cross and the Shamrock*, 74–75; Boyce, *Mary Lee*, 224.

75. Cannon, *Bickerton*, 98; Sadlier, *The Blakes and Flanagans*, 164; *Old and New*, 187.

76. Sadlier, *The Blakes and Flanagans*, 164; *Old and New*, 187.

77. Brownson, "Mission of America," 577; "The Native Americans," 283. Brownson eventually changes his mind.

78. Cannon, *Tighe Lyfford*, 133. See also Bryant, *Pauline Seward*, 1:266–67.

79. Boyce, *Mary Lee*, 269, 270.

Conclusion

1. Morris, *American Catholics: The Saints and Sinners Who Built America's Most Powerful Church*, 139. See also Fisher, who in *Communion of Immigrants* refers to "the uneasy triumph" of the Church in these years (114).

SELECTED
BIBLIOGRAPHY

Primary Sources

The best source for the novels covered in this book is the Wright American Fiction collection. Sadlier is the only one of the novelists who is not included in the collection. Wright has digitized the novels published between 1851 and 1875; those published from 1774 to 1850 are on microfilm. As the bibliography indicates, I used the Wright collection for all the novels except Charles Pise's 1829 *Father Rowland* and all of Sadlier. I used an alternative online source for the Pise work because Wright includes only the first edition of the novel rather than the second enlarged edition published two years later. For Sadlier, I relied on hard copy editions of her novels. When I used microfilm editions of the novels, for example with the Wright collection from 1774 to 1850, or hard copies, as with Sadlier, I noted in parentheses any available digitized copies of the complete work.

Early Catholic Novelists

Bryant, John D(elavan). *Pauline Seward: A Tale of Real Life*. 2 vols. Baltimore: John Murphy, 1847. Wright American Fiction, film 304, vol. 1 (1774–1850), reel B-13, no. 437. (Also available Internet Archive, American Libraries, https://www.archive.org.)

Dorsey, Anna Hanson. (Also wrote as Mrs. Anna H. Dorsey.) *The Oriental Pearl; Or, The Catholic Emigrants*. Baltimore: John Murphy, 1848. Wright American Fiction, film 304, vol. 1 (1774–1850), reel D-2, no. 856. (Also available Reprint, Baltimore: John Murphy, 1850, https://books.google.com.)

———. *The Sister of Charity*. 2 vols. New York: Edward Dunigan, 1846. Wright American Fiction, film 304, vol. 1 (1774–1850), reel D-2, no. 857.

———. *The Student of Blenheim Forest*. Baltimore: John Murphy, 1847. Reprint © 1867. Wright American Fiction, film 304, vol. 1 (1774–1850), reel D-3, no. 858.

Miles, George H. *The Governess; Or, The Effects of Good Example: An Original Tale*. Baltimore: Hedian & O'Brien, 1851. Wright American Fiction Project. Indiana University Libraries. http://purl.dlib.indiana.edu/iudl/wright/VAC 7242.pdf.

———. *Loretto; Or, The Choice*. Baltimore: Hedian & O'Brien, 1851. Wright American Fiction Project. Indiana University Libraries. http://purl.dlib .indiana.edu/iudl/wright/VAC7243.pdf.

Pise, Charles Constantine, Rev. *Father Rowland: A North American Tale*. Baltimore: Fielding Lucas Jr., 1829; 2nd enl. ed., 1831. Reprint 1841. HathiTrust Digital Library, http://babel.hathitrust.org.

———. *The Indian Cottage: A Unitarian Story*. Baltimore: Fielding Lucas Jr., 1831. Wright American Fiction, film 304, vol. 1 (1774–1850), reel PQ-5, no. 2049.

———. *Zenosius; Or, The Pilgrim-Convert*. New York: Edward Dunigan, 1845. Wright American Fiction, film 304, col. 1 (1774–1850), reel PQ-5, no. 2051. (Also available Sabin Americana, Gale, Cengage Learning, http://galenet .galegroup.com.)

Irish American Novelists

Boyce, John, Rev. (wrote fiction as Paul Peppergrass). *Mary Lee; Or, The Yankee in Ireland*. Baltimore: Kelly, Hedian & Piet, and Boston: Patrick Donahoe, 1860. Wright American Fiction Project. Indiana University Libraries. http:// purl.dlib.indiana.edu/iudl/wright/VAC5852.pdf.

Cannon, Charles James. "The Beal Fire." In *Facts, Feelings and Fancies*. New York: Bliss, Wadsworth, 1835. Wright American Fiction, film 304, vol. 1 (1774–1850), reel C-1, no. 474, 101–19.

———. *Bickerton; Or, The Immigrant's Daughter: A Tale*. New York: Patrick O'Shea, 1855. Wright American Fiction Project. Indiana University Libraries. http:// purl.dlib.indiana.edu/iudl/wright/VAC5982.pdf.

——— (written as Grandfather Greenway). "The Devil's Chimney." In *Ravellings from the Web of Life*, 255–364. New York: D. & J. Sadlier, 1855. Wright

American Fiction Project. Indiana University Libraries. http://purl.dlib
.indiana.edu/iudl/wright/VAC5983.pdf.

———. *Father Felix: A Tale.* New York: Edward Dunigan, 1845. Wright American Fiction, film 304, vol. 1 (1744–1850), reel C-1, no. 475. (Reprint, London: Dolman, 1850, at Internet Archive, European Libraries, https://www
.archive.org.)

———. *Harry Layden: A Tale.* New York: John A. Boyle, 1842. Wright American Fiction, film 304, vol. 1 (1744–1850), reel C-1, no. 476.

———. *Oran, the Outcast; Or, A Season in New York.* 2 vols. New York: Peabody, 1833. Wright American Fiction, Film 304, vol.1 (1744–1850), reel O-1, no. 1981.

———. *Mora Carmody; Or, Woman's Influence: A Tale.* New York: Edward Dunigan, 1844. Wright American Fiction, film 304, vol. 1 (1744–1850), reel C-1, no. 477.

———. *Scenes and Characters from the Comedy of Life.* New York: Edward Dunigan, 1847. Wright American Fiction, film 304, vol. 1(1744–1850), reel C-1, no. 478.

———. *Tighe Lyfford: A Novel.* New York: James Miller, 1859. Wright American Fiction Project. Indiana University Libraries. http://purl.dlib.indiana.edu
/iudl/wright/VAC5984.pdf.

——— (written as Grandfather Greenway). "The Two Spirits: A Legend." In *Ravellings from the Web of Life*, 211–54. New York: D. & J. Sadlier, 1855. Wright American Fiction Project. Indiana University Libraries. http://purl
.dlib.indiana.edu/iudl/wright/VAC5983.pdf.

McCorry, Peter (wrote fiction as Con O'Leary). *The Lost Rosary; Or, Our Irish Girls: Their Trials, Temptations, and Triumphs.* Boston: Patrick Donahoe, 1870. Wright American Fiction Project. Indiana University Libraries. http://purl
.dlib.indiana.edu/iudl/wright/VAC7145.pdf.

———. *Mount Benedict; Or, The Violated Tomb: A Tale of the Charlestown Convent.* Boston: Patrick Donahoe, 1871. Wright American Fiction Project. Indiana University Libraries. http://purl.dlib.indiana.edu/iudl/wright/VAC7146.pdf.

McElgun, John. *Annie Reilly; Or, The Fortunes of an Irish Girl in New York: A Tale Founded on Fact.* New York: J. A. McGee, 1873. Wright American Fiction Project. Indiana University Libraries. http://purl.dlib.indiana.edu/iudl
/wright/VAC7150.pdf.

Quigley, Hugh, Rev. Dr., *The Cross and the Shamrock; Or, How to Defend the Faith: An Irish American Catholic Tale of Real Life.* Boston: Patrick Donahoe, 1853. Wright American Fiction Project. Indiana University Libraries. http://purl
.dlib.indiana.edu/iudl/wright/VAC7532.pdf. (Reprint, Saddle River, NJ: Gregg Press, 1970.)

————. *Profit and Loss: A Story of the Life of the Genteel Irish-American, Illustrative of Godless Education.* New York: T. O'Kane, 1873. Wright American Fiction Project. Indiana University Libraries. http://purl.dlib.indiana.edu/iudl /wright/VAC7533.pdf.

Roddan, John T. Rev. *John O'Brien; Or, The Orphan of Boston: A Tale of Real Life.* Boston: Patrick Donahoe, 1850. Reprint, 1851.

Sadlier, Mary Anne. (Wrote as Mrs. James or Mrs. J. Sadlier.) *Alice Riordan, The Blind Man's Daughter: A Tale for the Young.* Boston: Patrick Donahoe, 1854. Reprint, Dublin: M. H. Gill, 1884. Reprint, Ulan Press, 2013.

————. *Bessy Conway; Or, The Irish Girl in America.* New York: D. & J. Sadlier, 1861. Reprint, New York: P. J. Kenedy, 1896. (Reprint, D. & J. Sadlier, n.d., Sabin Americana, Gale, Cengage Learning, http://galenet.galegroup.com.)

————. *The Blakes and Flanagans: A Tale Illustrative of Irish Life in the United States.* New York: D. & J. Sadlier, 1855. Reprint, P. J. Kenedy, n.d. (D. & J. Sadlier, 1855, Sabin Americana, Gale, Cengage Learning, http://galenet.galegroup .com.)

————. *Confessions of an Apostate; Or, Leaves from a Troubled Life.* New York: D. & J. Sadlier, 1864. Reprint, New York: P. J. Kenedy, 1903. Reprint, New York: Arno Press, 1978. (Internet Archive, University of Notre Dame Libraries, https://www.archive.org.)

————. *Con O'Regan; Or, Emigrant Life in the New World.* New York: D. & J. Sadlier, 1864. Reprint, New York: P. J. Kenedy, 1895. (Reprint, D. & J. Sadlier, n.d., Sabin Americana, Gale, Cengage Learning, http://galenet.galegroup .com.)

————. *Elinor Preston; Or, Scenes at Home and Abroad.* New York: D. & J. Sadlier, 1861. Reprint, n.d. (Internet Archive, University of Alberta Libraries, https://www.archive.org.)

————. *Old and New; Or, Taste Versus Fashion.* New York: D. & J. Sadlier, 1862. Reprint, P. J. Kenedy, 1895. Reprint, BiblioLife, n.d.

————. *Willy Burke; Or, The Irish Orphan in America.* Boston: Patrick Donahoe, 1850. Reprint, Boston: Patrick Donahoe, 1851. (Boston: Thomas B. Noonan, n.d., Internet Archive, University of Alberta Libraries, https://www .archive.org.)

Secondary Sources

Alba, Richard, and Victor Nee. *Remaking the American Mainstream: Assimilation and Contemporary Immigration.* Cambridge, MA: Harvard University Press, 2003.

Anbinder, Tyler. *Five Points: The Nineteenth-Century New York City Neighborhood That Invented Tap Dance, Stole Elections, and Became the World's Most Notorious Slum.* New York: Free Press, 2001.

Appleby, R. Scott, and Kathleen Sprows Cummings, eds. *Catholics in the American Century: Recasting Narratives of U.S. History.* Ithaca: Cornell University Press, 2012.

Armstrong, Nancy. "What Feminism Did to Novel Studies." In *The Cambridge Companion to Feminist Literary Theory*, edited by Ellen Rooney, 99–118. Cambridge: Cambridge University Press, 2006.

Bauer, Dale M., and Philip Gould, eds. *The Cambridge Companion to Nineteenth-Century American Women's Writing.* Cambridge: Cambridge University Press, 2001.

Baym, Nina. *Woman's Fiction: A Guide to Novels by and about Women in America, 1820–70.* 2nd ed. Urbana: University of Illinois Press, 1993.

Bayor, Ronald. H., and Timothy J. Meagher, eds. *The New York Irish.* Baltimore: Johns Hopkins University Press, 1996.

Becker, Penny Edgell. "'Rational Amusement and Sound Instruction': Constructing the True Catholic Woman in the Ave Maria, 1865–1889." *Religion and American Culture* 8, no. 1 (Winter 1998): 55–90.

Bednarowski, Mary Farrell. "Women, Spirituality, and History: Beyond Paralyzing Polarities." *Journal of Women's History* 17, no. 2 (2005): 184–92.

Bilhartz, Terry D. "Sex and the Second Great Awakening: The Feminization of American Religion Reconsidered." In *Belief and Behavior: Essays in the New Religious History*, edited by Philip R. Vandermeer and Robert P. Swierenga, 117–35. New Brunswick, NJ: Rutgers University Press, 1991.

Billington, Ray Allen. *The Protestant Crusade, 1800–1860: A Study of the Origins of American Nativism.* Chicago: Quadrangle Books, 1964.

Bodnar, John. *The Transplanted: A History of Immigrants in Urban America.* Bloomington: Indiana University Press, 1987.

Bolger, Stephen Garrett. *The Irish Character in American Fiction, 1830–1860.* New York: Arno Press, 1976.

Bontatibus, Donna R. *The Seduction Novel of the Early Nation: A Call for Socio-Political Reform.* East Lansing: Michigan State University Press, 1999.

Brown, Gillian. *Domestic Individualism: Imagining Self in Nineteenth-Century America.* Berkeley: University of California Press, 1990.

Brown, Thomas N. *Irish-American Nationalism, 1870–1890.* Philadelphia: J. B. Lippincott, 1966.

———. "Mary Anne Madden Sadlier." In *Notable American Women, 1607–1950: A Biographical Dictionary*, edited by Edward T. James, 3:219–20. Cambridge, MA: Harvard University Press, 1971.

Brownson, Orestes A. "Catholicity and Literature." *Brownson's Quarterly Review* (January 1856). Reprint, *The Works of Orestes A. Brownson*, edited by Henry F. Brownson, 19:447–64. New York: AMS Press, 1966.

———. "The Laboring Classes. An Article from the Boston *Quarterly Review*." Boston: Benjamin H. Greene, 1840. Originally published as "Article IV, Chartism, by Thomas Carlyle." *Boston Quarterly Review* 3, no. 3 (July 1840): 358–95.

———. "Literature, Love, and Marriage." *Brownson's Quarterly Review* (July 1864). Reprint, *Works*, 19:493–516.

———. "Mission of America." *Brownson's Quarterly Review* (October 1856). Reprint, *Works*, 11:551–84.

———. "The Native Americans." *Brownson's Quarterly Review* (July 1854). Reprint, *Works*, 18:281–300.

———. "Religious Novels." *Brownson's Quarterly Review* (January 1847). Reprint, *Works*, 19:143–54.

———. "Review of *The Blakes and Flanagans*." *Brownson's Quarterly Review* (April 1856). Reprint, *Works*, 20:23–39.

———. "Review of C. J. Cannon's Works." *Brownson's Quarterly Review* 2 (October 1857): 503–27.

———. "Review of *Mora Carmody*." *Brownson's Quarterly Review* 2 (January 1845): 134–36.

———. "Review of *Thornberry Abbey: A Tale of the Times*." *Brownson's Quarterly Review* (October 1846). Reprint, *Works*, 19:130–42.

———. "Review of *Tigh* [*sic*] *Lyfford. A Novel*." *Brownson's Quarterly Review* 4 (July 1859): 410–11.

———. "Review of *The Yankee in Ireland* [*Mary Lee*]." *Brownson's Quarterly Review* (January 1860). Reprint, *Works*, 20:83–93.

———. "Women's Novels." *Brownson's Quarterly Review* (July 1875). Reprint, *Works*, 19:595–605.

Burstein, Miriam Elizabeth. *Narrating Women's History in Britain, 1770–1902.* Burlington, VT: Ashgate, 2004.

Cappell, Ezra. *American Talmud: The Cultural Work of Jewish American Fiction.* New York: State University of New York Press, 2007.

Carby, Hazel. *Reconstructing Womanhood: The Emergence of the Afro-American Woman Novelist.* New York: Oxford University Press, 1987.

Carey, Patrick. *An Immigrant Bishop: John England's Adaptation of Irish Catholicism to American Republicanism.* New York: U.S. Catholic Historical Society, 1982.

Carroll, Michael P. *American Catholics in the Protestant Imagination: Rethinking the Academic Study of Religion.* Baltimore: Johns Hopkins University Press, 2007.

Casey, Daniel J., and Robert E. Rhodes, eds. *Irish-American Fiction: Essays in Criticism.* New York: AMS Press, 1979.

"Catholic Publisher Dies." *New York Times,* March 5, 1906.

Chinnici, Joseph. *Living Stones: The History and Structure of Catholic Spiritual Life in the United States.* New York: Macmillan, 1989.

Clarke, Brian. *Piety and Nationalism: Lay Voluntary Associations and the Creation of an Irish Catholic Community in Toronto, 1850–1895.* Toronto: McGill-Queen's University Press, 1993.

Cohen, Daniel A. "Miss Read and the Superiors: The Contradictions of Convent Life in Antebellum America." *Journal of Social History* 30 (Fall 1996): 149–84.

Connors, John R. "Patrick O'Shea." In *Dictionary of Literary Biography,* vol. 49. American Literary Publishing Houses 1638–1899, edited by Peter Dzwonkoski. 2 vols. Detroit: Gale Research, 1986.

Copeland, Ann. "Faith and Fiction-Making: The Catholic Context." *Cross Currents* 47 (Summer 1997): 173–94.

Cott, Nancy. *The Bonds of Womanhood: 'Women's Sphere' in New England, 1780–1835.* 2nd ed. New Haven: Yale University Press, 1977.

Cusack, Sr. Mary Francis. *Advice to Irish Girls in America.* New York: J. A. McGee, 1872.

Davidson, Cathy N. "Preface: No More Separate Spheres!" *American Literature* 70, no. 3 (1998): 443–63.

Delay, Cara. "Confidantes or Competitors? Women, Priests, and Conflict in Post-Famine Ireland." *Eire-Ireland: Journal of Irish Studies* 40, no. 1, 2 (2005): 107–25.

DeVries, Jacqueline. "Rediscovering Christianity after the Postmodern Turn." *Feminist Studies* 31, no. 1 (2005): 135–55.

Diner, Hasia R. *Erin's Daughters in America: Irish Immigrant Women in the Nineteenth Century.* Baltimore: Johns Hopkins University Press, 1983.

Dobson, Joanna. "Reclaiming Sentimental Literature." *American Literature* 69, no. 2 (1997): 263–88.

Dolan, Jay P. *The American Catholic Experience: A History from Colonial Times to the Present.* New York: Doubleday, 1985.

———. *Catholic Revivalism: The American Experience.* Notre Dame, IN: University of Notre Dame Press, 1978.

———. *The Immigrant Church: New York's Irish and German Catholics, 1815–1865.* Notre Dame, IN: University of Note Dame Press, 1983.

———. *The Irish Americans: A History.* New York: Bloomsbury Press, 2008.

Douglas, Ann. *The Feminization of American Culture.* New York: Doubleday, 1988.

Dowd, Christopher. *The Construction of Irish Identity in American Literature*. New York: Routledge, 2014.

Doyle, David Noel. "The Remaking of Irish-America, 1845–1880." In *Making the Irish American: History and Heritage of the Irish in the United States*, edited by J. J. Lee and Marion R. Casey, 213–52. New York: New York University Press, 2006.

Doyle, David Noel, and Owen Dudley Edwards, eds. *America and Ireland, 1776–1976: The American Identity and the Irish Connection*. Westport, CT: Greenwood Press, 1980.

Drudy, P. J., ed. *The Irish in America: Emigration, Assimilation and Impact*. Irish Studies 4. Cambridge: Cambridge University Press, 1985.

Dudden, Faye E. *Serving Women: Household Service in Nineteenth-Century America*. Middletown, CT: Wesleyan University Press, 1983.

Duncan, Jason K. *Citizens or Papists? The Politics of Anti-Catholicism in New York, 1685–1821*. New York: Fordham University Press, 2005.

Dunne, Robert. *Antebellum Irish Immigration and Emerging Ideologies of 'America': A Protestant Backlash*. Lewiston, ME: Edwin Mellen Press, 2002.

Eagan, Catherine. " 'White,' If 'Not Quite': Irish Whiteness in the Nineteenth-Century Irish-American Novel." *Eire-Ireland: Journal of Irish Studies* 36, no. 1, 2 (Spring/Summer 2001): 66–81.

Ellis, John Tracy, ed. *The Catholic Priest in the United States: Historical Investigations*. Collegeville, MN: Saint John's University Press, 1971.

Ellison, Julie K. *Cato's Tears and the Making of Anglo American Emotion*. Chicago: University of Chicago Press, 1999.

Enobong, Hannah Branch, and Melissa E. Wooten. "Suitable for Service: Racialized Rationalizations for the Ideal Domestic Servant from the Nineteenth to the Early Twentieth Century." *Social Science History* 36, no. 2 (Summer 2012): 169–89.

Ernst, Robert. *Immigrant Life in New York City, 1825–1863*. Syracuse: Syracuse University Press, 1994.

Ewens, Mary, O.P. *The Role of the Nun in Nineteenth-Century America: Variations on the International Theme*. Salem, NH: Ayer, 1984.

Fanning, Charles. *The Irish Voice in America: 250 Years of Irish-American Fiction*. 2nd ed. Lexington: University Press of Kentucky, 2000.

———, ed. *The Exiles of Erin: Nineteenth-Century Irish-American Fiction*. 2nd ed. Notre Dame, IN: University of Notre Dame Press, 1987.

———, ed. *New Perspectives on the Irish Diaspora*. Carbondale: Southern Illinois University Press, 2000.

Fegan, Melissa. *Literature and the Irish Famine*. Oxford: Clarendon Press, 2002.

Ferrie, Joseph. *Yankeys Now: Immigrants in the Antebellum United States, 1840–1860.* New York: Oxford University Press, 1999.

Fessenden, Tracy. "The Convent, the Brothel, and the Protestant Women's Sphere." *Signs: Journal of Women in Culture and Society* 25, no. 2 (2000): 451–78.

———. "Gendering Religion." *Journal of Women's History* 14, no. 1 (Spring 2002): 163–69.

———. "The Nineteenth-Century Bible Wars and the Separation of Church and State." *Church History* 74, no. 4 (December 2005): 784–811.

Fisher, James T. *Community of Immigrants: A History of Catholicism in America.* New York: Oxford University Press, 2000.

Flanagan, Thomas. *There You Are: Writings on Irish and American Literature and History.* New York: New York Review of Books, 2004.

Foik, Paul J., C.S.C. *Pioneer Catholic Journalism.* New York: United States Catholic Historical Society, 1930.

Franchot, Jenny. *Roads to Rome: The Antebellum Protestant Encounter with Catholicism.* Berkeley: University of California Press, 1994.

Frawley, Sister Mary Alphonise, S.S.J. *Patrick Donahue.* Washington, DC: Catholic University of America Press, 1946.

Gaustad, Edwin S., ed. *A Documentary History of Religion in America to 1877.* Grand Rapids, MI: William B. Eerdmans, 1982.

Gedge, Karin. *Without Benefit of Clergy: Women and the Pastoral Relationship in Nineteenth-Century American Culture.* New York: Oxford University Press, 2003.

Glazier, Michael, ed. *The Encyclopedia of the Irish in America.* Notre Dame, IN: University of Notre Dame Press, 1999.

Gleason, Philip, ed. *Catholicism in America.* New York: Harper & Row, 1970.

Glover, David, and Scott McCracken, eds. *The Cambridge Companion to Popular Fiction.* New York: Cambridge University Press, 2012.

Gordon, Michael A. *The Orange Riots: Irish Political Violence in New York City 1870 and 1871.* Ithaca: Cornell University Press, 1993.

Gorman, Robert, Rev. *Catholic Apologetic Literature in the United States, 1784–1858.* Washington, DC: Catholic University Press, 1939.

Griffin, Susan M. *Anti-Catholicism and Nineteenth-Century Fiction.* Cambridge: Cambridge University Press, 2004.

———. "Women, Anti-Catholicism, and Narrative in Nineteenth-Century America." In *The Cambridge Companion to Nineteenth-Century American Women's Writing*, edited by Dale M. Bauer and Philip Gould, 157–75. Cambridge: Cambridge University Press, 2001.

Groneman, Carol. "Working-Class Immigrant Women in Mid-Nineteenth-Century New York: The Irish Woman's Experience." *Journal of Urban History* 4, no. 3 (May 1978): 255–73.

Gudorf, Christine E. "Renewal or Repatriarchalization? Responses of the Roman Catholic Church to the Feminization of Religion." In *Horizons on Catholic Feminist Theology*, edited by Joann Wolski Conn and Walter E. Conn, 61–83. Washington, DC: Georgetown University Press, 1992.

Guglielmo, Thomas A. *White on Arrival: Italians, Race, Color, and Power in Chicago, 1890–1945*. New York: Oxford University Press, 2003.

Haddad, Yvonne, Jane I. Smith, and John L. Esposito, eds. *Religion and Immigration: Christian, Jewish, and Muslim Experiences in the United States*. Walnut Creek, CA: Altamira Press, 2003.

Hall, Mark David. "Beyond Self-Interest: The Political Theory and Practice of Evangelical Women in Antebellum America." *Journal of Church and State* 44, no. 3 (2002): 477–99.

Hamburger, Philip. "Against Separation." *The Public Interest* 155 (Spring 2004): 177–92.

———. *Separation of Church and State*. Cambridge, MA: Harvard University Press, 2002.

Handlin, Oscar. *Boston's Immigrants: A Study in Acculturation, 1790–1880*. Rev. ed. Cambridge, MA: Harvard University Press, 1979.

———. *The Uprooted*. 2nd ed. Boston: Little, Brown, 1973.

Harris, Ruth-Ann. "'Come You All Courageously': Irish Women in America Write Home." *Eire-Ireland: Journal of Irish Studies* 36, no. 1, 2 (Spring/Summer 2001): 166–84.

Hassard, John R. G. *The Life of the Most Reverend John Hughes*. New York: D. Appleton, 1866.

Higham, John. "Another Look at Nativism." *Catholic Historical Review* 44, no. 2 (1958): 147–58.

———. *Strangers in the Land: Patterns of American Nativism, 1860–1925*. New York: Atheneum, 1985.

Hotten-Somers, Diane M. "Relinquishing and Reclaiming Independence: Irish Domestic Servants, American Middle Class Mistresses, and Assimilation, 1850–1920." *Eire-Ireland: Journal of Irish Studies* 36, no. 1, 2 (Spring/Summer 2001): 185–201.

Howes, Marjorie. "Discipline, Sentiment, and the Irish-American Public: Mary Ann Sadlier's Popular Fiction." *Eire-Ireland: Journal of Irish Studies* 40, no. 1, 2 (Spring/Summer 2005): 140–69.

Hueston, Robert Francis. *The Catholic Press and Nativism, 1840–1860*. New York: Arno Press, 1976.

Hughes, John, Rev. *The Complete Works of the Most Rev. John Hughes, D. D. Archbishop of New York. Comprising His Sermons, Letters, Lectures, Speeches, etc.* 2 vols. Edited by Lawrence Kehoe. New York: Catholic Publication House, 1866.

Ibson, John Duffy. *Will the World Break Your Heart: Dimensions and Consequences of Irish-American Assimilation*. New York: Garland, 1990.

Ignatiev, Noel. *How the Irish Became White*. New York: Routledge, 1995.

Inglis, Tom. *Moral Monopoly: The Catholic Church in Modern Irish Society*. New York: St. Martin's Press, 1987.

Jackson, Pauline. "Women in 19th-Century Irish Emigration." *International Migration Review* 18, no. 4 (Winter 1984): 1004–1020.

Jacobson, Matthew Frye. *Roots Too: White Ethnic Revival in Post-Civil Rights America*. Cambridge, MA: Harvard University Press, 2006.

Jacoby, Tamar, ed., *Reinventing the Melting Pot: The New Immigrants and What It Means to Be American*. New York: Basic Books, 2004.

Jenkins, Brian. *Irish Nationalism and the British State: From Repeal to Revolutionary Nationalism*. Montreal: McGill-Queens University Press, 2006.

Jensen, Richard, "'No Irish Need Apply': A Myth of Victimization." *Journal of Social History* 36, no. 2 (Winter 2002): 405–29.

Joyce, William Leonard. *Editors and Ethnicity: A History of the Irish-America Press, 1848–1883*. New York: Arno Press, 1976.

Kane, Paula M. *Separatism and Subculture: Boston Catholicism, 1900–1920*. Chapel Hill: University of North Carolina Press, 1994.

Kane, Paula, James Kenneally, and Karen Kennelly, eds. *Gender Identities in American Catholicism*. New York: Orbis Books, 2001.

Katzenstein, Mary Fainsod. *Faithful and Fearless*. Princeton: Princeton University Press, 1999.

Keddie, Nikki R. "The New Religious Politics and Women Worldwide: A Comparative Study." *Journal of Women's History* 10, no. 4 (1999): 11–34.

Kelley, Mary. "Beyond the Boundaries." *Journal of the Early Republic* 21 (Spring 2001): 73–78.

Kelly, Mary C. *The Shamrock and the Lily: The New York Irish and the Creation of a Transatlantic Identity, 1845–1921*. New York: Peter Lang, 2005.

Kennelly, Karen, C.S.J., ed. *American Catholic Women: A Historical Exploration*. New York: Macmillan, 1989.

Kenny, Kevin. *The American Irish: A History*. Harlow, UK: Longman Pearson, 2000.

———. "Race, Violence, and Anti-Irish Sentiment in the Nineteenth Century." In *Making the Irish American: History and Heritage of the Irish in the United States*, edited by J. J. Lee and Marion R. Casey, 364–78. New York: New York University Press, 2006.

———, ed. *New Directions in Irish-American History*. Madison: University of Wisconsin Press, 2003.

Kete, Mary Louise. *Sentimental Collaborations: Mourning and Middle-Class Identity in Nineteenth-Century America.* Durham, NC: Duke University Press, 2000.

Kinealy, Christine. *Daniel O'Connell and the Antislavery Movement: The Saddest People the Sun Sees.* London: Pickering & Chatto, 2011.

Knobel, Dale T. *Paddy and the Republic: Ethnicity and Nationality in Antebellum America.* Middletown, CT: Wesleyan University Press, 1986.

Kucukalioglu, Elif Gozdasoglu. "The Representation of Women as Gendered National Subjects in Ottoman-Turkish Novels (1908–1923)." *Journal of Gender Studies* 16, no. 1 (2007): 3–15.

Lacombe, Michele. "Frying-Pans and Deadlier Weapons: The Immigrant Novels of Mary Anne Sadlier." *Essays on Canadian Writing* 29 (Summer 1984): 96–116.

Lannie, Vincent P. *Public Money and Parochial Education.* Cleveland: Press of Case Western Reserve University, 1968.

Larkin, Emmet. "The Devotional Revolution in Ireland, 1850–1875." *The American Historical Review* 77, no. 3 (June 1972): 625–52.

Lee, J. J. "Women and the Church since the Famine." In *Women in Irish Society: The Historical Dimension,* edited by Margaret MacCurtain and Donncha O Corrain, 37–45. Westport, CT: Greenwood Press, 1979.

Lee, J. J., and Marion R. Casey, eds. *Making the Irish American: History and Heritage of the Irish in the United States.* New York: New York University Press, 2006.

Leerssen, Joep. *Remembrance and Imagination: Patterns in the Historical and Literary Representation of Ireland in the Nineteenth Century.* Notre Dame, IN: University of Notre Dame Press, 1997.

Light, Dale B. *Rome and the New Republic: Conflict and Community in Philadelphia Catholicism between the Revolution and the Civil War.* Notre Dame, IN: University of Notre Dame Press, 1996.

Lindley, Susan Hill. *"You Have Stept Out of Your Place": A History of Women and Religion in America.* Louisville, KY: John Knox Press, 1996.

Lynch-Brennan, Margaret. "Ubiquitous Bridget: Irish Immigrant Women in Domestic Service in America, 1840–1930." In *Making the Irish American: History and Heritage of the Irish in the United States,* edited by J. J. Lee and Marion R. Casey, 332–53. New York: New York University Press, 2006.

MacCurtain, Margaret, and Donncha O. Corrain, eds. *Women in Irish Society: The Historical Dimension.* Westport, CT: Greenwood Press, 1979.

MacDonald, Mary Lu. *Literature and Society in the Canadas, 1817–1850.* Lewiston, NY: Edwin Mellen Press, 1992.

Maguire, John Francis, Rev. *The Irish in America.* London: Longmans Green, 1868. Reprint, New York: Arno Press, 1969.

Mannard, Joseph G. "Maternity . . . of the Spirit: Nuns and Domesticity in Antebellum America." *U.S. Catholic Historian* 5, no. 3, 4 (Summer/Fall 1986):
305–24.

Massa, Mark. "'As If in Prayer': A Response to 'Catholicism as American Popular Culture.'" In *American Catholics, American Culture: Tradition and Resistance*,
edited by Margaret O'Brien Steinfels, 2:112–18. New York: Rowman &
Littlefield, 2004.

McAvoy, Thomas T. *The Formation of the American Catholic Minority, 1820–1860.*
Philadelphia: Fortress Press, 1967.

———. "The Formation of the Catholic Minority in the United States,
1820–1860." *Review of Politics* 10 (January 1948): 13–34.

McCaffrey, Lawrence J. "Irish Americans." In *Multiculturalism in the United States:
A Comparative Guide to Acculturation and Ethnicity*, edited by John D. Buenker
and Lorman A. Ratner, 203–32. Westport, CT: Greenwood Press, 2005.

———. *The Irish Catholic Diaspora in America.* Rev. ed. Washington, DC: Catholic
University of America Press, 1997.

———. *Textures of Irish America.* Syracuse: Syracuse University Press, 1992.

———, ed. *Irish Nationalism and the American Contribution.* New York: Arno
Press, 1976.

McCarthy, Mark, ed. *Ireland's Heritages: Critical Perspectives on Memory and Identity.*
Burlington, VT: Ashgate, 2005.

McDannell, Colleen. "Catholic Domesticity, 1860–1960." In *American Catholic
Women: A Historical Exploration*, edited by Karen Kennelly, C.S.J., 48–80.
New York: Macmillan, 1989.

———. "Catholic Women Fiction Writers, 1840–1920." *Women's Studies* 19,
no. 3, 4 (1991): 385–405.

———. *The Christian Home in Victorian America, 1840–1900.* Bloomington: Indiana University Press, 1986.

———. *Material Christianity: Religion and Popular Culture in America.* New Haven:
Yale University Press, 1995.

McGreevy, John T. *Catholicism and American Freedom: A History.* New York: W. W.
Norton, 2003.

———. "Catholicism in America: Antipathy and Assimilation." In *American
Catholics, American Culture: Tradition and Resistance*, edited by Margaret O'Brien
Steinfels, 2:3–26. New York: Rowman & Littlefield, 2004.

———. "Introduction: The American Catholic Century." In *Catholics in the
American Century: Recasting Narratives of U.S. History*, edited by R. Scott Ap-
pleby and Kathleen Sprows Cummings, 1–10. Ithaca: Cornell University
Press, 2012.

M'Clintock, John, Rev., and James Strong. *Cyclopaedia of Biblical, Theological, and Ecclesiastical Literature* 9. New York: Harper and Brothers, 1894. http://books .google.com.

Meagher, Timothy J. *The Columbia Guide to Irish American History.* New York: Columbia University Press, 2005.

———. *Inventing Irish America: Generation, Class, and Ethnic Identity in a New England City, 1880–1928.* Notre Dame, IN: University of Notre Dame Press, 2001.

———, ed. *From Paddy to Studs: Irish-American Communities in the Turn of the Century Era, 1880–1920.* Westport, CT: Greenwood Press, 1986.

Meehan, Thomas F. "Catholic Literary New York, 1800–1840." *Catholic Historical Review* 4, no. 4 (January 1919): 399–414.

Merwick, Donna. *Boston Priests, 1848–1910: A Study of Social and Intellectual Change.* Cambridge, MA: Harvard University Press, 1973.

Messbarger, Paul R. *Fiction with a Parochial Purpose: Social Uses of American Catholic Literature, 1884–1900.* Boston: Boston University Press, 1971.

The Metropolitan Catholic Almanac and Laity's Directory. Baltimore: Fielding Lucas Jr., 1841.

The Metropolitan Catholic Almanac and Laity's Directory. Baltimore: John Murphy, 1860.

Miller, Kerby A. "Class, Culture, and Immigrant Group Identity in the United States: The Case of Irish-American Ethnicity." In *Immigration Reconsidered: History, Sociology, and Politics*, edited by Virginia Yans-McLaughlin, 96–129. New York and Oxford: Oxford University Press, 1990.

———. *Emigrants and Exiles: Ireland and the Irish Exodus to North America.* New York: Oxford University Press, 1985.

———. "For Love and Liberty: Irish Women, Migration and Domesticity in Ireland and America, 1815–1920." In *Irish Women and Irish Migration* 4, edited by Patrick O'Sullivan, 41–65. London: Leicester University Press, 1995.

———. *Ireland and Irish America: Culture, Class, and Transatlantic Migration.* Dublin: Kerby A. Miller, 2008.

Miller, Kerby A., and Bruce D. Boling. "Golden Streets, Bitter Tears: The Irish Image of America during the Era of Mass Migration." *Journal of American Ethnic History* 10, no. 1, 2 (Fall/Winter 1990–1991): 16–35.

Moloney, Deidre. "Who's Irish? Ethnic Identity and Recent Trends in Irish American History." *Journal of American Ethnic History* 28, no. 4 (Summer 2009): 100–109.

Moore, Laurence. *Religious Outsiders and the Making of Americans.* New York: Oxford University Press, 1987.

Morris, Charles R. *American Catholic: The Saints and Sinners Who Built America's Most Powerful Church*. New York: Random House, 1997.

Mott, Frank Luther. *Golden Multitudes: The Story of Best Sellers in the United States*. New York: R. R. Bowker, 1947.

Mulrooney, Margaret M., ed. *Fleeing the Famine: North America and Irish Refugees, 1845–1851*. Westport, CT: Praeger, 2003.

Murphy, Angela F. *American Slavery, Irish Freedom: Abolition, Immigrant Citizenship, and the Transatlantic Movement for Irish Repeal*. Baton Rouge: Louisiana State University Press, 2010.

———. "'Though Dead He Yet Speaketh': Abolitionist Memories of Daniel O'Connell in the United States." *American Journal of Irish Studies* 10 (2013): 11–38.

Murphy, Maureen. "Bridget and Biddy: Images of the Irish Servant Girl in *Puck* Cartoons, 1880–1890." In *New Perspectives on the Irish Diaspora*, edited by Charles Fanning, 152–75. Carbondale: Southern Illinois University Press, 2000.

———. "The Irish Servant Girl in Literature." In *Writing Ulster* 5; *America and Ulster; A Cultural Correspondence*, edited by William Lazenbatt, 133–47. Coleraine: University of Ulster, 1998.

Nelson, Bruce. *Divided We Stand: American Workers and the Struggle for Black Equality*. Princeton: Princeton University Press, 2001.

———. *Irish Nationalists and the Making of the Irish Race*. Princeton: Princeton University Press, 2012.

Neville, Grace. "'She Never Then after That Forgot Him': Irishwomen and Emigration to the United States in Irish Folklore." *Mid-America* 74 (October 1992): 271–89.

Nolan, Janet A. *Ourselves Alone: Women's Emigration from Ireland, 1885–1920*. Lexington: University Press of Kentucky, 1989.

———. *Servants of the Poor: Teachers and Mobility in Ireland and Irish America*. Notre Dame, IN: University of Notre Dame Press, 2004.

Noll, Mark A. *The Civil War as a Theological Crisis*. Chapel Hill: University of North Carolina Press, 2006.

"Obituary Patrick O'Shea." *Publishers' Weekly* 1780 (1906): 874.

O'Grady, Joseph P. *How the Irish Became Americans*. New York: Twayne, 1973.

O'Hanlon, John, Rev. *The Irish Emigrant's Guide for the United States*. Boston: Patrick Donahoe, 1851. Reprint, edited by Edward J. Maguire. New York: Arno Press, 1976.

Osofsky, Gilbert. "Abolitionists, Irish Immigrants, and the Dilemmas of Romantic Nationalism." *American Historical Review* 80, no. 4 (October 1975): 889–912.

O'Sullivan, Patrick, ed. *Irish Women and Irish Migration* 4. London: Leicester University Press, 1995.

Park, Robert E. *The Immigrant Press and Its Control: The Acculturation of Immigrant Groups into American Society*. Montclair, NJ: Patterson Smith, 1971.

Pearl, Sharrona. "White, with a Class-Based Blight: Drawing Irish Americans." *Eire-Ireland: Journal of Irish Studies* 44, no. 3, 4 (Fall/Winter 2009): 171–99.

Quinn, John F. *Father Mathew's Crusade: Temperance in Nineteenth-Century Ireland and North America*. Amherst: University of Massachusetts Press, 2002.

———. "Three Cheers for the Abolitionist Pope: American Reaction to Gregory XVI's Condemnation of the Slave Trade, 1840–1860." *Catholic Historical Review* 90, no. 1 (January 2004): 67–93.

Rafferty, Oliver. "Fenianism in North America in the 1860s: The Problems for Church and State." *History* 84, no. 274 (April 1999): 257–77.

Reher, Margaret Mary. *Catholic Intellectual Life in America: A Historical Study of Persons and Movements*. New York: Macmillan, 1989.

"Review of Cannon's *Scenes and Characters from the Comedy of Life*." In "Notices of Books." *Dublin Review* 25, no. 49 (September 1848): 258–59.

Reynolds, David S. *Faith in Fiction: The Emergence of Religious Literature in America*. Cambridge, MA: Harvard University Press, 1981.

Rice, Madeleine Hooke. *American Catholic Opinion in the Slavery Controversy*. Gloucester, MA: Peter Smith, 1964.

Roediger, David. R. *The Wages of Whiteness: Race and the Making of the American Working Class*. Rev. ed. New York: Verso, 2007.

———. *Working toward Whiteness: How America's Immigrants Became White*. New York: Basic Books, 2006.

Romero, Lora. *Home Fronts: Domesticity and Its Critics in the Antebellum United States*. Durham, NC: Duke University Press, 1997.

Rooney, Ellen, ed. *The Cambridge Companion to Feminist Literary Theory*. Cambridge: Cambridge University Press, 2006.

Roy, Jody M. *Rhetorical Campaigns of the Nineteenth-Century: Anti-Catholics and Catholics in America*. Lewiston, NY: Edwin Mellen Press, 2000.

Ryan, James Emmett. *Faithful Passages: American Catholicism in Literary Culture, 1844–1931*. Madison: University of Wisconsin Press, 2013.

———. "Orestes Brownson in Young America: Popular Books and the Fate of Catholic Criticism." *American Literary History* 15, no. 3 (Fall 2003): 443–70.

———. "Sentimental Catechism: Archbishop James Gibbons, Mass-Print Culture, and American Literary History." *Religion and American Culture* 7, no. 1 (Winter 1997): 81–119.

Ryan, Mary P. *Cradle of the Middle Class: The Family in Oneida County, New York, 1790–1865*. Cambridge: Cambridge University Press, 1981.

————. *The Empire of the Mother: American Writing about Domesticity, 1830–1860.* New York: Harrington Park, 1985.

Sadlier, Anna T. "Mrs. Sadlier's Early Life, Her Books and Friends." *Donahoe's Magazine* 49 (1903): 331–35.

Sadlier's Catholic Directory, Almanac, and Ordo. Annual. New York: D. & J. Sadlier, 1867–[1896].

Schrier, Arnold. *Ireland and the American Emigration, 1850–1900.* Chester Springs, PA: Dufour, 1997.

Schultz, April. "The Black Mammy and the Irish Bridget: Domestic Service and the Representation of Race, 1830–1930." *Eire-Ireland: Journal of Irish Studies* 48, no. 3, 4 (Fall/Winter 2013): 176–212.

Scott, Joan Wallach. "Feminism's History." *Journal of Women's History* 16, no. 2 (Summer 2004): 10–29.

————. *Gender and the Politics of History.* Rev. ed. New York: Columbia University Press, 1999.

Shaw, Richard. *Dagger John: The Unquiet Life and Times of Archbishop John Hughes of New York.* New York: Paulist Press, 1977.

Smith, Rogers M. *Stories of Peoplehood: The Politics and Morals of Political Membership.* Cambridge: Cambridge University Press, 2003.

Smith, Timothy L. "Religion and Ethnicity in America." *American Historical Review* 83, no. 5 (December 1978): 1155–85.

Sollors, Werner, ed. *Theories of Ethnicity: A Classical Reader.* New York: New York University Press, 1996.

Spalding, John Lancaster, Bishop of Peoria. *The Religious Mission of the Irish People and Catholic Colonization.* New York: Catholic Publication Society, 1880. Reprint, Arno Press, 1978.

Sparr, Arnold. *To Promote, Defend, and Redeem: The Catholic Literary Revival and the Cultural Transformation of American Catholicism, 1920–1960.* New York: Greenwood Press, 1990.

Stansell, Christine. *City of Women: Sex and Class in New York, 1789–1860.* Urbana: University of Illinois Press, 1987.

Steinfels, Margaret O'Brien, ed. *American Catholics, American Culture: Tradition and Resistance.* 2 vols. New York: Rowman & Littlefield, 2004.

Suarez-Orozco, Marcelo M. "Everything You Ever Wanted to Know about Assimilation but Were Afraid to Ask." In *The New Immigration: An Interdisciplinary Reader*, edited by Marcelo M. Suarez-Orozco, Carola Suarez-Orozco, and Desiree Baolian Qin, 67–84. New York: Taylor & Francis, 2005.

Sullivan, Eileen. "Community in Print: Irish American Publishers and Readers." *Journal of Irish and Irish American Studies* 8 (2011): 41–76.

Tate, Claudia. *Domestic Allegories of Political Desire: The Black Heroine's Text at the Turn of the Century*. New York: Oxford University Press, 1992.

Taves, Ann. *The Household of Faith: Roman Catholic Devotions in Mid-Nineteenth Century America*. Notre Dame, IN: University of Notre Dame Press, 1986.

Tavuchis, Nicholas. *Pastors and Immigrants: The Role of a Religious Elite in the Absorption of Norwegian Immigrants*. The Hague: Martinue Nijhoff, 1963.

Thernstrom, Stephan. *The Other Bostonians: Poverty and Progress in the American Metropolis, 1880–1970*. Cambridge, MA: Harvard University Press, 1973.

Thompson, Margaret Susan. "Sisterhood and Power: Class, Culture and Ethnicity in the American Convent." *Colby Library Quarterly* 25, no. 3 (September 1989): 149–75.

———. "Women and American Catholicism, 1789–1989." In *Perspectives on the American Catholic Church, 1789–1989*, edited by Stephen J. Vicchio and Virginia Geiger, 123–43. Westminster, MD: Christian Classics, 1989.

———. "Women, Feminism, and the New Religious History: Catholic Sisters as a Case Study." In *Belief and Behavior: Essays in the New Religious History*, edited by Philip R. Vandermeer and Robert P. Swierenga, 136–63. New Brunswick, NJ: Rutgers University Press, 1991.

Thorp, Willard. *Catholic Novelists in Defense of Their Faith, 1829–1865*. Boston: American Antiquarian Society, 1968. Reprint, New York: Arno Press, 1978.

Tocqueville, Alexis de. *Journey in Ireland, July–August 1835*. Edited and translated by Emmet Larkin. Washington, DC: Catholic University of America Press, 1990.

Tompkins, Jane. *Sensational Designs: The Cultural Work of American Fiction, 1790–1860*. New York: Oxford University Press, 1985.

Urban, Andrew. "Irish Domestic Servants, 'Biddy' and Rebellion in the American Home, 1850–1900." *Gender and History* 21, no. 2 (August 2009): 263–86.

Vandermeer, Philip R., and Robert P. Swierenga, eds. *Belief and Behavior: Essays in the New Religious History*. New Brunswick, NJ: Rutgers University Press, 1991.

Wald, Priscilla. *Constituting Americans: Cultural Anxiety and Narrative Form*. Durham, NC: Duke University Press, 1995.

———. "Immigration and Assimilation in Nineteenth-Century US Women's Writing." In *The Cambridge Companion to Nineteenth-Century American Women's Writing*, edited by Dale M. Bauer and Philip Gould, 176–99. Cambridge: Cambridge University Press, 2001.

Walker, Peter F. *Moral Choices: Memory, Desire, and Imagination in Nineteenth-Century American Abolition*. Baton Rouge: Louisiana State University Press, 1978.

Welter, Barbara. *Dimity Convictions: The American Woman in the Nineteenth Century*. Athens: Ohio University Press, 1976.

————. "From Maria Monk to Paul Blanshard: A Century of Protestant Anti-Catholicism." In *Uncivil Religion: Interreligious Hostility in America*, edited by Robert N. Bellah and Frederick E. Greenspahn, 43–71. New York: Cross-road, 1987.

White, Eva Roa. "Emigration as Emancipation: Portrayals of the Immigrant Irish Girl in Nineteenth-Century Fiction." *New Hibernia Review* 9, no. 1 (Spring 2005): 95–108.

Wills, Clair. "Women, Domesticity and the Family: Recent Feminist Work in Irish Cultural Studies." *Cultural Studies* 15, no. 1 (2001): 33–57.

Zoller, Michael. *Washington and Rome: Catholicism in American Culture.* Notre Dame, IN: University of Notre Dame Press, 1999.

INDEX

intermarriages portrayed in, 143
Irish drinking portrayed in, 224,
    265–66
Irish famine portrayed in, 47, 49
liberty portrayed in, 125–26
opposition to emigration in,
    154–55
poverty portrayed in, 268
priestly authority in, 184, 185
priests portrayed in, 92, 93, 151,
    173, 187, 307n42
role of Catholic community in, 66,
    138, 209
romance portrayed in, 198–99
threats to identity in, 62, 63
women portrayed in, 195–96, 206,
    214
work habits portrayed in, 220, 221,
    223
Bickerton (Cannon)
anti-Catholicism in, 79–80, 94,
    297n27
anti-Protestantism in, 110, 111–12,
    114, 117, 118, 119
audience and purpose of, 35, 36
convents portrayed in, 149
economic success in, 225–26
economic support systems in, 243
education addressed in, 250
emigration motives in, 39, 43
European reformers portrayed in,
    264
interfaith marriage in, 100,
    140–41
Irish Catholic identity in, 135
Irish drinking portrayed in, 265,
    266, 267
liberty portrayed in, 96–99, 128
nationalism addressed in, 158
obedience portrayed in, 223

patriotism portrayed in, 270, 271,
    272
politics portrayed in, 269, 272
poverty portrayed in, 43, 44, 46,
    267–68
priests portrayed in, 95, 170, 171,
    172, 174–75, 179–81
race portrayed in, 260
romance portrayed in, 200
wealth and status portrayed in,
    43, 46
women portrayed in, 115, 194–95,
    197, 206, 225–26
Blakes and Flanagans, The (Sadlier), *75*
anti-Catholicism in, 56, 70
anti-Protestantism in, 120, 299n66
audience and purpose of, 30
Catholic employers portrayed in,
    245
Church as community in, 38,
    137–38
Church authority portrayed in,
    146, 303n45
economic success in, 220, 227,
    228, 229, 237, 240, 243
education addressed in, 66, 74–78,
    79, 151–53, 249–51, 316n28,
    322n68
families portrayed in, 194, 202,
    211–13
intermarriage portrayed in, 153
Irish Catholic identity in, 136, 139
Irish community portrayed in,
    302n29
liberty portrayed in, 90, 122
materialism portrayed in, 239, 241
nationalism addressed in, 156
nuns portrayed in, 205
patriotism portrayed in, 272,
    273–74

EILEEN P. SULLIVAN

is lecturer in political science at Rutgers University.

CPSIA information can be obtained at www.ICGtesting.com
Printed in the USA
BVOW06s1908040416

442910BV00015B/111/P